C.A. to W.E.K.R.

Christmas 1955.

THE
GUINNESS BOOK
OF RECORDS

MOUNT EVEREST (29,160 feet)

The highest mountain in the world

THE GUINNESS BOOK OF RECORDS

GUINNESS SUPERLATIVES LIMITED
LUDGATE HOUSE, FLEET STREET, LONDON

ACKNOWLEDGEMENTS

The Admiralty
The Air Ministry
Bell Aircraft Corporation
Belships Company Ltd.
The Brewers' Society
Bristol Aeroplane Company Ltd.
The British Broadcasting Corporation
British Electricity Authority
British European Airways
British Mycological Society
British Overseas Airways Corporation
British Railways
British Speleological Association
The British Thomson-Houston Co. Ltd.
British Transport Commission
The British Travel and Holidays Association
British Waterworks Association
Burke's Peerage Ltd.
Caterers' Association of Great Britain
Central Office of Information
The Chemical Society
Church Commissioners
Conchological Society of Great Britain and Ireland
County Councils Association
Clerk of Dáil Eireann
Department of Industry and Commerce, Dublin
Diplomatic Mission of the Federal Republic of Germany
E. I. du Pont de Nemours & Co. Inc.
Fédération Aéronautique Internationale
Fédération Internationale de l'Automobile
Fédération Internationale des Hôpitaux
Fire Protection Association
Ford Motor Co. Ltd.
The Fur Trade Information Centre
General Motors Corporation
General Post Office
Geological Survey and Museum
The Home Office
Icelandic Legation
Imperial Chemical Industries Ltd.
Imperial War Museum
The Inland Waterways Association
Institut International des Châteaux Historiques
The Institute of Metals
International Association of Volcanology
International Civil Aviation Organization
Jaguar Cars Ltd.
Embassy of Japan
The Kennel Club
Kodak Ltd.
KWTV Oklahoma Television Corporation
The Library of Congress, Washington, D.C.
Liverpool Observatory and Tidal Institute
London County Council
London Transport Executive
J. Lyons & Co. Ltd.
Meteorological Office
Metropolitan Police
Ministry of Agriculture, Fisheries and Food
Ministry of Housing and Local Government
Ministry of Labour and National Service
Ministry of Pensions and National Insurance
Ministry of Supply
Ministry of Works
The Museums Association
National Coal Board
National Geographic Society
National Maritime Museum
National Physical Laboratory
The New York Times
New Zealand House
Jean Patou
Press Association—Reuters
Agent General for Queensland
Ransomes and Rapier Ltd.
Registrar General's Office, Edinburgh
Rolls-Royce Ltd.
Royal Botanic Gardens
Royal National Life-Boat Institution
Royal Norwegian Embassy
Sampson Low, Marston & Co. Ltd.
B. A. Seaby Ltd.
Sears, Roebuck & Co.
Siemens and Halske Aktiengesellschaft
Thomas Skinner & Co. Ltd.
Société Nationale des Chemins de Fer Français
Statutory Publications Office
The Treasury
Trinity House
U.N.E.S.C.O.
United States Coastguard
United States Department of Agriculture
United States Department of the Interior
The War Office
The Lady Wentworth
J. Whitaker & Sons Ltd.
World Health Organisation
Zoological Society of London

Third Impression

Printed in London
by
F. Howard Doulton & Co., Ltd.
(Associated Staples Press Company)
Stratford, London, E.15

FOREWORD

By the Rt. Hon. the Earl of Iveagh, K.G., C.B., C.M.G.

•

Wherever people congregate to talk, they will argue, and sometimes the joy lies in the arguing and would be lost if there were any definite answer. But more often the argument takes place on a dispute of fact, and it can be very exasperating if there is no immediate means of settling the argument. Who was the first to swim the Channel? Where is England's deepest well, or Scotland's highest tree, or Ireland's oldest church? How many died in history's worst rail crash? Who gained the biggest majority in Parliament? What is the highest point in our county? What is the greatest weight a man has ever lifted? And so on. How much heat these innocent questions can raise! Guinness in producing this book hopes that it may assist in resolving many such disputes, and may, we hope, turn heat into light.

Iveagh

Chairman

Arthur Guinness Son & Co., Ltd.,
Park Royal Brewery,
London.

September 1955

PREFACE

•

This book is a collection of facts—finite facts expressed in quantitative terms, predominantly those which by measurement are superlative or are records in their respective fields. The world's greatest man is, for this book, the man with the greatest girth rather than the man with the greatest intellect.

Many of the data contained within these pages are by their very nature constantly changing. In 1953 the Nebula Andromeda, the most distant heavenly body visible to the naked eye, was discovered to be twice as far away as had hitherto been thought. In February 1955, the Russians announced the discovery of a new mountain in Siberia higher than any in America, Europe or Africa. No reference book such as this can ever claim to have said the last word.

It would be impracticable to mention all the vast number of sources and references which attach to each of the items included in this volume. In the event of rival claims for a particular superlative, it has been the sole responsibility of the compilers to weigh up the evidence and to come to a decision.

We wish to acknowledge the generous assistance of countless experts from all over the world who have aided us, and we shall greatly welcome comments and suggestions from our readers who have reason for criticising our researches or can add to our information. In that way, we can hope to improve and enlarge any future editions.

The Compilers.

Guinness Superlatives Ltd.,
Ludgate House,
Fleet Street,
London.

CONTENTS

ILLUSTRATIONS

ACKNOWLEDGEMENTS

PLATE 1
- Chubb Crater—"By courtesy National Geographic Society"

PLATE 2
- Long-range gun—"By courtesy Imperial War Museum"

PLATE 3
- £100 stamp—"Reproduced from 'The Royal Philatelic Collection' by Sir John Wilson, Bt., edited and designed by Clarence Winchester; published by the Viscount Kemsley at the Dropmore Press Ltd., London"
- The Rt. Hon. C. P. Villiers, M.P.—"Picture Post Library"
- Smallest printed book—"Book by courtesy St. Bride's Typographical Library"

PLATE 4
- Hale telescope—"By courtesy Mount Wilson and Palomar Observatories"

PLATE 5
- Sandö Bridge—"By courtesy *AB Skånska Cementgjuteriet*"
- Teatro Olimpico—"*Edizione Chiovato, Vicenza*"

PLATE 7
- Grenville Steam Carriage—"By courtesy 'Bristol Evening Post'"
- Hammel car—"By courtesy of 'The Motor'"

PLATE 13
- Jose Meiffret—"By courtesy of 'Cycling'"

PLATE 16
- Paul Anderson—"By courtesy Strength and Health Magazine"
- Aeroplanes—"Copyright drawings by courtesy of 'Flight'"

Art-work by K. T. Toziczka.

ONE

THE UNIVERSE

The universe is the entirety of space and matter. The remotest known heavenly bodies are extra-galactic nebulæ at a distance of some 1,000 million light years or 6,000,000,000,000,000,000,000 miles. There is reason to believe that even remoter nebulæ exist but, since it is possible that they are receding faster than the speed of light (670,455,000 m.p.h.), they would be beyond man's "observable horizon". REMOTEST KNOWN BODIES

The largest nebulæ range up to 200,000 light years (1,200,000,000,000,000,000 miles) in diameter and have a luminosity up to 6,000 million times that of the sun. LARGEST NEBULÆ

The nearest heavenly body outside our own lens-shaped galaxy is the Greater Magellanic Cloud at a distance of 86,000 light years (505,000,000,000,000,000 miles). This is easily visible in our southern hemisphere. The nearest nebula is that of Andromeda (diameter 840,000,000,000,000,000 miles) visible in the northern hemisphere at a distance of 1,500,000 light years (9,000,000,000,000,000,000 miles). NEAREST NEBULA

Andromeda (see Photo Plate I), a spiral nebula, is also the remotest heavenly body visible to the naked eye. VISIBLE

Sirius (*Alpha Canis Majoris*), also known as the Dog Star, is the brightest star in the heavens with a magnitude of —1·6. It is in the constellation Canis Major and is visible in the winter months of the northern hemisphere, being due south at midnight on the last day of the year. Sirius is over 50 billion miles distant and has a luminosity twenty-six times greater than the sun. It has a diameter of 1,500,000 miles and a mass of 45,800,000,000,000,000,000,000,000,000 tons. The brightest southern hemisphere star is Canopus (magnitude —0·9). BRIGHTEST STAR

If all stars could be viewed at the same distance, the most luminous would be the faint Sigma Dodarus which is 300,000 times brighter than the sun.

Excepting the special case of our own sun, the nearest star is the very faint Proxima Centauri which is 4·3 light years (24,696,000,000 miles). Travelling in space, a 5,000 m.p.h. rocket would take 563,700 years or over 22,500 generations to reach it. The nearest star visible to the naked eye is the southern hemisphere star Alpha Centauri (4·33 light years). NEAREST STAR

LARGEST STAR

Of those measured, the star with the greatest diameter is Epsilon Aurigae at 2,500 million miles. So vast is this star that our own solar system of the sun and the six planets out as far as Saturn could be accommodated inside it.

The Alpha Herculis aggregation, consisting of a main star and a double star companion, is enveloped in a cold gas. This system, visible to the naked eye, has a diameter of 170,000,000,000 miles.

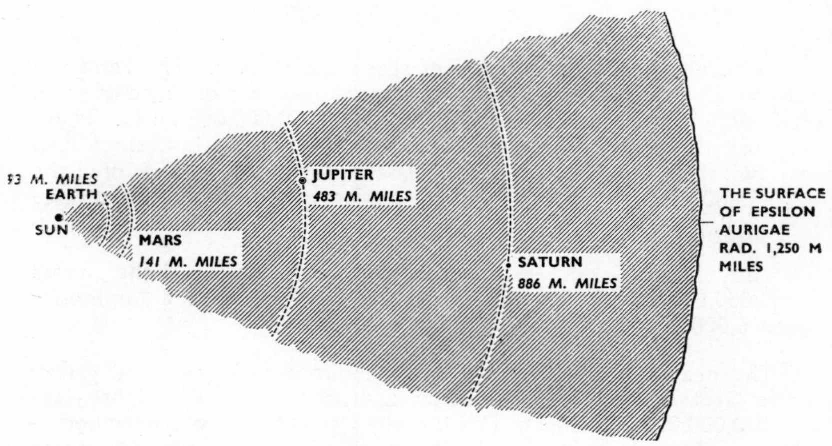

FASTEST STAR

The star with the largest proper motion is the tenth magnitude Munich 15040 (*Barnard's Star*). As viewed from the Earth, this star would move through an angle equivalent to the moon's diameter in less than 200 years.

HOTTEST STARS

The temperature of stars refers to their surface temperature and not to their interior temperature which is thought to attain scores of millions of degrees centigrade. Two O-type stars of the Wolf-Rayet class have an estimated surface temperature of 70,000°C.

DENSEST STAR

The densest stars are the 'white dwarfs'. The invisible companion to Sirius (see above) is 70,000 times as dense as water but there seems to be scarcely any limit to the density of this category of star. The limitation is at the neutron state, that is, when the atomic particles exist in a state in which there is no space between them.

SMALLEST STAR

The smallest stars are white dwarfs and black dwarfs some of which are only of planetary dimensions. The smallest is believed to be Maenan's Star.

REMOTEST PLANET

Planets are bodies (including the Earth) which belong to the solar system and which revolve round the sun in definite orbits. The remotest of these, as measured from the sun, is Pluto (discovered by Tombaugh in 1930). Its mean distance from the sun is 3,675,300,000 miles and its period of revolution is 248·4 years.

NEAREST PLANET

The planet whose orbit is closest to the sun is Mercury, which revolves at a mean distance of 36 million miles. The fellow planet closest to Earth is Venus which at times is less than 25¾ million miles distant inside our orbit as opposed to Mars's closest approach of just over 34 million miles.

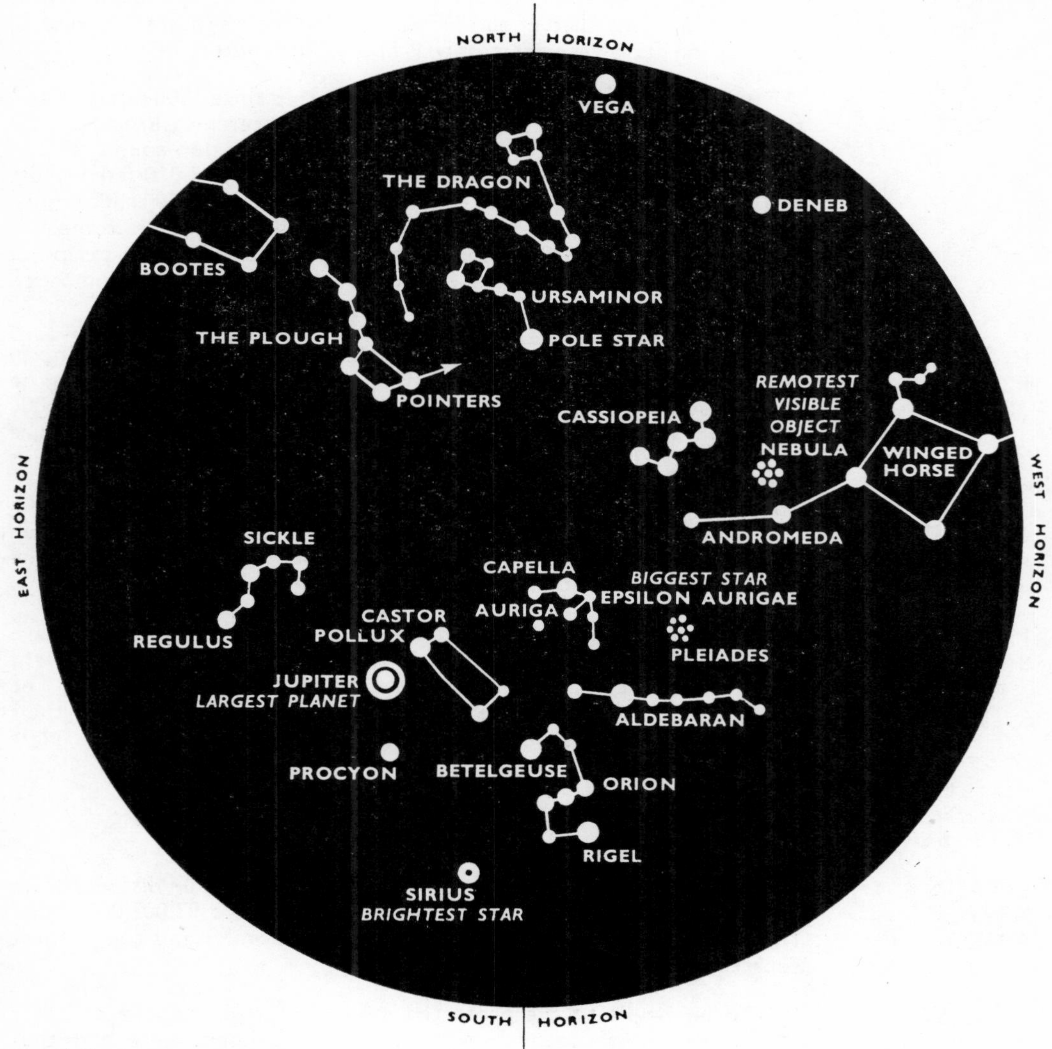

The chart shows the midnight December 1955 night-sky from the British Isles. To identify the celestial superlatives, face south where, if cloudless, you will easily pick out the brightest planet Jupiter and the brightest star Sirius. Now hold the map overhead so that you orientate the other main constellations, remembering that the centre of the map is the zenith (directly overhead).

BRIGHTEST PLANET

Viewed from the Earth, by far the brightest of the five planets visible to the naked eye (Uranus at Magnitude 5·7 is only marginally visible) is Venus (with a maximum magnitude of —4·4). The faintest is Pluto with a magnitude of 14.

LARGEST PLANET

Jupiter, with an equatorial diameter of 88,700 miles and a polar diameter of 82,790 miles, is the largest of the nine major planets with a mass 318 times that of the Earth. It also has the fastest period of rotation on its own axis at only 9 hours 50 minutes.

SMALLEST PLANET

Over 2,000 minor planets have been charted since 1800 but they are, for the most part, too small to yield to diameter measurement. Of the major planets, Mercury, whose period of revolution round the sun is only 87·97 days, is the smallest with a diameter of 3,010 miles and a mass only one-twentieth part that of the Earth, that is 300 trillion tons. Mercury also has the fastest velocity in orbit at 108,000 m.p.h. compared with the Earth's 66,600 m.p.h. Neither the density nor the period of rotation of the most recently discovered planet, Pluto (Tombaugh 1930) has yet been determined.

HOTTEST PLANET

The hottest of the planets is Mercury at an estimated mean temperature of 600°F. (315°C.). This depends upon its distance from the sun (surface temperature 5,500°C.) which varies between 28,566,000 miles and 43,455,000 miles. The planets with a surface temperature closest to Earth's 59°F. (15°C.) are Mars with 28°F. (-2·2°C.) and Venus with 68°F. (20°C.).

COLDEST PLANET

No estimate of the temperature of the remote Pluto has yet been made but it is reasonable to assume that it is even colder than the —400°F. (—240°C.) of Neptune.

MOST SATELLITES

Of the nine major planets, all but Mercury, Venus and Pluto have satellites. The planet with most is Jupiter with four large and eight small moons. Earth is the only planet with a single satellite. The distance of the solar system's thirty-one known satellites from their parent planets varies between the 5,830 miles of Phobos from Mars and the 14,700,000 miles of Satellite IX from Jupiter.

THE SUN

EARTH'S NEAREST APPROACH

Earth's orbit around the sun is elliptical, hence our distance from the sun varies. The average distance of the sun is 93,003,000 miles. The closest approach (perihelion) is 91,342,000 miles and the farthest departure (aphelion) is 94,452,000 miles.

LARGEST SUN-SPOT

To be visible to the protected naked eye, a sun-spot must cover about one two-thousandth part of the sun's hemisphere and thus have an area of 500 million square miles. The largest recorded sun-spot occurred on 8th April, 1947, in the sun's southern hemisphere. Its area was 7,000 million square miles with an extreme longitude of 187,000 miles and an extreme latitude of 90,000 miles. Sun-spots appear darker because they are over 2,000°C. cooler than the rest of the sun's surface.

ECLIPSES

EARLIEST RECORDED

The earliest date of an identifiable eclipse accurately recorded is one in Assyria in the year 911 B.C. From London there was no total eclipse of the sun visible for the 575 years from 20th March, 1140 to 3rd May, 1715. The most recent visible total solar eclipse from Great Britain was on 29th June, 1927 and the next will occur on the Cornish coast on 11th August, 1999.

LONGEST DURATION

The maximum possible duration of an eclipse of the sun is 7 minutes 40 seconds. This could only occur at the Equator, but the longest actually occurring for over 2,550 years was on 20th June, 1955 (7 minutes 8 seconds). The longest possible in the British Isles is 5½ minutes. Those of 885 A.D. and 1715 were both nearly 5 minutes as will be the eclipse of 2381 A.D. The longest totality of any lunar eclipse is 104 minutes. This has occurred on many occasions.

FREQUENCY

Seven is the greatest number of eclipses possible in a year, for example as in 1935 when there were five solar and two lunar eclipses, or four solar and three lunar eclipses as will occur in 1982. The least possible number in a year is two, both of which must be solar as in 1944.

COMETS

EARLIEST RECORDED

The successive appearances of Halley's Comet have been traced to 240 B.C. The first prediction of its return by Halley proved true on Christmas Day 1758, sixteen years after his death. Its next appearance will be in 1986.

CLOSEST APPROACH

On 1st July, 1770, Lexell's Comet, travelling at a speed of 23·9 miles per second (relative to the sun) came within 1,500,000 miles of the Earth. In May, 1910 however, the Earth is believed to have passed through the tail of Halley's Comet.

SHORTEST PERIOD

Of all the recorded comets (these are members of the solar system), the one which most frequently returns is Encke's Comet, first identified in 1786. Its period is 3·3 years and not a single return has been missed by astronomers. At the other extreme is the Great Comet of 1864 whose path was not accurately determined but which is not expected to return for perhaps 2,800,000 years.

LARGEST COMET

Comets are so tenuous that it has been estimated that even their heads contain no mass in excess of 20 miles in diameter and that 10,000 cubic miles of tail contain less matter than a cubic inch of air. These tails, as in the case of the Great Comet of 1843, may trail out to 200,000,000 miles.

MOON

NEAREST APPROACH

The moon, Earth's closest neighbour and only satellite, is at a mean distance of 238,857 miles. Its closest approach (perigee) is 221,463 miles and its extreme distance away (apogee) is 252,710 miles. The moon was first hit by radar on 10th January, 1946.

LARGEST CRATER

Only 59 per cent. of the moon's surface is visible from the Earth. The largest known crater is the walled plain Bailly towards the South Pole which is 183 miles across and with walls rising to 14,000 feet. The nearby Newton crater is the deepest crater with a floor 29,000 feet below its rim.

HIGHEST MOUNTAINS

There being no water on the moon, the heights of mountains can only be measured in relation to lower-lying terrain near their bases. The highest of all the-lunar mountains are the Leibnitz near the South Pole which rise to nearly 35,000 feet.

TEMPERATURE RANGE

When the sun is overhead, the temperature on the lunar equator reaches 214°F. (slightly above the boiling point of water). By sunset the temperature is 58°F. but after nightfall the temperature sinks to nearly —250°F.

LIGHT YEAR—is that distance travelled by light (speed 186,239 miles per second) in one year and is 5,873,185,800,000 miles.

MAGNITUDE—is a measure of stellar brightness such that the light of a star of any magnitude bears a ratio of 2·512 to that of a star of the next magnitude. Thus a sixth magnitude star is 2·512 times less bright than a fifth magnitude star, while one of the first magnitude is exactly one hundred or $(2{\cdot}512)^5$ times brighter. In the case of such exceptionally bright bodies as Sirius, Jupiter or the Moon, the magnitude is expressed as a minus quantity.

PROPER MOTION—that component of a star's motion in space, which, at right angles to the line of sight, constitutes an apparent change of position of the star in the celestial sphere.

TWO

THE NATURAL WORLD

1. Natural Phenomena

METEORITES

METEOR SHOWER

Meteors are mostly of cometary origin. The greatest meteor shower on record occurred on 12th November, 1833, when the Leonid meteors fell for several hours at an estimated rate of 200,000 per hour.

METEORITE CRATER

When a meteor penetrates to the Earth's surface, the remnant is described as a meteorite. The largest meteorite crater is the water-filled Chubb Crater in Northern Ungava, Canada. It was first sighted from a 'plane on 20th June, 1943 and was later found to have a rim 7½ miles round and to be 1,350 feet deep (see Photo Plate 1).

The largest dry crater is the Coon Butte crater near Canyon Diablo, Winslow, Northern Arizona, in the United States which is 4,000 feet in diameter and now about 550 feet deep with a parapet rising 130 to 155 feet above the surrounding plain. It has been estimated that a mass of 25,000 tons travelling at 36,000 m.p.h. would have been required to gouge this crater.

LARGEST METEORITES

The largest known meteorite is at Hoba West, near Grootfontein in South West Africa. This is a block about 9 feet long by 8 feet broad weighing approximately 60 metric tons (59 long tons). The heaviest meteorite housed by any museum is the "Tent" meteorite on exhibition at the Hayden Planetarium, 81st Street, Central Park West, New York. It weighs 32·5 tons and measures approximately 11 × 7 × 5 feet. It was recovered from Cape York in Greenland in 1897 by Admiral Peary.

The largest meteorite to hit the earth in historic times fell near Vanovara, Central Siberia, on the 30th June, 1908. The lowest estimate of the original mass before disintegration is 200 tons.

England

The heaviest meteorite known to have fallen in England weighed 56 lb. It fell on 13th December, 1795, at Wold Cottage, near Scarborough, Yorkshire.

Scotland

Scotland's largest recorded meteorite fell at Strathmore, Perthshire, on 3rd December, 1917. It weighed 22¼ lb. and was the largest of four stones totalling 29⅝ lb.

Ireland — The largest recorded meteorite to fall in the whole British Isles was the Limerick Stone of 65 lb. which fell on 10th September, 1813.

Wales — The only recorded meteorite to land in Wales was the 25½ oz. stone which went through the roof of a building in Beddgelert, Caernarvonshire, on 21st September, 1949.

AURORA

MOST FREQUENT — Polar lights, known as Aurora Borealis or Northern Lights in the northern hemisphere and Aurora Australis in the southern hemisphere, caused by electrical solar discharge, occur most frequently in high latitudes. The maximum auroral frequency, in excess of one hundred displays a year, occur in the region of the north magnetic pole near the Boothia Felix Peninsula, North Canada.

SOUTHERNMOST " NORTHERN LIGHTS " — Displays occur on an average ninety times a year in the Orkney Isles, twenty-five times a year in Edinburgh, seven times a year in London, and once a decade in Southern Italy. On 25th September, 1909, a display was witnessed as far south as Singapore. The greatest auroral display over the United Kingdom in recent times occurred on 25th January, 1938.

ALTITUDE — The extreme height of auroras has been measured at 620 miles while the lowest may descend to 45 miles.

EARTHQUAKES

WORLD'S GREATEST — Earthquakes are instrumentally measured on the Gutenberg-Richter scale. The highest readings yet obtained are magnitudes of 8·6 on two occasions. The earlier was the Colombian earthquake of 31st January, 1906, with a submarine epicentre Lat. 1°N., Long. 81½°W. and the more recent Assam earthquake of 15th August, 1950, with its epicentre Lat. 28°36′N., Long. 96°30′E. In Sagami Bay, Japan, the sea-bottom in one area sank 1,310 feet after the Kwanto shock of 1923.

WORLD'S WORST — The official total of persons killed and missing after the Kwanto earthquake in Japan on 1st September, 1923, was 142,807 people. The epicentre was in Lat. 24°58′N., Long. 139°21′E. Tokyo and Yokohama were largely destroyed. The damage was estimated at £1,000 million.

England — The East Anglian or Colchester " twin " earthquake of 22nd April, 1884 (epicentres Lat. 51°48′N., Long. 0°53′E. and Lat. 51°51′N., Long. 0°55′E.) caused damage estimated at £10,000 and the death of a child at Rowhedge. Langenhoe Church was wrecked. The only other recorded fatality in the British Isles was a man struck by falling masonry from a church in the City of London on 6th April, 1580.

Scotland — The strongest Scottish tremor occurred at Inverness on 13th August, 1816.

Wales — The strongest Welsh tremor occurred at Swansea on 27th June, 1906 (epicentre Lat. 51°38′N., Long. 4°W.).

Ireland — No earthquake with its epicentre in Ireland has ever been instrumentally measured, though the effects of remoter shocks have been felt. In August 1734 there was a shock which, however, damaged one hundred dwellings and five churches.

VOLCANOES

GREATEST ERUPTION

The total volume of matter discharged from Tambora, the East Indies volcano, on the island of Sumbawa, has been estimated as 36·4 cubic miles. The volcano lost over 4,000 feet in height and a crater 7 miles in diameter was formed. This compares with the 4·3 cubic miles ejected in the Krakatoa eruption (see below).

LOUDEST EXPLOSION

The greatest explosion in recorded history occurred at 2.56 G.M.T. on 27th August, 1883, with the eruption of Krakatoa, a small island lying in the Sunda Strait between Sumatra and Java in Indonesia. Rocks were projected to a height of 34·1 miles with dust falling 10 days later at a distance of 3,313 miles. The explosion was recorded 4 hours later on Rodriguez Island 3,000 miles away as the " roar of heavy guns " and was heard over 1/13th part of the surface of the globe. This explosion has been estimated to have had over a hundred times the power of the largest H-bomb test detonation.

HIGHEST

Active

Mount Antofalla (19,921 feet) in the Puna Atacama region of the Andes range in Argentina, South America.

Dormant

Though no eruptions are known, the dormant Andean peak Mount Llullaillaco (21,719 feet) on the borders of Chile and Argentina still occasionally emits gases and volatile substances.

Extinct

Mount Aconcagua (22,811 feet), first climbed in 1897, on the Argentine side of the Chile-Argentina border. This Andean peak is the highest mountain on the American continent.

Northernmost

This is Beerenberg (8,349 feet) on Jan Mayen Island in the Greenland Sea, north of the Arctic Circle. The island, probably discovered in 1614, was annexed by Norway in 1929.

Southernmost

The most southerly known active volcano is Mount Erebus (12,762 feet) on Victoria Land in Antarctica.

GEYSERS WORLD'S LARGEST

The Waimangu geyser, New Zealand in 1909 erupted to a height in excess of 1,000 feet but is now quiescent. Currently the world's largest active geyser is the " Giant " in the Yellowstone National Park, Wyoming, U.S.A. which erupts at intervals varying from 7 days to 3 months, throwing a spire 200 feet high at a rate of 700,000 gallons an hour. The " Great Geyser " in Iceland, from which all others have been named, spurts, on occasions, to 180 feet.

2. *Weather*

The meteorological records printed below necessarily relate largely to the last 100 to 120 years, since data before that time is both sparse and unreliable.

TEMPERATURE

The world average temperature is 59°F (15°C).

WORLD'S HIGHEST

On 13th September, 1922, at Azizia in North Western Libya, 25 miles south of Tripoli, a shade reading of 58·0°C (136·4°F) was obtained under standard conditions. The hottest place in the world considered over the year is generally allowed to be the Red Sea port of Massawa in Eritrea where the annual average (day and night) is 86°F (30°C).

BRITISH ISLES' HIGHEST

On 22nd July, 1868, at Tonbridge, Kent, England, a screen reading of 100·5°F (38°C) was obtained under standard conditions. A reading of 100°F (37·8°C) was obtained at the Royal Observatory, Greenwich, on 9th August, 1911. The warmest night recorded in London, was the 29th July, 1948, with a minimum night temperature of 74°F.

Ireland

The highest temperature ever recorded in Ireland was the 92°F noted at Phoenix Park, Dublin, on 16th July, 1876.

WORLD'S LOWEST

On 5th and 7th February, 1892, readings of 122 degrees of frost, or —90°F (—67·8°C), were obtained at Verkhoyansk, Siberia. Readings of —94°F (—70°C) were reported on 3rd January, 1885, and again during the winter of 1946-7 but were not verified by the Soviet Government. The coldest recorded place in the world considered over a year is the Antarctic station of Framheim where the annual average (day and night) has been —14°F (—25·5°C).

BRITISH ISLES' LOWEST

On 24th February, 1955, at Grantown-on-Spey, Morayshire, Scotland, a screen reading of —20°F (52 degrees of frost) was obtained The oft-quoted —23°F at Blackadder, Berwickshire, Scotland, on 4th December, 1879, is not accepted because the exposure of the thermometer was not standard.

England

The lowest temperature recorded for England is the 43 degrees of frost (—11°F) at Buxton, Derbyshire on 11th February, 1895. The —15°F reading at Cheadle, Staffordshire, on 25th December, 1860, was not standard. The London record is —9°F at Northolt on 29th January, 1947.

Wales

The lowest temperature recorded for Wales is the 42 degrees of frost (—10°F) at Rhayader, Radnorshire, on 21st January, 1940.

Ireland

The lowest air temperature ever recorded in Ireland was the 2°F at Markree Castle, County Sligo, on 16th January, 1881.

LONGEST FREEZE

The longest unremitting freeze in the British Isles (maximum temperature 32°F and below) is the twenty-five consecutive days from 26th January to 19th February, 1947, at Glenlivet, Banffshire, Scotland. Apart from a brief thaw during 19th and 20th February, 1947, this severe frost continued until 2nd March, 1947.

GREATEST TEMPERATURE RANGE

In the Siberian settlement of Yakutsk, a daily range of 181·4°F (100·7°C) has been recorded. This compares with the 120·5°F which separates the highest and lowest temperatures ever recorded over the whole of the British Isles.

RAINFALL

The world average is 33 inches per year.

WORLD'S GREATEST RAINFALL

Difficulties attend rainfall readings for very short periods but the figure of 1·03 inches in one minute recorded at San Gabriel Range, California, on 5th April, 1926, is regarded as the most intense ever attained.

Day

During a typhoon at Baguio on the island of Luzon, Philippines, 45·99 inches fell in the 24 hours on 14th-15th July, 1911. This deluge represented 4,645 tons of water per acre.

Month

During the July of the 1861 monsoon, 366 inches were reported from Cherrapunji in the Khasi Hills of Assam, North East India.

Year

The highest recorded figure for any given year was the 905 inches at Cherrapunji in 1861, but for annual average the Cherrapunji figure of 424 inches is surpassed by the 489 inches averaged over the last thirty years at Mount Waialeale, Island of Kauai, Hawaiian Islands, which has the largest rain gauge in the world.

BRITISH ISLES' GREATEST RAINFALL

Hour

In July 1901, 3·63 inches fell in one hour at Maidenhead (Lowood), Berkshire, England.

Day

From 9 a.m., 28th June to 29th June, 1917, at Sexey's School, near Bruton, Somerset, 9·56 inches fell, being equivalent to 965·6 tons of rain per acre. On 6th August, 1857, the measurement of a fall at Scarborough, Yorkshire, reached 9·5 inches in a day before the gauge overflowed.

The Welsh record is 8·31 inches at Lluest Wen Reservoir, Rhondda, Glamorganshire, on 11th-12th November, 1929, and the Scottish record is 8·20 inches at Kinlochquoich, Inverness-shire, on 11th October, 1916.

Week

The greatest rainfall in a week occurred at Ben Nevis, Inverness-shire, from 24th-30th January, 1903, when 20·57 inches fell.

Month

During October, 1909, 56·5 inches fell on Snowdon, Caernarvonshire, Wales.

Year

The highest rainfall for a year occurred at Borrowdale, Cumberland, England, in 1928 when 250·0 inches were recorded.

LONGEST RAIN SPELL

In 1923, it rained every day from 12th August to 8th November inclusive (89 days) both at Eallabus, Isle of Islay, off Western Scotland, and at Ballynahinch Castle, Galway, Ireland. At the latter station, 309 rainy days have been recorded in a year.

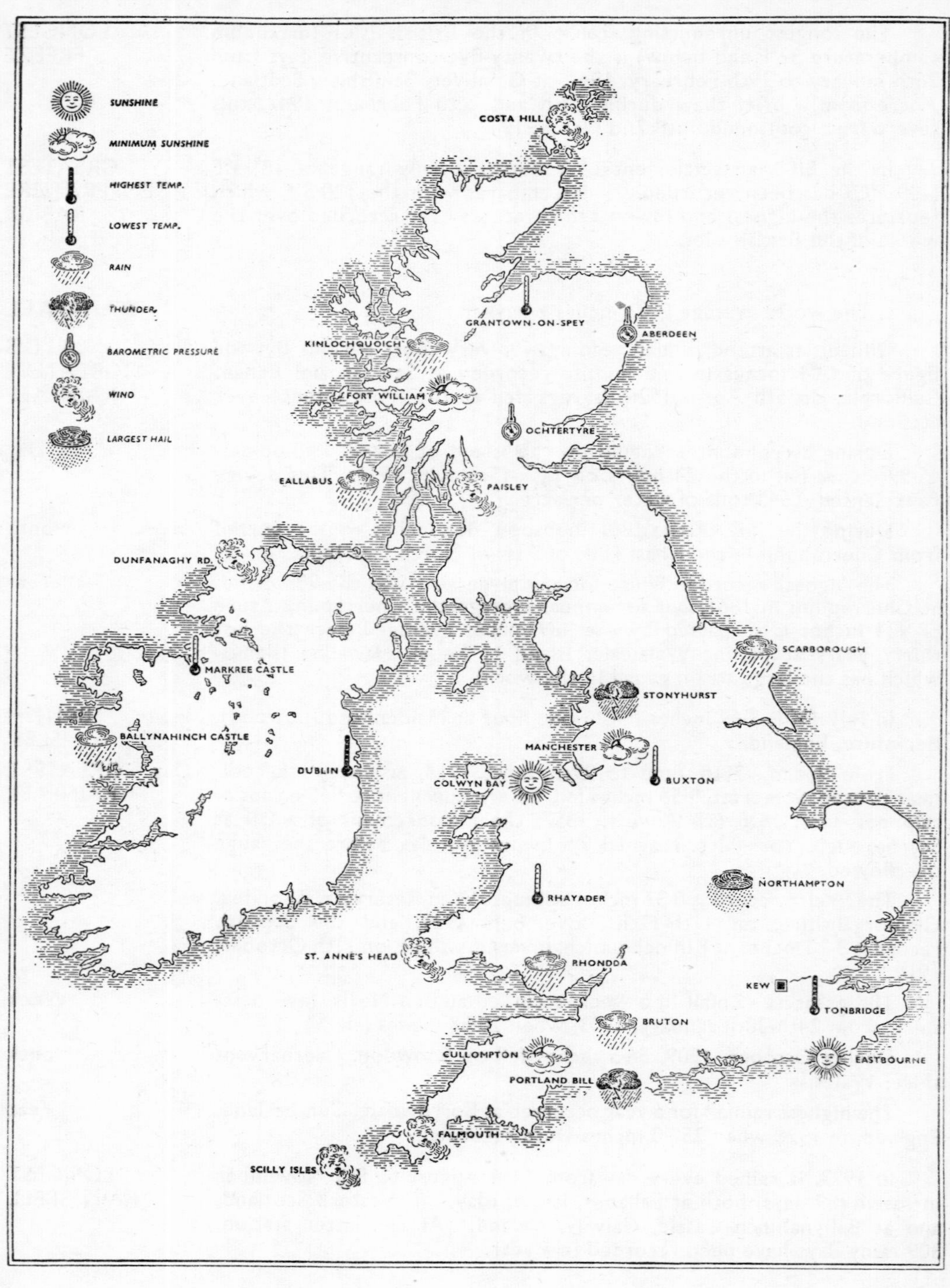
SUNSHINE
MINIMUM SUNSHINE
HIGHEST TEMP.
LOWEST TEMP.
RAIN
THUNDER
BAROMETRIC PRESSURE
WIND
LARGEST HAIL
COSTA HILL
GRANTOWN-ON-SPEY
ABERDEEN
KINLOCHQUOICH
FORT WILLIAM
OCHTERTYRE
EALLABUS
PAISLEY
DUNFANAGHY RD.
MARKREE CASTLE
BALLYNAHINCH CASTLE
DUBLIN
SCARBOROUGH
STONYHURST
MANCHESTER
COLWYN BAY
BUXTON
NORTHAMPTON
RHAYADER
ST. ANNE'S HEAD
RHONDDA
KEW
TONBRIDGE
BRUTON
CULLOMPTON
EASTBOURNE
PORTLAND BILL
FALMOUTH
SCILLY ISLES

FALSEST ST. SWITHIN'S DAYS

The legend that the weather on St. Swithin's Day, celebrated on 15th July since 912 A.D., determines the rainfall for the next forty days, is one which has long persisted. On 15th July, 1924, in London, there was a brilliant 13½ hours of sunshine but thirty of the next forty days were wet. On 15th July, 1913, there was a 15-hour downpour yet it rained on only nine of the subsequent forty days.

WORLD'S LARGEST HAILSTONES

The largest authenticated hailstones recorded were those weighed and measured, dissected and photographed at Potter, Nebraska, U.S.A. on 6th July, 1928. One weighed 1½ lb. and was 17 inches in circumference. There is an older and less well established record of 4½ lb. at Cazorla, Spain, on 15th June, 1829, but this may have been coalesced stones.

BRITISH ISLES' LARGEST HAILSTONES

The largest authenticated hailstone recorded to fall in the British Isles was 2 inches in diameter at Northampton on 22nd September, 1935. The damage done to St. Andrew's Hospital alone was over £600. One stone picked up at Rushden was stated to be as large as a tennis ball. A stone 5 inches by 3 inches was reported at Barton, Lincolnshire, on 3rd July, 1883.

BRITISH ISLES' LOWEST RAINFALL

In the entire year of 1921, only 9·29 inches of rain fell at Margate, Kent, England. The lowest London reading occurred in the same year with 12·16 inches.

LONGEST DROUGHT

At Hastings, Winchelsea, Lewes, and Haywards Heath in Sussex, England, there was an absolute drought (no day credited with 0·01 inches of rain or more) lasting sixty days from 4th March to 14th May, 1893. London's longest drought was the forty-six days during the " Battle of Britain " from 28th July, 1940, to 11th September, 1940.

SNOWFALL

The ratio of inches of snow to equivalent inches of rain vary between extremes from 5 to 1 (granular) to 50 to 1 (very loose). A common value is 11-12 inches to 1 inch of rain.

WORLD'S GREATEST

The heaviest falls of snow occur in polar regions and hence remain unrecorded. However, 883 inches (over 73 feet) were recorded in the single winter of 1906-7 at Tamarack, California, U.S.A.

BRITISH ISLES' HEAVIEST

Wind and drifting make statistics on snow depths unreliable. A level ground reading of 72 inches was recorded in 15 hours on south-east Dartmoor, west of Holne Chase, on 16th February, 1929. A snowdrift 60 feet deep in gullies near Harford, South Devon, was measured in 1927. The 300 feet deep drifts reported in Tavy Cleave, Dartmoor, in March, 1891, were not acceptably measured.

LATEST

The snow in the Great Corrie of Allt-a-Mhullin, north-east of Ben Nevis, remains unmelted during most summers. Snow fell as far south as the Isle of Wight on 11th July, 1888. London's latest snow was on 16th May in the years 1891, 1923 and 1935, and on the night 17th-18th May in 1955.

SUNSHINE

WORLD'S MAXIMUM

In latitudes higher than 66° in the polar summers the sun does not sink below the horizon. At the Canadian-U.S. Weather Station,

Alert, Dumb Bell Bay, Ellesmere Island, above 82°N, the sun does not set for 147 days. Observations in Antarctica showed conditions of cloudlessness permitting 60 hours of continuous sunshine during 9th-12th December, 1911.

HIGHEST SUN ANGLE The highest angle attained by the sun in London (Greenwich) is 61°58′ at midday on 21st June.

BRITISH ISLES

Day In the latitude 60°N in the Shetlands, there is a possible maximum June average of 18 hours 35 minutes sunshine a day. The possible maximum June average in London (Kew) is 16 hours 28 minutes. The highest durations actually recorded are 17 hours 6 minutes at Deerness, Orkney, on 14th June, 1920 (93·7 per cent. of possible) and 15 hours 48 minutes at Kew on 13th June, 1887 (95·9 per cent. of possible).

Week The highest sunshine duration for a week occurred at Colwyn Bay, North Wales, from 2nd-8th June, 1940, with 105·4 hours (91·6 per cent. of possible).

Month The record sunshine for a month in the British Isles is the 384·0 hours at both Eastbourne and Hastings, Sussex, England, in July, 1911 (77·6 per cent. of possible).

Year The highest annual duration recorded is 2,263 hours at Shanklin, Isle of Wight, in 1949. In Jersey in 1893, there was a total of 2,340 hours (52·6 per cent. of possible). The Irish record is 1,784 hours at Valentia, Co. Kerry, in 1887.

WORLD'S MINIMUM In polar winters, there are periods of months when the sun does not rise above the horizon. At Alert, the U.S.-Canadian arctic weather station, the sun sinks below the horizon for 145 days before again appearing.

BRITISH ISLES There are frequently days with no measurable sunshine. The maximum possible sunshine in the Shetlands (60°N) on an average December day is only 5 hours 55 minutes.

Month The lowest recorded sunshine readings for a month are 18 minutes both for Kew in December 1890, and for Manchester in December 1912. The lowest Scottish reading was 30 minutes at Fort William, Inverness-shire, in December 1936.

Year The record low annual sunshine figure for a year in England is the 1,101 hours at Cullompton, Devonshire, in 1912 (24·7 per cent. of possible). In 1933, the total duration at Fort Augustus, Inverness-shire, Scotland, was only 695 hours.

BAROMETRIC PRESSURE

The world average barometric pressure is 1,013 millibars—29·92 inches.

WORLD EXTREMES

Highest The highest barometric pressure ever recorded was at Irkutsk, Siberia, on 20th December, 1896, when there was a reading of 31·717 inches (1,074 m.b.). A reading of 31·75 inches (1,075 m.b.) has also been quoted for Siberia on 16th December, 1887.

Lowest The lowest recorded barometric pressure is the 26·29 inches (886·8 m.b.) in a typhoon in the Luzon Sea aboard the Dutch vessel "Sapoeroea" on 18th August, 1927.

BRITISH ISLES

Highest The highest barometric reading for the British Isles is 31·11 inches (1,054·7 m.b.) at Aberdeen, Scotland, on 31st January, 1902.

Lowest

The lowest barometric reading for the British Isles is 27·332 inches (925·5 m.b.) at Ochtertyre Crief, Perthshire, Scotland, at 8.30 p.m. on 26th January, 1884.

WIND EXTREMES

It has been calculated from the destructive effects produced that wind speed attained during tornadoes surpasses 500 m.p.h. Calculations have given values of 682 m.p.h. during the tornado at Mayfield, Ohio, U.S.A., on 4th February, 1842, and 558 m.p.h. at St. Louis, Missouri, U.S.A., on 27th May, 1896. Doubts, however, have been cast on these estimated figures. The highest instrumental reading obtained is 231 m.p.h. at 1·21 p.m. on 24th April, 1934, by Salvador Tagluica at Mount Washington Research Station, New Hampshire, U.S.A. (altitude 6,248 feet). It is known that in the upper atmosphere 'jet streams' attain speeds of over 300 knots (345 m.p.h.).

British Isles

The maximum wind velocity recorded in the British Isles was the 125 m.p.h. at Costa Hill, Orkneys, on 31st January, 1953.

England

The highest reading for the English mainland is 103 m.p.h. at Pendennis Castle, Falmouth, on 8th March, 1922, and 6th December, 1929. On the latter occasion 111 m.p.h. was measured in the Scilly Isles. The calmest place in the British Isles is Kew Observatory, London. The windiest place is the Butt of Lewis, Outer Hebrides.

Wales

On 18th January, 1945, the anemometer reached its limit at 113 m.p.h. on St. Ann's Head, Pembrokeshire.

Scotland

The highest wind speed recorded on the mainland of Scotland is 104 m.p.h. at Paisley, Renfrewshire, on 28th January, 1927.

Ireland

On the same day as the 1929 English record, the Irish record of 109 m.p.h. was recorded at Dunfanaghy Road, Donegal.

THUNDER World

The most thundery places in the world are in the tropics. The place with most thunderstorms a year is usually allowed to be Leon, Mexico, with an annual average of 142. The maximum range at which thunder can be heard is estimated variously from 24 to even 40 miles.

British Isles

The maximum reading for the British Isles is 38 thundery days at Stoneyhurst, Lancashire, in 1912. The best record of being thunder free is held by Portland Bill, Dorsetshire, where no thunder was recorded either in 1920 or 1922.

FOG

A condition of fog exists when the visibility is less than 1,100 yards.

World

The foggiest area of the Earth is recognized to be the Grand Banks of Newfoundland which are highly subject to advection sea fogs.

British Isles

The foggiest area in the British Isles is that around Huddersfield in the West Riding of Yorkshire where the visibility is less than 1,100 yards at 9 a.m. on more than fifty mornings a year. The greatest recorded duration of any fog in the British Isles is 114 hours (4 days 18 hours) in London on two occasions — 9 p.m. 26th November to 3 p.m. 1st December, 1948, and midnight of 4th December to 6 p.m. 9th December, 1952. Great fogs blanketed London during the period November 1879 to February 1880.

CLOUD EXTREMES

The highest standard cloud form is the cirrus averaging 27,000 feet and above but the rare mother of pearl formation sometimes reaches nearly 80,000 feet. The lowest is stratus, below 3,500 feet. The cloud form with the greatest vertical range is cumulo-nimbus which sometimes towers to 30,000 feet. Noctilucent ' clouds ' are believed to pass at a height of over 60 miles.

War-time statistics show that the point in the British Isles most frequently beset by cloud beneath 1,000 feet was St. Eval, Cornwall, with an annual average of 89 days for 1 p.m. readings.

The station with the best record of cloudlessness was Felixstowe, Suffolk, with 151 nights free from cloud below 8,000 feet (1 a.m. readings).

3. *Structure and Dimensions*

LARGEST DIAMETER

The Earth is not a true sphere. The polar diameter of the Earth (7,899·98 miles) is 26·7 miles less than the equatorial diameter (7,926·68 miles). As well as this spheroid departure from a true sphere, the Earth also has a slight ellipticity of the equator which shows it is a geoid form with a long axis (about longitude 0°) approximately 174 yards greater than the short axis. The greatest circumference of the Earth, at the Equator, is 24,901·96 miles.

SURFACE RANGE

The surface of the Earth, although broken by mountains, which rise to 29,160 feet and fissures which descend to 35,640 feet above and below sea level, has in relation to its size a very smooth surface. The total difference between the highest and lowest points being 64,800 feet or (estimating on the equatorial diameter of the Earth) a surface accuracy of 0·1545 per cent. On the basis of a billiard ball 2·1 inches in diameter, this would be represented by a scratch ·00315 inches, about 1/317th of an inch, deep.

EARTH'S STRUCTURE

The Earth weighs 5,900,000,000,000,000,000,000 tons and has a density of 5·53 times that of water. Modern theory is that the Earth has an outer shell or lithosphere about 25 miles thick, then an outer and inner rock layer extending 1,800 miles deep after which there is a molten iron-nickel core at a temperature of perhaps 5,400°F and at a pressure of 25,000 tons to the square inch. If the iron-nickel core theory is correct iron must be by far the most abundant element in the Earth. If calculations are confined to the Earth's crust, the most abundant element is oxygen particularly in the form of silica (silicon dioxide, SiO_2) constituting 59 per cent. of the crust and alumina (Al_2O_3) 15 per cent. of the crust.

The most abundant metal in the Earth's crust is aluminium at 7·5 per cent. to 8 per cent. Gold accounts for perhaps 0·0000005 per cent. while it has been contended that the existence in nature of masurium and illinium has not yet been established.

OLDEST ROCKS

The age of the Earth must of necessity be only an approximation but modern theory suggests 3,400,000,000 years.

Rocks estimated stratigraphically (by the study of their formation and structure) have been found in Africa and Canada which are regarded as the oldest outcrops in the world, being probably in excess of 3,000 million years old.

One of the modern methods of estimating age in geological formation is by measurement of the disintegration of radio-active substances in the sample.

The oldest reliably dated mineral is a monazite from ebonite tantalum claims in the Bikita District of Southern Rhodesia at a minimum of 2,600 million and a maximum of 2,680 million years. There is a less well founded claim for a 2,820 million year old lepidolite from Popes Claim near Salisbury, S. Rhodesia.

No British pre-Cambrian minerals have yet been dated but the oldest outcrops in England are believed to be quartz-mica-schists near Rushton, Shropshire, and schists and granalites of the Old Lizard Head Series in Cornwall. The oldest in Scotland are Lewisian gneisses in the north-west Highlands, the outer Hebrides and on Coll and Tiree. The oldest Welsh rocks are probably the gneisses in the Mona Complex of Anglesey.

OCEAN

LARGEST

The area of the Earth covered by the sea is approximately 139 million square miles, about 71 per cent. of the world's surface.

The largest ocean in the world is the Pacific. Including adjacent seas, it represents approximately 50 per cent. of the world's oceans and is 69,374,182 square miles in area.

DEEPS

The deepest ocean sounding in the world was made by the H.M. Survey Ship "Challenger" on 14th June, 1951. In the Western Pacific Ocean near the Mariana Islands, 200 miles south-west of Guam, the depth of the Mariana Trench was established at 35,640 feet. A metal object, say a pound ball of steel, dropped into the water above this deep would take approximately 62 minutes to fall to the sea-bed 6¾ miles below. The average depth of the Pacific Ocean is 13,215 feet.

The deepest sounding in the Atlantic Ocean is north of Puerto Rico and is 30,143 feet. The average depth of the Atlantic Ocean is 10,950 feet.

The deepest sounding in the Indian Ocean is the Sundar Trench 17,850 feet deep. The average depth of the Indian Ocean is 12,750 feet.

SALINITY

The most common elements by weight in sea-water are chlorine, approximately 1·9 lb., and sodium, approximately 1·05 lb. in every 100 lb. of sea water.

Although the proportions of the salts in the sea remain very much the same all over the world, salinity does vary. It is saltiest in the Red Sea where evaporation is high and the total salts may exceed 4 lb. in a 100 lb. of sea water.

In the Arctic and Antarctic regions, snow and melting ice tend to dilute the oceans and the total salts are approximately 3·2 lb. per 100 lb.

TEMPERATURE

The temperature of the water at the surface of the sea varies from approximately 28·5°F (—2°C) in the Polar regions to between 85°-90°F (31°C) in the Equatorial zones.

HIGHEST WAVE

The greatest possible height of a wave at sea is usually cited at 60 feet. However, the highest officially recorded sea-wave was measured from " U.S.S. Ramapo " proceeding from Manila to San Diego on the night 6th-7th February, 1933, during a 68-knot (78·3 m.p.h.) gale. The wave measured 112 feet from trough to crest.

The highest seismic sea wave, or tsunami recorded is that produced by the Krakatoa earthquake of 1883 (q.v.) at 135 feet. This type of wave has been observed to travel across oceans at over 460 m.p.h.

TIDES— WORLD'S GREATEST

The greatest tides in the world are found in the Bay of Fundy which separates Nova Scotia from the United States' north-easternmost state of Maine and the Canadian province of New Brunswick. Burncoat Head in the Minas Basin, Nova Scotia, has the largest mean spring range with 45·0 feet. Extreme ranges up to 53·0 feet have been recorded, for example, at Moncton on the Petitcodiac River, New Brunswick, in 1869.

England's

The place with the highest mean spring range in England and in the British Isles is New Passage on the Severn with 40·1 feet against a British Isles average of 15 feet.

Since records have been standardized, the highest tide recorded for the Thames (London Bridge) was on 6th January, 1929, when the water rose to 18·2 feet above the Ordnance Datum, Liverpool. The lowest recorded was on 14th March, 1914, when the water fell 10·3 feet below the Datum, though there is reason to believe an even lower level was reached in 1717.

Wales'

The record Welsh tides occur also in the Severn estuary at Newport, Monmouthshire, which has a mean spring range of 39·1 feet. Some 20 miles farther up on the north bank of the Bristol Channel at Chepstow an extreme range of 48·5 feet was recorded in 1883.

Scotland's

The point in Scotland with the highest mean spring range is Alloa, Clackmannanshire, on the north bank of the Firth of Forth with 17·8 feet.

Ireland's

The greatest mean spring tidal range in the whole of Ireland is at Mellon on the banks of the River Shannon at 18·3 feet. The largest range in Northern Ireland occurs at Newcastle, County Down, at 14·7 feet.

ICEBERG

The largest iceberg on record is one of 220 square miles in extent reported in the Antarctic in February 1955.

The southernmost iceberg reported in British home waters was one 60 miles from Smith's Knoll, near the Dogger Bank, in the North Sea.

LARGEST AND SMALLEST CONTINENT

Only 29 per cent. of the Earth's surface is land. The Eurasian land mass is the largest with an area of 20,750,000 square miles.

The smallest is the Australian mainland with an area of 2,974,581 square miles, which together with New Zealand and the Pacific Islands is included in Oceania.

LARGEST ISLANDS

Discounting Australia, which is usually regarded as a continental land mass, the largest island in the world is commonly cited as Greenland, with an area of 827,300 square miles. Recent exploration of its ice-cap suggests, however, that it may in fact consist of three islands. If this proves to be the case, New Guinea with an area of 316,861 square miles will be recognized as the world's largest island.

The mainland of Great Britain (Scotland, England and Wales) is by far the largest of the 187 inhabited islands forming the British Isles and is the eighth largest in the world with an area of 84,186 square miles. The remotest of the inhabited British islands is Foula in the Shetland group.

ATOLLS

The largest atoll in the world is Bikini in the Pacific, which encloses a lagoon of 280 square miles. Christmas Island, however, though its lagoon is only 89 square miles, has a coral area of 184 square miles.

REEFS

The largest reef in the world is the Great Barrier Reef off Queensland, North East Australia, which is 900 geographical miles in length.

MOUNTAINS HIGHEST

The Eastern Himalayan peak on the Tibet-Nepal border named Kang Chamolung (variously Cho-Mo-Lung-Ma) of 29,160 feet was discovered to be the world's highest mountain in 1852 by Radhanath Sikdar, Chief Computer to the Survey Department of the Government of India, from theodolite readings taken three years before. In 1860 its height was computed to be 29,002 feet. The $5\frac{1}{2}$-mile high peak was renamed Mount Everest in 1856 after Sir George Everest, former Surveyor-General of India. After the loss of eleven lives, Everest was finally conquered at 11·30 a.m. on 29th May, 1953, by Edmund P. Hillary of New Zealand, 33, (created K.B.E.) and the Sherpa, Tensing Norkay, 39, (awarded G.M.). The successful expedition was commanded by Col. H. C. J. Hunt, C.B.E., D.S.O., (created Knight Bachelor).

HIGHEST UNCLIMBED

With the successful climbing of K.2. (Mount Godwin-Austen) (28,250 feet), in the Jammu-Kashmir part of the Karakorums by Ardito Desio's Italian expedition on 31st July, 1954, and Kangchenjunga (28,166 feet) on the Nepal-Sikkim border by a British Expedition on 25th May, 1955, the highest unclimbed peak became Everest's neighbour, Lhotse I (27,890 feet).

LARGEST

The world's tallest mountain measured from base to peak is Mount Kea in the Hawaiian Islands at 30,750 feet of which 13,784 feet is above sea level. Another mountain whose dimensions exceed those of Everest is the Hawaiian peak, Mauna Loa of 13,680 feet. The greater and lesser diameter of its elliptical base, 15,000 feet below sea level, have been estimated at 74 miles and 53 miles.

MOST RECENTLY DISCOVERED

It was announced on 16th February, 1955, that Soviet surveyors had discovered a peak in N.E. Siberia 24,664 feet high. This mountain, higher than any in Africa, America, or Europe, was named Stalin Peak.

DEEPEST DEPRESSION

The deepest depression on the land surface of the Earth is the shores surrounding the Dead Sea, 1,286 feet below sea level.

BRITISH ISLES' HIGHEST MOUNTAINS

The highest mountain in Scotland and the British Isles is Ben Nevis (Gaelic for Snow Mountain) at 4,406 feet. It lies $4\frac{1}{4}$ miles south-east of Fort William, Inverness-shire.

England's highest mountain is Scafell Pike (3,210 feet) in the Lake District of Cumberland.

The highest mountain in Wales is Snowdon (Moel-y-Wyddfa) in Caernarvonshire, at 3,560 feet.

The highest point in Ireland is Carrantuohill (3,414 feet) in County Kerry.

HIGHEST POINTS
By Counties
England

County	Height	Location
Bedfordshire	780 feet	Dunshill Moor in Chilterns, nr. Dunstable
Berkshire	975 feet	Inkpen Beacon and Walbury Hill
Buckinghamshire	852 feet	Coombe Hill, nr. Wendover
Cambridgeshire	480 feet	300 yards south of the Hall, Great Chishill
Cheshire	1,908 feet	Black Hill
Cornwall	1,380 feet	Brown Willy
Cumberland	3,210 feet	Scafell Pike
Derbyshire	2,088 feet	Kinder Scout, between Crowden Head and Kinder Low
Devonshire	2,039 feet	High Willhays, 4 miles south of Okehampton
Dorset	909 feet	Pilsdon Pen, nr. Broadwindsor
Durham	2,430 feet	Burnhope Seat
Ely, Isle of	120 feet	North Hill, Haddenham
Essex	480 feet	in High Wood, nr. Langley
Gloucestershire	1,083 feet	Cleeve Hill, 3 miles north-east of Cheltenham
Hampshire	889 feet	Butser Hill, nr. Petersfield
Herefordshire	2,306 feet	Black Mountains
Hertfordshire	709 feet	Hastoe Hill, nr. Tring
Huntingdonshire	256 feet	1 mile north of Covington
Kent	808 feet	Between Westerham and Biggin Hill
Lancashire	2,633 feet	Coniston Old Man
Leicestershire	912 feet	Bardon Hill, $2\frac{1}{4}$ miles E.S.E. of Coalville
Lincolnshire	584 feet	nr. Normanby-le-Wold
London	443 feet	nr. Whitestones Pond on Hampstead Heath
Middlesex	504 feet	High Road, Bushey Heath
Norfolk	327 feet	nr. "Pretty Corner", Upper Sheringham
Northamptonshire	734 feet	Arbury Hill, nr. Daventry
Northumberland	2,676 feet	The Cheviot
Nottinghamshire	650 feet	Strawberry Bank, Huthwaite
Oxfordshire	836 feet	Portobello, Chilterns
Rutland	625 feet	Ranksborough Hill, north of Oakham
Shropshire	1,790 feet	Brown Clee Hill
Somerset	1,706 feet	Dunkery Beacon
Staffordshire	1,091 feet	Mow Cop
Suffolk	420 feet	Rede
Surrey	965 feet	Leith Hill, nr. Dorking

Sussex (East)	813 feet	Ditchling Beacon
(West)	918 feet	Blackdown Hill, Fernhurst
Warwickshire	854 feet	Ilmington Downs
Westmorland	3,118 feet	Helvellyn, on Cumberland border
Wiltshire	964 feet	Milk Hill, $1\frac{1}{4}$ miles north of Alton Barnes
Worcestershire	1,395 feet	Worcestershire Beacon, Malvern Hills
Yorkshire		
East Riding	808 feet	Garrowby Hill
North Riding	2,591 feet	Mickle Fell
West Riding	2,414 feet	Whernside
Isle of Man	2,034 feet	Snaefell
Isle of Wight	787 feet	St. Boniface Down, nr. Ventnor

HIGHEST POINTS
By Counties
Wales

Anglesey	720 feet	Mynydd Twr
Breconshire	2,906 feet	Penyfan or Cader Arthur
Caernarvonshire	3,560 feet	Snowdon (Y Wyddfa)
Cardiganshire	2,468 feet	Plynlimon
Carmarthenshire	2,460 feet	Carmarthen Van
Denbighshire	2,713 feet	Moel Sych and Cader Berwyn
Flintshire	1,820 feet	Moel Fammau (Mother of Hills)
Glamorgan	1,969 feet	Craig-y-Llyn
Merionethshire	2,972 feet	Aran Fawddwy, nr. Bala
Monmouthshire	2,228 feet	Chwarel-y-Fan
Montgomeryshire	2,713 feet	Moel Sych in the Berwyn mountains
Pembrokeshire	1,760 feet	Prescelly Top
Radnorshire	2,166 feet	In Radnor Forest

HIGHEST POINTS
By Counties
Scotland

Aberdeenshire	4,296 feet	Ben Macdhui
Angus	3,502 feet	Glas Maol
Argyllshire	3,766 feet	Bidean nam Bian
Ayrshire	2,520 feet	Shalloch on Minnoch
Banffshire	4,296 feet	Ben Macdhui
Berwickshire	1,749 feet	Meikle Says Law
Bute	2,866 feet	Goatfell, N.E. Arran
Caithness	2,313 feet	Morven
Clackmannan	2,363 feet	Ben Cleugh, Ochil Hills
Dumfriesshire	2,695 feet	White Coomb
Dunbartonshire	3,092 feet	Ben Vorlich
East Lothian	1,733 feet	Lammermuir Hills
Fifeshire	1,712 feet	West Lomond
Inverness-shire	4,406 feet	Ben Nevis
Kincardine	2,555 feet	Mount Battock
Kinross-shire	1,492 feet	Bishop Hill
Kirkcudbrightshire	2,764 feet	Merrick Mountain
Lanarkshire	2,454 feet	Culter Fell
Midlothian	2,136 feet	Blackhope Scar

Nairn	2,182 feet	Carn-Glas-Choire
Orkney	1,565 feet	Ward Hill, Island of Hoy
Peebles-shire	2,754 feet	Broad Law
Perthshire	4,004 feet	Ben Lawers
Renfrewshire	1,711 feet	Hill of Stake
Ross and Cromarty	3,877 feet	Carn Eite
Roxburgh	2,422 feet	Un-named peak, ½ mile S.E. of Auchop Cairn
Selkirk	2,269 feet	Ettrick Pen
Stirlingshire	3,192 feet	Ben Lomond
Sutherland	3,273 feet	Ben More Assynt
West Lothian	1,016 feet	The Knock
Wigtownshire	970 feet	Far Cairn
Zetland (Shetlands)	1,475 feet	Ronas Hill, North Mavain

RIVERS

LONGEST

The longest river in the world is the Nile which runs from the Victoria Nyanza to the Mediterranean, 4,160 miles long.

The longest river in the British Isles is the River Shannon. It rises in Co. Cavan and flows through a series of loughs to Limerick and is 240 miles long.

The longest river in England and Wales is the Severn which empties into the Bristol Channel and is 220 miles long.

The longest river in England is the River Thames which is 210 miles long.

The longest river in Wales is the Towy with a length of 68 miles.

The longest river in Scotland is the Tay with Dundee at the estuary. It is 117 miles long.

SHORTEST

The shortest river in the United Kingdom is the River Bain in Wensleydale, Yorkshire, approximately one mile in length. That with the shortest name is the River E in the Monadhliath mountains of Scotland.

The largest river basin in the world is that drained by the 3,900 mile River Amazon ; it covers approximately 2,053,000 square miles.

WORLD'S GREATEST RIVER BORE

The bore on the Tsientang-kiang (Hang-chow-fe) in Eastern China is the most remarkable in the world. At spring tides, the wave attains a height of up to 25 feet and a speed of 13 knots. It is heard advancing at a range of 14 miles. The bore on the Hooghly branch of the Ganges travels for 70 miles at over 15 knots.

The most notable river bore in the United Kingdom is that on the River Severn, which may attain a height of 5 feet.

WATERFALLS

The highest waterfall in the world is the Angel Falls, in Venezuela, on a tributary of the River Caroni, with a total drop of 3,312 feet—the longest single drop is about 2,650 feet.

GREATEST WATERFALLS

On the basis of the average annual flow, probably the greatest waterfall in the world is the Guayra in Brazil sometimes known as the Sete Quedas on the Alto Parana. Although only attaining an average height of about 110 feet, its estimated annual average flow over the 5,300 yard wide lip is 470,000 cubic feet per second. The amount of water this represents can be imagined by supposing that it was pouring into the dome of St. Paul's Cathedral—it would fill it completely in about three-fifths of a second.

During monsoon periods the Cauvery Falls in India attain an unsurpassed 650,000 cubic feet per second.

The highest waterfalls in the United Kingdom are in Ross-shire in Scotland, the 370 feet Glomach Falls.

LAKES AND INLAND SEAS

The largest inland sea or lake in the world is the Caspian Sea. It is approximately 795 miles long and its total area is approximately 169,500 square miles. Its maximum depth is 3,100 feet.

The largest lake in the British Isles is Lough Neagh in Northern Ireland. It is approximately 18 miles long and 11 miles wide and its area is 153 square miles. Its extreme depth is 102 feet.

The largest lake in England is Windermere in the south-eastern part of the Lake District in the county of Westmorland. It is 10½ miles long and has an area of 5·69 square miles. Greatest depth in the northern half of the lake is 219 feet.

The largest loch in Scotland is Loch Lomond which is approximately 23 miles long and it covers an area of 32·81 square miles. It is situated in the counties of Stirling and Dunbarton and its greatest depth is 630 feet.

The largest natural lake in Wales is Llyn Tegid with an area of 1·69 square miles, although it should be noted that the largest lake in Wales is that formed by the reservoir at Lake Vyrnwy where the total area is 3·18 square miles.

DEEPEST LAKE

The deepest lake in the world is Lake Baikal, Central Siberia. It is approximately 250 miles long and between 20 and 45 miles wide. It reaches depths of 5,650 feet.

The deepest lake in the British Isles is Loch Morar—its surface is 30 feet above sea level and extreme depth 1,117 feet.

LARGEST GLACIER

The world's largest glacier undoubtedly exists somewhere in the six million square miles of Antarctica which contains 87 per cent. of the world's glaciated surface. Comparative topography of the continent is not sufficiently developed to be more explicit. The largest glacier of the northern hemisphere is usually allowed to be the Muir Glacier in South East Alaska (59°N., 136°W.) which has an area of 350 square miles. The Malaspina Glacier of Alaska which results from the junction of several "expanded foot" glaciers, covers an area of 1,500 square miles. It has been estimated that, if returned to the sea, the 11 million cubic miles of the world's ice-sheets would raise the sea-level by 160 feet.

LONGEST GLACIER

The greatest measured valley glacier is the Fedtschenko Glacier in the Alai Pamirs of central Asia. It is 48 miles long. Some unsurveyed glaciers of Greenland and Antarctica may, however, exceed 100 miles in length.

WORLD'S LARGEST AVALANCHES

These probably occur in the remotest parts of the Himalayas, in Antarctica and Alaska, but few are observed in such unpopulated wastes and are thus less disastrous than many lesser avalanches in the European Alps where over 9,000 recognised avalanche paths have been charted.

Perhaps the worst disaster was that of 1689 when the town of Saas in Valais was wiped out.

In the great Glarnisch avalanche of 1890 (44° slope) the speed of snow was estimated at 217 m.p.h.

The most fatalities caused by an avalanche in the United Kingdom were the eight people killed at Lewes, Sussex, in 1836.

LARGEST DESERT

The Sahara Desert in North Africa is the largest in the world. At its greatest length, it is approximately 3,200 miles from east to west, from north to south it varies between 800 and 1,400 miles. The area covered by the desert is more than 3½ million square miles. The land level varies from below sea level to the mountain Emi Koussi (11,204 feet). The diurnal temperature range in the West Sahara may be more than 80°F. (45°C.) in 24 hours.

LARGEST GORGE

The largest gorge in the world is the Grand Canyon on the Colorado River in North Central Arizona, U.S.A. It extends from Marble Gorge to the Grand Wash Cliffs, a distance of approximately 280 miles. It varies in width from 5 to 15 miles and, in parts, is more than one mile in depth (see Photo Plate 1).

The Colorado River has, in the course of about a million and a half years, exposed rock beds ranging in age from the Pre-Cambrian era (more than 1,500 million years ago) to the Triassic period (about 160 million years ago).

DEEPEST CAVE

The deepest cave in the world is the Puits Berger, near Grenoble, 2,959 feet deep. In July 1955 its floor was reached by six French speleologists.

Recent tests carried out in the Gouffre Gachtiaggia Bella system in the French-Italian Maritime Alps suggest that there may be a cave system over 4,300 feet deep.

The biggest known underground chamber in the world is the Big Room of the Carlsbad Caverns in New Mexico. It is 4,000 feet long, 300 feet high and reaches 625 feet in width.

The deepest cave in the British Isles is Merregill Hole at Ingleborough, Yorkshire. A natural pothole, it is 520 feet deep.

CLIFFS

The highest cliffs in the British Isles are those on the north coast of Achill Island, County Mayo, Ireland, which at Croaghan are 2,192 feet sheer above the sea. England's highest cliffs are at Countisbury, North Devon, which drop 900 feet.

NATURAL BRIDGE

The longest natural bridge in the world is the Landscape Arch in Utah's Arches National Monument. This natural sandstone arch spans 291 feet and is set about 100 feet above the canyon floor. In one place erosion has narrowed its section to six feet.

4. *Flora*

WORLD'S LARGEST FOREST

The largest afforestated areas of the globe are the vast coniferous forests of Northern U.S.S.R. lying mainly between 55°N and the Arctic Circle. The total wooded areas amount to 2,275,000,000 acres.

LARGEST in BRITISH ISLES

The largest forest in England is Keilder Forest, Northumberland, at 70,875 acres.

The largest forest in Wales is the Gwydr Forest in Caernarvonshire and Denbighshire at 19,473 acres.

Scotland's most extensive forest is the Glen Trool Forest in Kirkcudbrightshire. It is 55,507 acres in extent.

WORLD'S LARGEST LIVING THING

The 272 feet 4 inches tall Californian redwood (*Sequoia gigantea*) tree named " General Sherman " in the Sequoia National Park, California, U.S.A. is the most massive living thing on Earth. It has a base circumference of 101 feet 7 inches and requires 17 men to encircle it with outstretched arms. Its mean base diameter is 32 feet 3 inches with a maximum of 34 feet.

WORLD'S TALLEST TREE

Of trees now standing, the tallest is the Californian redwood (*Sequoia sempervirens*) named the Founder's Tree in the Humboldt State Park, Dyerville, California. Measurements taken in 1947 showed it to be 364 feet high — 12 inches less than the height above street level of the cross on the dome of St. Paul's Cathedral, London.

A Douglas fir (*Pseudotsuga taxifolia*) felled by George Carey in Lynn Valley, North Vancouver, Canada, in 1895, stood 417 feet and was possibly the tallest tree of all time. The tree had a base circumference of 75 feet and was an estimated 1,800 years old.

England's

This is standing at Fonthill Abbey, Wiltshire, and is a Wellingtonia (*Sequoia gigantea*) which, when measured in 1954, was found to be 165 feet high.

Wales'

The famous Douglas fir (*Pseudotsuga taxifolia*) in the grounds of Powis Castle, Montgomeryshire, stood 175 feet when measured in 1954.

Scotland's

The Silver fir (*Abies alba*) at Kilbride, Inverary, Argyllshire, is the tallest tree in the whole British Isles at 176 feet (measured 1954).

Ireland's

This is a Sitka spruce (*Picia sitchensis*) at Curraghmore, County Waterford, which was 166 feet when measured in 1953.

GREATEST GIRTH IN THE WORLD

The Santa Maria del Tule tree, in the State of Oazaca, in Mexico, which is a Montezuma cypress (*Taxodium murcronatum*) has a base circumference of 160 feet and would require twenty-seven men with outstretched arms to encircle it.

ENGLAND'S GREATEST OAK

The Newland Oak at Newland, Gloucestershire, has a girth of 44 feet 9 inches.

WORLD'S OLDEST TREE

The ages of standing trees cannot be determined, but some of the Californian redwoods are thought to be 4,000 to 5,000 years old. The " General Sherman " tree (see above) has been cited as the " oldest living thing ".

OLDEST TREE IN THE BRITISH ISLES

Of all British trees that with the longest life is the yew (*Taxus baccata*) for which a maximum age of 2,800-3,000 years or more is usually conceded. The Fortingall Yew in Perthshire and Darley Yew near Matlock, Derbyshire (32½ foot girth) are regarded as the extreme examples.

WORLD'S FASTEST GROWING TREE

Discounting bamboo, which is not botanically classified as a tree, the fastest growing tree is the *Eucalyptus saligna* which in Uganda, Central Africa, has been measured to grow 45 feet in 2 years.

Bamboo (*Dendrocalamus giganteus*) has been observed, in Ceylon, to grow as much as 16 inches in a day on its way to a maximum height of 120 feet.

LARGEST LEAVES

The largest leaves of any plant belong to the Royal Water Lily (*Victoria Regina*) found in the back waters of the River Amazon in South America. They are circular up to 21 feet in diameter with upturned rim 2 inches high. The white blooms measure up to 15 inches across.

LARGEST BLOOM

The mottled orange-brown and white Rafflesia arnoldi has parasitic blooms which attach themselves to the Cissus vines of the Malaysian jungle and measure up to 3 feet across and attain a weight of 15 lb.

The largest bloom of any British flowering plant is that of the wild white Water Lily (*Nymphaea alba*), which measures 5 inches across.

WORLD'S LARGEST ROSE TREE

The 50-year old " Lady Banksia " rose tree at Tucson, Arizona, U.S.A. has a trunk 40 inches thick, stands 9 feet high and has arms spreading over 2,000 square feet supported by 32 posts so enabling 150 people to be seated under the arbour.

LARGEST ASPIDISTRA

The aspidistra (*Aspidistra elatior*) was introduced as a parlour palm to Britain from Japan and China c. 1822. The height attained by these plants is generally 24 to 30 inches though a plant growing in the shade may have its leaves elongated. A reported height of 42 inches is very much doubted by the Royal Botanic Gardens at Kew, Surrey.

LARGEST CACTUS

The largest of all cacti is the Saguaro (*Carnegiea gigantea*) found in Arizona, California, U.S.A., and Sonora, Mexico. The green fluted column is surmounted by candelabra-like branches rising, in some instances, to 70 feet. They have waxy white blooms which are followed by edible crimson fruit.

RAREST PLANTS

Hitherto unrecorded plants are discovered each year and there are thus many plants of which specimens are known in but a single locality. The flecked pink spurred coral-root (*Epipogium aphyllum*) is usually cited as Britain's rarest orchid, having been unrecorded between 1931 and 1953. The *homogyne alpina*, recorded by Don prior to 1814 in the mountains of Clova, Scotland, was not again confirmed until 1951.

LONGEST SEAWEED

Claims made that seaweed off Tierra del Fuego, South America, grows to 600 and even 1,000 feet in length have gained currency. More recent and more reliable records indicate that the largest species of seaweed is *macrocyctis pyrifera* which does not exceed 195 feet in length.

MOST POISONOUS TOADSTOOL

The yellowish-olive death cap (*Amanita phalloides*) is regarded as the world's most poisonous of all fungi. It is also found in England. Six to fifteen hours after tasting, the effects are vomiting, delirium, collapse and death. Among its victims was Pope Clement VII (1478-1534).

NORTHERNMOST PLANT LIFE

The seaweed *cryophilia* grows on the sea-ice in polar regions hundreds of miles north of the Arctic Circle.

THREE

THE ANIMAL KINGDOM

1. Mammalia

MAMMALS LARGEST and HEAVIEST

The Blue Whale (*Balaenoptera musculus*) is the largest animal which has ever inhabited the Earth. Specimens have been recorded up to a length of 108 feet and a weight of 131¼ tons. They inhabit the colder seas and can swim at 14 knots. The young can be 25 feet long at birth and weigh up to 7·14 tons.

LARGEST LAND ANIMAL

The largest bull African elephants (*Loxodonta africana*) stand 11 feet at the shoulder and may exceed 7 tons in weight.

The largest wild mammal in the British Isles, excluding wild ponies, is the Scottish red deer (*Cervus elaphus*). A full-grown stag reaches 4 feet 6 inches at the withers and weighs up to as much as 400 lb. The record antler span for a British animal is 42½ inches.

England's largest flying mammal is the great bat (*Pterygistes noctula*) with a wing span of nearly 14 inches.

TALLEST LAND ANIMAL

The giraffe (*Giraffa camelopardalis*) with neck erect measures up to 18 feet 5 inches in height (compare London trolleybus at 15 feet 7 inches). These are now found only in Africa, south of the Sahara.

SMALLEST

The species of shrew (*Suncus truscus*) found along the coasts of the northern Mediterranean has a body length of only 1½ inches.

The smallest mammal found in the British Isles is the lesser or pygmy shrew (*Sorex minutus*) which is only 1¾ inches long with a 1½ inch tail.

FASTEST LAND ANIMAL

Over very short distances the fastest of land animals is the cheetah (*Aciconyx jubatus*) at 70 m.p.h. Average specimens weigh 100 lb. They are found chiefly in Central India where they are trained for hunting. Tests in London in 1939 showed that on an oval track over 500 yards, the cheetah's average speed was 44 m.p.h.

LONGEST LIVED

No mammal can match the extreme proven age of 115 years attained by man (*Homo sapiens*) (see page 39). It is probable that the elephant makes the closest approach with about 70 years.

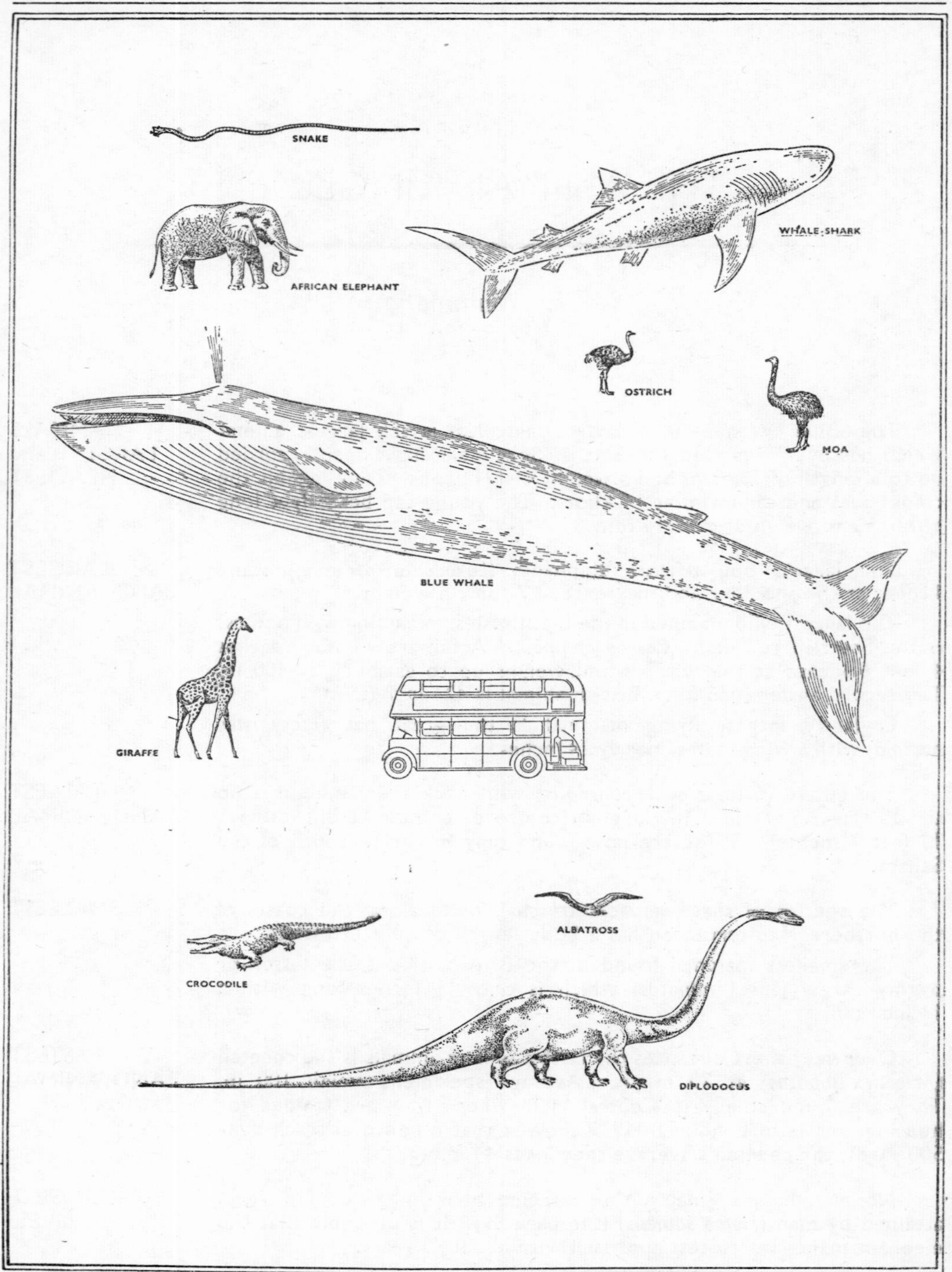

All drawings are to scale 1 : 275

RAREST

The Tasmanian wolf (*Thylacinus cynocephalus*), the largest of the carnivorous marsupials, is now confined to the wildest parts of Tasmania. So close is it to extinction that recent expeditions failed to find any specimens though there was evidence of their continued existence.

The rarest British mammal is the pine marten (*Mustela martes*) which is found both in the Lake District of England and the Highlands of Scotland. The largest specimens measure 32 inches from nose to tail.

HIGHEST

The highest altitude to which any animal has travelled is 80 miles by the Rhesus monkey " Mike " in an experimental Aerobee rocket in 1954.

GREATEST TUSKS

The longest recorded elephant tusks came from Kenya and are in the American National Collection. They are 11 feet 5½ inches and 11 feet in length, 18½ inches in circumference and weigh 293 lb. together. The world's heaviest, also from Kenya, (10 feet 5½ inches) weigh 214 lb. and 226½ lb., or together 440½ lb.

The longest walrus tusks on record are 37½ inches in length, 10¾ inches in circumference, weighing 10 pounds 13 ounces. The longest mammoth tusks on record are 13 feet long, weighing 200 lb.

LONGEST and SHORTEST GESTATION PERIODS

The longest of all mammalian gestation periods is that of the Indian elephant (*Elephas maximus*) with an average of 620 days and a maximum of 760 days (2 years and 30 days) — over 2½ times longer than a human. The gestation period of the young opossum (*Didelphis marsupialis*), which are born in a very immature stage of development, may be as little as 8 days though normally 12 days.

DOMESTICATED ANIMALS

HORSES
Age

The oldest recorded age for a horse is the 62 years credited to " Old Billy ", an English barge horse from the River Mersey believed to be a cross between a Cleveland and Eastern blood, which died in 1822. No reliable evidence confirms this claim and forty-five years more probably represents the extreme in the case of an Orkney mare which died at Fintray, Aberdeenshire, Scotland, in 1936.

Largest

The heaviest horse on record was the Shire mare Erfyl Lady Grey, London show champion 1924-26. She weighed 25 cwt. The tallest horse on record is a Clydesdale of 21 hands.

The largest mane on record was one of 13 feet—a Percheron—measured in Dee in 1891. The horse also had a 10 foot long tail.

Strength

A carefully conducted test carried out in Liverpool, England, in 1924 showed that two Shire geldings were able to pull an 18½ ton load.

DOGS
Age

Dogs over 18 are very rare but some live to a little over 20 and even 34 years has been accepted by some authorities. The oldest dog recently reported in the British Isles is a cross-bred terrier " Toss " of Studfold Farm, Horton-in-Ribblesdale, Yorkshire, which was 22 in 1955.

Largest Litter

The largest litter of puppies on record is the twenty-one thrown by the St. Bernard bitch, " Lady Millard ", owned by a Mr. Thorp of Northwold, Norfolk, on 9th February, 1895.

Most Popular

The most popular breeds change, as do fashions, but for the British Isles the cocker spaniel has held sway since 1935, reaching a popularity peak in 1947 with 27,000 Kennel Club registrations and a total estimated population of over 450,000. The most Kennel Club registrations are now among miniature poodles.

Longest Team

The longest dog team ever harnessed is the seventy-three dog team led by the Siberian husky " Waka " used in U.S. Army tests at the Chinook Kennels, Wonalancet, New Hampshire, in 1941, to pull a 10-ton Army truck.

CAT Oldest

Though 21 years is normally regarded as the limit for long lived cats, there is a well authenticated case of a female tabby " Ma " owned by Mrs. Alice St. George Moore of " Newton Barton ", Drewsteignton, Devon, attaining 32 years in 1955.

BIRDS

The talking bird with the greatest vocabulary in the world is " Sandy Paul ", a yellow brown-beaked budgerigar owned by Mrs. Irene Pauls of Staines, Middlesex, England. This bird, hatched in 1952, believed to be a female, knows twelve nursery rhymes straight through and has a total vocabulary of over 300 words. This compares with the 845 words devised by C. K. Ogden in 1930 for a Basic English vocabulary. *For auction prices, milk yield and prolificacy records for cattle, sheep and pigs, see under Agriculture.*

FURS

MOST VALUABLE

The most valuable single pelts are those of the now protected, and hence only illegally killed, sea otter (*Latax lutris*). A single pelt has been insured for £300.

Of legal furs, the most valuable is Siberian sable (*Mustela zibellina*) which consistently fetches over £50 per skin. Based on area, however, the most valuable fur is the topaz mutation of mink (*Mustela vison*) which fluctuates up to £28 a skin.

A coat made of the fur of chinchilla, the South American blue-grey rodent, rescued from extinction by the American, M. F. Chapman in 1923, fetched $35,000 (£12,500) in the United States, but it is believed that the unique azure blue mink coat purchased at an undisclosed price in Paris for the late Mme. Eva Peron was considerably more expensive.

HIGHEST PRICE

The highest price ever realised for the sale of live fur-bearing animals for breeding purposes was in the United States in 1913, when a pair of silver foxes changed hands for $35,000 or £6,250 apiece.

2. *Fishes*

LARGEST (Sea)

Though not comparable in size with the larger species of whales (mammals), the whale-shark (*Rhinedon typus*), first discovered off Cape Town in 1828, has been measured up to 45 feet in length. Specimens are creditably reported to reach lengths of 60 feet or even more, weighing up to 67 tons. The whale-shark, blackish with white dots, is harmless unless attacked and lives in the warmer areas of the Atlantic, Pacific, and Indian Oceans.

LARGEST (Freshwater)

The giant Russian sturgeon (*Acipenser*) found in the Volga river, has been measured to attain 26 feet in length and a specimen has been weighed at 3,221 lb. (1·44 tons).

Much the largest of British fishes is the sturgeon (*Acipenser sturi*) which occasionally travels some distance up our estuaries.

SMALLEST (Sea)

The fully grown male guppy fish (*Lebistes reticulatus*) is smaller than a queen bee. These tropical fish come from the waters around the Southern Caribbean and Venezuela.

SMALLEST (Freshwater)

The freshwater fish *Pandaka pygmaea* of the goby group found in the lakes of the Philippine Islands measure only fractionally over $\frac{3}{8}$ inch (9-11 mm.).

FASTEST

The swordfish, which include marlins (*Makaira mitsukurii*), are regarded as unrivalled for speed though the practical difficulties of measurement makes data extremely hard to secure. A maximum of 50 knots (57·5 m.p.h.) has been quoted, but 30 to 35 knots is the most that will be conceded by some experts.

LONGEST LIVED

Aquaria are of too recent origin to be able to establish which species of fish can fairly lay claim to the title of the longest lived. Early indications are that it is the European pike at 60 to 70 years. An 81 inch long, 215 lb., sturgeon caught on 15th July, 1953, in the Lake of the Woods, Kenora, Ontario, Canada, was believed to be 150 years old based on a growth ring (*annuli*) count in the spiny ray of its pectoral fin.

MOST ABYSSAL

The greatest depth from which living organisms have been recovered is 34,120 feet by the Danish Research vessel "Galathea" in the Pacific Ocean in 1950.

RAREST ONLY

Periodically specimens of fish never before identified are recovered. Such specimens, of which only a single known example exists, occur particularly among abyssal fauna.

SMALLEST YOUNG

The ocean sun-fish (*Mola mola*) weighing up to $\frac{1}{2}$ ton and 8 feet in length produces up to 300,000,000 eggs 1/10th inch long and 1/20th inch in diameter. The estimated increase in weight between young and adult is 60 million-fold, (human increase 22 fold).

3. *Reptiles and Amphibians*

(Crocodiles, snakes, turtles, tortoises and lizards).

REPTILES

LARGEST

The salt-water or estuarine crocodile (*Crocodilus porosus*) of South-East Asia may attain a length of 30 feet. Strictly carnivorous, they live in tidal waters and have been sighted far out at sea. They will devour anything they can overcome and will eat human corpses.

LONGEST

The rich yellow, brown and black reticulated python (*Python reticulatus*) is the longest of all snakes. It is found in Malaya, Burma and Indo-China and has been known to attain an extreme length of 33 feet. The shortest of all snakes is the burrowing *Typhlops braminus* which does not exceed 7 inches in length.

The longest British snake is the grass snake (*Natrix natrix*) with a record of 5 feet 10 inches. It is found throughout Southern England, and Wales and in Dumfriesshire, Scotland, but is absent in Ireland.

HEAVIEST

The leatherback turtle (*Demmochelys coriacea*) found rarely on Oceanic islands has been known to weigh up to 1,500 lb. and attain 9 feet in overall length.

LONGEST LIVED

The Royal Tongan tortoise " Tui Malila " is reputed to have been presented to Queen Salote's antecedent by Captain Cook in 1773, 1774 or 1777, thus indicating an age of 180 or more years.

The greatest proven age of a continuously observed tortoise is the 116 years of a Mediterranean spur-thighed tortoise (*Testudo graeca*) in Paignton Zoological Gardens, Devon, England.

The longest lived — and the heaviest — snake is the Anaconda which has been known to live 28 years (Washington D. C. Zoo) and weigh over 3 cwt.

MOST POISONOUS

The toxicity of the venom of the Australian tiger snake (*Notechis scutatus*) is unmatched by any other serpent. These snakes, tawny with dark bands, commonly grow to 4 or 5 feet in length. The only poisonous British snake is the adder or northern viper (*Vipera berus*). Though not vindictive, its bite has been known to cause death.

FASTEST MOVING SNAKE

The fastest measured speed for a snake is that of the Black Mamba (*Dendroaspis polylepis*) which, on a favourable surface, can attain nearly 7 m.p.h. The British grass snake has a maximum speed of 4·2 m.p.h.

SLOWEST MOVING REPTILE

Tests on a giant tortoise (*Testudo gigantea*) in Mauritius show that even when hungry and enticed by a cabbage it cannot exceed 5 yards in a minute (0·17 m.p.h.). Over longer distances its speed is greatly reduced.

AMPHIBIANS (Salamanders, toads, frogs, newts, etc.).

LARGEST

The giant salamander (*Megolobatrachus maximus*) found in Japan grows to over 5 feet in length and weighs up to 90 lb.

The largest frog is the rare goliath frog (*Rana goliath*) first found in 1906 in West Africa, which measures nearly 12 inches in length.

The largest British amphibian is the warty or Great Crested newt (*Trituris cristatus*) females of which attain 6 inches in length.

LONGEST LIVED

A toad in captivity in Copenhagen has reached the age of 54 years but there is evidence of giant salamanders attaining 60 years.

LONGEST FROG JUMP

The greatest distance achieved in a frog-jumping contest is 15ft. 6½ ins. by " Can't Take It " before a 30,000 crowd at Angel's Camp, California, on 17th May 1953.

4. *Birds*

LARGEST

Of living species, by far the largest is the ostrich (*Struthio camelus*) of Africa. Male examples of this flightless bird reach 300 lb. in weight and stand 8 feet tall. Ostriches are able to run at a speed in excess of 30 m.p.h.

LARGEST WINGSPAN

The wandering albatross (*Diomedea exulans*) of the southern oceans measures up to 11 feet 4 inches in wingspan. There is reason to believe that some unmeasured specimens may be in excess of 12 feet.

SMALLEST

One of the 600 varieties of humming birds, the *Lampornis prevesti*, found in the United States and in South America, is the smallest bird in the world with a total length of about 2½ inches. When hovering, their wings beat 55 times per second with a wing-tip velocity of 29 ft./sec. (19·8 m.p.h.).

RAREST

Claimant for this title is the North American ivory-billed woodpecker (*Campephilus principalis*) which may even be extinct. It is believed, however, that less than a dozen still exist in the Florida area.

There are over thirty species of birds which have been only once recorded in the British Isles. Among British birds which are not extinct but have not been seen in the British Isles for many years are Pallas's sandgrouse (1909), Savi's warbler (1916), and the Great Bustard (1936).

MOST ABUNDANT

The most abundant of all birds are the Wilson's petrels. They range as far south as Antarctica. The most abundant British birds are the Chaffinch and Blackbird (each 10 million).

LONGEST LIVED

Of those birds about which information is available the carrion crow is the only proven centenarian with the cockatoo second at 95 years.

FASTEST FLYING

The spine-tailed swift are alleged to have been timed to fly 2 miles in 36 seconds in India (200·0 m.p.h.) but experiments have shown that a bird of this size would be invisible even through binoculars at such a distance. The highest reliable ground speed recorded for any bird is the 93·55 m.p.h. average by a racing pigeon over an 80-mile course in Northern Ireland in 1914. Wood pigeons are reported to have attained an air speed of 150 m.p.h. (40 m.p.h. into a 110 m.p.h. wind) in Scotland in January, 1953.

LONGEST MIGRATION

The most extensive migration of any bird is that of the Arctic tern (*Sterna paradisaea*) which breeds in the Arctic within 8° of the North Pole and is found on the Antarctic coast in the northern winter after a flight of 11,000 miles.

HIGHEST FLYING

The celebrated example of a skein of 17 geese photographed crossing the sun from Dehra Dun, India, on 17th September, 1919, at a height variously estimated up to 58,000 feet has been discredited by experts. The highest acceptable altitudes are 24,000 to 25,000 feet by a lammergeier (*Gypaetus barbatus*) on Everest in 1922 and a chough (*Phyrrhocorax*) at approximately 26,000 feet in 1953.

LARGEST EGG

Of living birds, that producing the largest egg is the ostrich. These are found 6 to 7 inches in length and 4 to 6 inches in diameter. They require about 40 minutes for boiling.

SMALLEST EGG

The egg laid by the vervair humming bird of Jamaica looks like a pearl and is only ½ inch in length.

EARLIEST CUCKOO

Probably the earliest mention of the cuckoo was in 1490 B.C., when Moses publicly branded it as a bird to be held in abomination.

It is unlikely that in the British Isles the cuckoo has ever been heard earlier than 26th February in 1952, when it was independently reported to have been heard on the Hamworthy Marshes at Poole, Dorset.

5. *Insects*

LARGEST

The bulkiest of all insects is the beetle (*Macrodontia cervicornis*) which measures up to 5·85 inches (150 mm.) in length. Some tropical stick-insects (*Plasmidae*) have a body length up to 13 inches (330 mm.) while the Indian atlas moth (*Attacus*) has a wing span of fully 12 inches (305 mm.). The largest British insect is the silver water beetle (*Hydrous piceus*) which has a length of 1⅞ inch and a breadth of ⅞ inch.

SMALLEST

Several hundred new species of insect are discovered yearly, but of those known the smallest are minute beetles (*Coleoptera trichopterygidae*) and the *Hymenoptera mymaridae* known as the " battledore-wing fairy fly ", both of which are only 1/128 of an inch (0·2 mm.) in length. These could crawl through the eye of a needle with ease.

FASTEST FLYING

Experiments have proved that widely published statements that the female deer bot-fly could attain 800 m.p.h. are wildly exaggerated. The highest ground speed instrumentally measured is the 55-60 m.p.h. of the dragonfly *Austrophlebia*, but modern experiments have established that the highest maintainable air-speed of any insect is 27 m.p.h. rising to a maximum of 35 m.p.h. in short bursts.

LONGEST LIVED

Little data has been published but a *Cicada septemdecim* has been known to live 17 years of which 16 were in the larval stage.

BUTTERFLIES and Moths

Butterflies and moths form the order *Lepidoptera* of which there are 140,000 species.

LARGEST

The largest moths are the Indian atlas moths (*Attacus*) with a wing span of fully 12 inches (305 mm.). The world's largest butterfly is the New Guinea birdwing (*Troides Alexandrae*), the female of which has a span of 12 inches.

The largest of the species occurring in the British Isles is the great North American butterfly (*Danaus plexippus*) of which less than 250 have been recorded on the eastern side of the Atlantic; the wing-span of a fully grown specimen exceeds 4 inches.

The largest moth occurring in the British Isles is the death's-head moth (*Acherontia atropus*) with a wing span of up to 5¼ inches.

SMALLEST

The smallest *Lepidoptera* is the *Nepticula microtheviella* with a wing span of less than ⅛th of an inch (3 mm.).

The smallest British moth is the common blackthorn pygmy moth (*Nepticula plagicolella*), with a wing span of less than 2/5ths of an inch.

SPIDERS LARGEST

The world's largest spider is the (*Theraphosa blondi*) from the Guianas which is 3½ inches (9 cm.) in body length.

Of the 560 British species of spider covering an estimated population of over 200,000,000,000,000 the largest are the house spiders (*Tegenaria parietina*) in which the males have a leg span sometimes exceeding 5 inches.

The heaviest are the orb-weavers (*Aranea reaumuri*) which weigh over a gram.

SMALLEST

The smallest spiders in the world are the *Orchestina* and the *Cepheia longiseta* which have a body length of less than 1/30th of an inch (0·8 mm.).

The *Saloca diceros*, found among mosses in Dorsetshire and Staffordshire, are the smallest British spiders with a body length of less than 1/10th of an inch.

HIGHEST

Spiders are the highest permanent inhabitants of the Earth. Jumping spiders (*Salticidae*) have been collected at 22,000 feet on Everest. Spiders also live deep down in coalmines and caves.

MOST POISONOUS

The South American black widow spider (*Latrodectus mactans*) has a bite capable of killing a human being, but lethal results occur in less than one in ten instances.

SENSE OF SMELL

It has been successfully established that the male wax moth can detect the smell of a female at a range of one mile.

MOLLUSCS

(Squids, octopods, snails, shells, etc.).

LARGEST

The giant squid (*Architeuthis*) found on the Newfoundland Banks and occasionally washed up on British shores may have a body length of 8 feet and measure up to 40 feet overall. The largest snail is the *Achatina achatina* measuring 7 inches in length.

LARGEST SHELL

The largest of all shells is the marine bivalve (*Tridacna gigas*) found on the Indo-Pacific coral reef which may attain 4½ feet in length and weigh up to 500 lb. (nearly ¼ ton).

The largest British shell is the fan mussel (*Piana fragilis*) of which specimens found at Torbay, Devon, have reached 15 inches in length.

SMALLEST

The minute marine gastropod *Homalogyra atomus* from the Atlantic is only 1/30th inch in diameter, the smallest of all shells.

The smallest British shell is the land gastropod *Punctum pygmaeum* which is less than 1/25th inch in diameter.

PEARLS

Pearls are protective secretionary bodies produced by molluscs. Gem pearls come chiefly from the western Pacific (*genus Pinctada*) and the fresh water mussel (*genus Quadrula*).

The largest in the world is the Hope Pearl of 1,800 grains or nearly 3 ozs. It is fractionally over 3 inches in length and has a circumference at its globular end of 4½ inches. The largest known pearl of regular shape was known as " La Pellegrina " and weighed 111½ grains.

CRUSTACEA

(Crabs, lobsters, shrimps, woodlice, etc.).

LARGEST

The Japanese crab (*Macrocheiva*) possesses a body a foot across and legs capable of spanning 9 feet.

SMALLEST

The water-flea (*Alonella*) has an overall length of 1/100th of an inch.

MOST LEGGED

The animals with the biggest number of legs are the centipedes, some species having up to 173 pairs, i.e. 346 separate legs.

The millipede with the biggest number of legs (*Archestraptuo dodsoni*) has 66 segments, each bearing two pairs of legs, 264 in all.

6. Microbes

SMALLEST VISIBLE

The smallest object visible to the unaided human eye under the best possible conditions measures approximately 3·4 microns in diameter, roughly 1/7,500th of an inch. A micron is a thousandth part of a millimetre.

LARGEST BACTERIA

The largest of the bacteria is *Bacillus megatarium* which measures 1·5 × 4 microns, about 60 millionths by 160 millionths of an inch.

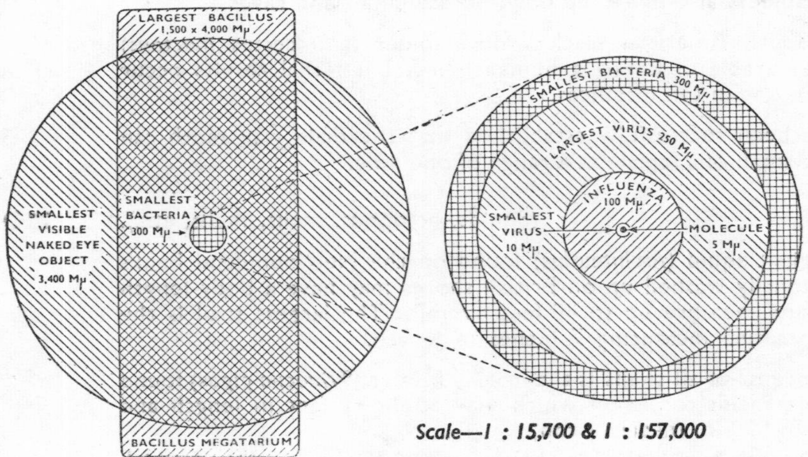

Scale—1 : 15,700 & 1 : 157,000

SMALLEST BACTERIA

The line between the smallest bacteria and the largest viruses is extremely difficult to draw since many of the organisms in this size group, 250-300 mμ (a mμ — or millimicron — is a millionth part of a millimetre) share various distinguishing characteristics. The rickettsiae, which causes typhus and similar fevers, are an example of what appears to be bacteria but also exhibit traits of viruses. They have in fact been variously classified as the largest virus and the smallest bacteria. The rickettsiae causing Psittacosis or parrot fever measure 275 mμ and are probably the largest virus-type particle.

SMALLEST VIRUS

The smallest virus is that of foot and mouth disease, approximately 10 mμ in diameter, 1/4,000,000th of an inch.

The smallest plant virus is the mosiac disease of alfalfa which is approximately 16 mμ in diameter.

SMALLEST MICRO-SCOPICALLY VISIBLE

The limit of resolution which can be obtained by the use of the normal optical system microscope and seen with the human eye is a particle about 250 mμ, the limiting factor being the wavelength of visible light which lies between about 7,500Å and 4,000Å (1 Ångstrom= 10^{-7} mm. or a tenth of a mμ). By using light of a shorter wave length than that visible to the human eye, e.g. ultra violet, and a specially equipped microscope, it is possible to obtain photographs of particles down to 100 mμ.

The development of the electron microscope, which uses a focusable beam of electrons with a wave length (dependent on the electron beam voltage) up to 100,000 times shorter than that of visible light, enables a resolution to be obtained down to 5 mμ. This is smaller than any virus yet discovered and is approximately the size of a haemoglobin molecule.

It is impossible to dogmatise on what could be fairly classified as the smallest particle of living matter because in this sphere there is no real definition of life.

Viruses grow, mutate and can be killed and seem to be alive, yet some of them, the plant viruses, can be transformed to a pure crystalline form and appear a type of protein, with a very high molecular weight, estimated at 1/1,000,000,000,000,000,000th of a gram. In this form they can be reintroduced to a "host" and again "live" at the host's expense. Viruses can only exist as parasites and can be artificially cultivated only on living tissue.

It should be remembered that since, for the successful operation of the electron microscope, it is necessary that the complete microscopic system be almost completely evacuated, all the specimens are dehydrated and therefore the sizes which have been quoted of virus particles measured under the electron microscope are not necessarily the living size of these organisms.

EXTINCT ANIMALS

LAND ANIMALS LARGEST

The giant dinosaur or thunder-lizard (*Diplodicus*) which roamed the swamps of North America 160 million years ago measured up to 87½ feet in length — nearly the length of three London trolleybuses and height of two. These semi-aquatic reptiles weighed over 40 tons.

The heaviest of prehistoric animals was the swamp-dwelling *Brachiosaurus* which is believed to have weighed 50 tons.

The largest prehistoric monster that ever roamed the British Isles was the amphibious dinosaur *Cetiosaurus* which measured up to 60 feet in length.

LARGEST MAMMAL

The *Baluchitherium*, a type of extinct rhinoceros, unearthed in Mongolia was found to measure 17 feet 9 inches to the shoulder and probably stood nearly 25 feet tall to the crown of its head.

LARGEST BIRD

The *Aepyornis titan* of Southern Madagascar which may have survived into the 18th century was a large flightless bird standing 10 feet in height. Its eggs were also the largest of any bird, being 13 inches in length with a diameter of 9½ inches and a capacity of 2 gallons—six times that of an ostrich egg. The extinct flightless bird from New Zealand, the moa, was probably taller, attaining a height of over 11 feet.

LARGEST FLYING CREATURE

The extinct winged lizard (*Pteramodon*) had an overall wing span of 20 feet.

EARLIEST BIRD

The earliest known of birds was the *Archaeopteryx*, belonging to the era of 150 million years ago, remains of which were first discovered at Solenhofen in Bavaria in 1861.

LONGEST SNAKE

The *Gigantophis*, inhabiting Egypt 60 million years ago, is estimated to have attained a length of 50 feet.

FOUR

THE HUMAN BEING

I. Dimensions

EARLIEST MAN

Five specimens of *telanthropus*, regarded by their discoverers as the earliest form of " true man ", were found at Swart Kranz, Transvaal, South Africa, in January 1953. These remains were declared to be 250,000 years earlier than the Java and Peking remains (*Pithecanthropus*).

HEIGHT

TALLEST GIANTS

The only admissible evidence upon the true height of giants is that of recent date made under impartial medical supervision. Biblical claims, such as that for Og, King of Bashan, at 9 Assyrian cubits (16 feet 2½ inches) are probably due to a confusion of units. Extreme mediaeval data from bone measurements refer invariably to mastodons or other non-human remains. Claims of exhibitionists, usually under contract not to be measured, are usually distorted for the financial considerations of promoters. There is an example of a recent "World's Tallest Man " of 9 feet 6 inches being an acromegalic of 7 feet 3½ inches.

Prior to 1872, medical literature tended to accept the claim confirmed by the French anthropometrist Paul Topinard (1830-1912) that the Finn, Kayanus, (Daniel Cajanus, died 1749) was the tallest man who had ever lived at 283 cms. (9 feet 3⅜ inches). His bones, now in Leyden Museum, were however, measured by Langer in 1872 giving a value of 222 cms. (7 feet 3⅜ inches).

Modern opinion now tends to the view that the tallest man of all-time of whom there is irrefutable evidence, was Robert Wadlow, born an 8½ lb. baby in 1918 in Alton, Illinois, U.S.A., and who died on 15th July, 1940, at Manistee, Michigan, weighing 35 stone 1 lb. and standing 8 feet 9½ inches (267 cms.) tall.

TALLEST GIANTESSES

Giantesses are much rarer than giants. The extreme example was Marianne Wehde of Germany (born 1866) who grew to 8 feet 4½ inches (255 cms.).

The tallest present-day giantess is Katja van Dyk of the Netherlands who is reputedly 8 feet 3 inches.

SHORTEST DWARFS

The strictures which apply to the evidence of the heights of giants apply as fully to dwarfs.

The smallest dwarf in medical literature is one who, at the age of 37, measured only 16 inches in height, recorded by Georges Buffon

E I *The nebula Andromeda, the most distant object visible to the naked eye. (Page 1)*

The world's greatest canyon, the Grand Canyon, Colorado, U.S.A. 280 miles long and up to 15 miles wide. (Page 24)

The Chubb Crater, northern Canada, is the world's largest known meteoric scar with a $7\frac{1}{2}$ mile circumference. (Page 7)

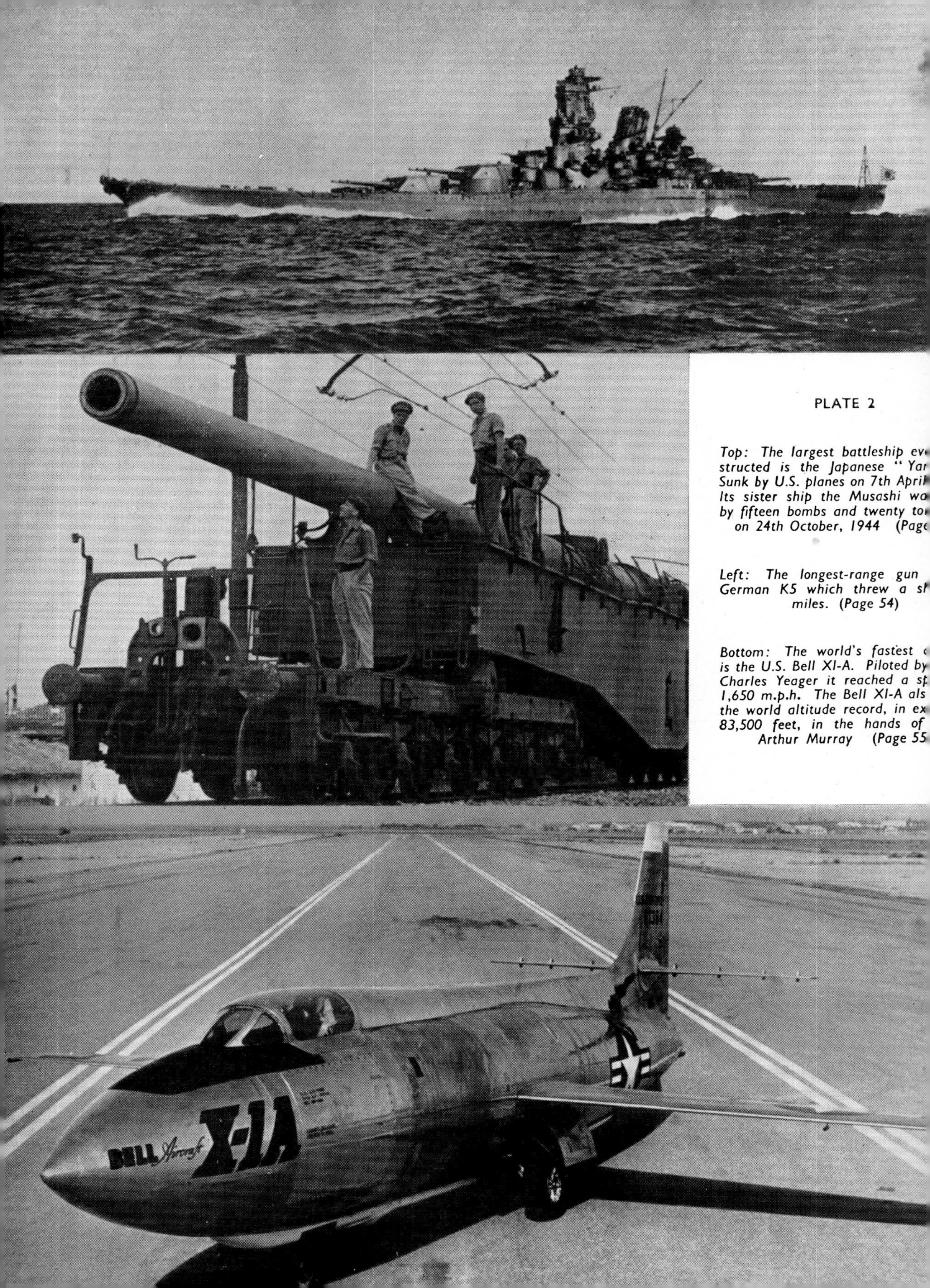

PLATE 2

Top: The largest battleship ev
structed is the Japanese " Yar
Sunk by U.S. planes on 7th April
Its sister ship the Musashi wa
by fifteen bombs and twenty to
on 24th October, 1944 (Page

Left: The longest-range gun
German K5 which threw a sh
miles. (Page 54)

Bottom: The world's fastest
is the U.S. Bell XI-A. Piloted by
Charles Yeager it reached a sp
1,650 m.p.h. The Bell XI-A als
the world altitude record, in ex
83,500 feet, in the hands of
Arthur Murray (Page 55

(1707-1788) in his "Histoire Naturelle". Of better-documented dwarfs, the smallest was the favourite of Queen Henrietta-Maria, Geoffrey Hudson (born Oakham, England, 1619) who, in 1649, was only 18 inches tall at the age of 30. He later grew to 3 feet 9 inches and was buried in Westminster, London, in 1682.

Walter Boehning, 48, claiming to be the smallest dwarf in the world died at Delmenhorst, Germany, in February, 1955, at a height of 20½ inches, while the smallest living dwarf in Britain is Miss Edith Barlow (born Yorkshire, 1929) who weighs 17 lb. and stands 22 inches.

WEIGHT

HEAVIEST HEAVYWEIGHTS

The heaviest man recorded in medical literature is Miles Darden who was born in North Carolina, U.S.A., in 1798. He grew to 7 feet 8 inches in height and attained a weight slightly in excess of 1,000 lb. (71 stone 6 lb.), dying in 1857 in Henderson County, Tennessee.

The heaviest recorded woman was a negress who died in Baltimore, U.S.A., in 1888, scaling 850 lb. (60 stone 10 lb.).

The heaviest human in the world today is Robert Earl Hughes, aged 27, of Fish Hook, Illinois, U.S.A., who is 6 feet tall and 946 lb. (67 stone 8 lb.). He was an 11 lb. baby and weighed 27 stone at the age of 10. He also possesses the greatest recorded girth at 109 inches, (9 feet 1 inch).

The heaviest recorded man in Great Britain was Daniel Lambert, born 13th March, 1770, at St. Margaret's, Leicester, died 21st July, 1809, at Stamford, weighing 739 lb. (52 stone 11 lb.).

The Irish record is the 728 lb. (52 stone) of Roger Byrne of Rosenalis who died aged 54.

THINNEST HUMANS

The lowest recorded human bodyweight was the 12 lb. of the Welshman, Hopkin Hopkins, at his death in Glamorganshire in March, 1754. At no time in his 17 years of life did he attain a weight of more than the 17 lb. he was at 14 years.

It is recorded that the biceps measurement of the Frenchman, Claude Seaurat (born 1798) was 4 inches at the age of 26 and that the distance between his back and his chest was 3 inches.

2. *Longevity*

OLDEST CENTENARIANS

Medical men, who have devoted themselves to the study of old age (gerontologists), do not give credence to reports of people living much beyond 110 years. Few subjects have been so obscured by deceit and falsehood. The most extreme claims are for a man of 185 years (variously 187) named Setrasch Czarten (also Petratsh Zarten) allegedly born near Teneswaer, in Hungary, in 1537, and alive in 1722 and for a woman of 175 years named Louisa Trousco, a South American negress, who died circa 1776.

The claims of such traditional English figures as Henry Jenkins (died at Ellerton-upon-Swale, 1670) allegedly 169 years, and Thomas Parr (died London, 1635) allegedly 152 years, are now regarded as spurious. Parish priests began only to register births and christenings in 1583 and births were not officially registered until 1837. The claim of the Research Institute of Biology of the Gorky University, Kharkov, Russia, made on 17th January, 1955, that there were then 717 centenarians over 110 years living in Russia is not based on the essential evidence of registered birth dates. Mahmud Eivazov in the Azervaijan village of Perassara, allegedly born in 1810, was at 144 the oldest of 4,425 persons cited as of over 100 years of age.

World

The greatest age which has survived official investigation is the 113 years of Pierre Joubert, a French Canadian bootmaker born in Charlesbourg, Canada, on 15th July, 1701, and buried in Quebec on 18th November, 1814. This case was personally investigated in 1870 by Dr. Tache, Official Statistician to the Canadian Government.

The greatest age for a woman for whom there exists acceptable evidence as to the date of birth is the 111 years 328 days of the Hon. Katherine Plunket, eldest daughter of the Rev. Thomas (later 2nd Baron) Plunket who was born at Kilsaran, County Louth, Ireland, on 22nd November, 1820, and who died at Ballymascanlan House, Co. Louth, on 14th October, 1932.

England and Wales

With birth registration introduced in 1837, the dates of birth of persons in excess of 110 only became subject to conclusive check in 1948 or 1949. In the period 1913 to 1946 four centenarians with reputed ages in excess of 110 years were recorded by the General Register Office at Somerset House, London. Of these, the oldest was Charles Alfred Nunez Arnold, who died in Liverpool, Lancashire, on 15th September, 1941. He was reputedly born on 11th July, 1829, and was baptised at St. George's Church, Bloomsbury, London.

On 20th November, 1948, there died at St. Asaph, Flintshire, Wales, Miss Isabella Shepeard, believed to be born in London on 5th August, 1833, and hence 115 years old and the last surviving inhabitant of the British Isles born before compulsory registration of births. Her brother died at 102.

Scotland

The oldest recorded ages in Scotland are: Man — 103 years 11 months (died 1945) and woman — 109 years 14 days (died 1936).

3. Reproductivity

MOTHERHOOD

WORLD

The greatest number of children produced by a mother in an independently attested case is that of the wife of the Russian, Fedor Vassilet (died 1872) who in 27 confinements, gave birth to 69 children (16 pairs of twins, 7 sets of triplets and 4 sets of quadruplets).

Mrs. Marie Cyr of Fort Kent, Maine, U.S.A., born 1911, married at 17 has produced a child every year of her first 26 married years (1929-1955) of whom 19 are living. Details of the insupportable case of Margarita Gonçalez, who was alleged in 33 confinements to have produced by two husbands 158 children (144 boys and 14 girls) of whom 99 lived to be baptised, have been reprinted from a report of 1585 by Henrique Cock in the New York Medical Journal.

Great Britain

The highest attested prolificacy from the British Isles is Atkinson's case (British Medical Journal, 1883) of a mother of 39 children (32 daughters and 7 sons) all of whom attained their majority.

DESCENDANTS

In polygamous countries, the number of a person's descendants soon becomes incalculable, but in monogamous Britain, perhaps, the most impressive of the many tombstone testimonies is that at Markshall Church, Essex, England, to Mrs. Mary Honeywood (née Waters) of Lenham, Kent, who died aged 92 on 11th May, 1620. She left 16 children, 114 grandchildren, 228 great-grandchildren and 9 great-great-grandchildren, totalling 367.

MULTIPLE BIRTHS

The celebrated case in 1278 of Countess Margaret, daughter of Florent IV, who is reputed, at the age of 42 to have produced 365 infants (182 males, 182 females and 1 hermaphrodite) may be an exaggerated report of a case of a hydatidiform or multiple molar pregnancy.

Other cases, such as Margaret, Countess Viröboslaus, who, on 20th January, 1296, in Krakow, Poland, is alleged to have produced 36 children at a single birth is similarly explicable. Medical opinion is that reported instances of multiple births in excess of 7 must be looked on with great suspicion. In this apocryphal class are Albucasis's case of 15 at one birth, the Countess of Altdorf's duodecaplets (12) and the English example of Ann Birch who, in 1781, is alleged to have produced decaplets of whom one girl survived to marry a Mr. Platt of Leeds.

Turning to medically more acceptable cases, the palm must be awarded to Mrs. Timothy Bradlee, herself a triplet, of Trumbell County, Ohio, U.S.A., whose production of octuplets (3 boys, 5 girls) in 1872 is recorded in the Boston Medical and Surgical Journal of 26th September, 1872.

Though there are also several instances of septuplets (e.g. Ibadan, Nigeria, in 1907) and sextuplets, there are only three examples of quintuplet births with all five surviving, namely Emilie (died 6th August, 1954, aged 20), Yvonne, Cecile, Marie and Annette, born to Mrs. Oliva Dionne, in Callander, Ontario, Canada, on 28th May, 1934 (aggregate weight 13 lb. 6 ozs.); Franco, Maria Fernanada, Maria Ester, Maria Christian and Carlos Alberto born to Franco and Vallotta de Diligenti in Buenos Aires, Argentina, on 15th July, 1943, and the birth of 5 boys in Turkey in July, 1944.

BABIES

LARGEST

The largest baby of which there is medical record was that of 23¾ lb. and 30 inches in length born in 1879 to the 7 feet 5½ inches Nova Scotia giantess, Mrs. Anna Bates (born 1847) reported in the New York Medical Record of 22nd March, 1879.

The heaviest recorded birth weight in Britain was a 20 lb. 2 ozs. boy born to a 33-year-old woman in Crewe, England, reported in "Lancet" in 1884. The heaviest recorded twins are 20 lb. 10½ ozs. (Jeff 10 lb. 5 oz., Danny 10 lb. 5¼ oz.) born in April 1955 to Mrs. Ferrel Maycroft, 22, of Michigan, U.S.A.

SMALLEST

Of full-term viable infants, the smallest on record was Home's case of a 16-oz. baby, 7 to 8 inches in length, born circa 1810 to a camp-follower of Wellington's Army, which survived to the age of 9 years.

4. Physiology

LONGEST BONE

The thigh bone or femur is the longest of the 206 bones in the human body. It constitutes usually 27½ per cent. of a person's stature.

SMALLEST BONE

The incus or anvil bone, one of the three auditory ossicles in the middle ear, is the smallest bone in the body.

LARGEST MUSCLE

Muscles normally account for 40 per cent. of the body weight and the bulkiest muscle in the human body is the gluteus maximus or buttock muscle which extends the thigh.

SMALLEST MUSCLE

The smallest muscle is the stapedius which controls the auditory ossicle known as the stirrup bone in the middle ear and which is less than 1/20th inch in length.

MOST FINGERS

Researching into polydactylism in 1930, De Linares recorded a case of a Spaniard with twenty-six digits.

LONGEST TRESSES

The longest recorded feminine tresses appear to be those of the 19th century exhibitionist named Miss Owens which were measured at 8 feet 3 inches.

LONGEST BEARD

Allworthy's case of hypertrichosis terminalis, reported in 1909, gives details of a 64-year-old patient with a beard 10 feet 10 inches long.

LONGEST MOUSTACHE

The longest moustache owned by a member of Britain's " Handlebar Club " is that of Mr. John Roy of Glasgow with a span of 16½ inches.

FASTEST REFLEXES

The results of experiments carried out in 1943 have shown that the fastest messages transmitted by the nervous system travel at 265 m.p.h.

LONGEST COMA

The longest period of human unconsciousness ever recorded was that of Robert Steger, who was severely injured in a factory accident in 1943 and died of deterioration at Bethesda Hospital, Cincinnati, U.S.A., in January 1952 after a coma lasting over 8 years.

BLOOD TRANSFUSION

The record number of donations notified by the Red Cross Blood Transfusion Service is 126 for a man and 91 for a woman.

The greatest recorded transfusion is six gallons in 23 hours received by Douglas H. McLeod, 31, at Brisbane on 4th August, 1955.

BLOOD GROUP

The preponderance of one blood group varies greatly from one locality to another. On a world basis Group O is the most common but in some areas, for example London and Norway, Group A predominates.

The full description of the commonest sub-group in Britain is O, MsNs, P+,Rr, La(a—), K—, Le(a—bt), Fy(a+b+), Jk(a+b+) which occurs in one in every 270 people.

The rarest blood group on the ABO system, one of 9 systems, is AB, which occurs in less than 3 per cent. of cases in the British Isles.

VOICE HIGHEST

The highest note ever achieved by the human voice is C in altissimo, sung by Lucrezia Agujari (1743-1783). Mozart heard her sing in Palma in 1770 and recorded the range of her voice. She paid many visits to London and is reported to have received as much as £100 a night.

The same note has also been sung by Ellen Beach Yaw, a singer of the early part of this century. C in altissimo is 2,048∿ (cycles a second).

LOWEST

The lowest note ever achieved is a full sounding A by Kaspar Foster (1617-1673) and Norman Allin. A " basso al ottava " is 44∿.

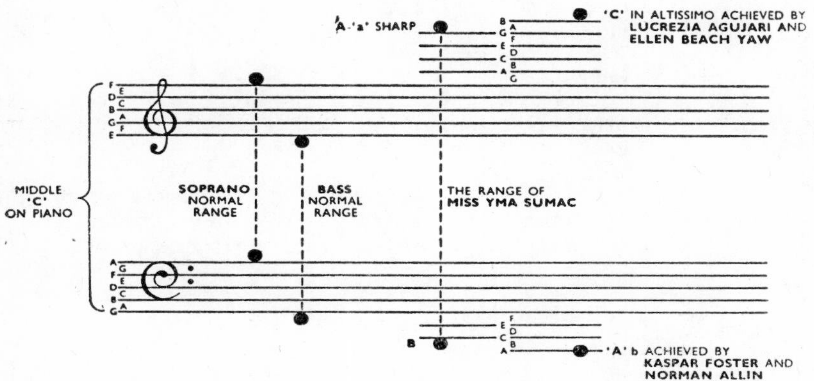

GREATEST RANGE

The singer with the greatest range is Miss Yma Sumac of Peru. She is reputed to have a range of five octaves from A♯ to B.

LOUDEST

The normal range of a human voice on a still day is 150 yards. There is a recorded case, under freak conditions, of a human voice being heard at a distance of ten and a half miles across still water at night.

TOUCH SENSITIVITY

The extreme sensitivity of the fingers is such that a vibration with a movement of ·02 of a micron can be detected.

SURGICAL INSTRUMENTS

The largest surgical instruments are axis-traction obstetric forceps which measure up to 17½ in. overall. The smallest are Elliot's eye trephine which has a blade 78/1000 in. in diameter.

ACROMEGALIC—The condition of an enlargement of the peripheries caused by over activity of the pituitary gland.

FIVE

THE HUMAN WORLD

1. Political

WORLD

The land area of the Earth is estimated at 58·16 million square miles, 29 per cent. of the world's surface area.

LARGEST POLITICAL DIVISION

The British Commonwealth of Nations, a free association of eight independent sovereign states together with their dependencies, covers an area of 14,435,060 square miles and has an estimated population of 625 million people.

COUNTRIES

LARGEST COUNTRY

The sixteen republics of the U.S.S.R. form the largest nation in the world, comprising 8,707,870 square miles, approximately 15 per cent. of the world's total land area.

The United Kingdom covers 93,035 square miles or ·16 per cent. of the total land area.

SMALLEST COUNTRY

The smallest political division in the world is the Vatican City with an area of 108·7 acres.

COUNTIES

The largest county in the United Kingdom and England is Yorkshire with 3,890,990 acres. The smallest county in England is London with 74,850 acres.

The largest county in Wales is Carmarthenshire with 588,472 acres and the smallest is Flintshire with 163,707 acres.

The largest county in Scotland is Inverness-shire with 2,695,094 acres. The smallest county in Scotland and the United Kingdom is Clackmannanshire with 34,937 acres.

The largest county in Northern Ireland is Tyrone with 779,548 acres and the smallest is Armagh with 312,767 acres.

The largest county in the Republic of Ireland, Poblacht na hÉireann, is Cork, the area of which, together with Cork County Borough, is 1,843,408 acres. The smallest county is Louth with 202,806 acres.

POPULATIONS

The population of the world is approximately 2,560 million, giving an average population density of 49 people per square mile.

The country with the largest population in the world is China with, according to the 1953 Census, approximately 602,000,000 people, 24 per cent. of the total world population.

The country with the smallest population is the Vatican City with 970 people.

DENSEST

The most densely peopled territories on Earth are Macao, a Portuguese colony on the coast of China, where 188,000 people crowd into five square miles—37,600 per square mile, and Gibraltar with 24,000 people on two square miles—12,000 per square mile.

Of territories over 250 square miles, Hong Kong's 391 square miles contain 2¼ million people giving it a density of 5,857 per square mile.

Of territories over 10,000 square miles, England and Wales, and Belgium contain about 750 people to the square mile, the highest figure recorded.

The least populated continent is Australia with just over three people per square mile.

The least populated territories, apart from Antarctica, are: Greenland 0·03 persons per square mile or one person to every thirty-three and a half square miles, Spitzbergen 0·12 persons per square mile or one person to every eight square miles, and Bechuanaland 1·1 persons per square mile.

EMIGRATION

More people emigrate from the United Kingdom than any other country. In 1953 emigrants totalled 144,122. The largest number in any one year being 360,000 in 1852.

In 1953 more than 32 per cent. of the total United Kingdom emigrants went to Canada, the greatest proportion to any one country.

IMMIGRATION

The country receiving the most immigrants during 1953 was the United States of America with a total of 184,324. The largest number from any one country—35,842, came from Canada and 17,155 from the United Kingdom. The United Kingdom, in the same year, received 77,764 immigrants, the largest number from any one country being 11,468 from Australia.

COUNTIES

The county in England with the largest population is Lancashire with 5,096,000 and that with the smallest is Rutland with 23,000.

The county in Wales with the highest population is Glamorgan with 1,207,000 people and that with the smallest is Radnor with 19,000 people.

The most populous Scottish county is Lanarkshire which, including Glasgow, totals 1,617,100 people.

The smallest county population in Scotland is Kinross with 7,300 people.

The most populous county in Northern Ireland is Antrim, the population of which, together with Belfast County Borough, totals 683,500 people.

The smallest county population in Northern Ireland is Fermanagh with 53,000 people.

The most populous county in the Republic of Ireland is Dublin, which, together with Dublin County Borough, has a population of 693,022 people.

The smallest county population in the Republic of Ireland is Carlow with 34,162 people.

CITIES

The largest conurbation in England and the world is London (Metropolitan Police District) with, according to the latest census, 8,346,137 people and an area in excess of 710 square miles. The fastest growing city in the world is Los Angeles, California, which has grown from 11,000 in 1881 to 2,100,000 with an area of 460 square miles.

The largest centre of population in Scotland is Glasgow, estimated in 1955 at 1,083,400 people.

The largest city in Wales is Cardiff, with an estimated 248,000 people.

The largest centres of population in Ireland are: Northern Ireland, Belfast with 449,100 people. Republic of Ireland, Dublin with 522,183 people.

BIRTH/DEATH RATES

The highest crude birth rate in the world for 1953 is on the Pacific Island of Guam with 60·8 live births per 1,000 population. The United Kingdom figure in this respect over the same period is 15·9. Owing to insufficient returns, the lowest birth rate figures are impossible to verify but Nyasaland with 8·8, West Berlin with 8·0 and Trieste with 9·4 are the lowest recorded.

The highest death rate of any country recorded during 1953 was Burma with 33·5 deaths per 1,000. The United Kingdom figure for the same period was 11·4.

The lowest figures recorded are for American Samoa 5·3 and Israel (Jewish population only) 6·3 per 1,000.

England

Birth rates and death rates, when calculated over relatively small areas or small numbers of people, naturally vary from year to year but the latest available figures show that in England, Helston Borough in Cornwall has the highest birth rate, 24 per 1,000 population, and the Urban District of Aldridge in Staffordshire has the lowest death rate, 5·9 per 1,000.

Wales

In Wales, the Borough of Pembroke, Pembrokeshire, has the highest birth rate, 21·1 per 1,000, and the Urban District of Caerphilly the lowest death rate, 9·3 per 1,000.

Scotland

In Scotland, the Burgh of Cumnock and Holmhead in Ayrshire has the highest birth rate, 25·7 per 1,000, while the lowest death rate, 7·4 per 1,000, is in the Burgh of Bathgate in West Lothian.

Northern Ireland

In Northern Ireland, the highest birth rate is in Londonderry County Borough with 29·4 per 1,000 and the lowest death rate is in the Borough of Carrickfergus in Co. Antrim, 8·8 per 1,000.

INFANT MORTALITY

Based on deaths before one year of age per 1,000 live births, the lowest rate is in Sweden where only 18·7 deaths are recorded per 1,000 live births.

The highest infant mortality rate is in Burma, 230·5 per 1,000. The United Kingdom figure over the same period was 26 per 1,000.

NATURAL INCREASE

On figures supplied by the World Health Organisation, the highest recorded natural increase in the world is recorded for Costa Rica with 35·9 per 1,000 per year. The United Kingdom figures are 2·9 per 1,000 increase for England and Wales, 4·9 per 1,000 increase for Scotland and 7·9 per 1,000 increase for Northern Ireland. The Republic of Ireland shows an increase of 8·7 per thousand.

The lowest recorded figures in the world, apart from the disturbed territories (for example, West Berlin a decrease of 3·4 per 1,000, Trieste a decrease of 1·5 per 1,000) is Austria with an increase of only 2·1 per 1,000.

LIFE EXPECTATION

At birth, the longest life expectancy in the world is: for males, in the Netherlands 69·4 years; for females, in Norway 72·65 years. The United Kingdom figures are England and Wales: for males, 66·73 years; for females, 71·88 years. Scotland: for males, 65·43 years; for females, 70·25 years.

The shortest life expectancy at birth in the world is in India, 32·45 years for males, 31·66 years for females. India and Ceylon are the only places in the world where expectation of life at birth is appreciably longer for men than for women.

At the age of 60, the longest life expectancy for both males and females is in Norway where men can look forward to an additional 18·39 years of life and women an additional 19·45 years. The United Kingdom figures on the same basis are, for England and Wales: men, 14·81 years; for women, 18·16 years. Scotland: 14·62 years for men, and 17·45 years for women.

MARRIAGES

There is no universally accepted definition of marriage for the purpose of international comparison of marriage rates. In some countries where the number of so-called " consensual " marriages is large, the apparent marriage rate, based on marriages registered, will appear to be low. Again, in countries where the statistics are based on the number of marriage licences issued, the apparent rate will be high since the marriage licence is a statement of intent only, and usually exceeds the number of marriages actually contracted.

However, during 1954, Hawaii shows the highest average rate of 10·1 new marriages for every 1,000 head of population.

The United Kingdom figure over the same period was 7·7 marriages per 1,000 and the lowest rate in the world was Peru with only 2·5 marriages per 1,000.

MOST TOURISTS

Based on latest available figures for a year Italy received 7,681,870 foreign visitors—more than any other country—and more than twice as many as Switzerland (3,217,715), the next most visited country. Visitors to the United Kingdom numbered 941,000.

By far the greatest proportion of Italy's visitors came from Switzerland, approximately 22 per cent. Most of the United Kingdom's foreign visitors (excluding visitors from the Republic of Ireland) came from the United States, approximately 29 per cent.

ROYALTY

OLDEST RULING HOUSE

Though historians claim to have traced the line of the Japanese Royal family back to Jimmu Tenno, who is reputed to have ascended to the throne 2,615 years ago in 660 B.C., there is doubt as to the authenticity of these claims.

The longest continuous reigning line is that of the Royal House of Denmark founded by Gorm the Old in A.D. 811. The present monarch, King Frederik IX (succeeded 20th April, 1947) is the direct descendent of Gorm and the fifty-second in line.

LONGEST AND SHORTEST REIGNS

The longest reign of any King of Great Britain was that of George III from 25th October, 1760 to 29th January, 1820 (59 years, 96 days) and the longest of a Queen that of Victoria from 20th June, 1837 to 22nd January, 1901 (63 years, 216 days).

The shortest reign of a King of England was that of Edward V from 9th April, 1483 to 26th June, 1483 (seventy-nine days) and the shortest of a Queen that of Jane, 6th July, 1553 to 19th July, 1553 (fourteen days).

The longest lived British monarchs were King George III who died on 29th January, 1820 at 81 years 7 months and Queen Victoria who at the time of her death, on 22nd January, 1901, had surpassed his age by four days.

The youngest monarchs to accede were Edward V in 1483 at the age of 12 years 5 months and Jane in 1553 at the age of 16 years.

MOST CHILDREN

The King with most children was James II (1685–1688) who had eight children by his first wife, Lady Anne Hyde, seven by his second wife, Mary of Modena, and four illegitimate children—totalling nineteen children.

The monarch with the greatest number of illegitimate children was Charles II (1649–1685) with fourteen.

Largest number of children produced by a Queen regnant was seventeen (all but one died in infancy) by Queen Anne (1702–1714) and the largest number by a Queen consort was fifteen by Queen Charlotte, wife of George III (1760–1820).

WELSH LONGEST REIGN

Of the independent Princes of Wales, the longest reigning was Gruffydd ap Cynan ap Iago from 1081 to 1137 (56 years) and the shortest Cadwallon ab Ieuaf (985–986).

SCOTTISH LONGEST REIGN

Of Scottish monarchs that with the longest reign was James VI of Scotland and I of England from 29th July, 1567 to 27th March, 1625 (57 years 8 months) and that with the shortest was Donald Ban, son of Duncan I, who reigned for a few months during 1093.

IRELAND

According to mainly traditional evidence Ireland had 247 native sovereigns from circa 1300 B.C. to A.D. 1172 of whom at least 190 died a violent death. The longest reign in the Christian era was the forty years of Eochaidh-Gundit (A.D. 213–253).

LEGISLATIVE

OLDEST PARLIAMENT

The earliest legislative body was the Althing of Iceland founded in A.D. 930. This body which originally comprised thirty-nine local chieftains was abolished in 1800, but restored by Denmark to a consultative status in 1843 and a legislative status in 1874. The legislative assembly with oldest continuous history is the Tynwald Court in the Isle of Man, which is believed to have originated over 1,000 years ago.

LARGEST

The largest legislative assembly in the world is the Houses of Parliament of the United Kingdom, of the Palace of Westminster, London consisting of 1,483 members (House of Lords 853, House of Commons 630).

HIGHEST PAID

The most highly paid of all the world's legislators are Congressmen of the United States who receive $12,500 plus $2,500 (tax free) and an additional $9,500 (£3,400) for "clerk hire" totalling $24,500 (£8,760) per annum.

ENGLAND'S EARLIEST

England's earliest parliament was that summoned by Simon de Montfort when, in 1264 in the reign of Henry III, he called for four knights to be elected by and to represent every county.

LONGEST AND SHORTEST

The longest English Parliament was the "Pensioners" Parliament of Charles II which lasted from 1661 to 1679. The longest United Kingdom Parliament was that of George V, Edward VIII and George VI lasting from 16th November, 1935 to 15th June, 1945, a span of 9 years 6 months and 25 days. The shortest United Kingdom Parliament was that of George III lasting from 15th December, 1806 to 29th April, 1807, a period of only 4 months and 14 days.

LONGEST SITTING

The longest sitting in the House of Commons was one of 41½ hours from 4 p.m. 31st January, 1881 to 2nd February, 1881 on the question of better Protection of Person and Property in Ireland.

LARGEST AND SMALLEST ELECTORATES

The largest electorate of all time was in 1941 the estimated 217,900 for Hendon, Middlesex, prior to redistribution. The largest electorate for any seat in 1955 was 85,124 in North Down for Northern Ireland and 77,298 for Dagenham, Essex for Great Britain. The smallest electorate of all time was in 1821 for Old Sarum (number of houses nil, population nil) in Wiltshire with eight electors who returned two members, thus being 54,475 times better represented than the Hendon electorate of 120 years later. The smallest electorate for any seat in 1955 was 25,311 for the Western Isles.

LARGEST AND NARROWEST MAJORITIES

The largest party majorities were those of the Liberals in 1832 with 370 seats and in 1906 with 356 seats. The narrowest party majority was that of the Whigs in 1847 with a single seat.

PERSONAL MAJORITIES

The largest individual majority of any member of parliament was the 62,253 by Sir Cooper Rawson, M.P. (Conservative) in 1931 at Brighton. He polled 75,205 votes against the 12,952 votes of his closer Labour opponent (L. C. Cohen) from an electorate of 128,779. The largest majority of any woman member of parliament was the 38,823 of the Countess of Iveagh, C.B.E., at Southend in the same General Election.

The smallest majority since "Universal" franchise was that of 2 by A. J. Flint, M.P. (National Labour) 17,587 votes over G. H. Oliver, D.C.M. (Labour) 17,585 votes at Ilkeston, Derbyshire in 1931.

HIGHEST POLLS

The highest poll in any constituency since " Universal " franchise, was the 92·55 per cent. at Fermanagh and South Tyrone, Ulster in the 1955 General Election when 60,797 of the electorate of 65,685 voted. The record for England is 91·64 per cent. at Clitheroe, Lancs. in the 1950 election, when 41,938 of the 45,758 electorate polled.

YOUNGEST AND OLDEST M.P.'s

Edmund Waller (1606–1687) was elected as Member of Parliament for Amersham, Buckinghamshire on 16th January, 1621 at the age of 16 years and 10 months. The official returns however do not show him as actually having taken his seat until two years later when, in the Parliament of 1623–24, he sat as Member for Ilchester. Minors were debarred in law in 1695 and in fact in 1832. Since that time the youngest Member of Parliament has been the Hon. Esmond Cecil Harmsworth (now second Viscount Rothermere) who was elected for Isle of Thanet, Kent on 28th November, 1919 when one day short of being 21 years and 6 months. The oldest sitting member in Parliamentary history was the Rt. Hon. Charles Pelham Villiers, P.C. (born 3rd January, 1802) who died while the Member for Wolverhampton on 16th January, 1898 aged 96. He was a Member of Parliament for 63 years 6 days having been elected at fourteen Elections. He was last seen in the House at the age of 95. See plate 3.

The oldest Member now sitting is David Gilbert Logan, C.B.E., M.P. (Labour) for the Scotland Division of Liverpool since 1929, who was 84 on 22nd November, 1954. The youngest is Peter Michael Kirk, M.P. (Conservative) for Gravesend, Kent, who was elected in the General Election of 26th May, 1955, aged 27 years and 8 days.

LONGEST SPEECH

The longest recorded speech in the House of Commons was that of Henry Peter Brougham on 7th February, 1828, when he spoke for six hours on Law Reform. He ended at 10·40 p.m. and the report of this speech occupied 12 columns of the next day's " Times." Brougham, created first baron in 1830, also holds the House of Lords record, also with six hours, on 7th October, 1831 speaking on the second reading of the Reform Bill.

The longest Budget Speech was that of W. E. Gladstone who, on 18th April, 1853, spoke from 4.35 p.m. to 9.20 p.m. (4¾ hours.)

The longest speech by a back bencher this century was the 137 minutes by Norman Harold Lever, M.P., Labour Member for Manchester, Cheetham on the Cinematograph Bill from 1.43 p.m. to 4.0 p.m. on 20th November, 1953.

LONGEST PREMIERSHIP

No Prime Minister has yet matched in duration the continuous term of office of the United Kingdom's first Prime Minister, Sir Robert Walpole (1676–1745) First Lord of the Treasury and Chancellor of the Exchequer from 3rd April, 1721 to 16th February, 1742. The office was not however officially recognised until 1905 since when the longest tenure has been that of Sir Winston Churchill, from 11th May, 1940 to 23rd May, 1945 and from 26th October, 1951 to 5th April, 1955.

LONGEST SPEAKERSHIP

Arthur Onslow (1691–1768) was elected Mr. Speaker on 23rd January, 1728 at the age of thirty-six which position he held for 33 years 43 days until 18th March, 1761.

REPUBLIC OF IRELAND

LONGEST AND SHORTEST DAILS

The longest parliament in the Dáil Éireann was the tenth Dáil from 30th June, 1938 to 26th June, 1943 (4 years 11 months) and the shortest the fifth Dáil from 23rd June, 1927 to 25th August, 1927 (64 days).

LONGEST SITTING

The longest sitting of the Dáil was 27 hours 40 minutes from 10.30 a.m. 14th July to 2.10 p.m. 15th July, 1933.

LARGEST PARTY MAJORITY

In the General Election of 17th June, 1938 the Fianna Fáil won 77 of the 138 seats.

LONGEST PREMIERSHIP

Éamon de Valéra, T.D., (Teachta Dála) was Premier from 9th March, 1932 to 18th February, 1948 (15 years 11 months) and again from 13th June, 1951 to 2nd June, 1954 (2 years 11 months), making a total of 18 years 10 months.

LONGEST SPEAKERSHIP

Frank Fahy, T.D., was elected Chairman of the Dáil on 9th March, 1932 and resigned after 19 years 3 months on 13th June, 1951.

MILITARY AND DEFENCE

WAR

Longest

The longest of history's countless wars was the " Hundred Years War " between England and France which lasted from 1338 to 1453 (115 years) though it may be said that the Holy War, comprising the nine Crusades from the First (1096–1104) to the Ninth (1270–1291), extended over 195 years. The last pitched land battle in Britain was at Cullodon Field, Inverness-shire on 16th April, 1746.

Bloodiest

By far the most costly war in terms of human life was World War II (1939–1945) in which, including military personnel and civilians of all countries, the total killed, according to a Vatican estimate, was 22,060,000 with an additional 34,300,000 wounded, making a total of 56,360,000 casualties.

In the case of the United Kingdom, however, the heaviest casualties arose in World War I (1914–1918) with 765,399 killed out of 5,500,000 engaged (13·92 per cent.) as opposed to 265,000 out of 5,896,000 engaged (4·49 per cent.) in World War II.

Most Costly

Though no satisfactory computation has been published, it is certain that the material cost of World War II transcended that of the rest of history's wars put together. In the case of the United Kingdom, the cost of £34,500 million was over nine times greater than World War I (£3,800 million) and over 170 times that of the Boer War of 1899–1902 (£217 million).

Greatest Invasion

The greatest invasion in military history was the Allied " Triphibian " operation against the Normandy coasts of France on D-day 6th June, 1944. Thirty-eight convoys of 745 ships moved in on the first three days supported by 4,066 landing craft and 347 minesweepers. Within a month, 1,100,000 troops, 200,000 vehicles and 750,000 tons of stores were landed.

GREATEST NAVAL BATTLE

The biggest naval action ever joined was the Battle of Leyte Gulf, Philippines, from 22nd to 27th October, 1944, with 166 U.S. and 65 Japanese warships engaged.

WORLD'S LARGEST ARMED FORCES

Numerically, the country with the greatest manpower under arms is the People's Republic of China (Chung-Hua Jen-Min Kung-ho Kuo) with 4,500,000 and an additional home guard militia of perhaps 13,000,000 from her population of 602,000,000. The U.S.S.R.'s regular armed forces have an estimated strength of 4,750,000 against the United States' 3,500,000. The peak war-time strength of United Kingdom forces was 5,120,000: Royal Navy 790,000 (plus W.R.N.S. 73,500); Army 2,930,000 (plus A.T.S.—now W.R.A.C.—210,300) and Royal Air Force 1,011,400 (plus W.A.A.F.—now W.R.A.F.—181,800).

NAVIES

The United States Navy is larger than the combined fleets of the rest of the world with a current strength of 101 aircraft carriers, 15 battleships, 75 cruisers, 354 destroyers and 200 submarines—and a total force of 5,000 ships of which 1,080 are active.

LARGEST BATTLESHIPS

The 72,200 ton Japanese battleships *Yamato* (sunk by U.S. planes on 7th April, 1945) and *Musashi* (sunk by fifteen bombs and twenty torpedoes on 24th October, 1944) were the largest battleships ever constructed. With an overall length of 863 feet, a beam of 127 feet and a full load draught of 36 feet they mounted nine 18-inch guns in three triple turrets. Each gun weighed 162 tons and was 75 feet in length firing a 3,200 lb. projectile. See Plate 2.

Britain's largest ever battleship is H.M.S. *Vanguard* with a full load displacement of 51,420 tons, overall length 814 feet, beam 108½ feet, and a maximum draught of 36 feet. She mounts eight 15-inch and sixteen 5·25-inch guns and has a war-time complement of 2,000. A shaft horse power of 130,000 gives her a sea speed of 29½ knots. The *Vanguard* was laid down in John Brown & Co., Ltd.'s yard at Clydebank on 20th October, 1941, launched on 30th November, 1944, and completed on 25th April, 1946, at a cost of £9,000,000.

LARGEST AIRCRAFT CARRIERS

The largest ship yet completed is the aircraft carrier U.S.S. *Forrestal* which has a full load displacement of 75,900 tons, an overall length of 1,036 feet, a maximum beam of 248 feet (129½ feet on the water-line) and a maximum draught of 37 feet. A shaft horse power of 260,000 gives her a speed of 33 knots. She was laid down by the Newport News Shipbuilding and Drydock Co. on 14th July, 1952, launched on 11th December, 1954, and completed at a cost of $218,000,000 (£77,857,000). She carries ninety aircraft and has a complement of 3,826. Her sister ship the U.S.S. *Saratoga*, launched 8th October, 1955, is reportedly 1,039 feet long.

Britain's largest ever aircraft carrier is H.M.S. *Ark Royal* with a full load displacement of 46,000 tons, overall length 808¼ feet, beam 112¾ feet, maximum draught 36 feet, mounting sixteen 4·5-inch guns and forty 40 mm.-A.A. guns with a war-time complement of 2,750 and a capacity of 110 aircraft. Her 152,000 shaft horse power gives her 31·5 knots. She was built at Birkenhead by Cammel Laird & Co., Ltd., being laid down on 3rd May, 1943, launched on 3rd May, 1950, and completed for sea-trials on 4th June, 1954.

SUBMARINES

The largest submarines ever constructed were the I-14, I-40 and I-400 of the Imperial Japanese Navy, completed in 1944 at Kawasaki, 400¼ feet in length, carrying three seaplanes, eight 21-inch torpedo tubes, one 5·5-inch gun, with a submerged displacement of 6,560 tons, and a complement of 144. The deepest diving and greatest range submarine yet constructed is the nuclear-powered U.S.S. *Nautilus*, which began sea-trials on 17th January, 1955. Costing $55 million (£20,000,000), she has an underwater speed in excess of 20 knots and a range of 30,000 miles.

The largest submarines in the Royal Navy are the " A " Class, completed 1945–48, with a submerged displacement of 1,620 tons, a length of 282 feet and a complement of sixty.

CONVOYS

The earliest Royal Navy convoy was across the English Channel in 1242.

The largest recorded convoy was the HX.S (Halifax, Slow) 306 in July, 1944, which comprised 167 ships of 1,056,413 tons and covered 26 square miles of sea.

MINES

The earliest use of metal explosive-filled mines was by the Imperial Russian Navy at Kronstadt during the Crimean war in 1854. The largest minefield ever laid was the barrier between Scotland and Iceland in which the Royal Navy, during 1943, laid 92,536 mines.

TORPEDOES

The torpedo was developed from David Bashnell's experiments in 1775 by the American engineer, Robert Fulton (1765–1815), in 1805 but was not perfected as an auto-mobile weapon until 1864 by the Scotsman, Robert Whitehead. The largest torpedoes constructed were those of 24-inch calibre used by major vessels of the Royal Navy.

ARMIES

Numerically, the world's largest army is that of the People's Republic of China with a first-line strength of 2,500,000 supported by 500,000 second-line troops, 1,750,000 regional troops, 800,000 public security troops and a militia believed to be 13,000,000 strong, making a total man-power of over 18½ million. This compares with the U.S.S.R.'s war-time peak of 12,500,000 of all arms.

The world's smallest Army died in April, 1939, with the death of Andreas Klieber, 95, the last survivor of the fifty-eight-strong Liechtenstein Army sent to aid Austria against Germany in the war of 1866.

OLDEST REGIMENT

The oldest regular regiment in the British Army is the Royal Scots, raised in French service in 1633, though the Buffs (Royal East Kent Regiment) can trace back their origin to independent companies in Dutch pay to as early as 1572. The Coldstream Guards, raised 1650, were, however, placed on the establishment of the British Army before the Royal Scots and the Buffs.

MOST BATTLE HONOURS ARMY

Battle Honours allowed to be carried on Regimental Colours in respect of the 1914–18 war were officially limited to ten while those for the 1939–45 war have not yet been awarded. The regiment with the greatest number of Battle Honours before the two world wars is the Gloucesters.

ROYAL NAVY

The earliest Royal Naval battle honour is " Armada 1588 " as borne by H.M. Cruiser " Swiftsure ".

The greatest number of battle honours carried by one ship is 20 by H.M.S. " Orion " but " Warspite ", a name now vacant, bears 25 battle honours.

GUNS

Earliest

Though it cannot be accepted as proved, the best opinion is that the earliest guns were constructed by the German, Berthold Schwarz, in 1313. The earliest representation of an English gun is contained in an illustrated manuscript dated 1326 at Oxford.

Largest

The remains of the most massive guns ever constructed were found in 1945 near Frankfurt, Germany. They were " Schwerer Gustav " and " Dora " each of which was 31·5 inch calibre with 105 feet long barrels designed to throw a 16,540 lb. projectile 51,000 yards with a 2,500 lb. charge. Each gun with its carriage weighed 1,344 tons.

Longest Range

The longest range ever achieved by any gun was that of the 20½ ton German 280 mm. (11·02 inch) K.5 with a 70 feet 8 inch long barrel which could send a 300 lb. projectile 93 miles. The 232 mm. (9·14 inch) " Big Berthas " which shelled Paris in 1918 had a ground range of 70 miles. See Plate 2.

Anti-Aircraft

The highest range anti-aircraft gun developed is the 30-ton U.S. " Stratosphere " 120 mm. gun developed in 1944 to attain an altitude of 11 miles. The record height for shooting down an aircraft was 36,000 feet (6·8 miles).

Mortar

The greatest mortars ever constructed were Mallet's mortar (Woolwich Arsenal, 1857) and the U.S. " Little David ". Both were of 36¼ inch (920 mm.) calibre—but neither was ever used in action.

TANKS

The prototype of all tanks was " Little Willie " built by William Foster & Co., Ltd., of Lincoln, England, and first tested in September 1915.

The heaviest operational tank used by any Army was the German panzerkampfwagen Tiger Model B (Royal Tiger) of 67 tons, mounting an 88 mm. gun and powered with 700 b.h.p. Heavier tanks up to 180 tons and one carrying a 380 mm. (14·97 inches) mortar were discovered in experimental stages in Germany.

AIR FORCES

The greatest Air Force of all-time was the United States Air Force which, in July, 1944, had 79,908 aircraft and in March, 1944, 2,411,294 personnel. Currently, it is probable that the U.S.S.R., with a reported annual production of 22,000 'planes, possesses the world's largest air force with 19,500 front line aircraft.

The oldest air force in the world is that of the United States which was started in the form of the Aeronautical Division of the Signal Corps with three men on 1st August, 1907.

LARGEST BOMBER

The world's largest bomber is the American Convair B-36 D which has a wing span of 230 feet, a length of 162 feet, a height of 46 feet 9 inches and is powered by six Pratt and Whitney R-4360 engines and four General Electric J47 turbojets giving a speed of 435 m.p.h. Its gross weight is 179 tons and it has a range, with a bomb load, of 10,000 miles.

IMPERIAL COINAGE

WEST DENOMINATION COIN—One third of a
thing (1/12d.). King George V, 1913. Bronze.

LARGEST COIN—Crown or five shilling piece (5s.). King George VI, 1937. Silver alloy 50%.

GHEST DENOMINATION COIN—Five pound
ece (£5). King George VI, 1937. Gold 22 carats.

SMALLEST COIN—One Maundy penny piece (1d.). King George VI, 1937. Silver 92.5%.

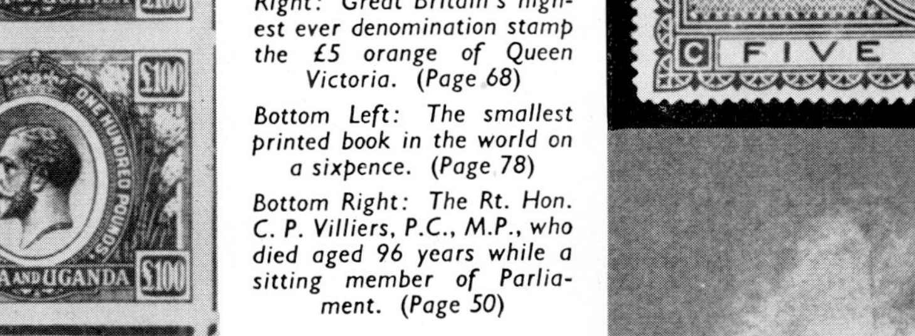

PLATE 3

Above: The Imperial coinage. (Page 64)

Left: The world's highest ever denomination stamp the King George V £100 red and black of Kenya. (Page 68)

Right: Great Britain's highest ever denomination stamp the £5 orange of Queen Victoria. (Page 68)

Bottom Left: The smallest printed book in the world on a sixpence. (Page 78)

Bottom Right: The Rt. Hon. C. P. Villiers, P.C., M.P., who died aged 96 years while a sitting member of Parliament. (Page 50)

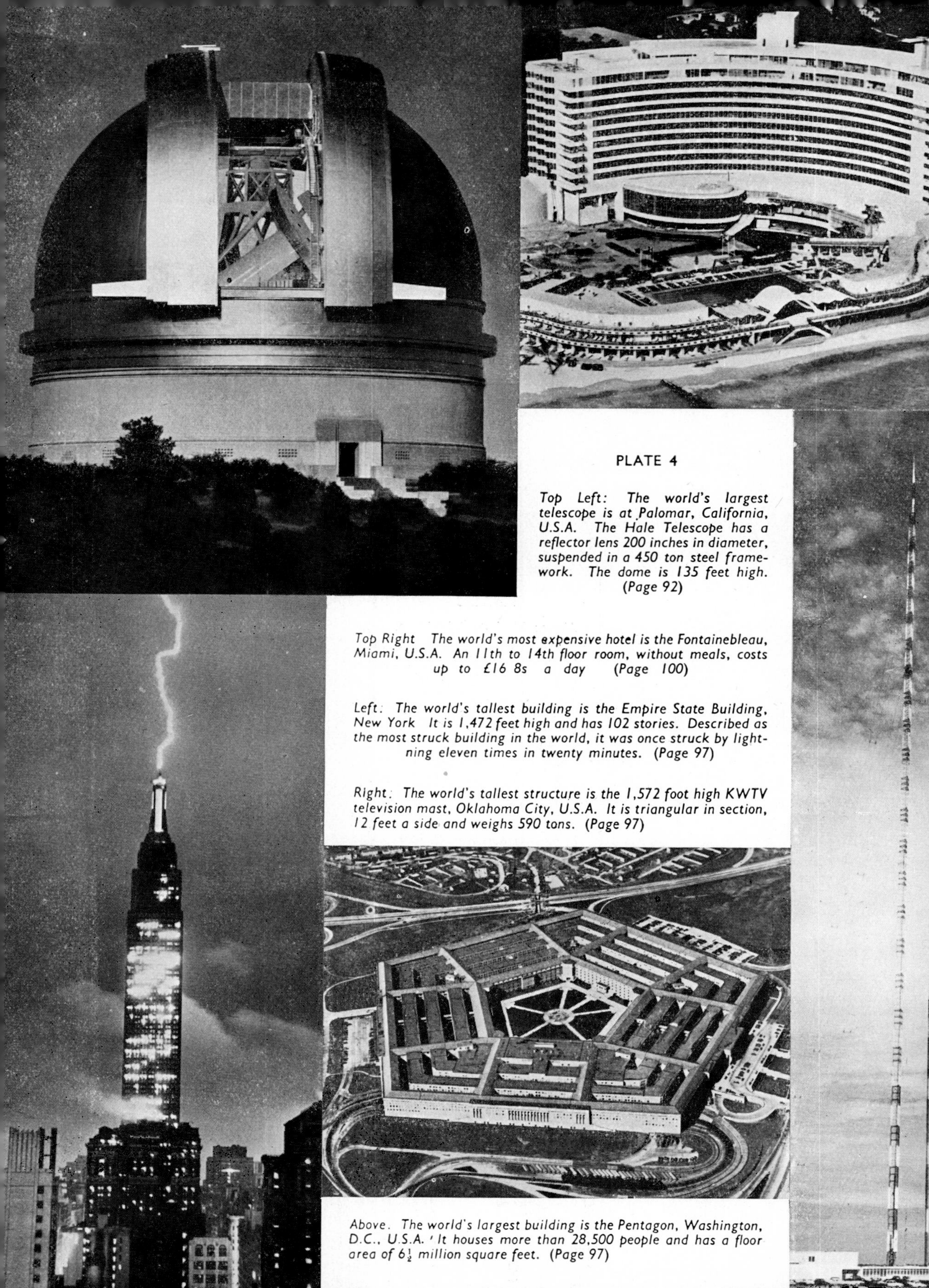

PLATE 4

Top Left: The world's largest telescope is at Palomar, California, U.S.A. The Hale Telescope has a reflector lens 200 inches in diameter, suspended in a 450 ton steel framework. The dome is 135 feet high. (Page 92)

Top Right The world's most expensive hotel is the Fontainebleau, Miami, U.S.A. An 11th to 14th floor room, without meals, costs up to £16 8s a day (Page 100)

Left: The world's tallest building is the Empire State Building, New York It is 1,472 feet high and has 102 stories. Described as the most struck building in the world, it was once struck by lightning eleven times in twenty minutes. (Page 97)

Right: The world's tallest structure is the 1,572 foot high KWTV television mast, Oklahoma City, U.S.A. It is triangular in section, 12 feet a side and weighs 590 tons. (Page 97)

Above. The world's largest building is the Pentagon, Washington, D.C., U.S.A. It houses more than 28,500 people and has a floor area of 6½ million square feet. (Page 97)

SPEED

The official International speed record is held at 755·149 m.p.h. over a 15–25 kilometre straight course by a North American YF-100A piloted by Lt.-Col. Frank K. Everest over Salton Sea, California, on 29th October, 1953. The YF-100A Super Sabre is powered by a Pratt and Whitney J57-P-7 turbojet, has a wingspan of 36 feet and a length of 45 feet.

The level flight record (altitude 40,000 feet) is 822·135 m.p.h. in an F-100-C Super Sabre by Col. Horace Hanes above the Mojave Desert, California, U.S.A. on 20th August, 1955.

FASTEST AIRCRAFT

The fastest aircraft was the American Bell Aircraft Corporation X-1A which, on 12th December, 1953, attained a speed of 1,650 m.p.h. over Edwards Air Force Base, California. The aircraft is powered by Reaction Motors Inc. rocket motors of four units using alcohol and liquid oxygen with a fuel duration of 4·2 minutes. Wingspan 28 feet, length 35 feet 7 inches, height 10 feet 8 inches. The pilot was Major Charles E. Yeager (born 13th February, 1923), Silver Star, D.F.C., Bronze Star, Air Medal, U.S.A.F. See Plate 2.

LONGEST FLIGHT

A U.S. B-47 bomber in December, 1954, stayed airborne 47 hours 35 minutes and covered 21,000 miles.

HIGHEST FLYING

The Bell X-1A also set the world's highest altitude performance on 16th June, 1954, at a figure in excess of 83,500 feet (probably 90,000 feet) over California. The pilot on this occasion was Major Arthur Murray.

LARGEST HELICOPTER

The world's largest operational helicopter is the U.S.A.F. Piasecki PV-15 Transporter (YH-16) which measures 134 feet overall and stands 25 feet in height. It is powered with Wright R-1820 engines.

LARGEST (NON-RIGID) AIRSHIP

The U.S. Navy Anti-Submarine airship ZP2N built by Goodyear is the world's largest non-rigid airship with a capacity of 970,000 cubic feet of helium.

LARGEST BOMB

The heaviest bomb ever used operationally was the R.A.F. 22,000 lb. "Grand Slam" dropped in 1944 in attacks on concrete U-Boat pens. In 1949, the United States Air Force tested a 42,000 lb. bomb at Muroc Dry Lake, California.

2. *Economic*

RESOURCES

The countries with the greatest resources of raw materials and basic industries arranged to show actual production figures from the latest available yearly reports and where possible, the proportion they represent of the world total. The United Kingdom figure has been included for comparison.

In many cases, authoritative figures for the U.S.S.R. are not available.

Agricultural

Arable land—U.S.S.R., 560 million acres, 16 per cent. of world total. The United Kingdom figure is 18·1 million acres.

Forest land—U.S.S.R., 2,270 million acres, 25 per cent. of world total. The United Kingdom figure is 3·9 million acres.

Cattle—India, 155 million head, 20 per cent. of world total. The United Kingdom figure is 10·7 million head.

Horses—U.S.S.R., 15·3 million, 26 per cent. of world total. The United Kingdom figure is 370,000.

Sheep—Australia, 123 million, 15 per cent. of world total. The United Kingdom figure is 22·8 million.

Pigs—U.S.A., 54·2 million, 16 per cent. of world total. The United Kingdom figure is 6·2 million.

Cotton (Ginned)—U.S.A., 3·5 million tons, 49 per cent. of world total.

Wool—Australia, 555,000 tons, 31 per cent. of world total. The United Kingdom figure is 47,000 tons.

Food

Wheat—U.S.A., 31·3 million tons, 21 per cent. of world total.* The United Kingdom figure is 2·6 million tons.

Meat—U.S.A., 11 million tons. The United Kingdom figure is 1·3 million tons.

Potatoes—U.S.S.R., about 74 million tons, 45 per cent. of world total. The United Kingdom figure is 8 million tons.

Suga—Cuba, 5·1 million tons, 16 per cent. of world total. The United Kingdom figure is 795,000 tons.

Rice—China, 47 million tons, 28 per cent. of world total.

Fish Landings—Japan, 4·5 million tons, 28 per cent. of world total. The United Kingdom figure is 76,200 tons.

Minerals

Coal—U.S.A., 371 million tons, 29·4 per cent. of world total. The United Kingdom figure is 223 million tons.

Petroleum—U.S.A., 304 million tons, 49·8 per cent. of world total. The United Kingdom figure is 159,000 tons.

Tin Ore—Fed. of Malay States, 60,600 tons, 37 per cent. of world total.* The United Kingdom figure is 944 tons.

Copper Ore—U.S.A., 770,000 tons, 32 per cent. of world total.

Gold—Union of South Africa, 11·6 million troy ounces, 37 per cent. of world total.

Iron Ore—U.S.A., 60 million tons, 40 per cent. of world total. The United Kingdom figure is 4·5 million tons.

Industrial

Electricity—U.S.A., 471,612 million k.w.h., 40 per cent. of world total. The United Kingdom figure is 73,370 million k.w.h.

Steel—U.S.A., 79 million tons, 44 per cent. of world total. The United Kingdom figure is 18·5 million tons.

Aluminium (Primary)—U.S.A., 1·3 million tons, 54 per cent. of world total. The United Kingdom figure is 32,000 tons.

Rubber (Nat.)—Indonesia, 750,000 tons, 40 per cent. of world total.

Communications

Merchant Fleets—U.S.A., 29·6 million tons, 36 per cent. of world total. The United Kingdom figure is 18·9 million tons.

Motor Vehicles—U.S.A., 56 million, 70 per cent. of world total. The United Kingdom figure is 4·6 million.

* No data for U.S.S.R.

PROPORTIONS OF TOTAL NATIONAL PRODUCT

It should be mentioned, with regard to these comparisons, that methods for the assessment and classification of these data vary from country to country. The figures, therefore, are approximations only indicating trends rather than quantitative comparisons.

AGRICULTURE

Agriculture and associated industries represent 57 per cent. of the domestic economy of Thailand and Turkey—more than anywhere else. In the United Kingdom, the same industries are only 5 per cent. of the total net product—the smallest proportion in the world.

MANUFACTURING

The United Kingdom, manufacturing and mining industries account for 43 per cent. of the total product — the largest proportion of any country in the world. Honduras, where these industries are 11 per cent. of the total, has the lowest figure.

TRADE

The percentage of the national product absorbed in retail and wholesale distribution is highest in Mexico—an estimated 31 per cent. The lowest proportion is that of 8 per cent. in Austria and the Belgian Congo.

PUBLIC ADMINISTRATION

The highest proportion of national income used for administration, defence, judicial, police is probably that of Israel with 15 per cent. The lowest figure under this heading is recorded for Honduras with 3 per cent.

TRADE

The country with the greatest value of exports at present is the United States. A total value of £5,350 million worth, about 19 per cent. of the world's total. The United Kingdom comes second on the list of world exporters with a total of £2,775 million or approximately 10 per cent. of the world's total.

The country with the greatest value of imports is again the United States, which during 1953 imported goods to the value of £3,700 million. The United Kingdom again ranks second with imports to the value of £3,400 million.

The country with the greatest excess of exports over imports, or favourable balance of trade, expressed as a percentage, was Venezuela. In 1953, their exports exceeded imports by 95 per cent. The greatest excess of exports over imports as an amount was shown by the United States, the value of the balance being £1,705 million or 33 per cent.

The country with the most greatly increased industrial production is Western Germany. Calculated on 1948, their production had increased by 182 per cent. compared with the United Kingdom's 29 per cent. Based on 1938, Western Germany has increased by 77·5 per cent. and the United Kingdom by 50 per cent.

INDUSTRIAL SHARES

During the five years since 1948, the year on which these figures are based, (1948 = 100) Japan has shown the greatest rise in the market price of her industrial shares. Throughout the years since 1948, the index has equalled, 100 — 211 — 119 — 145 — 252 — 383, expressed as an annual average.

The country showing the greatest fall over the same period, and on the same index number, is the Union of South Africa, the index number of whose shares fell from 100 to 56. The United Kingdom figure over the same period rose from 100 to 102.

STOCK EXCHANGE

The highest number of markings received in one day on the London Stock Exchange is 19,438 on the 20th January, 1947.

The greatest overall daily movement occurred on 24th February, 1955, when United Kingdom Ordinary shares fell some £200 million or 3·8 per cent.

The highest denomination of any share quoted on the London Stock Exchange is the £100 Preference shares of Baring Brothers & Co. Ltd., the bankers.

The lowest unit of quotation is in the case of the stock of Ice Rinks Ltd. at 1d.

COMPANIES

The greatest number of companies registered in the United Kingdom in any one year was 25,217 in 1946.

TRADE UNIONS

LARGEST

The world's largest trade union is the International Union, United Automobile, Aircraft and Agricultural Implement Workers of America. In 1954, their membership was approximately 1,479,000 of whom 180,000 were unemployed and 60,000 retired members of the Union. The U.A.W. is affiliated with the C.I.O. (Congress of Industrial Organisations) which has an estimated membership of 5·75 million in thirty-three national unions.

The largest union in the United Kingdom is the Transport and General Workers with a membership of approximately 1,300,000.

The largest labour organisation in the world is the A.F.L. (American Federation of Labour) which represents 111 national unions with an estimated 8·5 million members. In the United Kingdom, in 1955, the Trades Union Congress had 184 affiliated unions with a total membership of 8,093,837.

LIVERY COMPANIES

Of the eighty Livery Companies now in existence, the first in civic precedence is the Mercers Company (with a livery of 218), while the newest is the Farmers (livery 80). The Shipwrights is the largest company, with a livery of 500 and the smallest is the Waxchandlers with thirty-four.

LABOUR DISPUTES

The most serious single labour dispute in the United Kingdom was the General Strike of May, 1926, called by the Trades Union Congress in support of the Miners' Federation. During the nine days of the strike approximately 1,580,000 people were involved and about 14·5 million working days were lost.

During the year 1926 a total of about 2·75 million people were involved in 323 different labour disputes and the working days lost during the year amounted to 162·3 million, the highest figure ever recorded.

The biggest total of trade disputes to occur in any one year was 1,067 in 1920. The disputes involved roughly 1·6 million people and a total of 26·5 million working days were lost.

LONGEST STRIKE

The world's longest strike occurred at Dun Laoghaire, County Dublin. The dispute arose after a barman had been dismissed from his position in a public house. The Barmans' Union called the staff out on strike and arranged daily picketing of the premises, the strike commenced on the 6th March, 1939, and ended (when a new owner took over) on 5th December, 1953, more than fourteen and a half years later.

STANDARDS OF LIVING

COST OF LIVING INCREASE

The country with the greatest increase in the cost of living, based on an index figure of 1948 = 100 is Paraguay (primarily assessed on the capital Asunción) where in the seven years, 1948–1954 the cost of living rose to an index figure of 1,407, a rise of fourteen times. The prices of food alone rose a fraction more than fourteen and a quarter times.

An exceptional rise of sixty-five times, to an index figure of 6,519, occurred in Korea over the same period but, owing to the Korean war, it is not strictly comparable with the Paraguayan figure given above.

Over the same period, 1948–1954, the rise in the United Kingdom cost of living index, all items, was 32 per cent.

GREATEST DECREASE

The greatest decrease in the cost of living appears to be in Iraq where the figures (based on Baghdad) show a decrease in the price of all items of 29 per cent.

HOUSING

For these comparisons, dwelling units are defined as structurally separated room or rooms occupied by private households of one or more people and having separate access or a common passage way to the street.

The country with the largest number of separate dwelling units is the United States with, at the last assessment 44·8 million, about 360 people per 100 dwelling units.

The United Kingdom comes second in a world listing, in 1954, with 14 million. This equals 365 persons per 100 dwelling units. In both countries dwelling units with five to six rooms (of all types) comprise the major proportion of the total number—45 per cent. in the United Kingdom and 38 per cent. in the United States.

The highest density of occupation occurs in the municipality of Singapore where 29 per cent. of the dwelling units (mostly one to two room units) contain over five people in each room.

In the United Kingdom, 93 per cent. of the dwelling units have running water available and this is the highest proportion of all countries reporting such information.

Australia has the highest proportion of baths, 84 per cent. of their households being equipped with separate bathing accommodation; the United Kingdom figure is 62 per cent.

Norway, Portugal and Switzerland all report 100 per cent. coverage of electricity for lighting.

DOCTORS

The country with the most doctors per head of population is Israel where, in 1953, one doctor practised for every 390 people. At the opposite end of the scale is the Aden Protectorate, the 1952 figure for which was one doctor for 80,000 people. The figures for the British Isles are: one doctor for 1,000 people in the Republic of Ireland and in Scotland; one doctor for 1,200 people in England and Wales, and one for 1,700 in Northern Ireland.

HOSPITALS

The country with the greatest number of hospital beds per head of population is the Republic of Ireland with one bed for every sixty-seven people.

The lowest figure in the world is recorded for China, where available figures show a total of only 3,140 beds maintained by government services. This represents one bed for every 148,000 people.

The figures for the United Kingdom are: England and Wales 116 people for every bed, Scotland eighty-two people and Northern Ireland ninety-one people.

The largest medical centre in the world is the District Medical Center in Chicago, Illinois, which covers 478 acres, and contains among its institutions five hospitals, with a total of 5,600 beds, and eight professional schools with 3,166 students.

The Center, which has over 12,000 persons employed by or affiliated to it, was created by Act of Legislature in 1941 by the State of Illinois in order to advance the scope and usefulness of medical science. Out-patient visits amounted to more than 423,000 in 1954 and in the same year 13,661 babies were born in three of the hospitals.

The largest hospital in the United Kingdom is the St. James Hospital, Leeds, with 1,683 beds.

The largest mental hospital in the world is the Pilgrim State Hospital in New York State; it has 13,598 beds.

The biggest maternity hospital in the United Kingdom is Queen Charlotte's in London with 133 beds.

SOCIAL SECURITY

The United States is the country with the largest old age, invalidity and survivors social security scheme. In 1953, the number of participants was 46,000,000.

The country with the greatest number of recipients of old age pensions is the United Kingdom where there are 4,519,000 old age pensioners. This represents approximately 8·9 per cent. of the total population of the United Kingdom, the largest number of pensioners in any country of the world, and the highest proportion in the world.

In the United States, 2,977,000 people are in receipt of old age pensions, approximately 1·8 per cent. of the total population of the United States. The expenditure of the United States in this respect, £1,074,000,000, is more than three times as much as the United Kingdom's £340,000,000.

CONSUMPTIONS

FOOD CONSUMPTION

The figures relating to net food consumption per capita are based on gross available food supplies at retail level, less waste, animal feed, and that used for industrial purposes, divided by the total population. (The figures given are the latest available.)

CEREALS

Biggest consumers of cereal products—flour, milled rice, etc., are the Turkish people with a total of 430 lb. per head per year. United Kingdom figure is 216 lb.

POTATOES

The greatest eaters of potatoes are the people of the Republic of Ireland. They consume 405 lb. per head per year. The United Kingdom figure is 231 lb.

SUGAR

The figures for yearly sugar consumptions recorded since 1950 show Australians to be the heaviest users with a total of 119 lb. per head. The United Kingdom figure over the same period was 83¾ lb.

MEAT

The greatest meat eaters in the world—figures include offal and poultry—are the Uruguayans with a consumption of 277¾ lb. per head. United Kingdom figure is 116¾ lb.

MILK

Iceland consumes the greatest quantity of milk. Fresh consumption, and that used for dairy products (other than butter) totalled 666 pints per head per annum. The United Kingdom figure on the same basis was 345½ pints.

TOTAL CALORIES

Of all countries in the world, Ireland has the largest total of calories available per capita. Over twelve months, the intake averaged 3,500 per day. The United Kingdom figure over the same period was 3,060 per day.

TOTAL PROTEIN

Iceland has the highest consumption of protein per capita, a total of 113 grammes per day. United Kingdom figure 85 grammes per day.

The lowest figures in the world are: calories—India and Pakistan 1,590 per day; protein—also India and Pakistan 42 grammes per day.

ENERGY

To express the various forms of available energy, coal, liquid fuels and water power, etc., but omitting vegetable fuels and peat, it is usual to convert them all into terms of coal. On this basis, excluding the U.S.S.R. and China (for which data are not available), the world average consumption is the equivalent of 28½ cwts. of coal, or its energy equivalents, per year per person.

The highest consumption in the world is in the United States of America where the per capita consumption of coal equivalents is 157 cwts. per year. The comparable United Kingdom figure was 89 cwts.

MONETARY AND FINANCE

WORLD'S LARGEST BUDGET

The greatest annual expenditure of any national economy was that of the United States Government in 1945 with $98,416,219,788 (£35,145 million). The highest revenue was that of 1954 at $67,629,000,000 (£24,153 million) and the greatest national product that of 1953 at $364,857,000,000 (£130,306 million).

UNITED KINGDOM

The greatest annual expenditure of the United Kingdom was that of 1954–55 at £4,522 million and the highest revenue of the same fiscal year at £4,532 million.

The greatest annual surplus was the £853 million of 1948–49 and the greatest deficit the £2,825 million of 1944–45.

MOST TAXED COUNTRY

The most taxed country in the world is the United Kingdom. Between 38 per cent. and 40 per cent. of the national income is taken in central and local taxation compared with the figure of 25·6 per cent. in France, the next most taxed country.

HIGHEST LOWEST RATES

Income tax was introduced in Britain in 1799 at the standard rate of 2s. in the £. It was discontinued in 1815 only to be reintroduced in 1842 at a rate of 7d. in the £. It was at its lowest at 2d. in the £ in 1875, gradually climbing to 1s. 3d. in 1913. To finance World War I it had to be raised to 6s. by 1918 and during the inter-war years was never below the 4s. ruling between 1925 and 1930. From April 1941 until 1946 the record peak of 10s. in the £ was maintained to assist in the financing of World War II.

NATIONAL DEBTS

The country with the largest National Debt is the United States with a Gross Public Debt of $271,259 million (£96,780 million) or $1,670 (£596) per head. The United Kingdom National Debt, which became a permanent feature of England's economy as early as 1692, reached a peak of £25,630,644,900 in 1947–48 or £513 per head. This amount placed in a pile of brand new £1 notes would be over 1,650 miles in height.

GOLD RESERVES

The United States holds by far the largest gold reserve in the world at $22,100 million (£7,900 million). More than half is stored in the world's greatest treasure house, the United States Bullion Depository at Fort Knox, 30 miles south-west of Louisville, Kentucky. The gold is stored in standard mint bars of 400 troy oz. ($6\frac{3}{4} \times 3\frac{1}{2} \times 1\frac{3}{4}$ inches) each worth $14,000 (£5,000) and number some 900,000. The vault door weighs over 20 tons and no one person knows the whole combination.

The highest level ever attained for the United Kingdom's gold and dollar reserves was on 31st August, 1938, at $4,190,000,000 and the lowest of recent times $298,000,000 on 31st December, 1940.

LARGEST BANKING ORGANISATIONS

The International Bank for Reconstruction and Development, the United Nations " World Bank," in Washington, has a capital stock of $9,000 million (£3,215 million). The members' quotas to the International Monetary Fund, Washington, stand at $8,850 million (£3,160 million). Of private banks that with the greatest deposits is the Bank of America in California at a figure of $8,300 million (£2,960 million).

The largest United Kingdom Bank is the Midland Bank Ltd. with 2,127 branches, 17,000 employees and assets of £1,802,494,896 on its consolidated balance sheet. The bank is affiliated with the Clydesdale and North of Scotland Bank Ltd. and the Belfast Banking Co. Ltd. in Northern Ireland.

BANK RATE

The lowest the Bank Rate has ever been is 2 per cent., first on 22nd April, 1852, to 6th January, 1853. The highest ever figure was 10 per cent. first on 9th November, 1857, and most recently on 6th August, 1914. The highest yearly average was for 1864 (6 per cent. to 9 per cent.) at 7·35 per cent.

BANK NOTES

Paper money is an invention of the Chinese and though the date of 119 B.C. has been put forward, the innovation is believed to date from the T'ang dynasty of the 7th century A.D. The world's earliest bank notes were issued by the Bank of Sweden in 1661. The oldest surviving printed Bank of England note is one of £555 to bearer dated 19th December, 1699 ($4\frac{1}{2} \times 7\frac{3}{4}$ inches).

HIGHEST AND LOWEST DENOMINATIONS

Two Bank of England notes for £1,000,000 still exist dated prior to 1812 but these were used only for internal accounting. The highest issued denomination were £1,000 notes first printed in 1725, discontinued in 1943 and withdrawn on 30th April, 1945. The highest denomination notes currently issued are those for £5. The highest valued notes in the world are those for $100,000, bearing the head of President Wilson, issued by the United States Treasury. The lowest ever denomination Bank of England note was one for 1d. dated 10th January, 1828, which was adapted from a £5 note and doubtless used to adjust an overnight difference. It was purchased by the Bank from the landlord of the " Blue Last ", Bell Alley, in the City of London in 1868 for £1.

HIGHEST NOTE CIRCULATION

The highest ever bank note circulation in the United Kingdom was the £1,778,675,815 of June 1955—a pile of £1 notes 114 miles high.

WORST INFLATION

The world's worst inflation occurred in Hungary in June 1946 when the 1931 gold Pengo was valued at 1·3 quintillion ($1{\cdot}3 \times 10^{30}$) paper Pengös.

RATES and RATEABLE VALUES

RATING AREAS

The rating area with the largest rateable value in the United Kingdom is the county of the City of Glasgow, the rateable value of which, 1953/54, was £13,439,103.

In England, the City of Westminster has the largest rateable value of any rating area. Valuation in force in April 1953 was £11,231,401. The highest rate in the £ in England is the Borough of Wisbech, Isle of Ely—31s. 0d. in the £.

In Wales the highest rate is the urban district of Rhymney in Monmouthshire—35s. 6d. in the £. (It should be noted that Rhymney is differentially rated and therefore this figure only applies to part of the urban district). The estimated average (weighted) rate in the £ for England and Wales is 22s. 2d.

The lowest local rates in England are the 15s. 0d. in the £ of the County Boroughs of both Bournemouth and Eastbourne.

The lowest general rate in Wales is in the rural district of Pontypool, Monmouthshire, 14s. 6d. in the £.

In Scotland the highest rates are in Armadale in West Lothian County—29s. 2d., and the lowest county rate is 8s. in Orkney County.

On average, the rates levied per head of population in 1953/54 in England and Wales equalled £8 9s. 0d.

The highest per head figure was in the City of London where the collected rates equalled £1,234 14s. 0d. per head. It should be noted, however, that this figure is based only on the resident population and in the City of London, where the resident population is very low, it gives an abnormally high per head figure.

The lowest annual per head figure in England is £2 3s. 0d. in the rural district of Broadwoodwidger in Devon.

In Wales, the lowest annual per head figure is also £2 3s. 0d. in the rural district of Cemaes in Pembrokeshire.

COINS

WORLD OLDEST The earliest electrum (alloy of gold and silver) staters of Lydia in Asia Minor were coined about 700 B.C., probably in the reign of Candaules. Some numismatists believe that primitive money from China may be slightly earlier but the date of this remains uncertain.

HEAVIEST The Swedish copper 10 daler coins of 1644 attained a weight just under 20 lb.

HIGHEST DENOMINATION The Nepalese gold 200 mohur (£300) coins of the Moghul Emperor Shah Jehan (1628–1658) are both the highest denomination coins and those of the greatest intrinsic worth ever struck. Each weighs 33,600 grains (70 ozs. troy) and hence has an intrinsic worth of nearly £900.

RAREST There are more than 100 coins of which only one specimen is known. A famous example is the Indo-Greek gold 20 stater of Eucratides I (169-159 B.C.).

MOST EXPENSIVE One of the only six known specimens of the U.S. 1804 silver dollar fetched in 1946 in the open market $15,000 (£5,350). Some Greek coins are, however, known to have sold privately for sums in excess of this.

BRITISH OLDEST Bellovacian gold staters first appeared in the British Isles about 150 B.C., a century before the Roman invasion. Probably earlier were crude 'tin' coins found in south-east England, copies from Gaulish designs.

HIGHEST DENOMINATION Gold five-guinea pieces were minted from the reign of Charles II (1660-1685) until 1753 in the reign of George II.

LOWEST DENOMINATION Quarter farthings (1/16th d.) were struck for the Imperial coinage in copper in Victoria's reign in 1839 and 1851-53.

LEGAL TENDER OLDEST The oldest legal tender coins in circulation are silver half-crowns, shillings and sixpences of the reign of George III dated 1816. All gold coinage of or above the least current weight is legal tender to any amount dated onwards from 1838. The oldest legal tender bronze coinage is that also of Queen Victoria, dated 1860.

HEAVIEST HIGHEST DENOMINATION The gold five-pound (£5) piece or quintuple sovereign, is both the highest current denomination coin and also, at 616·37 grains (1·4066 ozs.), the heaviest. The most recent specimens available to the public are dated 1937 of which only 5,501 were minted. See Plate 3. Uncirculated Elizabeth II five pound pieces dated 1953 exist.

LIGHTEST SMALLEST

The silver Maundy penny piece is the smallest of the legal tender coins and at 7·27 grains (just over 1/60th oz.) the lightest. These coins exist for every date since 1822. Third of farthings were struck in 1866–85, 1902 and 1913.

LARGEST

The five-shilling (5s.) piece or crown is the largest of all current coins with a circumference of 4·84 inches.

RAREST

Only six specimens of the 1933 penny were struck but examples of the 1937 twelve-sided nickel-brass threepenny piece bearing the left facing portrait of King Edward VIII are the rarest in circulation.

BIGGEST CRASH

The biggest individual financial crash in history occurred in 1932 when a group of public utility companies in the U.S.A. — Insull Utility Investments — controlled by London born Samuel Insull, failed to fulfill its obligations.

Samuel Insull, at the time of the crash, was President of eleven companies, Chairman of 65 and on the boards of a total of eighty five. The group controlled more than 6,000 public utility plants.

The total loss to investors has never been accurately assessed but it has been estimated at more than £185 million. Some estimates even suggest £800 million. The group defaulted on its obligations to the amount of £54 million.

Charged with bankruptcy, fraud and embezzlement, Samuel Insull was acquitted and died in France in 1938. See BAIL p. 69.

TRANSPORT

AIRLINES

The country with the busiest airlines system is the United States where the latest available figures show a total of 18,150,000,000 passenger miles, domestic and international services, flown in one year. This equals an annual trip of 111 miles for every one of the 162·5 million inhabitants of the U.S.

The United Kingdom airlines carried out 1,430,000,000 passenger miles. This is equivalent to an annual flight of 28 miles for every person in the United Kingdom.

MERCHANT SHIPPING

The largest merchant fleet in the world is owned by the United States. In ships over 100 gross tons, American-owned ships accounted for 27,237,000 tons of the world's 93,352,000 tons of shipping.

The United Kingdom fleet, the second biggest in the world, accounts for 18,584,000 gross tons or approximately 20 per cent. of the world's total.

More vessels entered United States ports than any other country — a 1953 total of 83·3 million net registered tons. The United Kingdom figure over the same period was 69·4 million tons.

BUSIEST PORT

The largest and busiest dock complex in the world is that administered by the Port of London Authority. The five main dock systems which are run by the P.L.A. cover an area of 4,140 acres of which 700 are water. In 1954 the Port handled a total of 53,793 ships with a total net registered tonnage of 68,550,917 tons. The wet docks alone handled 17,024 ships of 33,385,060 net registered tonnage of this total.

The total tonnage of goods imported and exported was 51,405,555 tons.

RAILWAY

The country with the greatest length of railway is the U.S.A. with 237,500 miles of track. This equals a density of one mile of railway for every 12·7 square miles. Belgium is the country with the greatest railway density — one mile of track for every 1·43 square miles. British Railways with 51,600 miles of track comes second in a density table with one mile of railway for every 1·71 square miles.

British Railways carry more people than any other railway system. In 1952, the figure was 988,997,000.

The Japanese State Railway system carries out more passenger miles (one passenger for one mile) than any other system — in 1953 51,950 million. The United Kingdom figure was 20,810 million.

The freight record is held by the United States with, in 1953, a total of 543,000 million ton miles. The United Kingdom figure for the same year was 22,750 million ton miles.

ROADS

The country with the greatest length of road is the United States with 2,600,000 miles of graded roads, not including some 600,000 miles of dirt roads.

The country with the most motor vehicles is again the United States with a total number of private cars, commercial vehicles and passenger vehicles of 51,425,600.

The country with the greatest number of vehicles per mile of road is the United Kingdom. Its 184,000 miles of road carry 3,871,100 motor vehicles, approximately 20 vehicles a mile, or, if motor cycles, tractors, etc. are included, a total of 5,282,222 vehicles — nearly 29 vehicles of all types for every mile of road. If they were all equally spaced on public roads, there would be a vehicle every 60 yards.

The country with the greatest length of road compared on an area basis is Belgium with 3·3 miles for every square mile. The United Kingdom figure is 1·98 miles per square mile.

The highest traffic density at any one point in the United Kingdom is at Hyde Park Corner, London. It is used by 81,446 vehicles a day. The busiest Thames Bridge is Putney with an average of 28,700 vehicles a day in 1955.

London's slowest traffic lights are those at the junction of Pratt Street and Delancy Street with Camden High Street, N.W.1, with a delay of 69 seconds.

The greatest reported number of driving " L " test failures is 17, in May, 1939, by a man, who triumphed at his 18th attempt.

INLAND WATERWAYS

The country with the greatest length of inland waterways is Finland. The total of navigable lakes and rivers is 31,000 miles.

In the United Kingdom the total navigable length of rivers and canals is 3,920 miles.

The busiest canal in the world is the Sault Ste. Marie connecting Lakes Superior and Huron in North America.

COMMUNICATIONS

The country with the greatest number of available transmitting frequencies is the United States, where there were, in 1953, a total of 4,433 stations and wavelengths. In the United Kingdom there are 63 transmitting frequencies.

There are more than 232 million radio sets in use throughout the world — approximately 95 for every 1,000 people or roughly one receiver for every ten people all over the world.

RADIO SETS

The country with the highest number of radio receivers is the United States of America where approximately 110,000,000 sets are in use. This figure represents approximately 47 per cent. of the world's total of 232 million sets for a population of 6½ per cent. of the people of the world.

This figure gives the United States the highest concentration of radio receivers with 701 sets per 1,000 people.

The equivalent United Kingdom figure is 277 per thousand on the basis of 14,067,394 broadcast and broadcast/television licences current in July 1955.

The lowest density appears to be Tanganyika where some 2,000 sets are distributed among 7·9 million people — 0·25 sets per 1,000 persons, one set to 3,950 people.

Television services and the numbers of sets in use are growing in nearly every country. For this reason, the figures are only rough estimates to be regarded more as proportionate than actual.

The country with the largest number of T.V. sets is the United States where approximately 32 million are in use, equalling 192 per thousand.

The United Kingdom figures are 4,725,583 sets or 94 sets per thousand.

TELEPHONE

The country with the greatest number of telephones is the U.S.A. with an estimated 50 million; this provides 31 per 100 population against a U.K. figure of 3·77 million subscriber lines — 10th in world rating with 12 instruments and 7·5 lines per 100 population.

In the U.S.A. every one of the 165 million population makes an average 368 calls a year. United Kingdom average 67 calls a year per person, but the biggest telephone users in the world are the Canadians, who make an average of 459 calls a year.

POSTAL SERVICES

The country with the largest domestic letter mail in the world is the United States, whose population posts 51,000 million letters a year. The British figure, for the same period, was 8,658,000,000 letters.

The United States also takes first place in the number of letters which each person posts during one year. The most recent figure totalled 308. The British figure in this respect was 170 per year.

Of countries reporting to the International Bureau of the Universal Postal Union, French Somaliland returned the lowest figure for domestic mail showing 7,980 letters in 1953.

POSTAGE STAMPS
Earliest

The earliest adhesive postage stamps in the world are the "Penny Blacks" of Great Britain, bearing the head of Queen Victoria, placed on sale on 1st May for use on 6th May, 1840.

Size

The largest postage stamps ever issued were the Express delivery stamps of China in 1913 which measured 9¾ inches by 2¾ inches.

The smallest stamps ever issued are those of the Colombian State of Bolivar, 1863-1866, at 10 cents and at 1 peso, measuring 5/16ths inch by ⅜ inch.

Denomination The highest denomination stamp ever issued was the King George V £100 red and black Kenya stamp of 1925-27. The highest denomination Great Britain stamp ever issued was £5 orange Queen Victoria stamp issued on 21st March, 1882. Owing to demonetization it is difficult to determine the claimant for the lowest denomination stamp though this probably is the French ½ centime stamp of 1919-22, then representing 1/20th of a penny. See Plate 3.

Rarest There are a number of stamps of which but a single specimen is known. Of these the most celebrated is the famous British Guiana 1 cent black on magenta of 1856 which was originally bought from a schoolboy for 6 shillings.

Most Expensive The highest price ever paid for a stamp is the £12,720 paid in October 1953 for a Swedish 3 skilling Banco yellow of 1855.

POSTAL ADDRESSES The commonest postal place name in the British Isles is Newport. There are 8 Newports with Post Offices in the United Kingdom and two in the Republic of Ireland. The highest road numbering in the British Isles is that in Dumbarton Road, Glasgow, in which there is a house numbered 2,562.

POSTAL DISTRICTS Of London's 118 postal sub-districts the largest is London, E.4., embracing the Chingford, Essex, area and the smallest is London, E.C.3., which covers the oldest parts of the City and the Tower of London.

PILLAR BOXES Pillar boxes were introduced by the novelist Anthony Trollope (1815-82). The oldest standing is one of the round type in Cumberland Terrace, London, N.W.1., erected on 12th December, 1867. An older hexagonal type box is still standing at Wellington Place, St. John's Wood, London, but it was erected later on 29th May, 1868.

TELEGRAMS The most telegrams are sent by the people of the United States who send approximately 152 million telegrams per year, one for each inhabitant of the United States. The United Kingdom figure is 36,400,000.

NEWSPAPERS The country with the largest number of different daily newspapers is the United States. Every day 1,865 newspapers issue approximately 55,370,000 copies.

The country with the most daily newspapers per head is the United Kingdom where 122 newspapers issue 31,000,000 copies a day, to give the figure of 615 papers per thousand people. This compares with the United States figure of 353 copies for every 1,000 people.

Many countries and territories do not produce a daily newspaper but the lowest recorded readership figure is for Ethiopia, where one daily newspaper is issued — one copy for every 30,000 inhabitants.

The world's biggest consumer of newsprint is the United States who in 1954 used 5,400,000 tons. This equals a per head consumption of 75 lb.

The United Kingdom consumption over the same period equalled 34 lb. per head — a total of 821,000 tons.

3. Judicial

LEGAL AND LITIGATION

OLDEST STATUTE

The oldest statute in operation to-day is a section of the Statute of Marlborough of 1267, retitled in 1948 " The Distress Act, 1267 ".

LONGEST STATUTE

Measured in bulk the longest statute by far is the Income Tax Act 1952, which runs to 507 pages. However, its 532 sections are surpassed by the Merchant Shipping Act, 1894.

SHORTEST STATUTE

The shortest statute is the Parliament (Qualification of Women) Act, 1918, which runs to twenty-seven words — " A woman shall not be disqualified by sex or marriage for being elected to or sitting or voting as a Member of the Commons House of Parliament ".

MOST PROTRACTED LITIGATION

The dispute over the claim of the Prior and Convent (later the Dean and Chapter) of Durham to administer the spiritualities of the diocese during a vacancy in the See grew fierce in 1283. It smouldered until 1939, having flared up in 1672, 1890 and 1920. In 1939 the Archbishop of Canterbury exercised his metropolitan rights and appointed the Dean as guardian of spiritualities of Durham " without prejudice to the general issue " then 656 years old.

BAIL

The highest recorded bail is that for $200,000 (£71,400) granted to Samuel Insull (1859-1938) in Chicago, Illinois, U.S.A., in May 1934, before the investigations into the finances of Insull Utility Investments.

In April 1937, £1,000,000 was demanded by a Bolivian Court in La Paz for alleged armament offences by two Britons.

The highest bail figure in a British court is the bail of £22,000 granted to Alec Edward Morton Wilcox at the Mansion House Court in the City of London on September, 1954. In the Leopold Harris arson case of July 1933, a total of £81,500 was required for the 10 defendants.

LONGEST TRIAL

The longest trial in the annals of British justice was the Tichborne personation case. The first trial lasted 103 days and collapsed on 6th March, 1872. The new trial went on for 188 days resulting in a sentence for perjury (14 years imprisonment and hard labour) on 28th February, 1874, on the Australian, Thomas Castro, otherwise Arthur Orton, who claimed to be Sir Alfred Tichborne's elder brother Roger. The whole case thus spanned 827 days, and cost £55,315.

The impeachment of Warren Hastings, which began in 1788, dragged on for 7 years but the trial lasted only 145 days.

LONGEST ADDRESS

In the Globe and Phoenix case of 1916-1917 Mr. W. H. Upjohn, K.C., addressed the court for 50 days.

GREATEST COMPENSATION

The greatest compensation paid for wrongful imprisonment was the £6,000 in 1929 to Oscar Slater who had been arraigned for the murder of the elderly Miss Gilchrist in Glasgow on 6th May, 1909.

RECORD DAMAGES IN BRITAIN
Personal injury

The greatest figure yet awarded for personal injury in a British Court is the £47,720 to Mr. Harold J. F. Gourley, 67, a civil engineer, maimed (loss of left leg and right arm) in the Weedon, Northants, railway disaster of September 1951. The award against the British Transport Commission was made before Mr. Justice Pearce on 1st April, 1954.

The highest figure awarded for injury in a road accident was the £24,000 at Chelmsford Assizes to Dr. Lionel Moore Billingham, 51, on 23rd July, 1948. The figure was subsequently reduced to £14,000. The highest sum awarded and paid was the £17,000 to Pauline Pitcher, 20, on 23rd May, 1955, against the owners and drivers involved in a collision on 6th March, 1952, at Chiswick.

BREACH OF CONTRACT

The highest damages ever awarded for a breach of contract was the £610,392 awarded in the House of Lords on 28th April, 1932, to the Bank of Portugal against the London printers Waterlow & Son, Ltd. on 16th July, 1930, arising from the fraudulently authorized printing of 580,000 five-hundred escudo notes in 1925. One of the perpetrators, Arthur Virgilio Alves Reis served 16 years (1930-1946) in gaol.

BREACH OF PROMISE

The largest sum involved in a breach of promise suit was the £50,000 accepted by Miss Daisy Markham (Mrs. Moss) in settlement against the Marquis of Northampton in 1913.

DEFAMATION

The highest damages for defamation was the £25,000 awarded in March 1934 before Mr. Justice Avory to Princess Irina Alexandra Youssoupoff against Metro-Goldwyn-Mayer Pictures Ltd. concerning imputations upon her morals in the film "Rasputin, the Mad Monk".

DIVORCE

The highest award made to the dispossessed party in a divorce suit was the £25,000 awarded to Mr. Demetrius Sophocles Constantinidi against Dr. Henry William Lance for bigamous adultery with his wife Mrs. Julia Constantinidi who married Lance seven days after obtaining a divorce in Sioux Falls, U.S.A., on 27th February, 1902.

GREATEST REDUCTION

The greatest reduction of damages on appeal was in the "Sunshine Roof Case" (Mechanical and General Invention Co. *v.* Austin Motor Company and Sir Herbert Austin) when on 27th March, 1934, the £98,000 awarded by a jury was reduced to 40 shillings.

ALIMONY

The world's record alimony was that paid by Reuben Hollis Fleet, the American millionaire aircraft manufacturer, to his second wife Dorothy (née Mitchell) in 1945, after their separation following 'verbal abuse'. The sum amounted to £4,125,000.

The highest alimony awarded in a British Court is £5,000 per annum but the 2nd Duke of Westminster settled £13,000 per annum upon his first wife, Constance, Duchess of Westminster (née Cornwallis-West) in 1919.

CRIME AND PUNISHMENT

HIGHEST MURDER RATE

Taking figures for the decade (1940-1950) that part of the world with the highest annual average murder rate is the State of Georgia, U.S.A., with 167·3 per million. That with the lowest over the same period is Scotland with 2·7 per million population.

In Great Britain the highest annual total of murders this century was 242 in 1945, and the lowest 124 in 1937.

WORLD'S BIGGEST MURDERERS

The most prolific murderer in history was H. H. Holmes of U.S.A., who between 1892 and 1896 killed over 150 women at his specially equipped "employment agency" in Wallace Street, Chicago, U.S.A. He was hanged on 7th May, 1896.

The greatest number of victims ever ascribed to a murderess were the 49 known victims of Belle Gunness of La Porte, Indiana, U.S.A., who lured over 40 would-be suitors to her farm before, on 28th April 1908, she lost her own life when the farmhouse caught fire.

Britain's most prolific murderer was probably the perpetrator of the infamous series of Jack the Ripper murders in 1888 when six women and probably four others were accounted for. Among identified murderers Gordon Frederick Cummins, 28 (executed at Wandsworth on 25th June, 1942) accounted for at least four, and probably six women. A total of at least six women were also killed by John Reginald Halliday Christie, 55 (hanged 15th July, 1953) while as many as nine victims were ascribed to John George Haigh, the acid bath murderer (hanged 10th August, 1949).

GREATEST MASS MURDERS

In 1486 at Tenochtitlan, near Mexico City, 20,000 Aztecs had their hearts cut out in a ritual ceremony.

At the S.S. camp at Auschwitz, Silesia, where 4,000,000 people were exterminated in 1943–44, the greatest number killed in a day was 24,000.

SUICIDE

The country with the highest suicide rate (based on latest available figures) is Alaska with 24·8 per 100,000.

The latest England and Wales figure is 9·9, and Scotland 5·5, per 100,000. In the United Kingdom there are, on average, 14 suicides every day.

EXECUTIONS

Capital punishment in the British Isles dates from A.D. 450 but fell into disuse in the 11th century only to be revived in the Middle Ages, reaching a peak in the reign of Edward VI (1547-1553), when an average of 560 persons were executed annually at Tyburn alone. The most people executed at one hanging was 24 at Tyburn in 1571. Even into the 19th century, there were 223 capital crimes, though people were, in practice, only hanged for 25 of these.

Between 1830 and 1955, the largest number hanged in a year was 27 (24 men, 3 women) in 1903 and the least 5 in 1854, 1921 and 1930.

Largest Crowd

The earliest use of the " drop " was at the hanging of Earl Ferrers on 5th May, 1760, though it did not become general until 1783. The greatest crowd at a public execution was the estimated 100,000 present when Henry Fauntleroy was hanged for forgery on 30th November, 1824, in London.

The last public execution in England took place outside Newgate Prison on 26th May, 1868, when Michael Barrett was hanged for his part in the Fenian bomb outrage near Clerkenwell Prison, London. The earliest non-public execution was on 13th August, 1868, of the murderer of Thomas Wells.

YOUNGEST and OLDEST EXECUTED

Though the hanging of persons under 18 was only expressly excluded in the Childrens' and Young Persons' Act, 1933 (Sect. 33), no person under that age has, in fact, been executed since 1887. The youngest persons executed this century have been eighteen year olds in 1904, on 7th January, 1922 (Henry Jacoby), 1925 (Bishop), 1932 and 1949. The oldest person hanged was a man of over 70 in 1914.

EXECUTIONER

The longest period of office of a Public Executioner was that of John Calcroft (1800-1879) who was in office from 1828-1871 and who officiated at nearly every hanging outside Newgate Prison, London.

LONGEST ESCAPES

The record prison escape was the 179 days' freedom achieved by Stanley Hilton Thurston who broke out of Lewes Prison, Sussex, with a wooden key in 1939 and was finally recaptured after a struggle in Oxford Street, London. His three prison and two police station escapes are estimated to have cost the tax-payer some £10,000. The longest escape from Broadmoor was the 668 days of John Edward Allen, the " Mad Parson " who got away on 7th July, 1947.

BLOODIEST ASSIZES

In the West Country Assizes of 1685 (Winchester to Wells), Lord Jeffreys of Wem (1648-1689) sentenced 330 persons to be hanged, 841 to be transported for periods of 10 or more years and larger numbers to be imprisoned and flogged.

HEAVIEST SENTENCES

The heaviest sentences imposed by a Judge in the 20th century were 205 years (121 years allowing for concurrence) by Mr. Justice Stable on a group of I.R.A. offenders at Manchester on 10th March, 1939. In the United Kingdom, a life sentence is, being subject to review, indeterminate. Cases of prisoners actually serving 20 years are recorded (Edward Wild Hilton 1913 to 1933) and on 28th November, 1948, Francis O'Neill, 24, of Belfast, was sentenced to 26 years for his part in two armed robberies. On 17th May, 1939, William Burkitt, thrice acquitted of murder by a jury (1915, 1925 and 1939), was sentenced by Mr. Justice Cassells " to be kept in prison for the rest of your natural life ". Burkitt, whose appeal against the sentence failed in 1948, had served 34 years up to 1954. The longest single period served by a reprieved murderer in Great Britain this century was the 22 years of a man released in 1907.

The longest determinate sentence imposed for a single offence was 25 years penal servitude for manslaughter in 1879.

LYNCHING

Lynching still persists in the United States. The worst year in the 20th century was 1901 with 130 lynchings (105 negroes, 25 white) and 1952 the first year with no reported cases.

BIGGEST ROBBERIES

The biggest " inside job " was that at the National City Bank of New York from which the Assistant Manager, Richard Crowe, removed $883,660 (£315,590). He was arrested on 11th April, 1949.

The biggest robbery of Royal Mails occurred on 21st May, 1952, with the loss of over £200,000 in soiled bank-notes from a Post Office van in Eastcastle Street, London, W.1.

BIGGEST BIGAMIST

It has been recorded that, on trial in Sheffield, England, on 19th December, 1922, Mrs. Theresa Vaughan (or Vaughn), 24, confessed to 61 bigamous marriages in the space of five years. A male record of 72 has been noted.

PRISONS LARGEST IN WORLD

The largest prison in the world is Lubianka Jail, Moscow, with an estimated capacity of 80,000. The largest penal camp in the world is the complex of concentration camps at Vorkuta in Northern Russia which was opened in 1943. Recent estimates are that there are 223,000 prisoners working in 40 mines guarded by 12,000 militia.

In British Isles

The largest prison in the United Kingdom and England is Wormwood Scrubbs, West London, with 1,355 cells.

The oldest English prison is Oxford built c. 1640.

The largest jail in Scotland is Barlinnie with 952 single cells. Ireland's largest prison is Mountjoy Prison, Dublin, with 808 cells.

SMALLEST

The smallest prison in the world is usually cited as that on the Isle of Sark, Channel Islands, which has a capacity of two. The smallest in England is Gloucester Prison with 134 cells. The smallest in Scotland is Dumfries Jail with only 11 single cells. Ireland's smallest prison is that at Sligo with 100 cells.

POPULATION

The highest prison population for England and Wales was in 1952 with an average of 23,670, with a peak in July touching 24,000. In Scotland the average prison population for 1954 was 2,169 — slightly below the peak attained in 1914.

4. Humanities

RELIGIONS and BELIEFS

LARGEST RELIGIONS

Religious statistics are necessarily the roughest approximations. The test of adherence to a religion varies widely in rigour, while many individuals, particularly in China, belong to two or more religions.

Christianity is the world's prevailing religion with at least 750 million and probably an additional 250 million Protestants who are not in membership with the Church of their baptism. It would appear that the total of 200 million practising and 250 million non-practising Protestants is slightly outnumbered by the 460 million who have received baptism into the Roman Catholic Church. The title of the largest non-Christian religion lies between the Confucians and the Mohammedans, each with over 300 million adherents.

In the United Kingdom the Anglicans, made up of members of the Established Church of England, the Dis-established Church in Wales, the Episcopal Church in Scotland and the Church in Ireland, have the greatest number of adherents, estimated at 6,200,000. In Scotland the most numerous group are the Presbyterians, who number 1,280,000.

LARGEST CATHEDRALS

The largest cathedral in the world is St. Peter's in the Vatican City, Rome. The length of the cathedral, measured from the apse, is 611 feet 4 inches. The area is 18,110 square yards. The inner diameter of the famous dome, the largest in the world, is 137 feet 9 inches and its centre is 390 feet 5 inches high. The external height is 457 feet 9 inches.

The largest cathedral in the British Isles is the Anglican Cathedral of Liverpool. Built in modernized Gothic Style, work was begun on 19th July, 1904, and when completed will have cost over £3,000,000. The building encloses 100,000 square feet and has an overall length of 671 feet. The Vestey Tower is 331 feet high.

SMALLEST

The smallest cathedral in the United Kingdom is St. Asaph in Flintshire. It is 182 feet long, 68 feet wide and has a 100 foot high tower.

The longest Gothic church in the United Kingdom is Winchester Cathedral ; it is 560 feet long.

Longest nave in the United Kingdom is that of St. Albans Cathedral — 285 feet long.

OLDEST CHURCH

The oldest church in the United Kingdom is acknowledged to be St. Martin's Church, Canterbury. It was founded on the remains of a Roman chapel which probably dates back to the first century A.D. It was restored in A.D. 560 as part of the marriage contract of the Christian Bertha, daughter of the King of Paris, to the heathen King Ethelbert. Later King Ethelbert was converted, and it is very probable that it was in this church that he was baptised by Augustine in A.D. 597. Various additions have, of course, been made to the remaining original fabric. The chancel arch is 13th century, the roof of the nave and the church tower 14th century.

The oldest church in the United Kingdom of which a considerable part of the original fabric remains is All Saints Church, Brixworth, Northampton. The date of dedication is between A.D. 680-685 and it is built in the "Early Christian" or Basilican style and the building is original up to roof level.

The oldest church in Ireland is the Gallerus Oratory near Kilmalkedar, Co. Kerry, which is believed to date from the mid 6th century (A.D. 550).

HIGHEST SPIRE

The highest church spire in the world is that of the Protestant Cathedral of Ulm in Germany. The building is early Gothic and was begun in 1377. The tower, in the centre of the west façade, was not finally completed until 1890 and is 528 feet high.

The highest spire in the United Kingdom is that of the church of St. Mary — Salisbury Cathedral. Except for the spire, the cathedral was built in the years 1260-1266. The spire was added later, 1330-1375, and reaches a height of 404 feet. St. Paul's Cathedral, London, once possessed a 493 feet spire but this was struck by lightning in 1561.

SAINTS MOST and LEAST RAPIDLY CANONIZED

The shortest interval that has elapsed between the death of a Saint and his canonization was in the case of St. Peter, the Martyr, (born in Verona in 1206) who was murdered at Borlasina on 5th April, 1252. Struck on the head by a hatchet, he was unable to speak but dipped his finger in his blood and wrote "Credo in Deum" on the dusty road. He was canonized the following year.

The other extreme is represented by St. Bernard of Thiron, 20 years Prior of St. Sabinus, who died in 1117 and was made a Saint in 1861 — 744 years later.

COMMONEST SAINT'S NAME

Hagiologists have not yet succeeded in identifying all the Saints but it is established that the commonest of the Saints' names is Mary which is sometimes borne by male Saints.

EARLIEST PATRON SAINT

Of the four patron Saints of the British Isles the earliest was St. George of England who was martyred at Nicomedia on 23rd April, A.D. 303. He was not adopted as Patron Saint till the reign of Edward III (1327-1377), whereas St. Andrew has been recognized as the Patron Saint of Scotland since the 8th century.

STAINED GLASS OLDEST

The oldest stained glass in the world is certain figures of the Prophets in a window in the cathedral of Augsburg, Germany, dating from the 11th century. The oldest stained glass in the British Isles is 12th century fragments in the Tree of Jesse in the north side of the clerestory of the York Minster nave dated prior to 1170.

LARGEST

The largest ancient stained glass window in the British Isles is the Five Sisters window in York Minster, each panel of which is 5 feet in breadth and 53½ feet high.

The largest stained glass window in the United Kingdom is the east window of the Anglican Cathedral at Liverpool (76 by 44 feet).

The latest parish population figures date from 1930. The most populous parish at the present time is the Parish of Great Greenford (Holy Cross), Greenford, Middlesex, with more than 60,000 parishioners. The least populous is Iham Parish in the diocese of Chichester, Sussex, with a nil population.

BENEFICES

The net benefices of parishes fluctuate greatly but in the case of the six which have reached around £2,000 per annum schemes are being put into effect to reduce them. The Parish of All Saints, Loughborough, Leicestershire, has been listed at £2,010 per annum.

OLDEST CLERGYMAN

The oldest clergyman of the Church of England was the Rev. W. H. R. Longhurst (1838-1943), Canon of Worcester, who died eight days before he would have reached his one hundredth and fifth birthday.

OLDEST BISHOP

The oldest Church of England Bishop is the Rt. Rev. Lennox Waldron Williams, consecrated Lord Bishop of Quebec on 25th January, 1915, retired 1935 and who reached the age of 96 on 12th November, 1954.

PAINTING

EARLIEST

The earliest known painting is probably the Stag's head, painted by finger tip, in the La Pileta Cave at Benoajan, Malaga, Spain, belonging to the Upper Palaeolithic period 30,000 to 15,000 B.C. Ceiling paintings in the Pech-Merle Cave at Lot, France, also belong to this period.

LARGEST

John Banvard's "Panorama of the Mississippi", completed in 1846, showing the river scene for 1,200 miles in a strip 15,000 feet in length and 12 feet wide is the largest painting in the world with an area of over 4¼ acres. It is housed on rollers in America.

The largest flat painting ever executed was the "Panthéon de la Guerre" (just over 400 feet long by over 40 feet high) showing the life-size portraits of 6,000 1914-18 war heroes. The work occupied four years with as many as 130 artists contributing.

The largest Old Master is "Il Paradiso" by Jacopo Robusti (Tintoretto) (1518-1594) and his son Domenico on Wall "E" in the Sala del Maggior Consiglio in the Palazzo Ducale in Venice, Italy. The work was completed between 1587 and 1590 and is 72 feet 2 inches long and 22 feet 11½ inches high.

HIGHEST PRICED

The highest price ever fetched by a painting in public auction was the $360,000 (£128,570) bid for Gainsborough's "Harvest Wagon" in New York on 20th April, 1928.

The highest price established for a private treaty sale is that for the altar piece "Alba Madonna" by the Italian Raphael (1483-1520), purchased by the American, Andrew W. Mellon, from the Soviet Government in July 1930. The exact price has not been disclosed but is known to have been in excess of $1,000,000 (£357,000). The picture was transferred from the former Imperial Gallery, The Hermitage, Leningrad, and is now housed in the National Gallery of Art, Washington, D.C.

The highest price paid for a painting in the life-time of an artist is £17,400 for " Dancers at the Bar " by the French impressionist, Hilaire Degas (1834-1917), just before his death.

LANGUAGE and THE WRITTEN WORD

EARLIEST LANGUAGE

It is possible that formalized language dates from the Azilian (France) culture of 15,000 B.C. The oldest known formally written language is Sumerian dating from 5,000 B.C.

COMMONEST LANGUAGE

The language spoken by more people than any other is Chinese, including Mandarin, to an estimated 475 million. Excluding the Indic group of 12 major tongues, the next most commonly spoken language is English in the case of 265 million.

In the British Isles there are eight languages :— English, Scots Gaelic, Welsh, Irish Gaelic, Manx, Romany (Gipsy) and Jersey and Guernsey *patois*. Of these English is, of course, predominant, and Manx has almost followed Cornish (1777) into extinction.

MOST PRIMITIVE LANGUAGE

Of the 3,080 languages, living and dead, known to scholars probably the most grammatically primitive is Arunta, an aboriginal Australian tongue which has no pronouns and in which numbers are only vague expressions of place. Words are indeterminate in meaning and form.

MOST COMPLEX

The K'ang-hsi dictionary of Chinese characters has 40,000 entries. Of the eighty-four meanings of the fourth tone of " i " in Chinese the same sound includes " dress ", " hiccup " or " licentious ". The written language provides 92 different characters of " i^4 " so that the meaning intended identifies itself.

LONGEST WORDS

The longest word in the Oxford Dictionary is floccipaucinihilipilification, meaning estimating as worthless, first used in 1741.

Literature

The longest word in English literature is honorificabilitudinitatibus, occurring in William Shakespeare's "Love's Labour Lost", Act V, Scene I.

Medical

The longest technical term is that for a lung disease which attacks miners — pneumonoultramicroscopicsilicovolcanokoniosis — a 45-letter term.

PLACE-NAMES

The longest place-name in the world is the 83-letter New Zealand village Taumatawhakatangihangakoauotamateaturipukakapikimaungahoronukupokaiwhenuakitanatahu in the Southern Hawkes' Bay district of the North Island. The name, in Maori, means " the place where Tamatea, the man with the big knee who slid, climbed and swallowed mountains, known as Land-eater, played on his flute to his loved one ".

The longest place name in the British Isles is the 58-letter name of the Anglesey village Llanfairpwllgwyngyllgogerychwyrndrobwllllantysiliogogogoch which is translated : " St. Mary's Church in a hollow of white hazel, close to a rapid whirlpool and St. Tysilio's Church ".

LONGEST PERSONAL NAMES

The longest surname in the British Isles was the six barrelled one borne by the late Major L. S. D. O. F. Tollemache Tollemache de Orellana Plantagenet Tollemache Tollemache, born 1884, died of wounds in France 20th February, 1917.

SHORTEST

There exists among the 37 million names on the Ministry of Pensions and National Insurance index a single example of a one-lettered surname. Its identity has not been disclosed, but is believed to be " O ".

In Burma there is a surname written " apostrophe aitch " " 'H ".

COMMONEST

The commonest name in the world is Mahommed which can be spelt in many ways. The commonest given name in the English-speaking world is John.

The commonest name in Great Britain is Smith, of whom there are 510,000 nationally insured, of whom 6,500 are plain John Smith and another 10,000 are John (plus one or more given names) Smith. Including uninsured persons there are over 800,000 Smiths in England and Wales alone, of whom 90,000 are A. Smiths.

There are, however, estimated to be 1,540,000 persons with M' Mc, or Mac (Gaelic ' son of ') before their surnames.

LONGEST TITLE

The world's longest title is borne by Lieutenant-General His Highness Shri 108 Maharajadhiraj, Raj Rajeshwar Shri Maharja-i-Rajgan Maharaja Sir Yadvindra Singh Mahendra Bahadur, Yadu Vanshavatans Bhatti Kul Bhushan, G.C.I.E., G.B.E., LL.D., Rajpramukh of Patiala and East Punjab States Union since its formation in August 1948. The appellation " Shri 108 " indicates that in its fullest form this title contains the word " Shri " 108 times.

OLDEST TEXTS

The oldest known written text is the cuneiform expression of Sumerian speech of about the 5th millennium B.C. In 1952, some clay tablets of this writing were unearthed from the Sumerian temple of Inanna at Erech (c.3,500 B.C.). The earliest known vellum document is Demosthene's *De Falsa Legatione* of the second century A.D.

BOOK
OLDEST PRINTED

The oldest surviving printed book is in the British Museum and is a 16-foot long Buddhist scroll Diamond Sutra of A.D. 868. The earliest known book of folded pages is another Buddhist work dated A.D. 949.

MECHANICALLY PRINTED

Recent opinion is that the 192-leaved Constance Missal (Missale Speciale Constantiense), from Basle, Switzerland, the first of the three known copies of which was rediscovered in 1880, may have priority over the more generally accepted earliest mechanically printed book — the 42-line Gutenberg Bible of c.1455. The earliest dated printed work is the Psalter completed by Fust and Schoeffer on 14th August, 1457.

SMALLEST

The smallest book in the world is a handwritten one — Poems by Edgar Guest. It was written by Burt Randle in 1942. It is less than $\frac{1}{8}$ inch square and is held by a metal clasp.

The smallest printed books in the world were probably those produced by N. V. Lettergietery " Amsterdam " — a firm of Dutch typefounders on the occasion of their 100th year of business. They are approximately 4·1 mm. (5/32 inch) square, leather-bound, stamped in gold, and contain 20 pages. On the first page is a reproduction of the Lord's Prayer.

The smallest book in the world printed from movable type was made by Salmin Brothers of Padua in Italy in 1896 — The Galileo a Madama Cristina di Lorena. It has 207 pages and a portrait of Galileo as a frontispiece. The size of the book is $\frac{5}{8}$ inch high and 7/16 inch wide.

HIGHEST PRICED

The highest prices ever paid for printed books are for Gutenberg bibles, a copy of which crossed the Atlantic in 1954 under a private treaty sale for $200,000 (£71,400). The highest price for a printed book at auction is $151,000 (£53,900) paid in New York on 28th January, 1947, for Stephen Day's " Whole Booke of Psalms " printed in Cambridge, Mass., U.S.A. in 1640.

BIBLE OLDEST

The oldest known Bible is the Yonan manuscript of the complete New Testament in Syriac-Aramaic of A.D. c.350 presented to the U.S. Library of Congress on 27th March, 1955.

LONGEST and SHORTEST BOOKS

The longest book in the Bible is the Book of Isaiah with 66 chapters and the shortest is the Second Epistle of John with 13 verses.

PSALMS VERSE and SENTENCE

Of the 150 Psalms, the longest is the 119th with 176 verses and the shortest the 117th with two verses. The shortest sentence in the whole Bible is in the Gospel according to St. John, Chapter II, verse 35, consisting of the two words " Jesus wept ". The total number of letters in the Bible is 3,566,480 or, with the Apocrypha, 4,291,480.

MOST PROLIFIC AUTHOR

The most prolific author in the world is Georges Simenon who in June 1955 published his one hundred and fifty-third novel under his own name. Prior to these, under seventeen pen-names, he had published, calculated on the normal length of his present-day novels, another two hundred works making a total of over three hundred and fifty novel-length books.

For a lifetime output no author has rivalled that of Voltaire (François Marie Arouet) (1694–1778) who in seventy-four years of writing produced over fifty-five plays, countless poems and *prose romances*, many historical and philosophical works and a vast correspondence which is still being augmented by new discoveries.

PUBLISHING

The principal book publishing country in the world is the United Kingdom where, during 1953, 18,257 titles were produced. This figure includes re-editions and 12,734 first editions.

MAPS

OLDEST

The oldest map in the world is a cadastral clay tablet of c.2,200 B.C., depicting areas for land taxation, preserved in Istanbul Museum, Turkey. The oldest papyrus map is the Turin Papyrus of an unidentified Egyptian gold mine dated 1,320 B.C.

The earliest representation of Great Britain is that by Ptolemy dated A.D. c.150. The oldest native map of the British Isles is the Anglo-Saxon map from Battle Abbey dated A.D. c.980, now in the British Museum.

Atlas

Creator of the earliest atlas was the Greek Ptolemy (A.D. 90–168) probably A.D. c.150. His work was first printed in Bologna, Italy, in 1477.

The best mapped area in the world is the British Isles in which the Ordnance Survey was founded in 1791 and began to produce maps on the largest scale of 25 inches to the mile in 1853.

LIBRARIES

LARGEST

The largest library in the world is the United States Library of Congress, Washington, D.C. It contains 33,152,852 items, including 10,155,307 volumes and pamphlets, 14,282,594 manuscripts, 2,307,534 maps and views, 2,002,277 volumes and pieces of music and 438,881 gramophone records.

The greatest library in the United Kingdom is that in the British Museum, London, containing 6,000,000 books and manuscripts.

MEDICAL

The world's largest medical library is the Surgeon General's Library in Washington, D.C., while the largest in the British Isles is that of the Royal Society of Medicine in Wimpole Street, London, W.1.

NEWSPAPERS

OLDEST

The " Berrow's Worcester Journal ", published in Worcester, England, enjoys the distinction of being the oldest continuously produced newspaper in the world. It was founded in 1690 and has appeared weekly since June 1709. Of daily 'papers the oldest is " Lloyd's List " which is the shipping intelligence bulletin of Lloyd's, London, established in 1734.

LARGEST

The most massive single issue of a newspaper yet published was the 490 page edition of the New York Times of 12th September, 1954, at a cost of 20 cents (1s. 5d.).

The largest page size of any newspaper is the 30-inch by 22-inch of the " Nantucket Inquirer and Mirror " published in Rhode Island, U.S.A.

HIGHEST CIRCULATION

The highest circulation of any newspaper in the world is that of the London Sunday 'paper " News of the World " printed in Bouverie Street, London, which rises to 9,000,000 copies with an estimated readership of over 19,000,000. The 'paper first appeared on 1st October, 1843, and averaged 12,971 copies a week in its first year and surpassed the million mark in 1905. To provide sufficient pulp for the 62,400 five-mile reels, over half a million trees have to be felled each year.

The highest circulation of any daily paper is that of the London " Daily Mirror " founded in 1903, which has attained $4\frac{3}{4}$ million copies daily. The highest circulation of an evening paper in the world is the London " Evening News " established 1881, which reached an average daily net sale of 1,752,166 in the first six months of 1950.

PERIODICALS

LARGEST CIRCULATION

The largest circulation of any periodical is that of "The Reader's Digest." There are 28 international editions in 12 languages (circulation over 7,000,000) which, added to the U.S. home edition (circulation 10,500,000), make a total monthly circulation of 17½ million.

The highest circulation periodical in the British Isles is the "Radio Times". The average print order is 8,223,612 copies a week. The materials used include 885 tons of paper, 9½ tons of ink and 355 miles of stapling wire, per issue. The full page advertising rate, facing matter, is £4,000, the highest in the U.K.

INDEXES

The longest index in the world is that maintained by the U.S. Social Security Administration Department of Health, Education and Welfare, known as the National Employee Index. It occupies 27,800 square feet and contains 148,463,911 names.

The largest index in the British Isles is that maintained by the Ministry of Pensions and National Insurance at Newcastle with 37,000,000 names.

MUSIC

OLDEST

The world's oldest surviving musical notation is a Sumerian hymn recorded on a clay tablet dated c.800 B.C. but it has defied interpretation. Musical history is, however, able to be traced back to the 3rd millennium B.C. when in Chinese Temple music the yellow bell (*huang chung*) had a recognized standard musical tone.

INSTRUMENTS

The harps and flutes of ancient Egypt are known to have dated from at least as early as 4,000 B.C.

LARGEST ORGAN
World

The largest musical instrument ever constructed is the Atlantic City Auditorium Organ, Atlantic City, New Jersey, U.S.A. Completed in 1930, this heroic instrument has two consoles (one with seven manuals and another movable one with five), 1,225 speaking stops and 33,112 pipes ranging from 3/16th inch to 64 feet in length. It is powered with blower motors of 365 h.p. and cost $500,000 (£178,600).

British Isles

The largest organ in the British Isles, and the largest Cathedral organ in the world, is that installed in Liverpool Cathedral in 1926 with one 5-manual and one 4-manual console, and 10,925 pipes.

ONE MAN BAND

The most complex "one-man band" ever constucted was the "Panomonico" built by the Austrian Karl Waelzel. It incorporated 150 flutes, 150 flageolets, 50 oboes, 18 trumpets, 5 fanfares, 2 timbals and 3 large drums. It was bought by Archduke Charles of Austria (1771-1847) for 100,000 French francs for the express purpose of annoying people at his court.

The largest stringed instrument ever constructed was a pantaleon with 270 strings stretched over 50 square feet used by George Noel in 1767.

LARGEST DRUM

The largest drum in the world is that owned by the University of Texas Longhorn Band made in Elkhart, U.S.A. It is 25 feet 0¾ inch in circumference and is mounted on wheels and is towed by a tractor.

The most musicians required to operate a single instrument were the six required to play the gigantic orchestrian, known as the Appollonican, built in 1816 and played till 1840.

The largest double bass ever constructed was the 10 foot high octo-bass built by J. B. Vuillaume (1798-1875) in c. 1845. The stretch being too great for any musician's finger-span the stopping was effected by foot levers. It was played in London in 1851.

The longest Swiss alpenhorns, which are of wooden construction, attain 14 feet in length and are of pine.

The earliest piano in existence is the Cristofori piano built in Florence in 1721 and now preserved in the Metropolitan Museum of Art, New York.

ORCHESTRA

The vastest orchestra ever assembled was that for the World Peace Jubilee staged in Boston on 17th June, 1872, with 2,000 musicians supported by a choir of 20,000 voices. Johann Strauss conducted this array in a ' rendition ' of " The Beautiful Blue Danube ".

BRASS BAND

The oldest band in Great Britain is the New Mills Old Prize Band of Stockport, Cheshire, established in 1812. Originally a combination of brass and reed instruments it finally became a full brass combination in 1935. The Black Dyke Mills Band (established 1819) celebrated its centenary as a brass band in 1955.

HIGHEST and LOWEST NOTES

The extremes of orchestral instruments range between the highest represented by the piccolo or octave flute with 4,752 cycles per second and the lowest with the double bassoon as used in Haydn's " Creation " with 32 cycles a second. The highest note on a standard pianoforte is 4,096 cycles.

The limitations of the human ear are generally between 16 cycles and 18,000 cycles such that a note three octaves above the top note of a piano would be inaudible.

BELLS

HEAVIEST

The heaviest bell in the world is the Tsar Kolokol cast in 1733 in Moscow. It weighs approximately 193 tons and is 22 feet 8 inches in diameter and about 20 feet high, and its greatest thickness is 24 inches. The bell is cracked and a fragment, weighing about 11 tons, broken from it. The bell now stands on a platform near the Kremlin in Moscow.

The heaviest bell hung in the United Kingdom is Great Paul at St. Paul's Cathedral in London. It weighs 16 tons 14 cwts. 2 qrs. 19 lb. and has a diameter of 9 feet 6½ inches.

The heaviest bell ever cast in England and the biggest tuned bell in the world is the bourdon bell of the Laura Spelman Rockefeller Memorial carillon, Riverside Church, New York City, which weighs 18 tons 5 cwts. 1 qr. 18 lb. and is 10 feet 2 inches in diameter.

OLDEST

The oldest bell in the world is reputed to be that found by Layard in the Babylonian Palace of Nimrod and is approximately 3,000 years old.

The oldest dated bell in England is that hung in St. Chad's, Claughton, in the parish of Hornby with Claughton, Lancashire. It weighs about 2½ cwts., is 21¼ inches in diameter and 16½ inches high. Still in perfect condition and in regular use, it is dated 1296.

BIGGEST CARILLON

The biggest carillon in the world is the Laura Spelman Rockefeller Memorial carillon, Riverside Church, New York City, U.S.A. It consists of 72 bells with a total weight of approximately 102 tons.

HEAVIEST CARILLON

The heaviest carillon in the United Kingdom is in St. Nicholas' Church, Aberdeen, Scotland. It consists of 48 bells, the total weight of which is 25 tons 8 cwts. 2 qrs. 13 lb. The bourdon bell weighs 4 tons 9 cwts. 3 qrs. 26 lb. and the carillon comprises four octaves, less the bottom semi-tone.

BELL RINGING

Eight bells have been rung to their full " extent " (40,320 changes) only once, in 1751, by relays of thirteen bell ringers working continuously for twenty hours. In modern competition rules, set by the Central Council of Church Bell Ringers, relays are forbidden and under these conditions the best that has been done so far is 21,600 changes in 12 hours 56 minutes by a Cheshire team at St. Chad's, Winsford, Cheshire, on 4th November, 1950.

COMPOSER

MOST PROLIFIC

The most prolific composer of all-time was Filippo de Monte (c.1521-1603) who composed 1,000 madrigals, of which 600 were published, together with 300 motets and other work.

MOST RAPID

Among composers of the classical period the most prolific was Wolfgang Mozart (1756-1791) who produced 600 operas, operettas, piano and string quartet concertos, violin sonatas, divertimenti, serenades, motets, masses and litanies of which only 70 were published before he died, aged 35. His opera " The Clemency of Titus " (1791) was written in 18 days while three symphonic masterpieces " Symphony in E flat ", " Symphony in G minor " and the " Jupiter Symphony in C " were written in the space of 42 days in 1788. His overture " Don Giovanni " was written in full score at one sitting.

OLDEST

The longest lived of any major composer is Jean Sibelius of Finland, writer of " *Finlandia* " and " *Tapiola* ", who was born on 8th December, 1865, and in 1954 surpassed the eighty-eight years of the Italian Guiseppe Verdi (1813–1901).

EARLIEST OPERA

The first real opera with the complete drama sung to instrumental accompaniment was " La Dafne ". With words by Ottavio Rignucci and music by Jacopo Pevi, it was produced in Florence in 1597.

THEATRE

LONGEST RUNS

The longest run of any show at one theatre anywhere in the world is by the play " The Drunkard " written by W. H. Smith and a " Gentleman ". First produced, as a moral lesson, by the American showman P. T. Barnum in 1843, it was not used commercially again until the Theatre Mart in Los Angeles, California, revived it on 6th July, 1933. From that date, it ran continuously, one show a night, until 6th September, 1953. Starting on 7th September, 1953, a new musical adaptation of " The Drunkard ", called the " Wayward Way ", started to play alternate nights with the original version and is still playing. During this time, more than two million people have seen the play at over eight thousand consecutive nightly performances. Two members of the cast, Miss Marie Duvall and Mr. Neely Edwards, are still playing the parts they originated more than twenty years ago.

The longest continuous run of any show at one theatre in the United Kingdom was the first World War favourite " Chu Chin Chow ". It commenced on 31st August, 1916, at His Majesty's Theatre, London, and ran for 2,238 performances.

The longest run of any straight play in the United Kingdom at one theatre, was Noel Coward's " Blithe Spirit " which ran for 1,997 performances. It opened on the 2nd July, 1941, at the Piccadilly Theatre, London.

LONGEST CHORUS LINE

The world's longest chorus line are New York Radio City Music Hall's Rockettes. Thirty-six girls dance precision routines across the 144-foot wide stage. The whole troupe, which won the *Grand Prix* in Paris in July 1937 is forty-six strong but ten girls are always on alternating vacation.

EDUCATION

ILLITERACY

Literacy is variously defined as " ability to read simple subjects " and " ability to read and write a simple letter ". The looseness of definition precludes anything more than approximations but the world percentage of illiteracy has been reliably estimated at between 45 per cent. and 55 per cent., roughly 1,250 million people.

The continent with the greatest proportion of illiterates is Africa, where more than 170 million people—approximately 80 per cent. of the continent's total can neither read nor write.

Mozambique has the highest illiteracy rate anywhere in the world with 99 per cent. of all age groups of its people being unable even to read.

This figure is matched, although measured on a different basis, by the Somaliland Protectorate where only one person in every hundred can read and write.

Of those countries for which figures are available, Sweden records the highest literacy rate. Less than one in a 1,000 is unable to read and write.

UNIVERSITY OLDEST

Probably the oldest educational institution in the world is the Egyptian university of Al-Azhar. According to the Egyptian Education Bureau, Al-Azhar was first established as an academy in A.D. 989 and evidence suggests that such subjects as mathematics, astronomy, medicine and geography were taught there at that time.

The oldest University in the British Isles is the University of Oxford which came into being c.1167. The oldest college is quoted as University College (1249), though its foundation is less well documented than that of Merton College in 1264.

The earliest college at Cambridge University, is Peterhouse College founded in 1284. The largest college at either university is Trinity College, Cambridge. It was founded in 1546.

The oldest university in Scotland is the College of St. Salvator, now the United College of St. Salvator & St. Leonard of the University of St. Andrews, Fifeshire. It was established in 1411.

The largest university building in the world is the Lomonosov University of Moscow on the Lenin hills, which stands 787 feet, has 32 stories and contains 40,000 rooms. It was constructed in 1949–1953.

LARGEST in the BRITISH ISLES

		No. of Students	
England	University of London (1836)	17,220	(women 4,687)
	external students—	23,928	
Wales	University of Wales (1893)	4,454	(women 1,282)
Scotland	University of Glasgow (1451)	5,598	(women 1,082)
N. Ireland	The Queen's University of Belfast (founded 1908)	2,144	(women 570)
R. of Ireland	National University of Ireland, Dublin (founded 1909)	5,732	(women 1,262)

LARGEST SCHOOL

The largest school in the British Isles is Kidbrooke Comprehensive Secondary School, Corelli Road, London, S.E.3, opened on 7th September, 1954. It has 2,000 pupils, an assembly hall to seat 1,400, five gymnasia and sixteen acres of playing fields, including eight hard tennis courts.

OLDEST SCHOOL

The title of the oldest school in Britain is contested. It is claimed that King's School, Canterbury, was a foundation of Saint Augustine, some time between his arrival in Kent in A.D. 597 and his death in c.604.

MOST EXPENSIVE

The most expensive school in the world is La Rosey in Switzerland where the expense of maintaining a boy is nearly £1,000 p.a.

The most expensive school in the British Isles is Millfield at Street, Somerset, where the basic fees are £435 per annum for boys and £540 per annum for girls over 17 in the co-educational sixth form.

The highest annual fees in a girl's school are £330 15s. at Heathfield, Berks.

BROADCASTING

GREATEST AUDIENCES

Accurate figures as to the total number of people who listened to the B.B.C. broadcasts or re-broadcasts of the 1953 Coronation are, of course, impossible to obtain, but it is authoritatively estimated that well over 100 million people viewed or listened to the B.B.C. programmes, broadcast by the B.B.C. and those re-broadcast by the major United States networks and by over 2,000 stations throughout the world.

Probably the world's most widespread radio programme is " The Lutheran Hour ". It is sponsored by the Lutheran Laymen's League, a body of approximately eighty thousand who form an agency within the Missouri Synod of the Lutheran Church in the United States. It is transmitted by 1,200 radio stations in sixty-five countries, and the programme is broadcast regularly in fifty-six languages.

The Lutheran Church also sponsor a television programme which, carried as a public service by 260 television stations, is the most widespread television programme in the world.

OLDEST

The programme which has been on the air for the longest time is "The Children's Hour". It dates from the very beginning of broadcasting in 1922.

LONGEST

The longest duration of a B.B.C. broadcast was the reporting of the Coronation of Queen Elizabeth II on 2nd June, 1953. It began at 10.15 a.m. and finished at 5.30 p.m. — 7 hours 15 minutes.

PROGRAMMES

Light music forms the greatest proportion of all broadcasting time on the Home Service with 17·5 per cent of the total weekly 115 hours, averaging twenty hours every week.

In the Light Programme (weekly total 107 hours), light music also forms the greatest proportion of the broadcasts — 30·6 per cent or approximately thirty-two hours forty-five minutes per week.

On the Third Programme, serious music takes by far the greatest proportion of the transmitting time of forty-two hours per week with 53·8 per cent, approximately twenty-two and a half hours.

Children's programmes take up the greatest proportion of the television average programme duration of thirty-seven and a half hours per week with 17·7 per cent or approximately six and a half hours.

MOST POWERFUL TRANSMITTER

The most powerful radio transmitter in the United Kingdom is the 400 kW Droitwich Transmitter which broadcasts the Light Programme on 1,500 metres band at a frequency of 200 k/cs. per second.

The most powerful television transmitters in the B.B.C. system are the four 100 kW transmitters at Kirk o'Shotts, Wenvoe, Holme Moss and Sutton Coldfield.

BIGGEST CONTRACT

The biggest contract ever signed for television appearances was between Jackie Gleason, the American comedian, and the Columbia Broadcasting System on behalf of the Buick Division of General Motors, in December 1954. Under this contract, Jackie Gleason will receive £2½ million over the next two years for a once weekly half-hour programme. He also has an option to continue for another fifty-two weeks which, if taken up, will be worth another £1,400,000.

MUSICAL BEST SELLERS

GRAMOPHONE RECORDS

The greatest seller of any gramophone record to date is Irving Berlin's "White Christmas" which has now sold 18,000,000 copies. This figure includes the total of Bing Crosby's recording of this song which, alone, accounted for more than 9,000,000.

The biggest seller of the pre-electric recording era is "Dardanella" composed by Johnny Black and Felix Bernard which sold more than 6½ million without the present day impetus to sales of radio and motion picture exploitation.

Figures relating to the gramophone productions of the United Kingdom are unpublished, but Eddie Calvert's recording of "O Mein Papa" has sold more than 1,000,000 copies.

FASTEST SELLING

The fastest selling record of all time is "The Ballad of Davy Crockett" by Tom Blackburn and George Burns, U.S.A. The record has sold more than seven million copies on twenty different labels in its first six months on the markets.

OLDEST RECORD

The oldest gramophone record in the B.B.C. library is a record made by Emil Berliner of himself reciting the Lord's Prayer. It was made in 1884.

INSTRUMENTAL WORKS

The greatest selling instrumental work is "The Glow Worm" by Paul Lincke, published in 1902. It has sold over 4,000,000 copies in various arrangements in the ensuing fifty years.

Among non-copyright instrumental works — on which exact figures do not exist — it is generally agreed that "The Blue Danube" waltz by Johann Strauss, is the all-time biggest seller of the world.

BIGGEST SELLING SONGS

The title of the biggest selling song is shared by "Till We Meet Again" by Raymond B. Egan and Richard Whiting, published in 1918 and "Let Me Call You Sweetheart" by Beth Slater Whitson and Leo Friedman, published in 1910. Up to 1954, "Till We Meet Again" had sold more than 6,000,000 copies. Precise figures relating to "Let Me Call You Sweetheart" are unknown.

In recent years the biggest selling song is "White Christmas" by Irving Berlin. First published in 1941, by the end of 1947, it had sold over 3,000,000 copies and it still sells at the rate of 300,000 copies a year, particularly at Christmas time, bringing its present total sales to something over 5,000,000.

Figures relating to the largest selling English songs are not obtainable but the following each sold more than 1,000,000 copies — "It's a Long Way to Tipperary", published in 1914; "Keep the Home Fires Burning", published in 1915; "Roses of Picardy", published in 1916; "The Bells of St. Mary's", published in 1917 and "Among My Souvenirs", published in 1927.

MUSICAL COMEDY

The world's most successful musical comedy is "Oklahoma!" created by the Americans Rodgers and Hammerstein, which already 10 million people have paid £12,500,000 to see.

FILM

There is no exact definition of long films throughout the world. Various countries make definition by length but the following data refers to so-called feature films. The biggest producer of feature films is the United States, where, in 1953-54, 344 films of feature length were made. The United Kingdom figure was 138 during the same period.

CINEMA

The people of the United Kingdom go to the cinema more often than any other country in the world. Each week on average half the total population visit a cinema, of which there are a total of 4,595, with a total seating capacity of 4,200,000, or one cinema seat for every twelve persons.

Australia and New Zealand have more cinema seats per total population than any other country in the world, with one cinema seat for every 7·5 persons.

The film which has made the most money to date is "Gone With The Wind", which is reputed to have earned £12 million gross.

PLATE 5

ft: Radio City Music Hall, 'ork, U.S.A. (Page 101)

ght: Sandö Bridge over ver Angerman, Sweden. (Page 105)

The Britannia Assembly Filton, Gloucester. (Page 98)

Left: The Chacaltaya tory (17,180 feet), in Bolivia. (Page 97)

m Right: The Teatro co, Vicenza, Italy. (Page 101)

PLATE 6

Top Right: The Smith's Arms, Godmanstone, Dorset. (Page 102)

Above: The world's deepest boring at Palomar Field, California. (Page 108)

Right: World's largest sculptures — Mount Rushmore, U.S.A. (Page 104)

Bottom Right: World's highest fountain at Geneva — 426½ feet high. (Page 110)

Below: World's highest bridge — Royal Gorge Bridge, 1,053 feet above the Arkansas River. (Page 105)

OSCARS

Walt Disney has won more " Oscars "—awards of the United States Academy of Motion Picture Arts and Sciences instituted 1929 than any other person. His total is twenty-four from 1931 to 1955.

FILM STUDIOS

The largest film studio in the British Isles is that of British Lion Film Corporation at Shepperton with a working area of 115,306 square feet. The Pinewood Studios at Iver Heath, Bucks., has, however, more employees with over 1,050.

ARTISTS

The actor who has appeared in more films than any other is the American Samuel Hinds with a total of 159.

The highest total of films for a British actor is eighty-two, by Sir C. Aubrey Smith.

The oldest cinema actor was Cyril Maude (b. 1862) who appeared at the age of 89 years.

SIX

THE SCIENTIFIC WORLD

ELEMENTS

All matter in the Solar System is made up of 92 natural chemical elements comprising 2 liquids, 11 gases and 79 solids.

GASES
Lightest

Hydrogen, a colourless gas discovered by H. Cavendish (British) in 1766, is 14·39 times lighter than air, weighing only 0·005611 lb. per cubic foot or 0·08988 grams per litre.

Heaviest

Radon, a colourless gas discovered by F. E. Dorn (Germany) in 1900, is 111·5 times heavier than hydrogen. It is also known as Niton and is an emanation from radium salts.

Lowest and Highest Melting and Boiling Points

Of all substances, helium has the lowest boiling point (—268·94°C). This element, which is at normal temperatures a colourless gas, was discovered in 1868 by Sir Joseph Lockyer (British) and Pierre Jannsen (French) working independently. Helium was first liquefied by the Dutch physicist, Kammerlingh Onnes, in 1908. Liquid helium, which exists in two forms, can only be solidified under pressure.

Of the elements that are gases at normal temperatures, chlorine has the highest melting point (—101·6°C) and the highest boiling point (—34°C). This yellow-green gas was discovered by the Swede, C. W. Scheele, in 1774.

Commonest

The Earth's atmosphere has been computed to weigh 5,000,000,000,000,000 tons of which nitrogen constitutes 78·09 per cent. by volume in dry air.

Rarest

By far the rarest of the eleven elemental gases, which constitute the atmosphere is radon, (see above) which probably accounts for only ·00000000000000006 per cent. of the atmosphere.

METALS
Lightest

Lithium (Li), a silvery white metal discovered by the Swede, J. A. Arfvedson, in 1817, is the lightest of all metals with a specific gravity of 0·534 grams per millilitre (c.c.) or a density of 33·32 lb. per cubic foot. It is over 42 times lighter than osmium.

Densest

Osmium (Os), a grey-blue metal of the platinum group, discovered by S. Tennent (British) in 1804, is the densest of all metals with a specific gravity of 22·48 grams per millilitre (c.c.) or a density of 1,403 lb. per cubic foot. A cubic foot of uranium would weigh only 1,164 lb.

Lowest and Highest Melting and Boiling Points

Excluding mercury, which is liquid at normal temperatures, caesium (Cs), a silvery-white metal discovered by the Germans, R. W. von Busen and G. R. Kirchoff in 1860, melts at 28°C (82·4°F).

Tungsten or wolfram (W), a grey metal discovered by the Spaniard, D. F. de Elhuyar, in 1784, melts at 3,370°C.

Excluding mercury as above, the metal which vaporises at the lowest temperature is caesium at 670°C.

Tungsten has to be heated to 5,900°C (2,530°C above its melting point) before it vaporizes.

Expansion

The highest linear thermal expansion of any metal is that of caesium which, at about 20°C., is 97×10^{-6} in. per inch per one degree C°.

The lowest linear expansion is that of the alloy Invar, containing 36·1 per cent. nickel, the remainder being iron: the linear thermal expansion of this being a maximum of 2×10^{-6} in. per inch per one degree C° at ordinary temperatures.

Ductility

The most malleable, or ductile, of metals is gold; either pure or in the form of an alloy containing 97 per cent. gold, the remainder being copper and silver, can be beaten down without annealing from 1/1000 inch thickness to about 1/250,000 inch thickness. One ounce of gold (avoirdupois) can be drawn in the form of a continuous wire thread to a length of fifty-one miles.

Rarest

Of the natural elemental metals, a number of the 15 described as the Rare Earths have not yet been separated into metallic purity. Doubt has been expressed even as to the existence in nature of element 43 named masurium and element 61 named illinium.

The rarest form of matter on earth was the 17 atoms of mendelevium (Element 101, Symbol Mv) synthesized in the University of California's Cyclotron at Berkeley, California, U.S.A., by Dr. Glenn T. Seaborg early in 1955. This transuranic element, which has properties similar to thallium, was found to have a half-life not much more than thirty minutes.

Commonest

Though ranking behind oxygen and silicon in abundance, aluminium is the commonest of all metals, constituting 7·5 per cent. of the Earth's crust.

Newest

Beginning in 1940 with neptunium (Element 93) artificial transuranic elements have been created by cyclotron bombardments as follows :— plutonium (Element 94) 1940, americium (Element 95)

1944, curium (Element 96) 1944, berkelium (Element 97) 1949 and californium (Element 98) 1950. Reports in 1954 indicated the achievement of einsteinium (Element 100), and in 1955, mendelevium (Element 101) see above.

HARDEST SUBSTANCE

Diamond, a crystalline form of carbon (Element 6) is the hardest of all known substances. The hardest of man-made compounds is tungsten carbide.

STRONGEST ACID

The strength of acids and alkalis is measured on the pH scale. The pH of a solution is the logarithm to the base 10 of the reciprocal of the hydrogen-ion concentration in gram molecules per litre. True neutrality, pH 7, occurs in pure water at 22°C. The strongest acid is hydrochloric acid (HCl) (an aqueous solution of hydrogen chloride gas discovered by B. Valentine in 1644).

STRONGEST ALKALI

The strength of alkalis is expressed by pH values rising above the neutral 7·0. The strongest are caustic soda or sodium hydroxide (Na OH) and caustic potash or potassium hydroxide (KOH).

SMELLIEST SUBSTANCE

The most powerfully smelling substance is ethyl mercaptan (C_2H_5SH). This can be detected in a concentration of 4 by 10^{-8} milligrams per litre of air. Thus 4 mg. completely volatilized would still be detectable in an enclosed space with a floor the size of a full-sized football pitch and a roof 45 feet high.

MOST EXPENSIVE PERFUME

The costliest perfume in the world is Jean Patou's "Joy" from Paris. It is based on the finest of rose oils, rosa damascena, and jasmin oil blended with over one hundred other flower essences. It retails at 103s. 6d. per $\frac{1}{4}$ oz. or £225 per pint. The biggest and most expensive listed bottle of perfume is the one litre ($1\frac{3}{4}$ pints) size of Chanel No. 5. Made in France, it retails in the United Kingdom at £94 10s. a bottle.

DRINK

MOST ALCOHOLIC

The strength of spirituous liquor is gauged by degrees proof. Proof spirit is that mixture of alcohol (C_2H_5OH) and water which at 51°F. weighs 12/13ths of an equal measure of distilled water. Such spirit in fact contains 57·06 per cent. alcohol by volume so that pure or absolute alcohol is 74·5° over proof (O.P.).

The strongest drink was Royal Navy issue rum which prior to 1948 was 40° O.P. or 79·8 per cent. alcohol. Since that time it has been reduced to $4\frac{1}{2}$° U.P. or 54·5 per cent. alcohol. The most potent standard drink now obtainable is Swiss absinthe, an aromatized spirit flavoured with wormwood (*artemisia absinthium*), angelica root, fennel and hyssop, which contains up to 75 per cent. alcohol.

WEAKEST BEER

The weakest liquid ever marketed as beer was the sweet ersatz beer with an original gravity of 1000·96. Brewed by Sunner, Colne-Kalk, in Germany 1918, it had a strength one thirtieth of the weakest beer now obtainable in the United Kingdom.

MOST EXPENSIVE

The most expensive bottle of wine obtainable would be a bottle of Feinste Trockenbeeren Auslese of 1949 or any other good vintage. This is a white wine made in the Rhine Valley in very small quantities from specially selected grapes and retails at £8 or more.

The most expensive standard bottle of spirits obtainable from stock in this country is antique liqueur brandy (vintage 1858) at 105s. a bottle. The most expensive liqueur is the raspberry liqueur Eau de Vie de Framboise at 71s. per 26 oz. bottle.

Largest bottle used in the wine and spirits trade is called the Rehoboam. It holds one and a third gallons. (Equivalent of eight normal bottles.)

GEMS

Most Precious

A flawless emerald of good colour is carat for carat the most precious gem and may cost in excess of £1,000 per carat. A carat = 3 grains (see page 94).

Rarest

Only two stones are known of the pale mauve gem Taaffeite first discovered in a cut state in Dublin, Ireland, in November 1945. The bigger of the two examples is of 0·84 carat.

Hardest

Hardest of all gems and the hardest known substance is diamond which chemically is pure carbon. Diamond is 90 times harder than the next hardest gem corundum (Al_2O_3) and those from Borneo and New South Wales have a particular reputation for hardness. Hardnesses are compared on Moh's scale on which the finger nail is $2\frac{1}{2}$, window glass $5\frac{1}{2}$ and diamond 10.

Densest

The densest of all gems is Cassiterite or tinstone (SnO_2), a colourless to yellow stone found in Australia, Bolivia, Malaya, Mexico and in Cornwall, England. It has a specific gravity of 6.90 rising to 7·1 in opaque mass.

Highest Refractive Index

Rutile, the reddish titanium oxide TiO_2, has a refractive index of 2·903 compared with the 2·421 of a diamond.

Largest

The largest gem ever found was a 520,000 carat aquamarine near Marambaia, Brazil, in 1910, which yielded over 200,000 carats of gem quality stones.

DIAMONDS

The largest white diamond ever discovered was a 3106 metric carat (over $1\frac{1}{4}$ lb.) stone by Captain M. F. Wells, in the Premier Mine, Pretoria, South Africa, on 26th January, 1905. It was named after Sir Thomas Cullinan, D.S.O., Chairman of the mining company, and was presented to King Edward VII. The Star of Africa No. I in the Royal Sceptre, cut from it, is the largest cut diamond in the world at 530·2 metric carats with 74 facets. The largest coloured diamond known is the 44·4 metric carat vivid blue Hope diamond found in the Killur mines, Golconda and purchased by Jean Baptiste Tavernier in 1642.

EMERALDS

Emerald is green beryl. Hexagonal prisms up to $15\frac{3}{4}$ inches long and $9\frac{3}{4}$ inches in diameter have been recorded from the Ural mines. The largest cut green beryl crystal is the Austrian Government's 2,680 carat unguent jar carved by Dionysio Miseroni in the 17th century. Of gem quality emeralds, the largest known is the Devonshire stone of 1,350 carats from Muso, Columbia.

SAPPHIRES

Sapphire is blue corundum (Al_2O_3). Vague reports exist of a 1,988 carat sapphire found in a mine in Burma but the largest identified stone was a 951 carat specimen housed in the King of Ava's treasury in Burma in 1827.

RUBIES

Ruby is red corundum (Al_2O_3). Though there have been reports of a semi-transparent 2,000 carat Tibetan ruby, the largest gem stone known was a 1,184 carat stone of Burman origin.

PEARL

Pearls are protective secretinary bodies produced by molluscs. Gem pearls come chiefly from the western Pacific genus Pinctada and the fresh water mussel genus Quadrula. See Molluscs, page 35.

OPAL

The largest known opal is one of 2,975 carats found in the Czerwenitza mines of Hungary (now Cervenica, Czechoslovakia) in 1770 and now in the Imperial Museum, Vienna. The rarest variety of opal is the Ilouiznandos.

CRYSTAL

The largest crystal ball is the Warner 106-pound sphere of Burman quartz in the U.S. National Museum in Washington, D.C.

NUGGET

The largest gold nugget ever found was the 7,560 oz. Holtermann Nugget taken from Hill End, New South Wales, Australia, in 1872.

TELESCOPES

EARLIEST

Although there is evidence that the early Arabian scientists understood something of the magnifying power of lenses, their first use to form a telescope has been attributed to Roger Bacon (c.1214-92) in England. The prototype of modern refracting telescopes was that completed by Hans Lippersheim for the Dutch government on 2nd October, 1608.

LARGEST

The largest refracting (i.e. magnification by lenses) telescope in the world is the 62 feet long, 40-inch Yerkes telescope located at Williams Bay, Wisconsin, and belonging to the University of Chicago, U.S.A. The largest in the British Isles is the 28-inch at the Royal Greenwich Observatory, completed in 1894.

The largest reflector telescope in the world is the 200-inch Hale Telescope of the California Institute of Technology on Palomar Mountain, 66 miles north of San Diego, California, U.S.A. The project took 20 years to complete, the telescope being dedicated on 3rd July, 1948. The essential reflecting surface consists of an ounce of aluminium spread on a polished parabolic pyrex-type glass lens of over 15½ tons operated in a 450 ton steel frame-work. Stars can be photographed, the brightness of which is no greater than that of a candle flame at a range of 40,000 miles. Its astronomical range is 1,000 million light-years (see page 6) and stars of magnitude 23·5 can be located.

The largest reflectors in the British Isles are of 36 inches. Plans are in progress for the installation of a 98-inch reflector at Herstmonceux Castle in Sussex.

PHOTOGRAPHY

EARLIEST

The earliest photograph was taken by the French scientist, Nicephore Niepce, in 1826. It probably took something like eight hours to expose, and was taken on a sensitized polished pewter plate and showed the courtyard of his home.

The world's earliest aerial photograph was taken by " Nadar " from a captive balloon over the Arc de Triomphe, Paris, in 1858.

FASTEST CAMERAS

The world's fastest cine camera is at the Los Alamos Scientific Laboratory in the United States. It exposes at the rate of 14·4 million frames a second—ninety-six exposures on 36 mm. film in 1/150,000 seconds. It contains a revolving mirror rotating at 23,000 revolutions a second.

The fastest cine camera in the United Kingdom is part of the equipment of the Atomic Energy Authority, The Kerr Cell cine-camera, which takes photographs at the rate of 24 million a minute. The optical system of the camera is such that it could define an object ⅛ inch long 100 yards from the camera.

LARGEST PHOTOGRAPHS

The largest colour transparency in the world is at Grand Central Station, New York. An advertising photograph, it is 18 feet high and 60 feet long with rear illumination by a 61,000 watt bank of lights.

The world's largest radiograph was made at the University of Rochester, New York. The subject was a jeep, and the size of the complete X-ray was 12 feet long, 4 feet 9 inches high.

HIGHEST PHOTOGRAPHS

The highest photographs ever taken on earth were the Kodachrome 35 mm. transparencies exposed by Sir Edmund Hillary on the summit of Everest in 1953.

The highest photograph ever taken by man was exposed from the balloon Explorer II of the National Geographical Society by Capt. A. W. Stevens in 1935. From a height of 72,395 feet over South Dakota, the photograph shows the horizon 330 miles away and includes an area larger than the state of Indiana (36,291 square miles).

BRIGHTEST LAMP

The brightest lamp in the world is the Mazda Type F.A.5 Flash Tube, produced by British Thomson-Houston. The lamp, which contains xenon in a cylindrical arc tube of hard glass, has an electrode sealed into each end of the tube to give an arc gap of only a few millimetres. The tube gives a top brightness intensity of 1,000,000 candles per square inch for periods of 1/25 of a second. This compares with the brightness of the sun which is about 800,000 candles per square inch.

LARGEST SCIENTIFIC INSTRUMENT

The world's largest scientific instrument is the Radio Telescope of the Manchester University Experimental Station, Jodrell Bank, Cheshire, England. Work began in September 1952. The filigree skeletal bowl and 180 foot high supports weigh 1,500 tons and is fully steerable. Its cost is believed to be in excess of £500,000.

METROLOGY

In metrology the following prefixes have these meanings :—

Mega	=	×	1,000,000	1 million.
Kilo	=	×	1,000	1 thousand.
Centi	=	×	0·01	1 hundredth.
Milli	=	×	0·001	1 thousandth.
Micro	=	×	0·000001	1 millionth.

In dealing with large numbers scientists use the notation of 10 raised to various powers to eliminate a profusion of noughts, for example, 19,160,000,000,000 miles would be written $19{\cdot}16 \times 10^{12}$ miles. Similarly a very small number ·0000154324 grain would be written $15{\cdot}4324 \times 10^{-6}$ grain.

EARLIEST MEASURES

The earliest measures were measures of length based on the proportions of human limbs. The cubit (elbow point to tip of middle finger) is believed to have been in use as a timber measure as early as 7,000 B.C.

LONGEST MEASURE

The longest linear measure is an astronomical unit used in measuring stellar distances known as the parsec, which is the distance at which the semi-major axis of the Earth's orbit would subtend one second of arc, that is 19,160,000,000,000 miles.

SHORTEST MEASURE

The shortest linear measure used for visible objects is normally the millimetre (1/1000th of a metre = 0·0393701 inch). The micro-millimetre or micron is hence a millionth of a metre or 1/25,490th part of an inch. For microscopy, the unit of a millimicron ($M\mu$) is used, being 1/1,000th part of a micron. In work on light waves, however, the Ångstrom unit (1/10th of a millimicron) is employed which represents 1/254,900,000th of an inch.

CUBIC MEASURE

If the parsec is accepted as the largest linear measure, then it follows that the cubic parsec must be the greatest measure of capacity. Similarly the cubic millimicron is the smallest measure of capacity.

HEAVIEST WEIGHT

The heaviest Imperial measure of weight is the ton (2,240 lb.). The Spanish ton, however, is 31·64 lb. heavier while the Chilean cajon is 2·90 tons or 6,496 lb. The metric ton or tonne is 2,204·622 lb., hence the megatonne is 984,206 tons.

LIGHTEST

The lightest unit for measuring weight is the Imperial grain which is 0·323995 of a metric carat, 15·4324 to the gram and 437½ to the ounce avoirdupois. The microgram one millionth of a gram (μg or γ) is, however, 0·0000154324 of a grain.

In sub-atomic physics the smallest constant is the mass of an electron (at rest) which is $(9{\cdot}1066 \pm 0{\cdot}0032) \times 10^{-28}$ gram which equals nine thousand-quadrillionths of a gram.

SMALLEST TIME MEASURE

The fundamental unit of time is provided by the Earth's daily axial rotation. The smallest standard subdivision of the day is the second which is 1/24th part (hour) divided into 1/60th part (minute) and further subdivided by sixty.

For scientific purposes, the micro-second (a millionth part of a second) is employed.

LONGEST TIME MEASURE

The terms such as an age, epoch or aeon used to express time are all indeterminate. The term millennium, however, expresses 10 centuries or 1,000 years. The most fundamental year is the sidereal year of 365·2563604 days.

SHORTEST YEAR

The year 1752 lasted only 271 instead of 365 days. Prior to 1752 the year was reckoned to begin on 25th March. Owing also to discrepancies between the old style (Julian) and the new style (Gregorian) calendar, 2nd September was followed by 14th September. A legacy of the old style remains in the income tax year in which 5th April is a new style version of the old 25th March date for the beginning of a new year.

LONGEST AND SHORTEST DAYS

The longest and shortest days depend upon the local time at which the summer and winter solstices fall. Confining the consideration to Greenwich, if the solstice falls on 21st June in one year later than 6 p.m., it may fall after midnight of 21st June the year following, thus making 22nd June the longest day. The six hour annual advance in the solstice is corrected by the Leap Year cycle so does not progress. At the present time the shortest days are 21st December, though later in the century they will sometimes overlap into 22nd December.

LONGEST AND SHORTEST DAYLIGHT

At Greenwich the daylight on 21st December lasts 7 hours 50 minutes and on 21st June 16 hours 39 minutes. The evenings begin lengthening on 14th December when the sunset (for a sea-level horizon) is two seconds later than on the 13th December. Similarly the evenings begin drawing in on 13th June.

LONGEST MILE

Of the six major varieties of mile the longest is the Swedish mile, which is 10,000 metres, or 6 statute miles 376 yards. The longest in the British Isles is the Irish mile of 2,240 yards. The shortest is the statute or land mile of 1,760 yards.

LARGEST ACRE

Of the six recognised variations on the Imperial acre of 4,840 square yards, the largest is the Lancashire acre of 7,866 square yards and the smallest the customary North Wales acre of 3,240 square yards.

LARGEST GALLON

Of the nine major variations on the Imperial gallon which is the volume occupied by 10 lb. of water weighed in air against brass weights at 62°F and at 30 inches of mercury, atmospheric pressure, the largest is the Scottish gallon at 3·007 Imperial gallons and the smallest that used in Bolivia, Ecuador and Costa Rica at 0·74 gallons.

LARGEST PINT

Of the five major variations on the Imperial Pint (one eighth part of an Imperial gallon) the largest is the Glasgow pint which equals 4 Imperial pints and the smallest is the U.S. pint which is 0·8327 of an Imperial pint.

CALENDAR

EARLIEST EASTER

The earliest date upon which Easter can fall is 22nd March. This last occurred in 1818 and will not occur during the 20th century.

LATEST EASTER

The latest date upon which Easter can fall is 25th April. This last occurred in 1943 and will not recur during the 20th century.

Summer time in the United Kingdom normally begins at 02·00 G.M.T. on the day following the third Saturday in April, or if Easter Sunday, then the day following the second Saturday in April, and ends at 02.00 G.M.T. on the day following the first Saturday in October.

EARLIEST and LATEST FOR PUTTING CLOCKS FORWARD AND BACK

Summer Time (clocks one hour in advance of Greenwich Mean Time) was introduced on 21st May, 1916. Apart from wartime years 1941-45 and in 1947, when double summer-time was enforced, the earliest date for putting clocks forward was 14th March in 1948. The latest, apart from the inaugural year, was 22nd April in the years 1923, 1928 and 1934.

Apart from the six years of double summer-time the earliest date for putting the clocks back was 16th September, 1923, and the latest 19th November, 1939. The earliest and latest dates for the operation of double summer-time were 2nd April in both 1944 and 1945 and 17th September in 1944.

PHYSICAL EXTREMES

HIGHEST TEMPERATURE

The highest published temperature yet attained is one in excess of 600,000 degrees centigrade officially disclosed in a report of the Monte Bello Island Atom Bomb Test of 3rd October, 1952.

LOWEST TEMPERATURE

The lowest temperature reached is 0·0015°K or within 1/1,500th of a degree of absolute zero (−273·16°C) by Dr. Kurti at the Clarendon Laboratory, Oxford, announced on the 25th October 1954.

HIGHEST ENERGY

The highest energy ever artificially given to atomic nuclei is about 5 GeV (five thousand million volts). This was achieved with the bevatron of the University of California's Radiation Laboratory at Berkeley.

Two machines to give higher energies are at present in the design stage, the proton synchrotron at Brookhaven, U.S.A., and the one for the European Council for Nuclear Research (C.E.R.N.) at Geneva. Both of these have design energies of 20-30 GeV.

LARGEST MAGNET

The largest magnet in the world is that of the bevatron of the University of California. It has an external diameter of 135 feet and a weight of 10,000 tons.

HIGHEST PRESSURE

The highest static maintained pressure ever measured under laboratory conditions is the 6·25 million pounds per square inch achieved by Prof. P. W. Bridgeman of the Lyman Laboratory of Physics, Harvard University, Massachusetts.

HIGHEST VACUUM

The highest vacuums obtained in scientific research are of the order of 10×10^{-9} atmospheres. This compares with an estimated pressure in inter-stellar space of 10×10^{-19} atmospheres.

WIND TUNNELS

The world's largest wind tunnel is the low-speed tunnel with an 80 ft. wide test section at Ames Aeronautical Laboratory, U.S.A. The most powerful is the 216,000 h.p. installation at the Arnold Engineering Test Centre at Tullahoma, Tennessee. The highest Mach number attained with air is Mach 13 (9,880 m.p.h.), but Mach 15 was reached at Princeton, U.S.A., with helium early in 1954. For periods of micro-seconds, shock Mach numbers of the order of 30 have been attained in impulse tubes at Cornell University, New York, U.S.A.

SEVEN

THE WORLD'S STRUCTURES

I. Buildings for Working

TALLEST BUILDING

The tallest building in the world is the Empire State Building, New York. Standing on approximately two acres of ground, it is 1,472 feet high to the top of the television tower, which was added to the existing 1,250 feet building in 1950.

In its 102 stories, 950 firms employ approximately 20,000 people. About 1,000 people are constantly employed in day to day maintenance in the operation of the building, including the cleaning of the 6,500 windows. There are 63 passenger lifts, or, if you prefer to walk, 1,860 steps from top to bottom. Completed on 1st May, 1931, it cost nearly £15,000,000 and occupied 7,000,000 man hours.

HIGHEST BUILDING

The highest inhabited building in the world is the Chacaltaya High Altitude Laboratory. Maintained by the Laboratorio de Física Cósmica for Cosmic Ray Research, it stands at a height of 17,180 feet above sea level. It is situated in the Andes about 22 miles from the Bolivian city of La Paz. The laboratory can accommodate about 20 people. Usually four or five are maintained constantly at the laboratory, each person staying only for five to seven days.

NORTHERNMOST & SOUTHERNMOST HABITATION

The most northerly habitation in the world is the Danish Scientific Station set up in 1952 in Pearyland, Northern Greenland, over 900 miles north of the Arctic Circle.

The most southerly permanent human habitation is the Australian Antarctic research base at Mawson at 67°30′S.

LARGEST OFFICE BUILDING

The largest office building in the world is the Pentagon, Washington, U.S.A. Built to house the U.S. Government's war offices, it was completed in January 1943, and cost approximately $83,000,000 (£29,660,000). Each of the outermost sides of the Pentagon is 921 feet long and the perimeter of the building is approximately $\frac{7}{8}$ mile. The five stories of the building enclose a floor area of approximately $6\frac{1}{2}$-million square feet. During the day 28,500 people work in the building. The telephone system of the building has over 44,000 telephones connected by 160,000 miles of cable and its 220 staff handle 280,000 calls a day. Two restaurants, six cafeterias and ten snackbars and a staff of 675 form the catering departments of the building.

The United Kingdom's largest office building is Shell-Mex House, between the Strand and the Embankment. From Embankment level to the top of the clock tower, it is 201 feet high and the fifteen floors enclose a total gross floor area of 584,444 square feet. The sixteen lifts of the building can carry altogether 10,000 persons an hour and their maximum speed is one floor per second.

CHIMNEYS

The world's highest smokestack is the 585 feet tall brick chimney at the Anaconda Copper Mining Co. smelting works in Anaconda, Montana, U.S.A.

The highest chimney ever built in the United Kingdom was at the chemical works of Joseph Townsend, Ltd., at Port Dundas, Glasgow, at 474 feet. It was built in 1857–59 and was demolished in 1928.

LARGEST HANGAR

The largest hangar is the Britannia Assembly Hall at the Bristol Aeroplane Company's works at Filton in Gloucester. Originally intended for the construction of a flight testing base for the Bristol Brabazon, it now houses the construction of the Britannia. The overall width of the Hall is 1,054 feet and the overall depth of the centre bay is 420 feet. It encloses a floor area of 7½ acres. The cubic capacity of the Hall is 33 million cubic feet. The building was begun in April 1946 and completed by September 1949.

LARGEST PRE-STRESSED CONCRETE BUILDING

The British European Airways servicing bays at London Airport are the largest pre-stressed concrete buildings in the world. The two hangar buildings each measure 900 feet by 110 feet. The long side of each hangar building contains five doors each with a clear opening 150 feet wide × 30 feet high which gives access to a concrete apron 900 feet long × 300 feet wide. The total installation will cover an area of 4½ acres and approximately 2,000 engineers and maintenance men will be employed there.

LARGEST GARAGE

The largest garage in the world is beneath Grant Park, Chicago, and has a capacity of 2,350 cars. The largest in the United Kingdom is the Metropolis Garage, Ltd., Olympia, London. Completed in 1937, it has eleven floors built on the mezzanine principle and can accommodate eleven hundred cars.

LARGEST SEWAGE WORKS

The largest sewage works in the world is the West and South-West Plant in Chicago, U.S.A., opened in 1940. It serves an area containing 3,250,000 people.

The largest in the United Kingdom is the £5½ million Mogden works at Isleworth, Middlesex, completed in 1935. Mogden works serves the West Middlesex area of 15 local authorities and a total population of approximately 1,400,000 people. The amount of sewage treated is 70 million gallons a day. During wet weather it has reached a daily peak of 450 million gallons.

The system is linked by 70 miles of main trunk sewers of up to 12¾ feet in diameter.

WAREHOUSE

The world's largest warehouse is that at Collingwood Dock, Liverpool, which has 14 stories and 36 acres of floor space.

BARN

The largest barn in Britain is that at Manor Farm, Cholsey, near Wallingford, Berkshire. It is 303 feet in length and 54 feet in breadth.

2. *Buildings for Living*

EARLIEST CASTLES

Castles in the sense of unfortified manor houses existed in all the great early civilizations including that of Ancient Egypt prior to 3,000 B.C. Fortified castles in the more accepted sense only existed much later. The oldest in the world is that at Gomdan in the Kingdom of Yemen in Arabia which originally had twenty stories and dates from prior to A.D. 100.

The oldest stone castle in the British Isles is Richmond Castle, Yorkshire, built A.D. c.1075.

LARGEST CASTLES

The largest castle in the world is that at Aleppo in Syria which is oval in shape and was built with a surrounding wall 1,230 feet long and 777 feet wide. It dates, in its present form, from the Hamanid dynasty of the tenth century A.D.

The most massive keep in the world is that in the thirteenth century Chateau-fort de Courcy, in the Department of l'Aisne, France. It is 177 feet high, 318 feet in circumference and has walls over twenty-two and a half feet in thickness.

The largest castle in the British Isles is the Royal residence of Windsor Castle which is primarily of twelfth century construction and is in the form of a parallelogram, 1,890 feet on its longest side by 540 feet. The overall dimensions of Carisbrooke Castle (450 feet by 360 feet), Isle of Wight, if its earthworks are included, are 1,350 feet by 825 feet. The largest castle in Scotland is Doune Castle built c.1425.

LARGEST PALACE

The largest palace in the world is the Vatican Palace, Vatican City, in Rome. Covering an area of 13½ acres, it has 1,400 rooms, chapels and halls of which the oldest date from the 15th century. The Papal Library has approximately 700,000 printed books and 70,000 manuscripts.

LARGEST FLATS

The largest block of flats in Britain is Dolphin Square, London, covering a site of 7½ acres. The building occupies the four sides of a square enclosing gardens of about 3 acres. Dolphin Square contains 1,220 separate and self-contained flats, an underground garage for 300 cars with filling and service station, a swimming pool, eight squash courts, a tennis court and an indoor shopping centre. There are twenty-six lifts to the various floors and a restaurant. The water supply of the building comes from four 600 feet deep wells which supply a total of 14,500 gallons per hour into the three large reservoirs which have a total capacity of half a million gallons. The building employs a staff of over 200 people, including domestic workers, electricians, engineers, decorators, and clerical staff.

LARGEST HOTELS

The largest hotel in the world based on number of rooms is the Conrad Hilton in Chicago. Its twenty-five floors contain 3,000 guest rooms. It would thus take more than eight years to spend one night in each room in the hotel. The hotel employs about 2,000 people of which more than 70 are telephone operators and supervisors and 72 lift operators. The laundry of the hotel, with nearly 200 employees, handles 530 tons of flat work each month as well as some 30,000 shirts, and 18,000 pairs of socks.

The largest hotel in the world on the basis of cubic footage is the Waldorf Astoria, Park Avenue, New York. It occupies a complete block just under two acres in extent and reaches a maximum height of 625 feet 7 inches. The Waldorf Astoria has 47 stories and about 2,200 guest rooms and maintains the largest hotel radio receiving system in the world. Any house or overseas programme that the visitor wishes to hear can be transmitted to his suite, as well as speeches and music from the public rooms of the hotel.

The biggest hotel in the United Kingdom is the Regent Palace Hotel, Piccadilly Circus, London. It has 1,140 rooms accommodating 1,670 guests. The total staff numbers 1,200.

MOST EXPENSIVE

The most expensive " big " hotel in the world is the Fontainebleau, Miami Beach, Florida. Built in 1954 at a cost of approximately £5·3 million, it stands on five acres of a 14-acre ocean-front estate. A yacht basin, capable of accommodating 50 boats, and two open-air swimming pools are in the grounds. The main building of the hotel contains 565 guest rooms in 15 floors and there are 265 cabins with private bathrooms in the grounds facing the private beach.

The daily standard room rate for 11th to 14th floor rooms with terraces facing the ocean, during the peak season (January to March) is £16 8s. 0d., or £114 16s. 0d. per week. Nine " presidential " suites are available at daily rates of £51 17s. 6d.

HOLIDAY CAMP

The largest holiday camp in the world is Butlin's Filey Holiday Camp. Every year more than 150,000 people spend a holiday there, and, in 1955, 9,000 holidaymakers were accommodated during the peak weeks. The camp covers 498 acres and in 1954 there were 2,574 guest chalets with hot and cold water. On the camp are two theatres, two ballrooms, each able to hold 3,000 dancers, boating lake, swimming pool, tennis courts, putting and bowling green, Church of England and Roman Catholic churches. The total staff is approximately 1,000.

LARGEST HOUSE

The largest house in the United Kingdom is Wentworth Woodhouse, near Rotherham, Yorkshire, formerly the seat of the Earls Fitzwilliam. The main part of Wentworth Woodhouse, built over 300 years ago, has more than 240 rooms with over 1,000 windows, and its principal façade is 600 feet long.

3. *Buildings for Entertainment*

LARGEST STADIUM

The world's largest stadium is the Strahov Stadium, Prague completed in 1934 to accommodate 240,000 spectators of mass displays of up to 40,600 gymnasts.

The largest football stadium in the world is the Maracaña Stadium in Rio de Janeiro, Brazil, which has a normal capacity of 150,000. On 1st July, 1950, Brazil *v.* Yugoslavia, a crowd of 200,000 was accommodated. A nine foot moat protects players from spectators.

The largest stadium in the United Kingdom is that at Hampden Park, Glasgow, which has accommodated a football crowd of over 149,500.

AUDITORIUM

The world's largest auditorium is the Atlantic City, New Jersey, U.S.A., municipal auditorium and convention hall. The Auditorium seats 41,000 people and covers seven acres. The Main Hall is 488 feet long and 288 feet wide and 137 feet high. The total floor space available for exhibitions is 300,000 square feet and each stand is independently equipped with water, gas, electricity, steam, compressed air and sewerage. A regulation American football field (360 feet × 160 feet) can be laid out in the Main Hall and still leave room for 12,000 seats.

LARGEST THEATRE

The largest indoor theatre in the world is the Radio City Music Hall, Rockefeller Center, New York. It seats more than 6,200 persons and the average annual attendance is more than 8,000,000 people.

The stage is 144 feet wide and 66 feet 6 inches deep, equipped with a revolving turntable 43 feet in diameter and three 70 feet long elevator sections. It is one of the most modern and mechanised in the world. The orchestra lift — large enough to house 75 musicians — rises from sub-basement level 27 feet below the stage to form an extension to the main stage and it can then travel 60 feet backstage under its own power. The theatre is equipped with dressing rooms to accommodate 600 persons. Usually 600 staff are employed in the theatre, including artists, management, electricians and stage hands. See Plate 5.

The largest theatre in the United Kingdom is the Opera House, Blackpool. It was opened in July 1939 and has seats for 3,000 people. Behind the 45 foot wide proscenium arch the stage is 110 feet high, 60 feet deep and 100 feet wide, and there is dressing room accommodation for 200 artists.

The largest open-air theatre in the world is at Mendoza in Argentina. It can seat 40,000 people.

OLDEST THEATRE

The oldest theatre in the world is the Teatro Olimpico in Vicenza, Italy. Designed by Palladio in the Roman Style, it was finished after his death by his pupil Scamozzi in 1582. It is preserved today in its original form. See Plate 5.

The oldest theatre in the United Kingdom, still in use, is the Theatre Royal, Bristol. The foundation stone was laid on 30th November, 1764, and the theatre was opened on 30th May, 1766, with a "Concert of Music and a Specimen of Rhetorick". Since then it has been more or less continuously in use as a theatre. It is the home of the Bristol Old Vic Company.

LARGEST BALLROOM

The largest ballroom in the United Kingdom is the Great Room of the Grosvenor House, Park Lane, London. The room is 192 feet long and 120 feet wide and the floor covers a total area of 23,040 square feet.

PLEASURE BEACH

The biggest pleasure beach in the world is Coney Island, New York. As well as its five mile beach it features more than 350 business and amusement places, side-shows, "rides" and penny arcades. During the season it is conservatively estimated that 50,000,000 people visit Coney Island and each of them spend about $1·25 (8s. 11d.).

The longest pleasure pier in the world is Southend Pier, 1⅓ miles in length. It is decorated with more than 75,000 lamps.

LARGEST CINEMA

The largest open-air cinema in the world is in Berlin in the British Sector. Converted from the Olympic Stadium Amphitheatre, it seats 22,000 people.

The largest cinema in the United Kingdom is the Playhouse, Glasgow, with 4,235 seats.

The largest cinema in England is the Gaumont State, Kilburn, London, which has a seating capacity of 3,996.

The oldest building designed as a cinema is the Biograph Cinema, Wilton Road, Victoria, London. It was opened in 1905 and originally had seating accommodation for 500 patrons. Its present capacity is 700.

PUBLIC HOUSES

LARGEST PUBLIC HOUSE

The largest public house in the United Kingdom is the Downham Tavern, near Bromley, Kent. Built in 1930 to serve the Downham Estate, it employs twenty permanent staff with an additional eighteen to twenty people during rush periods.

The two large bars, counter length 45 feet, are able to hold a thousand customers. Altogether the Tavern has a capacity of about 1,800 people. During the peak periods, Christmas week and bank-holiday weekends, 50,000 bottled beers and 40,000 pints of draught beer are served.

SMALLEST PUBLIC HOUSE

The smallest pub in the United Kingdom is " The Smith's Arms " at Godmanstone, Dorset. It is ten feet wide and about four feet high at the eaves. Its licence was granted personally by Charles II (1660–1685). See Plate 6.

HIGHEST PUBLIC HOUSE

The highest public house in the United Kingdom is the Tan Hill Inn in Yorkshire. It is 1,732 feet high on the moorland road between Reeth in Yorkshire and Brough in Westmorland.

The highest in Wales is the Sportsman's Arms on the road that crosses the Denbigh Moors between Denbigh and Pentre Foelas.

OLDEST PUBLIC HOUSE

There are various claimants to the title of the United Kingdom's oldest inn: " The Angel and Royal " at Grantham, which has cellar masonry dated 1213; the " Fountain Inn " at Canterbury; " The George " at Norton St. Philip near Bath, 1290, and the " Fighting Cocks", St. Albans, which is reputed to be built on the foundations of a monks' fishing lodge dating back to A.D. 795.

LONGEST NAMED

The pub with the longest name is " The Thirteenth Mounted Cheshire Rifleman Inn " at Stalybridge, Cheshire.

SHORTEST NAMED

The shortest pub name is the " XL " Bar, 65 Fountainbridge, Edinburgh.

LONGEST BARS

The longest bar in the world is that built in 1938 at the Working Men's Club, Mildura, Victoria, Australia, which has a counter 285 feet in length, served by 32 taps.

The longest bar in the British Isles is the Long Bar in the Blackpool Tower, Blackpool, Lancs., which extends over 144 feet.

WINE CELLAR

The largest wine cellars in the world are at Paarl near Cape Town, in the centre of the wine-growing district of the Union of South Africa. They have a capacity of 20 million gallons.

e 1875 Grenville Steam Carriage. *(Page 111)*

PLATE 7

The Danish Hammel of 1887. *(Page 111)*

The Mercedes 300 SL. *(Page 111)*

The " D " type Jaguar. *(Page 112)*

The £9,800 Pegaso Z102. *(Page 113)*

The Rolls Royce Silver Wraith. *(Page 113)*

The Most powerful United Kingdom built prime mover — The Thornycroft Mighty Antar. *(Page 114)*

PLATE 8

Top Left: The heaviest roa
a 185 ton casting made by
Steel Corporation, Ltd. (Pa

Top Right: The heaviest se
a 190 ton lighter, one o
shipped from Rotterdam t
by Belships. (Page 120)

Left: The Euclid LLD. (Pa

Below: The Bristol Olymp
(Page 122)

The L.N.E.R. 4-6-2 Mallard which hauled seven coaches weighing 240 tons at 126 m.p.h. (Page 114)

The Al-Malik-Saud-Al-Awal, 28,738 ton oil tanker which sails under the Saudi-Arabian flag. (Page 118)

4. Specialised Structures

WORLD'S TALLEST STRUCTURE

The tallest structure in the world is the 1,572 foot television transmitting tower of station KWTV in Oklahoma City, U.S.A.

The tower is triangular in cross section, 12 feet a side, to the 1,420 feet level. Above that point the tower tapers to the two antennae which it carries. One is a 79-foot RCA fourteen-layer supergain and the other a 73-foot RCA twelve-bay superturnstile, with a total effective radiated power of 316,000 watts.

The tower, which weighs 1,323,000 pounds (approximately 590 tons) rests on a set of porcelain insulators designed to withstand a crushing load of 11,200,000 pounds (5,000 tons). The tower is guyed by twenty-four stranded steel cables which vary in diameter from $1\frac{1}{2}$ to 2 inches and radiate 950 feet from the base. An electric lift runs to the 1,340 foot level and the tower carries nine 1,000 watt flashing beacons and eighteen obstruction lights. From the top of the tower the line of sight to the horizon is 60 miles. See Plate 4.

The pre-stressed concrete Brussels Telecommunication Tower, due to be completed for the 1958 Exhibition, has been planned to reach a height of 1,935 feet 5 inches and will be the highest structure in the world.

BRITAIN'S TALLEST STRUCTURE

The tallest structures in the United Kingdom are the General Post Office radio masts outside Rugby, Warwick. The masts, each weighing 170 tons, were erected in 1925 and stand 820 feet high.

TALLEST TOWER

The tallest tower in the United Kingdom is the Blackpool Tower. The height to the top of the tower is 518 feet 9 inches. In its construction 3,478 tons of steel and 352 tons of cast iron were used. The Tower was opened in 1894. Every year, four tons of red lead and one and a half tons of lead oxide are used to paint the steel work.

TALLEST FLAGSTAFF

The world's tallest flagstaff is the eighteen and a half-ton, 214 feet high Douglas fir flagstaff at Kew, London. It was towed across the Atlantic from Canada and erected on 18th October, 1919.

CONCRETE DAM

The world's biggest concrete dam, and the biggest concrete structure in the world, is the Grand Coulee Dam on the Columbia River, Washington State, U.S.A. 4,173 feet long and 550 feet high, it contains 10,585,000 cubic yards of concrete, and weighs about 21,600,000 tons. The hydro-electric powerplant has a capacity of 1,249,800 kilowatts and is the largest installation of its type in the world.

Measured by volume, the Fort Peck Dam, across the Missouri River in Montana, is the largest in the world. It contains 128 million cubic yards of earth and rock fill, and is 21,026 feet long. It maintains a reservoir containing 19·4 million acre feet.

HIGHEST DAM

The highest dam in the world is the Grand Dixence in Switzerland. It is 932 feet from base to rim and the total volume of concrete in the dam is 520,000 cubic yards.

BIGGEST RESERVOIR

When the Owen Falls scheme is completed, Lake Victoria, Uganda, will be the biggest reservoir in the world, both in area, approximately 27,000 square miles, and in volume. The dam at Jinja is 2,500 feet long and has a maximum height of 100 feet and contains 230,000 cubic yards of concrete. Eventually ten turbines will be installed producing 50,000 kilowatts.

At the present moment, the reservoir with the largest capacity in the world is Lake Mead formed by the Hoover Dam in the United States. Lake Mead is 119 miles long.

The largest dam in the United Kingdom is the Claerwen Dam in Wales, opened on 23rd October, 1952. It is a concrete gravity dam and materials weighing more than 700,000 tons were used in its construction. The dam is 240 feet maximum height from base to sill and its overall length is 1,166 feet. It cost more than £2,000,000 and forms a reservoir containing approximately 10,625,000,000 gallons.

The largest reservoir in the United Kingdom is the Ladybower Reservoir in Derbyshire. It covers an area of 504 acres and has a maximum depth of 135 feet.

LARGEST MONUMENTS

The largest monument ever constructed is the Pyramid of Cheops (Khufu) at Gizeh near Cairo, built in the 4th Egyptian Dynasty c. 2800 B.C. Its original height was 481 feet (now 451 feet) with a base covering 12½ acres. It has been estimated that it required 100,000 slaves 20 years to manoeuvre the 2½ ton stone blocks, totalling nearly 7 million tons, into position.

The Pyramids of Egypt, of which the earliest is the step pyramid at Saqqara, were reckoned among the Seven Wonders of the World. Of these ancient wonders only fragments remain of the Temple of Diana of the Ephesians built c. 500 B.C. at Ephesus (destroyed A.D. 262) and of the Tomb of Mausolus built at Halicarnasus c. 325 B.C. No trace remains of the Hanging Gardens of Babylon (c. 600 B.C.), the Statue of Zeus, the Colossus of Rhodes (destroyed by earthquake 224 B.C.), or the Pharos Lighthouse (destroyed by earthquake in A.D. 1375).

LARGEST SCULPTURE

The world's largest sculptures are the Mount Rushmore National Memorial in the U.S.A. Known as the Shrine of Democracy, these sculptures, in granite, take the form of the busts of Presidents Washington, Jefferson, Theodore Roosevelt and Lincoln. The busts are proportionate to men 465 feet high, and the distance between the top of Washington's head to his chin is 60 feet. See Plate 6.

LARGEST STATUE

When completed the world's largest statue will be that of the Sioux Indian chief, Crazy Horse, begun in 1939 near Mount Rushmore, South Dakota. A projected 561 feet high and 641 feet long, it will require the removal of 6 million tons of stone.

BRIDGES

Modern bridges fall into three main groups: arch, cantilever, and suspension. (See diagram).

LONGEST SPAN SUSPENSION

The longest single span bridge in the world is the Golden Gate Bridge in California. It spans the entrance to San Francisco Bay joining San Francisco to Marin County in the north. A suspension bridge, it is 4,200 feet between uprights. The two towers of the bridge are 746 feet high and it carries six lanes of roadway and two footways on a deck 90 feet wide, 220 feet above the water level. It was opened to traffic in May 1937 at a cost of approximately $35,000,000 (£12·5 million).

The longest suspension bridge in the United Kingdom is that designed by I. K. Brunel spanning the Clifton Gorge of the River Avon, near Bristol, it is 702 feet between uprights. It was completed in 1864.

HIGHEST

The highest suspension bridge in the world is the bridge over the Royal Gorge of the Arkansas River 1,053 feet above the water level. It has a main span of 880 feet. See Plate 6.

LONGEST SPAN CANTILEVER

The Quebec Bridge over the St. Lawrence river in Canada has the longest cantilever span of any in the world—1,800 feet. It carries two railway tracks. Begun in 1904, it was finally completed in 1918.

The largest cantilever bridge in the United Kingdom is the Forth Bridge. Its two main spans are 1,710 feet long. It carries a double railway track over the Firth of Forth 150 feet above the water level. Work commenced on the bridge in 1882 and was completed eight years later.

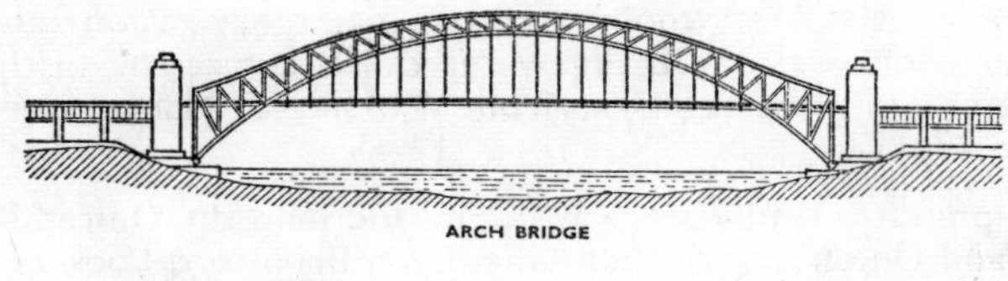

ARCH BRIDGE

SUSPENSION BRIDGE

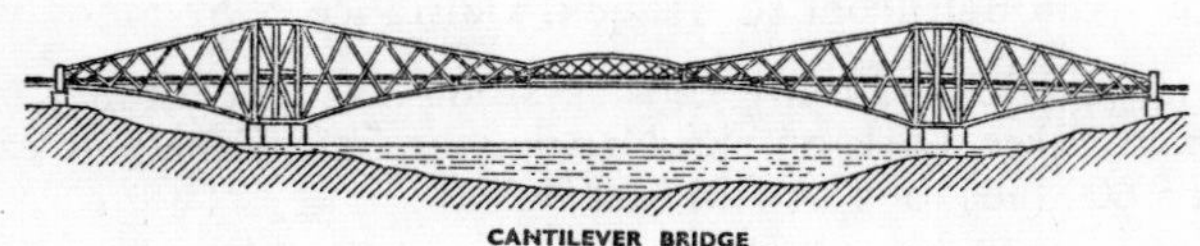

CANTILEVER BRIDGE

LONGEST SPAN STEEL ARCH

The longest steel arch bridge in the world is the Bayonne Bridge which connects New York to Staten Island. Its span is 1,652 feet—two feet longer than the Sydney Harbour Bridge.

LARGEST SPAN STEEL ARCH

The largest steel arch bridge in the world is the Sydney Harbour Bridge. Its main span is 1,650 feet wide and it carries four railway tracks, six lanes of roadway, two footways, 172 feet above the waters of Sydney Harbour. It took seven years to build and was completed in March 1932 and cost approximately £4½ million.

The longest span steel arch in Great Britain is the Newcastle-upon-Tyne Bridge carrying the Great North Road across the River Tyne. Its span is 531 feet and width 64 feet. It carries road and passenger traffic 84 feet above the level of the river.

LONGEST CONCRETE ARCH

The longest reinforced concrete span is that of the Sandö Bridge of the Ångerman River, Sweden. It is a hingeless, hollow-box section arch and spans 866 feet 5 inches. The bridge carries a motor road 132 feet above the river. See Plate 5.

LONGEST SPAN

The longest brick-built span in the United Kingdom and most probably in the world is the Maidenhead Railway Bridge which carries the Western Region tracks over the River Thames. Completed in 1839 to a design of I. K. Brunel, it includes two 128-feet brick spans with a rise of only 24½ feet.

LARGEST CANALS

The world's longest big ship canal is the Suez, 100 miles in length.

The world's biggest canal, measured in cross section area, is the Panama which varies from 22,000 to 45,000 square feet.

The world's deepest lock is the Donzère-Mondragon lock on the River Rhône at 86 feet. It takes 8 minutes to fill.

EARLIEST CANALS

The first canals in Britain were undoubtedly cut by the Romans. In the Midlands — the Fossdyke Canal — between Lincoln and the Trent, is an example of their work, part of which is still in use today.

However, the first wholly artificial major navigation canal in the United Kingdom was the Bridgewater canal, cut at the instigation of the Duke of Bridgewater, it ran from Worsley to Manchester and was opened in 1761.

LONGEST CANAL

The longest inland waterway in England (and the United Kingdom) is the Grand Union Canal, Main Line, from Brentford Lock Junction to Langley Mill, a total distance of 167⅜ miles. The voyage along the whole length of the Grand Union Canal, Main Line, would involve the negotiation of 169 locks.

The longest inland waterway in Scotland, apart from the 62 mile navigable portion of the River Forth from the Isle of May to Stirling, is the Caledonian Canal which runs from Clachnaharry to Corpach, a total navigable length of 60 miles in which there are 29 locks.

The longest inland waterway in Northern Ireland is the Loch Erne Navigation from Belturbet to Belleek, a distance of 52 miles.

LARGEST LOCKS

The largest lock on any canal system in the United Kingdom is the Eastham Large Lock on the Manchester Ship Canal. It can handle craft up to 600 feet long and 80 feet beam.

The longest flight of locks in the United Kingdom is at Tardebigge where a flight of 30 consecutive locks raises the canal level 217 feet. The 2½ mile long Tardebigge flight is on the Worcester and Birmingham Canal.

CANAL TUNNEL

The longest canal tunnel in the United Kingdom is the Standedge Tunnel on the Huddersfield Narrow Canal. It is 5,415 yards long. The Huddersfield Narrow Canal is also the highest in the United Kingdom reaching a height at one point of 638 feet above sea level.

LONGEST AQUEDUCT

The longest aqueduct in the United Kingdom is the Pont Cysyllte, on the Frankton to Llantisilio branch of the Shropshire Union Canal. It is 1,007 feet long and crosses the Valley of the Dee. Constructed by Telford, it was opened for use in 1803.

LARGEST DRY DOCK

The largest floating dock in the world is the King George V Dock at Southampton. It has a total length on the floor of 960 feet and a clear available width of 130 feet 8 inches. The dock itself weighs 18,990 tons and its total lifting capacity is 60,000 tons.

WORLD'S LONGEST TUNNEL

The world's longest continuous tunnel is the London Transport Executive underground railway line from Morden to East Finchley, via Bank. It is 17 miles 528 yards long and the diameter of the tunnel is 12 feet and the station tunnels 21 feet $2\frac{1}{2}$ inches.

The world's longest main-line tunnel is the Simplon Tunnel, completed after eleven years' work in 1906. Linking Switzerland and Italy under the Alps, it is 12 miles 559 yards long.

The longest road tunnel in the world is the Mersey Tunnel, joining Liverpool and Birkenhead—2·13 miles long, including branch tunnels 2·87 miles. Work was begun in December 1925 and it was opened by H.M. King George V in July 1934. The total cost was £$7\frac{3}{4}$ million. The 36-feet wide roadway carries nearly $7\frac{1}{2}$ million vehicles a year.

LIGHTHOUSES

The most powerful lighthouses in the world are Belle Île (Anse de Goulphar) and Gatteville (Pointe de Barfleur) lighthouses on the French coast. Each has an intensity of 20 million candlepower.

The light with the greatest visible range is an air light in Heda, Japan. Placed at an altitude of 3,251 feet and with a candlepower of 1·6 million it can be seen for 65 miles.

The brightest lighthouse in England is the St. Catherine's Light, Isle of Wight, at 5,250,000 candlepower.

The brightest in Scotland is Isle of May Lighthouse, 1,250,000 candlepower and in Ireland the Aranmore light on Aran Island, Donegal —3,000,000 candlepower.

The tallest lighthouse in the United Kingdom is the Bishop Rock, 146 feet high.

Remotest

The most remote Trinity House lighthouse is the Smalls, approximately sixteen nautical miles off the Pembrokeshire Coast. The most remote Scottish lighthouse is Sule Skerry thirty miles off shore. The most remote Irish light is Blackrock nine miles off the Mayo coast.

WINDMILLS

The earliest recorded windmills are those used for corn grinding in Persia in the seventh century A.D. The earliest in England was the twelfth century Post-mill at Bury St. Edmunds, Suffolk, but the oldest mill still complete is the Bourn Mill, Cambridgeshire, dated 1636.

The largest conventional windmill in England is the disused one at Sutton, Norfolk, while the largest working mill is at Sibsey, Lancashire. Of modern steel erections for the harnessing of wind-power the most powerful ever constructed was Putman's 1,250 kilowatt plant in Vermont, U.S.A., in 1941. Of those in Britain the most powerful is the experimental windmill at St. Albans, Hertfordshire, built in 1953, which is 140-feet high to the tip of its $4\frac{1}{4}$ ton propeller and has an output of 100 kilowatts in a 30 m.p.h. wind.

ZOO

EARLIEST

Egyptian tomb inscriptions indicate that animals, other than domestic animals, were kept in captivity as early as 2,000 B.C. but the earliest zoo of which there is definite evidence is one in China dated c.1100 B.C.

The earliest zoo in the United Kingdom was that founded by Henry I (1100–1135) at Woodstock, Oxfordshire.

LARGEST

The collection of the Zoological Society of London, the oldest privately owned zoo in the world, was founded in 1828. Its collection, housed partly in Regent's Park, London (36 acres), and partly at Whipsnade, Bedfordshire (600 acres), is the most comprehensive in the world. The 1955 census showed there were 3,372 animals, birds and reptiles being housed and 2,782 fish in the aquarium. The record attendances are over 3,000,000 in 1950 for Regent's Park and 593,075 in 1954 for Whipsnade.

AQUARIA

LARGEST

The world's largest aquarium is the John G. Shedd Aquarium, 12th Street in Grant Park, Lake Michigan, U.S.A. completed in November 1929 at a cost of $3¼ million (£1,162,000). The total capacity of its display tanks is 450,000 gallons with reservoir tanks holding 2,000,000 gallons. 10,000 specimens of 250 species are housed. Salt water is brought in rail tankers from Key West, Florida. Record attendances are 78,658 in a day on 21st May, 1931, and 4,689,730 visitors in the single year of 1931.

OCEANARIA

EARLIEST

The world's first oceanarium is the Marine Studios, eighteen miles south of St. Augustine, Florida, opened in 1938. Up to seven million gallons of seawater is pumped daily through two major tanks, one rectangular (100 feet long by 40 feet wide by 18 feet deep) containing 450,000 gallons and one circular (233 feet in circumference and 12 feet deep) containing 400,000 gallons. The tanks are seascaped, including a seven-ton coral reef and even a ship-wreck.

LARGEST

The largest salt water tank in the world is that at the Marineland of the Pacific, Palos Verdes, Los Angeles, California, U.S.A. It is 251½ feet in circumference and 22 feet deep with a capacity of 640,000 gallons. The total capacity of the whole oceanarium is 1,190,000 gallons.

BORINGS

Man's deepest penetration into the Earth's crust is at the "A" 7-4 test oil well at Paloma Field, near Bakersville, California, U.S.A. Boring for 737 days an Ohio Oil Company drilling crew reached 21,482 feet (4 miles 362 feet) on 30th October, 1953. The bottom-hole temperature at 20,000 feet was 334°F. (167·7°C.). The drilling was carried out with 4½ inch drilling pipe from a 178 feet high derrick. The core barrel stuck and the project was abandoned on 31st December, 1954. See Plate 6.

The deepest oil well in the United Kingdom is the Duke's Wood No. 146 well at Eakring, Nottinghamshire, at 7,476 feet.

MINES

The world's deepest mine is the Ooregum section of the Champion Reef gold mine in the Kolar Gold Field, Mysore State, India, where the Auxiliary Main Winze is 9,811 feet below the surface.

The deepest mine in the British Isles is in England in the Crombouke Seam, Bradford Colliery, at 3,550 feet. The deepest in Scotland is the Barncraig Seam at Michael Colliery, East Fife, at

3,198 feet. The deepest in Wales is the Six Feet Seam at Duffryn Rhondda Colliery, Glamorganshire, at 3,000 feet. The deepest shaft in Britain is No. 2 shaft Hem Heath Colliery at 3,408 feet.

Note.—Owing to the oblateness of the Earth, the Ooregum miners cannot claim to have set the record for the closeness to the earth's centre. This distinction was achieved on 6th April, 1909, by the polar explorers Robert E. Peary, Matthew Henson, and the Eskimos Ooqueah, Ootah, Egingwah and Seegloo when they reached the North Pole which is 70,488 feet nearer the Earth's centre than sea-level points on the equator and is nearly 9,000 feet nearer than the South Pole which is on the Antarctic plateau.

LARGEST GOLD MINE

The largest gold mining area in the world is the Witwatersrand gold field near Johannesburg, South Africa. At one time it produced more than half the world's gold, and employed over 180,000 miners. Its gold-bearing reefs extend over a distance of 60 miles.

The largest goldmine in Britain is that in Merionethshire, Wales, where gold was discovered in 1834.

QUARRIES

The world's largest man-made excavation is the Kimberley Open Mine in South Africa dug over the period of forty-three years (1871 to 1914) to a depth of nearly 4,000 feet and with a diameter of about 1,500 feet and a circumference of nearly a mile, covering an area of thirty-eight acres. About three tons of diamonds were extracted from the 25 million tons of earth dug out.

The largest quarry in Britain is Imperial Chemical Industries Ltd.'s Tunstead Quarry, near Buxton, Derbyshire, the working face of which is 1½ miles in length and 120 feet high.

WATER WELLS

The world's deepest water well is that in the Blackall Ranges in Queensland, Australia, at just over 7,000 feet deep. The deepest well in the British Isles is a water table well in the Staffordshire coal measures at Smestow at 2,842 feet.

The deepest artesian well in Britain is that at the White Heather Laundry, Stonebridge Park, Willesden, London, N.W.10, bored in 1911 to a depth of 2,225 feet.

LONGEST FENCE

The longest fence in the world will be the dingo-proof fence enclosing the main sheep areas of Queensland, Australia. The wire netting fence, to be completed in about two years, will be six feet high and stretch for 3,437 miles.

LARGEST DOOR

Because of the difficulty of definition there does not appear to be a world record for doors, our researches, however, indicate the following as being the two largest in the world.

The largest doors in the United States are those made for the U.S. Navy dirigible hangar, 250 feet wide and 120 feet high.

The largest doors in the United Kingdom are those to the Britannia Assembly Hall at Filton, Bristol. The doors are 1,045 feet in length and 67 feet high, divided into three bays of 345 feet long.

LARGEST WINDOW

The largest plate glass window ever made was one 50 feet long by 8 feet high exhibited at the Festival of Britain, South Bank, London, in 1951. This was made by Pilkington Bros. Ltd. at St. Helens, Lancashire, but was later cut up.

LONGEST STAIRS

The world's longest stairs are at the Aura power station, Western Norway. Built of wood in 1952, these are 3,462 feet in length rising in 3,715 steps at an angle of 45 degrees to a total height of 2,450 feet.

LONGEST LADDERS

The longest pole ladders manufactured are those of 77 rungs, 53 feet 4 inches in length. Steel backed sliding ladders, however, are made to extend to a length of 70 feet. The highest fire brigade ladder in Britain is a turntable with a 120 feet extension operated by the Hull Fire Brigade.

LARGEST MARQUEE

The largest marquee in the world is one made by Piggott Brothers in 1951 and used by the Royal Horticultural Society at their annual show in the grounds of the Royal Hospital, Chelsea. The marquee is 310 feet long × 480 feet wide, and consists of 18¾ miles of 36 inch wide canvas.

LONGEST CURTAIN

The world's largest curtain is that covering Jan Styka's painting "The Crucifixion" at Forest Lawn Memorial-Park, Glendale, Calif. It is of velvet, 195 feet wide, 45 feet long and weighs 1·56 tons.

LARGEST CHANDELIERS

The largest chandeliers in the world are those in the central Lecture Hall of the University of Moscow. Each of the eight has six tiers of lights and weighs 2½ tons. They were hung in 1953.

HIGHEST FOUNTAIN

The world's highest fountain is the Jet d'Eau de La Rade, Geneva, Switzerland. The 1,360 h.p. pump, installed in 1951, can throw the column in calm weather to a height of 426 feet. See Plate 6.

CEMETERIES

The largest cemetery in the United Kingdom is Brookwood Cemetery, Brookwood, Surrey. It is owned by the London Necropolis Co. and is approximately 500 acres in extent.

The largest crematorium in the United Kingdom is the Golders Green Crematorium, London, which has a 12 acre garden.

EIGHT

THE MECHANICAL WORLD

1. Road Vehicles

OLDEST

The oldest "horseless carriage" in the world still in running order is the Grenville Steam Carriage, designed by R. Neville Grenville of Glastonbury, and built in 1875. The three-wheeled carriage, which weighs about 45 cwt., is powered by a two-cylinder, slide-valve steam engine, bore and stroke 5 inches × 6 inches. The steam was supplied by a coal-fired upright boiler working at a pressure of 100 lb., placed between the rear wheels.

Two bench-type seats were fitted across the machine, each seating three people, the steersman sat front and centre with the brakesman on his right. One man at the rear would stoke the boiler and change gear.

The top speed of the machine was said to be 15 m.p.h. The carriage was used by its designer until well into the 1890's as a conveyance. It was then used as a stationary engine driving a cider mill in Glastonbury until the 1940's, and is now in the Bristol Museum. See Plate 7.

OLDEST I.-C. CAR

The oldest internal-combustion engined car still in running order is the Danish "Hammel". Designed by Albert Hammel, who took out the original patents in 1886, it was completed in 1887.

The engine is a twin-cylinder, horizontal water-cooled four-stroke with a capacity of 2,720 cc., bore and stroke 104·5 × 160 mm. and a compression ratio of 3·5 : 1. The inlet valve gear is automatic, exhaust by push-rod. The carburettor is of the surface type and the ignition by tube burner. The engine is governed by a valve on the induction manifold and recently, on a test bed, it produced 3·5 b.h.p. at 500 r.p.m.

The transmission is by chain and sprockets, forward gear from the crankshaft and the reverse from the camshaft. No differential was fitted, a differential effect being achieved by cone clutches allowing rear wheel slip. In 1953 it completed the London-to-Brighton run in 12½ hours. See Plate 7.

FASTEST SALOON

The fastest "closed" car in the world is the Mercedes Benz 300 SL Sports Coupé produced by Daimler Benz A.G. of Stuttgart, Germany.

The 300 SL is powered by a six-cylinder engine of 2996 cc. capacity with bore and stroke 85 × 88 mm., compression ratio of 8·55 : 1, which developes 240 b.h.p. at 6000 r.p.m. The 300 SL has no carburettors but utilises a system of direct petrol injection into the cylinders by means of a special Bosch pump which ensures extremely accurate metering of fuel.

The transmission is effected through a single dry plate clutch to a 4-speed synchromesh box and maximum speed in top is c. 165 m.p.h. The all-round independent suspension is by helical springs, unequal wishbones at front and swing axles at rear.

It sells in the United Kingdom at £4,932 15s. 0d. See Plate 7.

MOST POWERFUL CAR

The most powerful standard car in the world is the Ferrari 375 Millemiglia produced by Ferrari of Modena, Italy.

An open two-seater, with an all-up weight of 2,000 lb., the Millemiglia is equipped with a twelve cylinder 4522 cc. engine arranged as a 60° V-12.

The bore and stroke ratio is oversquare (84 × 68 mm.), and the compression ratio 9 : 1, the carburation is by three quadruple choke Weber carburettors, and the transmission is through a multiple plate clutch to a 4-speed synchromesh gear box. The maximum b.h.p. of the Millemiglia is c. 340 at 7000 r.p.m. which indicates a power weight ratio around 5·9 and maximum speeds with 3·4 back axle ratio and without modifications of 1st gear 74 m.p.h., 2nd 104 m.p.h., 3rd 144 m.p.h., top gear c. 180 m.p.h.

FASTEST MOST POWERFUL

The fastest and most powerful United Kingdom built car is the " D " type Jaguar, made by Jaguar Cars Ltd. of Coventry.

The car is powered by a 6-cylinder in-line engine of 3442 cc., bore and stroke 83 × 106 mm., working at a compression ratio of 9 : 1. It developes 250 b.h.p. at 6000 r.p.m. The power unit is basically the same as the XK 120 engine with twin overhead camshafts and hemispherical combustion chambers, but with dry sump lubrication system and carburation by three double-choke Webers.

The transmission is by close ratio 4-speed synchromesh box through a hydraulically operated three plate clutch to a hypoid bevel final drive.

The suspension is by torsion bars throughout, independent wishbones in the front and trailing links at the rear. The brakes are Dunlop disc type, three pairs of pads at front, two pairs at rear, hydraulically operated. See Plate 7.

MOST POWERFUL SALOON

The most powerful saloon car in the world is the Chrysler 300 manufactured by the Chrysler Corporation, Detroit, U.S.A.

The two-door, 4-5 seater hardtop is powered by a 300 h.p. Firepower V-8 engine of 5432 cc. capacity, bore and stroke 96·7 × 92·2 mm. and a compression ratio of 8·5 : 1. The engine, which develops peak horsepower at 5,200 r.p.m., is fitted with two four-choke carburettors.

Automatic gearbox and power assisted steering are standard equipment. The " 300 ", which costs in the U.S.A. ex works $3,758 (£1,340), has been timed in the U.S. Stock Car Speed Trials Championships at 127·58 m.p.h.

MOST EXPENSIVE

The most expensive standard cars in the world are the Pegasos, manufactured in Spain by the Empresa Nacional de Autocamiones, S.A. The Pegaso, for which a wide variety of body styles is offered, is powered by a 3·2 or 2·8 litre engine. The 90° V-8 engine has twin overhead camshafts on each bank of cylinders, an oversquare bore-stroke ratio, and such refinements as sodium-cooled valves. The power developed is about 250 b.h.p. at 6,500 r.p.m.

From the single dry plate clutch the propeller shaft transmits the drive to the 5-speed constant mesh box mounted behind the rear axle. The drive then passes forward to the ZF limited slip differential. The rear axle is a modified De Dion set forward of the gearbox and differential housing. The suspension is by torsion bars throughout.

The most expensive version of the Pegaso available in the United Kingdom is the type 102 Thrill Berlinetta, 2-door aerodynamic saloon (2·8 litres). It sells at £9,800. See Plate 7.

MOST EXPENSIVE IN U.K.

The most expensive standard United Kingdom built car is the Rolls-Royce Silver Wraith chassis fitted with a four-door saloon body by James Young Ltd.

The Silver Wraith chassis is powered by a 6-cylinder in-line engine of 4,566 cc. with overhead inlet and side exhaust valves. The bore and stroke is 92 × 114 mm., compression ratio 6·4 : 1.

The transmission is by either 4-speed synchromesh box through single dry plate clutch or by 4-speed fully automatic gearbox through a fluid coupling (£99 3s. 4d. extra).

The 4-5 seater body designed for the owner-driver is fitted with all leather upholstery and refinements such as folding tables in the back seats, heater, de-misters, radio, cigar lighter, etc., are included in the total price of £7,041 19s. 2d. of which £2,071 19s. 2d. is Purchase Tax. See Plate 7.

LEAST EXPENSIVE

The least expensive car in the world in volume production is the Ford " Popular ". The four-seater, two-door Popular saloon is powered by a 4-cylinder side valve engine of 1172 cc. bore and stroke 63·5 × 92·5 mm. with a compression ratio of 6·16 : 1. The transmission is by single dry-plate clutch through a 3-speed gearbox with synchromesh on 2nd and top. The engine develops maximum horse-power, 30·1, at 4,000 r.p.m. and the car has a maximum speed of 60 m.p.h. The car retails in the United Kingdom at a basic price of £275, which, with Purchase Tax, totals £390 14s. 2d.

BIGGEST ENGINE

The Russian Zis has the largest engine capacity of any standard car in the world. A design closely based on the pre-war American Packard, it has a capacity of 5,998 cc. The engine is a straight-eight with a compression ratio of 6·85 : 1 and it develops 138 b.h.p. at 3,600 r.p.m. and has a maximum speed of 87 m.p.h.

MOST POWERFUL TRUCK

The most powerful dumper truck in the world is the Euclid LLD 50-tonner, sold by Blackwood Hodge & Co. Ltd. The LLD is powered by two 12·2 litre, 300 h.p. Cummins diesels, the total horse-power developed is 600 at 2,100 r.p.m. The transmission is by two 3-speed and reverse automatic Allison torque converters each driving one of the tandem rear axles. The net weight empty is 46 tons and maximum speed 36 m.p.h. The truck is 36 feet 5 inches long and is mounted on ten 5 feet 9 inches diameter wheels. The maximum payload is 45 tons, bringing the gross weight of vehicle and maximum load to about 92 tons, with a top laden speed of 32 m.p.h. See Plate 8.

The most powerful United Kingdom built prime mover is the Thornycroft " Mighty Antar ". It is powered by a V-8 Meteorite Mk 101 diesel engine developing 260 b.h.p. The power is transmitted through a main and auxilliary gear box providing 12 forward speeds. The maximum gross train weight is 100 tons. See Plate 7.

FASTEST TRUCK

The fastest truck in the world is the open-bodied transporter used by Daimler Benz to transport their racing cars. It is fitted with a Mercedes 300 SL sports engine and, fully laden with a car on the back has been timed at 106 m.p.h. Its cab will hold three people.

HEAVIEST LOAD

The heaviest loads ever conveyed by road in this country were four 185-ton castings made by English Steel Corporation Ltd., of Sheffield, for a vertical hydraulic press being constructed in America. They were conveyed by Messrs. Pickfords' Heavy Haulage service from Sheffield to Liverpool for eventual shipment to the United States of America. Over the 110-mile route, bridges had to be tested and some strengthened and police escorts were provided throughout the journey. It took eight men and three, sometimes four, 220 h.p. tractors three days to move each casting from the works to the docks. The immense twenty-four-wheeled trailer cost £30,000 and the total all-up weight of one casting, the trailer and tractors, was over 300 tons. See Plate 8.

2. *Railways*

FASTEST

The world rail speed record is held jointly by two French Railway electric locomotives, the CC7107 and the BB9004. On 29th and 30th March, 1955, hauling three carriages of a total weight of 100 tons, they both achieved a speed of 205·6 m.p.h. The runs took place on the 1500 volt D.C. Bordeaux-Dax line, and the top speed was maintained for nearly $1\frac{1}{4}$ miles. See Plate 9.

Both locomotives were selected from those running under ordinary service conditions but the transmission system of both was modified to raise the gear ratio to allow for higher than normal speeds.

The CC7107 weighs 106 tons and has a continuous rating at 1500 volts of 4300 h.p.

The BB9004 weighs 81 tons and has a continuous rating of 4000 h.p.

STEAM

The world's speed record for steam locomotives is held by the L.N.E.R. 4-6-2 Mallard, which, hauling seven coaches weighing 240 tons gross, achieved a speed of 126 m.p.h. on 3rd July, 1938. See Plate 8.

FASTEST REGULAR RUN

The fastest regular run is the " Twin Zephyrs " diesel traction train which runs from East Dubuque to Prairie du Chien, U.S.A., at an average speed of 86·2 m.p.h. over the 54·6 mile journey.

Fastest electric traction run is the French National Railways' " Mistral " from Paris to Lyons, a distance of 317·4 miles at an average speed of 76·2 m.p.h.

Fastest steam traction run is the Union Pacific "Overland Limited" between North Platte and Kearney, Nebraska, covering the 95 miles in 79 minutes — 72·1 m.p.h.

LONGEST NON-STOP

The longest daily non-stop run in the world is the "Elizabethan" from King's Cross, London, to Edinburgh. It covers the 392·75 miles in 390 minutes at 60·5 m.p.h. average speed, hauling a 400-ton train of eleven coaches.

MOST POWERFUL

The world's most powerful steam locomotives, reckoned on tractive effort, are the Class M4- 2-8-8-4 loco's built by the Baldwin Locomotive Works, U.S.A., for the Duluth, Missabe & Iron Range Railroad in 1941–1943. They have a tractive force of 140,000 lb.

PERMANENT WAY

For lengths by country and square mile, see Part 5, Section 2.

The longest straight in the world is over the Nullabor Plain, Southern and Western Australia, 328 miles dead straight although not level. The longest straight on British Railways is the 18 miles between Selby and Hull, Yorks.

The longest length of unbroken four-lane track in the world is between Castleton and Dunkirk, New York, in the United States, and is 342½ miles in length.

The longest stretch of continuous four-lane track in the United Kingdom is between St. Pancras, London, and Glendon North Junction, Northamptonshire, and is 75 miles in length.

The longest stretch between consecutive stations open for passenger traffic on British Railways is between York and Malton — 21 miles.

WIDEST GAUGE

Widest gauge in standard use is 5 feet 6 inches. This width is used in India, Pakistan, Ceylon, Spain, Portugal, Argentina and Chile.

HIGHEST ALTITUDE

The highest altitude standard track in the world is on the Peruvian Central Railways at La Cima, where the track rises to 15,806 feet.

The altitude record for non-standard track is also in South America at Montt, on the Collahausi branch of the Antofagasta and Bolivian Railway. It reaches a height of 15,809 feet.

The highest point on the British Railways system is on the Perth-Inverness main line at Druimauchdar with a height of 1,484 feet above sea level.

The highest British railway, non-standard 2 feet 7½ inches gauge, is the Snowdon Mountain Railway which rises to just below the mountain summit, 3,493 feet above sea level.

The lowest point on British Railways is in the Severn Tunnel — 144 feet below sea level.

STEEPEST GRADIENTS

The world's steepest standard gauge gradient by adhesion is 1 : 11. This figure is achieved by the Guatemalan State Electric Railway — between River Samala Bridge and Zunil.

This gradient is matched by the 1 metre gauge Chamonix line of the South-East Region of French National Railways between Chedde and Servoz.

The steepest sustained adhesion-worked gradient on a main line in the United Kingdom is the two-mile Lickey incline at 1 : 37·7 in Warwickshire.

The steepest rack and pinion railway in the world is 1 : 2 on the Pilatus Mountain Railway, Switzerland.

The steepest funicular (cable drawn by stationary engine) railway in the world is between Piotta and Piora, Lake Ritom, Switzerland, with a maximum gradient of 1 : $1\frac{1}{8}$ or 88 per cent.

BUSIEST JUNCTION

The world's busiest railway junction is Clapham Junction on the Southern Region of British Railways with over 2,500 trains every 24 hours.

LONGEST VIADUCT BRIDGE

The longest railway viaduct or bridge in the world is largely a matter of definition. The following are the longest in their various types.

The Great Salt Lake Viaduct is a pile trestle bridge nearly twelve miles long. It carries the tracks of the Southern Pacific Railroad across the Great Salt Lake in Utah.

The Huey P. Long bridge, Louisiana, 23,235 feet long (4·4 miles) including approach roads, has spans each 262 feet 6 inches in length.

Longest bridge in British Railway system is the Tay Bridge, joining Fife and Angus. It is 11,653 feet (2·2 miles) long and bridges 10,289 feet of waterway.

The highest standard gauge viaduct in the world is at Fades, in the Puy de Dome, between Clermont Ferrand and Mont Lucon. It is a 472 feet span, 435 feet above the river.

TUNNELS

The longest main line railway tunnel in the world is the Simplon between Switzerland and Italy — 12 miles 559 yards long.

The longest in the British Railways system is the Severn Tunnel. It is 4 miles 628 yards long and links Gloucester to Monmouthshire.

The longest tunnel in the world in an underground railway system is on the Northern Line of the London Transport Executive between Morden and East Finchley — a total length of 17 miles 528 yards.

STATIONS

The world's biggest railway station is the Grand Central Terminal New York. It covers 48 acres on two levels with 41 tracks on the upper level and 26 on the lower.

The largest railway station in extent on the British Railways system is Clapham Junction, London, covering $27\frac{3}{4}$ acres. The station with the largest number of platforms is Waterloo, London, with 21 main line and two Waterloo and City Line platforms. It covers an area of $24\frac{1}{2}$ acres.

The smallest passenger station is Blackwell Mill, Derbyshire, part of the former L.M.S. system.

The highest station in the world on standard gauge railways is Ticlio, at 15,610 feet, on the Peruvian National Railways.

The place farthest from a railway station in England is Lynton in North Devon. It is 18 miles from Barnstaple station.

PLATFORM

The longest platform in the world is at Sonepur on the North-Eastern Railway of India and is 2,415 feet long.

The longest platform in the British Railways system is at Victoria and Exchange Station, Manchester, at 2,194 feet in length.

LONGEST RAILWAY JOURNEY

The longest railway journey in the world, continuous and without more than three or four hours wait at connections, is from Paris to Pyongyang in Korea. The route passes through seven countries, France, Belgium, Germany, Poland, U.S.S.R., Manchuria and Korea, and is more than 9,000 miles. Thomas Cook & Son Ltd. can provide a ticket which, based on the official exchange rates now prevailing, costs £194 for a single journey. This includes sleepers where available,

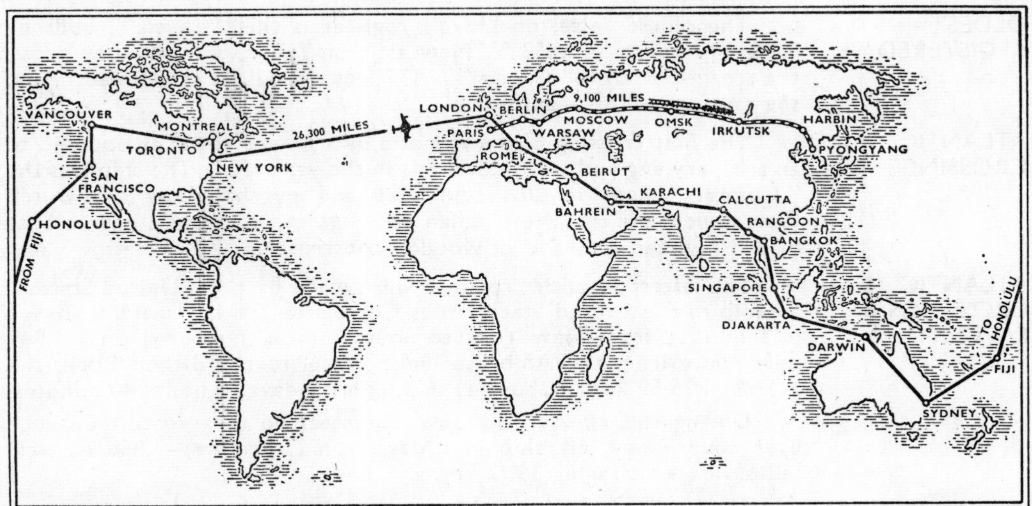

but no meals. The journey would last 12 days and pass through Liege, Cologne, Berlin, Warsaw, Smolensk and Moscow. After Moscow, the Trans-Siberian Railway passes through Kazan, Omsk, Otpor, Sin-chu to Pyongyang.

The longest railway journey in the United Kingdom is from Penzance in Cornwall to Wick, North Scotland. The route passes through Exeter, Bristol, Hereford, Shrewsbury, Crewe, Wigan, Carlisle, Glasgow, Stirling, Perth and Inverness on this 920-mile journey. The fare is 134s. 2d. for a third class single.

3. *Ships*

EARLIEST

The earliest known references to sea-going vessels are dated approximately 2,000-3,500 B.C. and are of Egyptian origin. Propelled by oars and a square-rigged sail, they were used for trading in the Mediterranean.

EARLIEST POWER

Generally accepted as the earliest mechanically propelled vessel was a boat designed by James Rumsey in the United States in 1786. Working on a jet principle driven by a pump, it reached about four miles an hour.

The "Charlotte Dundas" was the first really successful power-driven vessel. She was a paddle-steamer built by Symington in Scotland in 1801-2.

The earliest regular steam run is reputed to be by the " Phoenix " which maintained a service from New Jersey to Philadelphia in 1809.

EARLIEST TURBINE

The first turbine ship was the " Turbinia " built in 1894 to the design of the Hon. Charles Parsons. The " Turbinia " was 100 feet long and of 44½ tons displacement with machinery consisting of three steam turbines totalling about 2,000 shaft horse-power. At the first demonstration of the vessel, she reached a speed of over 32 knots.

OLDEST REGISTERED

The oldest vessel on Lloyd's register is the " Galicia ", built by T. & W. Smith in 1853 at Newcastle-on-Tyne. Of 279 tons gross, the steam-powered " Galicia " is 137 feet overall, 21 feet breadth, and she sails under the Spanish flag.

ATLANTIC CROSSINGS

The first crossing of the Atlantic by a power vessel as opposed to an auxiliary engined sailing ship was in the year 1827. The ship was the " Curacao " built in Dover in 1826 and purchased by the Dutch Government for the West Indian mail service. She was a paddle boat of 438 register tons and of wooden construction.

ATLANTIC CROSSINGS FASTEST

The fastest Atlantic crossings were made by the " United States " flagship of the United States Lines Company. On her maiden voyage in July 1952 from New York to Southampton, measured on a 2,949 mile route from the Ambrose Light Vessel to the Bishop Rock, she averaged 35·59 knots, about 41 m.p.h., for 3 days 10 hours 40 minutes.

During this run, on 6th July, she steamed the greatest distance ever covered by any ship in a day's run (24 hours) — 868 nautical miles, hence averaging 36·17 knots.

The greatest distance ever covered by a sailing ship in one day was the 465 mile run of the clipper " Champion of the Seas ". Commanded by Capt. Newlands, she was on her maiden voyage from Liverpool to Melbourne and made her record run in the South Indian ocean on the 12th December, 1854.

The fastest crossing of the Atlantic by a British ship is 3 days 20 hours 42 minutes by the Cunarder " Queen Mary " on 10th-14th August, 1938. On a 2,938 mile route from the Ambrose Light Vessel to Bishop Rock, she averaged 31·69 knots.

NORTHERNMOST

The farthest north ever reached by a ship is 83° 11′ N. at 49° 3′ E. by the Russian ice-breaker " Feodo Litke " on 12th September, 1955.

PASSENGER LINER LARGEST

The " Queen Elizabeth ", of the Cunard fleet, is the largest passenger vessel in the world and also has the largest displacement of any ship in the world, with a gross tonnage of 83,673. She has an overall length of 1,031 feet, and is 118 feet 7 inches in breadth. She is powered by steam turbines which develop about 200,000 h.p. The " Queen Elizabeth's " normal sea speed is about 28½ knots.

LARGEST TANKER

The largest tanker in the world is the " Al-Malik Saud Al-Awal " of 28,738 gross tonnage. The tanker, launched at Hamburg in 1954, was built for the Onassis fleet, and sails under the Saudi-Arabian flag. She is a single screw steam turbine vessel and is 725 feet long, 95 feet in breadth and draws 39 feet 8½ inches and has a capacity of 47,000 tons of oil. See Plate 8.

PLATE 9

ft: The BB9004 French Nat. Railways, joint record holder at 205·6 m.p.h. (Page 114)
ght: The Ransomes & Rapier W.1400, largest dragline excavator in the world. (Page 126)
The Marion Power Shovel, largest land vehicle weighing 2,200 tons. (Page 126)
Noble & Lund Lathe, a turbine gear blank being lowered into position. (Page 126)
Left: The Olsen Clock, containing the world's slowest mechanism. (Page 128)
Right: The Craven Boring Mill, the largest machine of its type. (Page 125)

PLATE 10

Above: *The English Electric 11 ft. diameter straight flow* (Page 127)

Top Left: *The Wyman-Gordon 35,000 ton press.* (Page 1.

Below: *Colonel Charles Yeager (1,650 m.p.h.) and Major Murray (90,000 ft.).* (Pages 55 and 144)

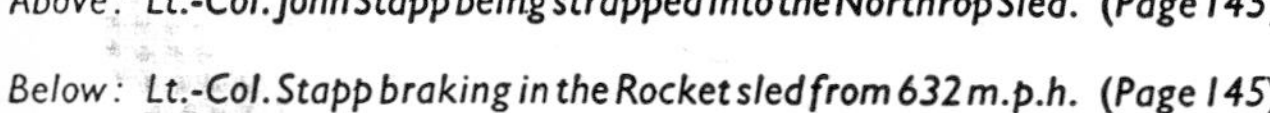

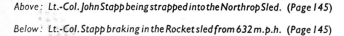

Above: *Lt.-Col. John Stapp being strapped into the Northrop Sled.* (Page 145)

Below: *Lt.-Col. Stapp braking in the Rocket sled from 632 m.p.h.* (Page 145)

QUEEN ELIZABETH
H.M.S. VANGUARD
H.M.S. ARK ROYAL
MUSASHI
U.S.S. FORRESTAL
FRANCE II

Scale 1 : 2900

WHALING FACTORY SHIP

The largest whaling factory ship in the world is the "Juan Peron" of 30,000 tons gross. It was built for the Argentine Mercantile Marine at Harland and Wolff's, Belfast, and completed in 1951.

MOST FUNNELS

The ship with the greatest number of funnels was the "Leviathan" built in New York in the 19th century. The "Leviathan" had a cigar-shaped hull 700 feet in length and was equipped with sixteen engines and thirty-two funnels. Designed to exceed 30 knots, it only reached 4 on trials and the project was eventually abandoned.

LARGEST ANCHOR

The largest anchors in the world are those designed for the 57,000 tons U.S. aircraft carrier "Forrestal". The anchors, which are of the stockless type, are approximately 14 feet overall and weigh 30 tons each. The "Forrestal" has been equipped with two.

HEAVY LOADS

Heaviest single items ever carried by sea were probably a consignment of three large lighters shipped from Rotterdam to India in 1931. Each lighter weighed 190 tons and the three were carried as deck cargo by the M.S. "Belpareil", a vessel in the Belships fleet, who specialised in the transport of heavy loads. See Plate 8.

SAILING SHIPS

LARGEST

The largest sailing vessel ever built was the "France II" launched at Bordeaux in 1911. The "France II" was a steel-hulled, five-masted barque (square-rigged on four masts and fore and aft rigged on the aftermost mast). She had a tonnage of 5,806 gross and her hull measured 368 feet overall. Although principally designed as a sailing vessel with a stump topgallant rig, she was also fitted with two steam engines.

The largest "fully rigged" sailing ship (square-rigged on all masts) ever built was the steel-hulled German "Preussen" launched at Geestemund in 1902. She was 408 feet in length and of 5,081 tons gross.

On each of her five masts, she carried six yards and could set 47 sails with a total area of about 50,000 square feet. She had more than 19 miles of running rigging and about 6½ miles of standing rigging.

The largest schooner (fore and aft rigged on all masts) ever designed was the "Thomas W. Lawson" built in 1902 in Massachusetts, U.S.A. She was 385 feet overall and 5,218 tons gross and constructed of steel. Her rig was unique; she was the only vessel ever to have seven masts and set seven similar fore and aft sails.

4. *Aircraft*

AIRCRAFT

(For Military Aircraft see under Military & Defence).

LARGEST

The largest British aircraft ever constructed was the Bristol Brabazon I with a wingspan of 230 feet, a length of 177 feet and a height of 50 feet and an all-up weight of 150 tons. It was powered by eight Centaurus engines, developing 20,000 h.p. Its total wing area was 5,317 square feet and its first flight trials took place on 4th September, 1949.

The largest aircraft ever constructed was the Hughes "Hercules" flying boat, which was raised a few feet into the air in a test run in Los Angeles Harbour, Calif., U.S.A., in November, 1947. The eight-engined, 190 ton aircraft has a wing span of 320 feet, and a length of 219 feet. It has never again flown.

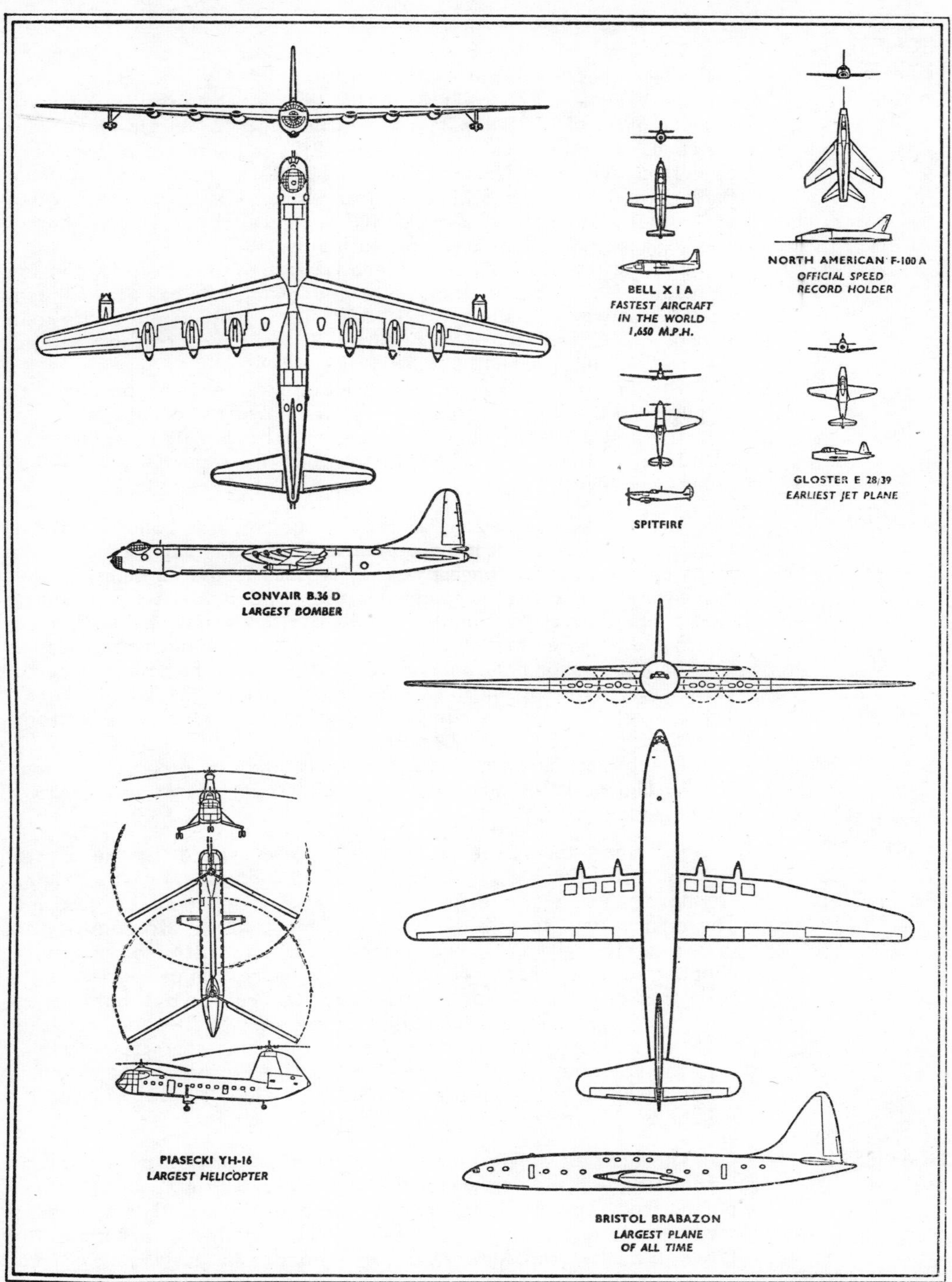
CONVAIR B.36 D
LARGEST BOMBER
BELL X I A
FASTEST AIRCRAFT
IN THE WORLD
1,650 M.P.H.
NORTH AMERICAN F-100 A
OFFICIAL SPEED
RECORD HOLDER
SPITFIRE
GLOSTER E 28/39
EARLIEST JET PLANE
PIASECKI YH-16
LARGEST HELICOPTER
BRISTOL BRABAZON
LARGEST PLANE
OF ALL TIME

Scale 1:955

FASTEST, HIGHEST FLYING

See under Military Aircraft.

EARLIEST FLIGHTS

The first controlled power-driven flight occurred at 10.30 a.m. on 17th December, 1903, near Kill Devil Sand Hill, North Carolina, when Orville Wright (1871-1948) flew the 12 h.p. chain-driven "Flyer" at an airspeed of 30-35 m.p.h. at an altitude of 8-12 feet for 12 seconds, watched by his brother Wilbur (1867-1912) and a crowd of five. The earliest cross-English Channel flight was achieved from 4.35 a.m. from Barraques, France, to 5.12 a.m. near Dover Castle, England, when Louis Blériot flew his "Blériot XI", powered by a 23 h.p. Anzani engine, across in 37 minutes on 25th July, 1909.

The earliest trans-Atlantic flight was achieved from 5.13 p.m. on 14th June, 1919, from St. John's, Newfoundland, to a bay near Clifden, County Galway, Ireland, at 9.25 a.m. 15th June when Capt. John Alcock, D.S.C. and Lt. Arthur Whitten Brown flew across in a Vickers "Vimy" at times only 10 feet above the waves.

The first true jet flight was achieved in Germany on the 27th August, 1939, when the Heinkel 178 was flown a short distance.

The first British jet flight occurred on 7th April, 1941, at Gloster's aerodrome, when P. E. G. Sayer, O.B.E., flew the Gloster E28/39 (wing span 29 feet, length 25 feet 3 inches, height 9 feet 3 inches).

AIRPORT

The largest international airport in the world is London Airport, Hounslow, Middlesex. It covers an area of 2,874 acres (roughly 2½ miles by 2 miles). Its longest runway is 9,504 feet (1·79 miles) long.

Twenty-eight airline companies use London Airport and during 1954 there were a total number of 79,649 aircraft movements, handled by the estimated 14,000 staff employed by the various companies and the Ministry of Transport and Civil Aviation. The total number of passengers, both incoming and outgoing during 1954 was 1,724,139. The longest civil airport runway in the world is at Tucson, Arizona, U.S.A., and is 11,500 feet (2.18 miles) long.

The busiest airport in the world is Midway Airport, Chicago, U.S.A. During 1954 Midway handled 348,909 aeroplanes and 7,935,879 passengers.

MOST POWERFUL JET ENGINE

The most powerful jet engine in the world is the Bristol Olympus 101 turbojet. The Olympus 101 is based on the original Olympus which was the first "twin spool" engine to be designed. The term "twin spool" defines a system in which two compressors in series are driven by two separate turbines with no mechanical coupling between them. The first, low pressure, compressor feeds the high pressure compressor so that each can run at optimum speed. This design gives greatly increased power at high altitudes together with lower fuel consumption and easier handling characteristics.

The Olympus 101 — 13 feet 1 inch long, 40 inches in diameter and weighing 3,650 lb. — develops a thrust of 11,000 lb. with a specific weight of ·302 lb. for each pound of thrust. See Plate 8.

HEAVIEST LOAD

The heaviest single piece of freight ever handled by air was an automatic mesh welder weighing 6,500 kilos (6 tons 7½ cwts.) transported from Zurich, Switzerland, to London Airport. The equipment measured 15 feet 6 inches × 5 feet 6 inches × 4 feet 8 inches and was flown in a chartered Airwork DC 4 Skymaster in May 1955.

LONGEST JOURNEY

The longest bookable journey by air, London to London, by the quickest standard route around the world, would cost £547 4s. 0d. and take four days. Leaving London, the route passes through Rome, Beirut, Bahrein, Karachi, Calcutta, Rangoon, Bangkok, Singapore, Djarkarta, Darwin, Sydney, Nandi (Fiji), Canton Is., Honolulu, San Francisco, Vancouver, Calgary, Regina, Winnipeg, Toronto, Montreal, New York and London. See Chart page 117.

The fastest round-the-world flight on commercial airlines is 107 hours 20 minutes, eastwards from San Francisco by Susan Bryan in August 1955.

5. *Power Producers*

WINDMILLS

The earliest recorded use of wind power was for grinding corn in Persia about the 7th century A.D. The earliest known English example is a 12th century corn-grinding post mill at Bury St. Edmunds, Suffolk. The largest conventional type mill still working is at Sibsey, Lancashire.

The largest " depression " type wind-driven generator ever built in the United Kingdom is the Enfield 100 kW anemo-electric plant designed for the British Electricity Authority and made by Enfield Cables Ltd., in collaboration with De Havilland Propellers Ltd., to test the possibilities of large-scale operation of wind-driven generators.

The unit, which is 100 feet high from the foundations to the axis of the propeller, weighs 40·5 tons. The propeller consists of two hollow blades with automatic hydraulically controlled pitch with a swept diameter of 80 feet.

The air passages in the hollow bladed propellers are connected through the propeller boss to the main tower of the unit. When the propeller revolves, the air inside the blades is ejected by centrifugal force—thus creating a partial vacuum in the tower and an updraught. It is this updraught which is used to rotate a vertically arranged axial flow turbine of 48 inches diameter. The generator is a 100 kW, 415 volt, and reaches maximum output at 1,000 r.p.m., at wind speed of 30 m.p.h.

In the U.S.A. in Vermont in 1941, a wind-driven generator of this type was built to produce 1,250 kilowatt but a mechanical failure on test occurred and the project was abandoned.

BIGGEST BOILER

The biggest single boiler ever designed in the world is at present under construction by Babcock and Wilcox at the River Rouge plant of the Detroit Edison Company in U.S.A.

More than 150 feet high, it will have an evaporative capacity of 1,720,000 pounds of steam per hour and deliver steam to the turbine at 2,000 pounds per square inch.

The main pressure drum of the boiler is 82 feet long and the thickness of its steel walls is nearly 6 inches. Of welded construction, it weighs 193 tons.

The boiler will supply steam to a turbine producing 273,000 kW.

BIGGEST BOILER United Kingdom

The largest single boiler unit in the United Kingdom is the Babcock & Wilcox plant completed in 1955 for the Castle Donnington Power Station. The boiler is of the radiant type and supplies power to a turbine unit of 100,000 kW.

Fired by pulverised fuel the boiler has a maximum continuous rating of 830,000 lb. of steam per hour. The final steam temperature is 1,060°F. (571·1°C.) at a superheater outlet pressure of 1,600 lb. per square inch.

POWER PLANT LARGEST

The largest concentration of electric generating plant on any one site in the United Kingdom is at Barking, where the three power stations in the London Generation Division of the Central Electricity Authority have a total installed capacity of 747,250 kW or approximately one million h.p.

The largest power station under one roof in the United Kingdom is the Battersea Power Station, also in the London Generation Division, which has an installed capacity of 511,700 kW, nearly 800,000 h.p.

The largest hydro-electric plant in the United Kingdom is the Loch Sloy Power Station of the North of Scotland Hydro-electric Board. The installed capacity of this station is 130,450 kW or 175,000 h.p.

GENERATOR LARGEST

The largest generator in the world is being built by Allis-Chalmers Manufacturing Co. for the River Rouge plant of the Detroit Edison Co.

The unit will have a capacity of 300,000 kW (400,000 h.p.) and is designed to be the most economical ever built. It will produce a kilowatt hour of electricity (one unit) for less than three-quarters of a pound of coal.

The cross-compound turbine is designed for an initial pressure of 2,400 pounds per square inch and an exhaust pressure of 1 in. Hg. absolute. The initial temperature is 1050°F and reheat temperature 1,000°F and both high and intermediate pressure turbines are on the 3,600 r.p.m. shaft.

LARGEST PUMP TURBINE

The world's largest reversible pump-turbine is being made by Allis-Chalmers for the extension to the Tennessee Valley Authority's Hiawassee Dam in North Carolina, U.S.A.

The single unit is intended to operate in one direction as a pump and in the reverse direction as a turbine. A directly connected electrical machine serves as a motor for pump operation and as a generator for turbine operation. As a turbine, it will have a maximum rating of 120,000 h.p., and when used as a pump will have a rated pumping capacity of 3,900 cubic feet per second against a 205 feet head, or 3,300 million gallons a day.

LARGEST ELECTRIC MOTOR

This same electrical unit, when used as a motor, is the world's largest, rated at 102,000 h.p. at 106 revolutions per minute. As a generator it is rated at 70,000 kW, 13,800 volts.

In a normal cycle of operations, the water from the Hiawassee reservoir will drive the turbine to provide power during peak demand periods. During off-peak periods when surplus power is available from other plants, the unit will operate as a pump to lift water back to the reservoir. The operation of the unit is economically practicable because the off-peak power for pumping will cost less than the value of that produced during peak demand periods, and will also improve the load factor on the local system.

LARGEST GAS WORKS

The largest gas works in the world is the Beckton plant of the North Thames Gas Board, London. The Beckton Works, which covers 300 acres and employs 3,500 people, contains over seventy miles of standard gauge railway line on which there are fifty locomotives and 1,100 wagons.

The coal handling plant, the largest in the United Kingdom, is equipped with two deep water piers, and it can handle 2,000 tons of coal an hour or 2 million tons a year. The maximum gas-making capacity is 164 million cubic feet a day from about six thousand tons of coal.

6. *Engineering*

LARGEST MACHINE TOOLS

The largest machine tool in the world in operation is the 35,000 ton closed die forging press at the Wyman-Gordon plant in Worcester, Massachusetts, U.S.A.

The press is used mainly for producing die castings in aluminium of up to 500 lb. in weight and 10 feet 5 inches in length, principally aircraft components. It weighs 7,180 tons and the total moving weight is 4,050 tons. It stands 44 feet 8 inches above, and extends 62 feet 5 inches below the operating floor. The excavations for the machine went down 100 feet to bed rock.

The press is hydraulically operated by water pressure delivered at 4,500 pounds per square inch and during press operations pressures up to 6,000 lb. per square inch are reached. To withstand these pressures, the water lines are of forged steel with walls five inches thick. The standard die set is 20 feet by 10 feet and the stroke 6 feet.

Wyman-Gordon also have under construction a 50,000 ton press, the total weight of which will be 10,605 tons. See Plate 10.

LARGEST BORING MILL

The largest boring mill ever produced in this country was made by Craven Bros. (Manchester), Ltd. for a Canadian firm in 1953.

The mill, which weighs a total of approximately 650 tons, can accept work up to 42 feet 6 inches in diameter and up to 13 feet 4 inches in height and up to 140 tons in weight.

The main work table is 41 feet in diameter and weighs approximately 170 tons. It is driven by two 150 h.p. variable speed motors, which give it, in conjunction with a three-speed gearbox, a speed range of 0·15 to 3·5 r.p.m.

The machine is operated by 28 separate motors and generators and the electrical system includes special interlocking devices to ensure the maximum degree of safety. The main control desk (lower right in our photograph) incorporates, as well as the principal electrical switches and gear-changing controls, a tachometer, ammeter, temperature indication dial and thirteen coloured warning lights. See Plate 9.

LARGEST PLANER

The largest planing machine in the United Kingdom is the 16 feet wide heavy duty machine produced by Noble & Lund of Gateshead, Durham. Work can be accepted up to 16 feet wide, 11 feet high and 30 feet long. The main drive is by a 100 h.p. variable speed motor supplemented by two 20 h.p. motors for cross-planning and power traverse and a 10 h.p. feed motor. The cutting speeds are variable between 15 feet and a 100 feet per minute and the cross-planing between 25 feet and 50 feet per minute. Approximate weight of the planer is 230 tons.

LATHE LARGEST

The largest centre lathes produced in the United Kingdom are the 112 inches centre lathes made by Noble & Lund. They are designed mainly for turning turbine gear blanks up to 200 inches in diameter and marine crankshafts up to 30 feet long.

The main bed is 54 feet long and 20 feet wide and is made in eight sections bolted together, the headstock spindle bearings are 22 inches diameter front, and 14 inches diameter rear.

The main drive motor is 75 h.p. with an additional four 3 h.p. saddle motors and a 7½ h.p. tailstock motor. Change speed gearing is incorporated in the headstock to give four rates of speed to the spindle and this, with the speed variation of the motor, gives a total speed range of 0·33 to 18·4 r.p.m. The machine without its electrical equipment weighs 280 tons. See Plate 9.

EXCAVATOR SHOVEL

The largest stripping shovel (mechanical excavator) in the world and, as well, the biggest land vehicle in the world, is now being built for an American coal mining company for open cast working, by Marion Power Shovel Co. of the U.S.A.

The machine has been designed to remove approximately a 90 feet depth of overburden, and the bucket size is 60 cubic yards in capacity. On the machine's normal operating cycle it will be removing 100 tons of earth every 50 seconds.

The excavator, which weighs approximately 2,200 tons, is carried on eight caterpillar tracks mounted in pairs, each 8 feet high, 22 feet long and having a 54 inch tread width.

It is powered by sixteen electric motors having an available total of 4,500 h.p. Our illustration shows an example of a similar type shovel, currently the world's largest, of 50 per cent. less capacity—the Marion 5561 with a 45 cubic yard bucket. See Plate 9.

DRAGLINE

The largest dragline excavator in the world is that designed and made by Ransomes & Rapier Ltd. for Stewart & Lloyds' opencast ironstone workings at Corby, Northamptonshire. The excavator has a bucket size of 20 cubic yards with a capacity reach of 260 feet. The tubular steel boom has a length of 282 feet and the overall height is 175 feet. It is powered by two generator sets of 1,500 h.p. each and its working weight is 1,650 tons.

The two walking shoes set on eccentrically mounted legs are 48 feet long and 9 feet 6 inches wide and weigh 56 tons each; they have a " stride " of 6 feet 10½ inches. See Plate 9.

LARGEST CRUSHER

The world's largest gyratory crusher is a 56 ton Allis-Chalmers unit, crushing taconite in Minnesota. Powered by two 500 h.p. electric motors the crusher can accept pieces of rock up to 5 feet in one dimension and crush them to a maximum of nine inches in any one dimension. The rock can be handled at the rate of 3,500 tons an hour.

WEIGHING MACHINE

Construction of the world's largest weighing machine, 52 feet 9 inches high with a capacity of 669 tons per hour, was begun in The Hague in July 1955 for shipment to Australia. Britain's largest scale is one with a capacity of 300 tons per hour at Tate & Lyle's London sugar refinery.

LONGEST OIL PIPE

The longest crude oil pipe line in the world is the Interprovincial Pipe Line Company's installation from Redwater, Alberta to Sarnia, Ontario, a distance of 1,775 miles. Along the length of the pipe thirteen pumping stations maintain the flow of oil. Just after a pumping station the pressure in the pipe is between 900 and 1,000 pounds per square inch but this high pressure falls to 50 pounds per square inch before it reaches the next pump. Approximately 6·9 million gallons of oil a day are pumped along the line.

LARGEST VALVE

The largest straight-flow valves in the world are those made by the English Electric Co., Ltd., for the Castelo-do-Bode and Gabril Hydro-electric power stations in Portugal. They have a bore of 11 feet. See Plate 10.

SMALLEST TUBING

The smallest tubing in the world is made by Accles & Pollock, Ltd., of Birmingham. Produced in anticipation of an industrial demand, it is ·0017 inches—seventeen ten-thousandths of an inch outside diameter and the bore is five ten-thousandths of an inch in dimaeter. The average human hair measures twenty to thirty ten-thousandths of an inch in diameter. The tubing which is stainless has been used for the artificial insemination of queen bees and "feeding" nerves.

LARGEST INGOT

The largest steel ingot ever to be produced in the United Kingdom was cast by the English Steel Corporation of Sheffield. It weighed 275 tons and was 29 feet long and 14 feet overall diameter.

TRANSFORMER

The world's biggest transformer was made by Siemens-Schuckertwerke A.G. of Germany in 1955. The transformer is equipped with built-in cooling radiators, is nearly fifty feet long and weighs 238 tons. It is rated at 200,000 kVA and has a voltage ratio of 10·5 kV:245 kV.

HIGHEST ROPEWAY

The highest and longest aerial ropeway in the world links Chamonix and Aiguille du Midi on the French side of Mont Blanc. The ropeway is in two sections, intermediate and upper. From the intermediate station, the rope to the upper mountain station is 3,170 yards long and the negotiated height of the upper section is 4,840 feet—(higher than Ben Nevis). The main carrier rope is 1·96 inches in diameter with a breaking strain of 228 tons.

The two cars work on the pendulum system—the carrier rope is locked and the cars are hauled by means of three pull ropes powered by a 230-h.p. motor. They have a maximum capacity of forty-five persons, travel at thirty-two feet per second (nearly twenty-two m.p.h.).

FASTEST PASSENGER LIFTS

The fastest lifts in the world are those fitted in the R.C.A. Building, Rockefeller Plaza, New York. They rise a total of 795 feet at a speed of 1,400 feet per minute, or 15·9 miles per hour.

The fastest lifts in the United Kingdom are those at the Hampstead station Underground railway of the London Transport Executive. They rise at 800 feet per minute, just over nine miles per hour.

FASTEST ESCALATOR

The fastest escalators in the United Kingdom are those at the Leicester Square station Underground railway of the London Transport Executive. They have a step speed of 180 feet per minute.

The escalators with the highest rise are those fitted at the Tyne Tunnel, Newcastle. They have an overall length of 180 feet and a vertical rise of 85 feet and were the first escalators to be designed for use by people with bicycles. They were opened on 24th July, 1951.

CLOCKS

WORLD'S LARGEST

The world's biggest clock is on the Colgate-Palmolive plant in Jersey City, U.S.A. The dial is 50 feet in diameter and covers an area of 1,963 square feet. The minute hand is 27 feet 3 inches long and the hour hand 19 feet 6 inches. It was started at noon 1st December, 1924.

The largest clock in the United Kingdom is on the Singer Sewing Machine factory at Clydebank, Scotland. It has four faces, each 26 feet in diameter, and the minute hand is 12 feet 9 inches long and the hour hand 8 feet 9 inches.

MOST ACCURATE

The most accurate and complicated clock in the world is the Olsen clock installed in the Copenhagen Town Hall. The clock, which has more than 14,000 units, took ten years to make and the mechanism of the clock functions in 570,000 different ways. The celestial pole motion of the clock will take 25,700 years to complete a full circle, the slowest moving piece of mechanism in the world. See Plate 9.

OLDEST

Perhaps the oldest church clock in the United Kingdom is that in the tower of the Parish Church of St. Mary the Virgin, Rye, Sussex. The clock, which is still in working order with its original parts, was made by Lewys Billiard of Winchelsea in the year 1560. The clock mechanism has to be wound twice daily.

A weight-driven clock, of which the original working parts have been renewed, is at Wells Cathedral, Somerset, dating from c.1335.

TIME MEASURER

The most accurate mechanism for the measurement of short periods of time has been developed by Dr. C. H. Townes of Columbia University, New York, U.S.A.

Using a new principle, the design permits direct amplification of high frequency microwaves without the use of vacuum tubes. Using, for instance, the energy of the ammonia molecules, the clock can produce microwaves with frequencies to the order of 24,000,000,000 cycles per second. Two of these " masers " (abbreviation for microwave amplifier by stimulated emission of radiation) have been compared to an accuracy of one part in one hundred thousand million, which is likely to be the most accurate comparison of physical quantities yet made.

WATCHES

OLDEST

The oldest watch (portable clock-work time keeper) is that made of iron by P. Hele in Nürnberg, Germany, c.1504, now in the Memorial Hall, Philadelphia, U.S.A.

SMALLEST

The smallest watches in the world are produced by Jaeger Le Coultre of Switzerland. A fifteen jewelled movement with a jewelled-lever escapement, it measures just over half an inch long and three-sixteenths of an inch in width. The movement, with its case, weighs under a quarter of an ounce.

NINE

THE BUSINESS WORLD

1. Commerce

LARGEST MANUFACTURING CONCERNS
World

The largest manufacturing company in the world is General Motors Corporation of Detroit, Michigan. During 1953, they sold approximately $10,028 million (£3,581 million) of products. Their unit sales of cars and trucks equalled 3,760,000. Their total assets are $4,405 million (£1,527 million). Their total capital is $2,982 million (£1,066 million). Their shareholders total 494,632. Their products include Chevrolet, Oldsmobile, Buick, Cadillac and Pontiac cars and in America include heavy off-the-road vehicles, household appliances and air conditioning plants, refrigerators, diesel engine locomotives, aluminium castings, turbo-jet and turbo-prop aircraft engines. In this country they are the parent of Vauxhall Motors, Bedford Trucks and Frigidaire Refrigerators, in Germany the Opel car and in Australia the Holden car. Their average employment figure during 1953 was 576,667 men and women. In the United States alone, they employed 385,929 hourly-rate workers who earned an average of $92·27 (£32 19s. 6d.) per week for an average of 41·9 hours work per week. One of their most recent achievements was on 23rd November, 1954, when General Motors produced its fifty millionth U.S. built car since 1908.

The United Kingdom registered company with the greatest assets is the Imperial Chemical Industries, Ltd., with £523,516,725 as at 1st January, 1955.

LARGEST INSURANCE COMPANY

The largest insurance company in the world is the Metropolitan Life Insurance Company of New York, U.S.A. The company's 1954 annual report showed a total assets figure of $13,091,375,527·88 or £3,672,638,190 and unassigned assets after all future obligations are deducted of $59,968 million (£21,400 million).

The largest insurance company in the United Kingdom, is the Prudential Assurance Co., Ltd. At the beginning of 1954, their total funds, life assurance and annuity, for both ordinary and industrial branches totalled £648,686,342. The total sums assured, at the beginning of 1953, were £908·9 million for the ordinary branch and for the industrial branch £1,001·2 million. The combined total of the sums assured was £1,910,136,048. During 1953 their ordinary and industrial branch premium income, including annuity considerations, was £85,832,003 and new business assured by them totalled £198,902,856.

BUILDING SOCIETIES

The largest building society in the world is the Halifax Building Society of Halifax, Yorkshire, England. It was established in 1853 and had total assets as at 1st January, 1955, of £237,786,000. It has 1,241 employees and 118 branch offices. The oldest society in the world is the Chelmsford and Essex Society, established in July 1845.

GROCERY CHAINS

The largest grocery chain in the world is The Great Atlantic and Pacific Tea Company in the U.S.A., with over 4,500 stores, including some 400 supermarkets. They operate thirty-nine bakeries, two laundries for the uniforms of their 120,000 employees, a printing plant an alaskan fishing fleet and a monthly magazine "Woman's Day" with a circulation of three million.

Last year their net sales of the three-thousand-odd products they stock was $3,989,103,161 (£1,426,000,000) and their net earnings after taxes were $30,395,806 (£10,920,000), less than 0·77 per cent. or 0·77 cents. in the dollar (1¾d. in the £).

DEPARTMENT STORE CHAINS

The largest department store chain in the world is the United States' J. C. Penney Co. Inc. They operate stores in 1,646 communities and in every one of the forty-eight states of America. In 1954, their turnover amounted to $1,107,152,173 (£395,000,000).

DEPARTMENT STORE

The store with the largest number of sales in the world is the Gosudarstvenny Universalny Magazin (G.U.M.—State Universal Shop) in Red Square, Moscow. It was opened in 1922 and remodelled in 1953. It can accommodate 25,000 customers simultaneously and 150,000 a day with ease. Selling everything "required for stomach, body or mind" the store served thirty million customers in the last six months of 1954 who made fifty million purchases worth £178 million. The store has a sales area of 11½ acres and 1½ miles of counters.

The largest department store in the United Kingdom is Harrods, London. It has a total selling floor space of 13 acres, employs 5,200 people and has a total of nine million transactions a year.

SHOE STORE

The largest shoe store in the world is Lilley & Skinner, Ltd., 356–360 Oxford Street, London. The shop has a floor area of 70,000 square feet spread over four floors. With a total staff of more than two hundred and fifty people, it offers, in ten departments, a choice of some 200,000 pairs of shoes. Every week, on average, 24,000 people visit this store.

BOOK SHOP

The world's biggest book shop is that of Messrs. W. & G. Foyle of London. First established in 1904 in a small shop in Islington, Foyle's now maintain a stock of four million books on approximately thirty miles of shelving in their Charing Cross Road premises. The total staff is approximately six hundred people and they handle about nine million letters a year, more than four thousand every working hour. Foyle's sell more than five million books every year.

MAIL ORDER

The largest mail order house in the world is the Sears Roebuck Co. of Chicago, Illinois, U.S.A., with assets of $1,388 million (£395 million). In 1953 the total volume of sales was $2,981,925,000 (£1,067 million). The company issues seven different catalogues annually with a total circulation of over fifty million copies, listing 103,000 items.

The largest mail order house in the United Kingdom is Littlewoods of Liverpool who serve more than six million customers a year.

NEWSPRINT

The largest newsprint mills in the United Kingdom are the Kemsley Mills of the Bowater Paper Corporation near Sittingbourne in Kent. The Bowater Paper Corporation produce 60 per cent. of all the newsprint manufactured in the United Kingdom and in 1955 became the largest producers of newsprint in the world.

BREWERY

The biggest brewery in the world is Anheuser-Busch, Inc., of St. Louis, Missouri, U.S.A. In 1953 they produced 6,733,124 barrels of beer, or 1,390,455,443 United Kingdom pints, the greatest volume ever produced by a single brewery. Anheuser-Busch employ approximately eight thousand five hundred persons and in 1954 produced about seven and a half million bottles and cans of beer a day.

The largest brewery in the United Kingdom and Republic of Ireland is the Guinness Brewery at St. James's Gate, Dublin.

BRICKWORKS

The largest brickworks in the world is the London Brick Company plant at Stewartby, Bedford. The works, established in 1898, now cover 160 acres and produce over twelve million bricks every week.

ROPEWORKS

Established in 1876, the Belfast Ropework Company, Ltd., has grown to be the biggest ropeworks in the world. It now covers an area of forty acres and employs some 2,000 people. Between two hundred and three hundred tons of finished products are produced each week at their Connswater, Belfast, factory.

The longest ropewalk in the factory is 1,000 feet long and they have produced rope up to thirty-six inches in circumference.

SHIPYARD

The largest shipbuilding yards in the United Kingdom are the Harland and Wolff yards at Belfast, Northern Ireland, where more than twenty thousand people can be employed.

RESTAURATEURS

The largest restaurateurs in the United Kingdom are J. Lyons & Co., Ltd. They run a total of 250 teashops, four Corner Houses, and special restaurants and staff canteens and in them serve a yearly total of 280,000,000 meals. Some of their 30,000 staff produce 25 miles of Swiss roll every day, 12½ million pieces of chocolate and sugar confectionery every week, 7 million small cakes and buns weekly and 3 million portions of ice cream and 5 tons of bullseyes every day.

COMMERCE

The largest motor manufacturing group in the United Kingdom is the British Motor Corporation, the principal products of which are Austin, Morris, Riley, M.G., Wolseley, Austin-Healy, Nash, Nuffield Tractors, S.U. Carburettors and Vanden Plas. Some 45 per cent. of all the cars on the roads of Britain were built by members of this group. The total of employees number approximately fifty-seven thousand people. The total wage bill of the group of companies is £600,000 per week. B.M.C. as a group achieved a production of nearly ten thousand units a week in 1955.

BIGGEST EXPORTER

The biggest motor exporting factory in the world is Ford Motor Company at Dagenham, Essex. During 1954 they exported 154,503 units, cars, trucks and tractors, to 148 different countries to a total value of about £62,200,000. The Dagenham factory, the largest completely self-contained motor manufacturing unit in Europe, covers an area of 26·5 million square feet. The number employed at Dagenham is about thirty-five thousand. In 1954 they produced 297,788 units and current production is in excess of 1,500 units a day.

LARGEST SIGN

The largest advertising sign in the world is the Pepsi-Cola sign in Times Square, New York, U.S.A. It includes two five storey Pepsi-Cola bottles, 35,000 light bulbs and a 50,000 gallon a minute waterfall.

LAND VALUES

The most expensive land in the British Isles is that in the vicinity of the Bank of England, Royal Exchange and Stock Exchange in the City of London. When land in this area last changed hands, prior to 1939, it realized as much as £121 per square foot—a parcel of land almost exactly equal to the size of this book lying open. There is reason to believe that the present day sale value would be well in excess of the rate of £527,000 per acre.

DIRECTORSHIPS

The man with the greatest number of directorships listed in the "Directory of Directors" is Mr. George Maurice Wright, Chairman of Debenhams, Ltd., with sixty-seven companies. The man with the largest number of directorships of public companies with Stock Exchange quoted shares is Mr. Harold Charles Drayton with thirty companies. The film magnate Mr. J. Arthur Rank is, however, reputed to have a total of 135 directorships of all kinds which, if he attended all their annual general meetings, would entail him, in a working year, in an A.G.M. once every 15·2 normal office hours.

2. *Agriculture*

MOST AND LEAST AGRICULTURAL COUNTRIES

Agriculture and associated industries represent 57 per cent. of the domestic economy of Siam (Thailand) and Turkey—the highest proportion of any country. In the United Kingdom the same industries provide only 5 per cent. of the total national net product—the lowest of any country in the world. Over 13 per cent. of the land surface of the United Kingdom is urbanized.

FARMS

The largest farms in the world are collective farms in Russia upon which there are no data available.

The largest farms in the British Isles are Scottish hill farms in the Grampians. The largest arable farm is that of Elveden in Suffolk farmed by the Earl of Iveagh. Here 9,500 acres are farmed on an estate of 23,000 acres, the greater part of which was formerly derelict land. This farm is the size of 324 average English farms of 71 acres.

The world's largest single wheat field is probably that sown in 1951 near Lethbridge, Canada, extending over 35,000 acres.

RANCH

The world's largest ranch is the Gang Ranch, British Columbia, which is over 3,900,000 acres.

CROP YIELDS
Wheat

Crop yields for highly tended small areas are of little significance. The world record wheat yield is 70½ cwt. per acre on a 8·96 acre field in 1952 at Wiggenhall St. Mary, Norfolk, by Turrell Bros. This compares with the average United Kingdom yield of 20½ cwt. per acre—double that which obtains in North America.

FOOT AND MOUTH DISEASE

The worst recorded pandemic of foot and mouth disease, a febrile virus infection, was that centred on South Germany in 1920 where there were 181,067 affected premises and a further 37,000 in France. The earliest positive outbreak in the British Isles occurred in 1839.

The worst year in Great Britain was 1923 with 1,929 outbreaks calling for £2,208,786 in compensation for 69,256 cattle and 59,529 other animals slaughtered, and the best year was 1948 with fifteen outbreaks calling for £54,554 in compensation for 104 cattle and 589 other animals.

WORLD RECORDS MILK YIELD

The highest life-time milk yield of any cow is that given by the British Friesian " Manningford Faith Jan Graceful " owned by R. and H. Jenkinson of Oxfordshire, England. Now aged 17 years, this cow has yielded 325,130 lb. (145·14 tons) to 3rd July, 1955. See Plate 11.

The world record for one lactation (365 days) is 45,081 lb. (20·13 tons) by R. A. Pierson's British Friesian " Bridge Birch " in England in 1947.

The world record for milk yield in a day is 198 lb. by R. A. Pierson's British Friesian " Garsdon Minnie ".

BUTTER FAT

The world record butter fat yield for a life-time was set in the United States at 10,936 lb. by the Jersey cow " Silken Lady's Ruby of F " in its twenty-one years of life.

The world's record butter fat yield in a lactation is 1,799 lb. (33,184 lb. milk at 5·42 per cent.) by A. Drexler's " Zenda Bountiful " at Manor Farm, Kidlington, Oxfordshire, England, for the year ended 3rd March, 1953, sufficient to produce 2,116 lb. of butter.

The record for butter fat in one day is 6·44 lb. (57 lb. milk at 11·30 per cent.) by the Hon. Mrs. W. P. A. Bradshaw's Guernsey cow " Fillette 3rd of Les Videclins " in October 1953.

LIVESTOCK RECORDS

CATTLE

Bull

The highest price ever fetched by a bull is the $100,000 (£35,714) paid by Dr. Hammer at the International Chicago Agricultural Show in November 1950, for a Black Aberdeen, Prince Eric of Sunbeam. This price was also paid in May 1954 at Fair Oaks Ranch, Boerne, Texas, for Hillcrest Larry 25th. However, the same figure of $100,000 (£35,714) was paid in February 1955 by J. Danciger for a one-third share in the Black Angus bull " Prince 105 SAF " owned by J. V. Hampton and Simon of Decatur, Texas.

The British auction record for a bull is 14,500 guineas (£15,225) paid at Perth by Ralph L. Smith of Missouri, U.S.A., for Laidlow Smith's Shorthorn bull " Pittodrie Upright " in 1946. In January 1953 $45,000 (£16,070) was paid by American interests in a private treaty for Capt. R. S. de Quincey's Hereford bull " Vern Diamond ".

Cow

The world record price for a cow is the $40,600 (£14,500) paid by R. Pavin Davies of England, for a Shorthorn " 8th Duchess of Geneva " at the 1873 New York Mills auction.

WORLD AND BRITISH BREED RECORDS

Milking frequencies and special feeds may influence abnormal milk and butter fat output, hence uniform comparisons are unobtainable. The data below represent extreme recorded yields. W = World, B = British.

	AYRSHIRE	BRITISH FRIESIAN	DAIRY SHORTHORN	GUERNSEY	HOLSTEIN	JERSEY
MILK LIFETIME YIELD	B 206,410 lb. "Cowgrove Nora" to 1947 (James Gibson)	W and B (see above)	B 223,917 lb. "Winton Gentle 2nd" (J. R. Burge & Son)	W 194,276 lb. "Caumsett Ida" U.S.A. B 171,425 lb. "Shiwa Cherquis Doris" (R. W. Godfrey)	W 281,193 lb. "Pansco Hazel" to 1953 of Whittier, Cal., U.S.A. (F. F. Pellisser)	W 196,457 lb. "Silken Lady's Ruby of F" of California, U.S.A. B 171,846 lb. "Hockley Lila" (Mrs. Lionel Corbett)
LACTATION YIELD (Limit 365 days)	B 30,910 lb. "Nether Craig Janet", 1936 (Alexander Cochrane)	W and B 45,081 lb. (see above)	W and B 41,644 lb. "Cherry" in 1939 (Wort and Way)	W 26,672 lb. "Welcome In Forward's Clara" U.S.A. B 25,333 lb. "Hazelby Fancy" in 1948 (Capt. Cosmo Douglas)	W 42,805 lb. "Green Meadow Lily Pabst" in 1951, Michigan, U.S.A. (Merle H. Green)	W and B 24,734 lb. "Stranges Musical" in 1952 (J. R. Proctor)
YIELD in 24 HOURS	B $103\frac{1}{2}$ lb. (two milkings) "Faulkners Rosebud" May 1953 (James Alexander)	W and B 198 lb. (see above)	B $129\frac{1}{2}$ lb. "Eva" in 1930 (Mrs. Kate Hollas)	B $98\frac{1}{2}$ lb. "Hazelby Sea Fancy" 1949 (Capt. Cosmo Douglas)	W 165·1 lb. "Ravensworth Skylark Johanna" 1948, Virginia U.S.A. (Smith and Janney)	B $120\frac{3}{4}$ lb. "Moors Pacified Diana" Feb. 1950 (Prof. R. W. Wheldon)
BUTTER FAT LACTATION YIELD (Limit 365 days)	—	W and B 1,799 lb. (see above)	W 1,614 lb. "Melba 15th of Darbalara" 1923 Australia B 1,217 lb. (305 days) "Boxgrove Barbara 4th" 1954 (S. M. Roberts)	W and B 1,383·9 lb. "Fascination 3rd of the Pastures" 1954 (Sir Robert Black)	W 1,511·8 lb. "Carnation Homestead Daisy Madcap" 1953 Carnation, Wash., U.S.A.	W and B 1,476·6 lb. (361 days) (24,734 lb. milk at 5·97%) "Stranges Musical" 1952 (J. R. Proctor)
YIELD in 24 hours	—	—	—	W and B 6·44 lb. from 57 lb. milk at 11·30% (see above)	—	B 4·12 lb. from 71·8 lb. milk at 5·73% "Lady Spotted Pearl" 1930 London (R. G. W. Berkeley)

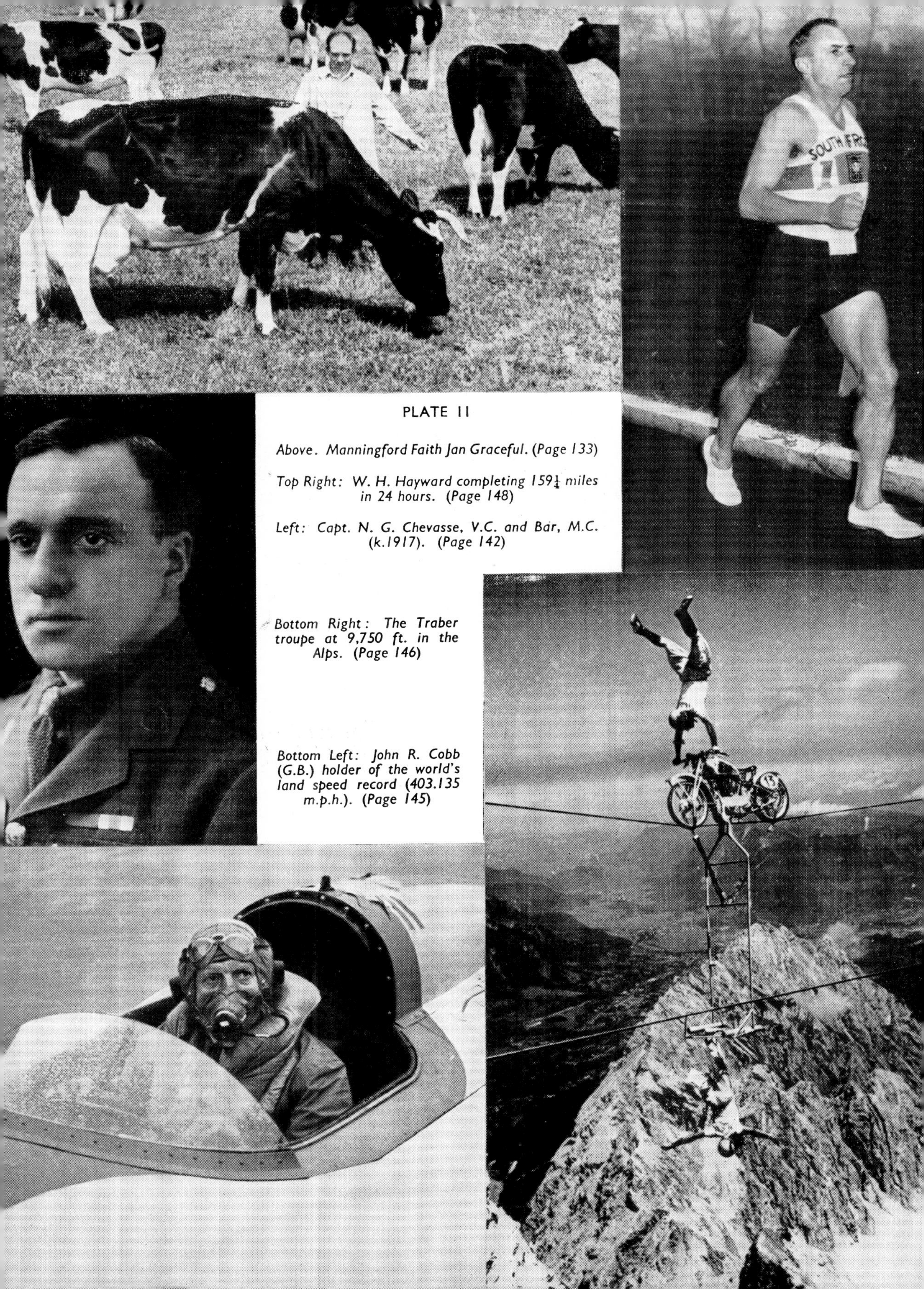

PLATE 11

Above. Manningford Faith Jan Graceful. (Page 133)

Top Right: W. H. Hayward completing 159¼ miles in 24 hours. (Page 148)

Left: Capt. N. G. Chevasse, V.C. and Bar, M.C. (k.1917). (Page 142)

Bottom Right: The Traber troupe at 9,750 ft. in the Alps. (Page 146)

Bottom Left: John R. Cobb (G.B.) holder of the world's land speed record (403.135 m.p.h.). (Page 145)

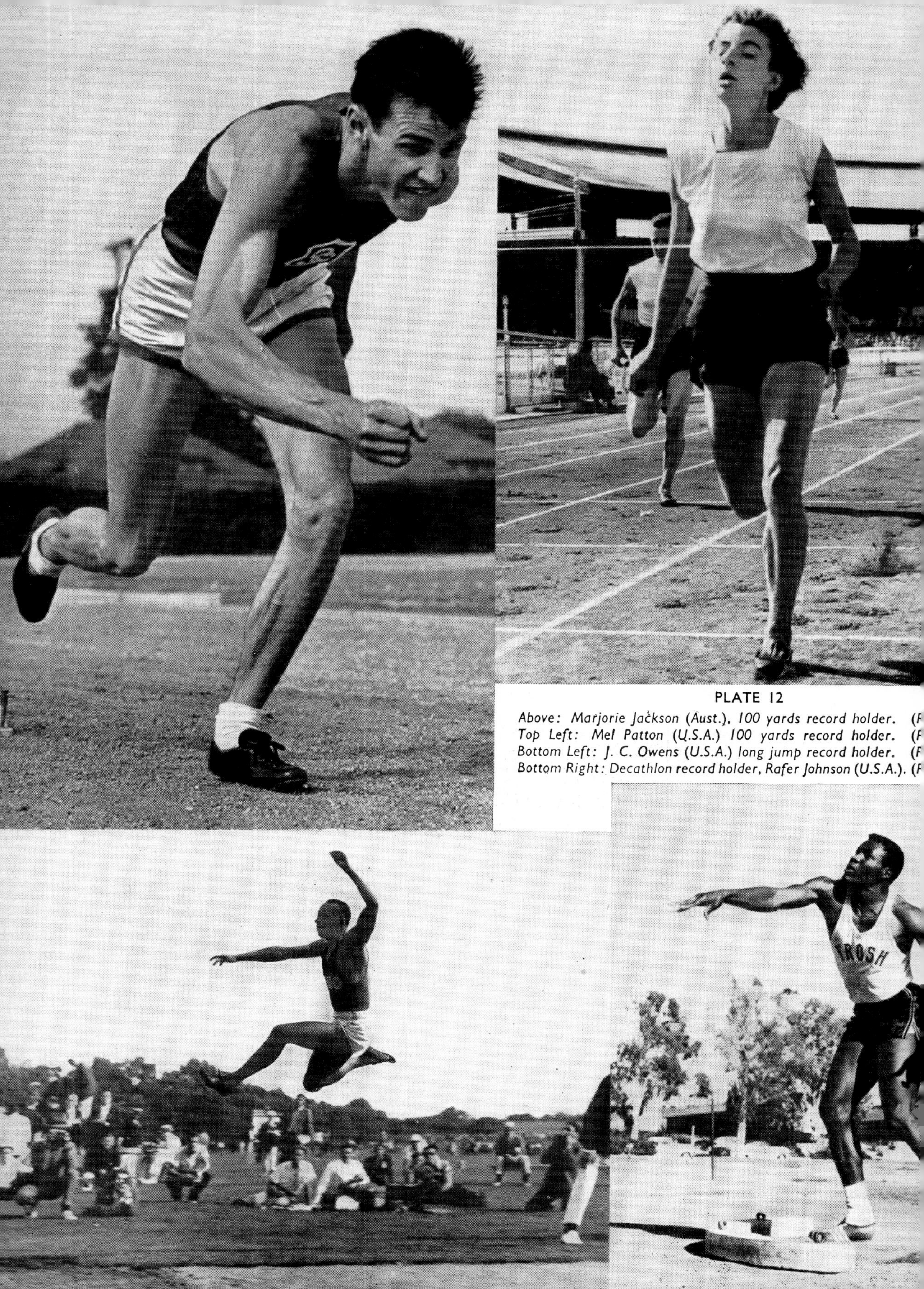

PLATE 12

Above: Marjorie Jackson (Aust.), 100 yards record holder. (F
Top Left: Mel Patton (U.S.A.) 100 yards record holder. (F
Bottom Left: J. C. Owens (U.S.A.) long jump record holder. (F
Bottom Right: Decathlon record holder, Rafer Johnson (U.S.A.). (F

The British auction record for a female is 6,000 guineas (£6,300) for the imported Dutch Friesian heifer "Berber 13th" at Peterborough in November 1950.

Sheep

The world record for any breed of sheep is 5,500 guineas (£5,775) for a Kent ram at Fielding, New Zealand, in January 1951.

The British auction record is £2,500 by B. Wilson for a Scottish Blackface ram lamb owned by J. M. Wilson at Lanark in October, 1954.

Pigs

The world's record price for a pig is $10,200 (£3,643) paid in 1953 for a Hampshire boar "Great Western" for a farm at Byron, U.S.A.

The British record is 3,300 guineas (£3,465) paid for the Landrace gilt "Bluegate Ally 33rd" at Reading on 2nd March, 1955.

Horses

The highest price ever paid for a farm horse is 9,500 guineas (£9,975) for the Clydesdale stallion "Baron of Buchlyvie" paid by W. Dunlop in Scotland in December 1911.

DIMENSIONS

Cattle

The live weight record for cattle was set in 1807 when the 10 year old "Durham Ox" scaled 34 cwt. (3,808 lb.). Reputedly the largest ox now living is the 9 year old Hereford-Friesian "Big Bill Campbell" at Major C. H. Still's Hall Farm, Upton, Northamptonshire, England, weighing 30 cwt. (3,360 lb.), standing over 6 feet in height and 12 feet 6 inches from nose to tail.

Reputedly the smallest cow in the world "Sally", a Dexter breed standing only 34 inches, is on the same farm.

The highest recorded birthweight for a calf is 172 lb. (12 stone 4 lb.) from a South Devon cow owned by J. H. Pears & Sons of Berry Pomeroy, Devon, in September 1952.

Pigs

The heaviest pig ever recorded in Britain was one of 12 cwt. 66 lb. (1,410 lb.) bred by Joseph Lawton of Astbury, Cheshire. In 1774, it stood 4 feet 8½ inches in height and was 9 feet 8 inches long.

The highest recorded weight for a piglet at weaning (8 weeks) is 74½ lb. in the case of a Wessex gilt from a litter of 9 (average weight 57·1 lb.) owned by T. T. Casson of Silecroft, Cumberland, reported in January 1952.

The world prolificacy record is 31 piglets (26 survived) thrown by the sow "Liz" at Eye, Suffolk, England in June 1955.

Sheep

The highest recorded birthweight of a lamb in Britain is 25 lb. reported by C. Hardwick from Bristol, Somerset, in 1927.

EGG LAYING

The greatest authenticated egg-laying record is 355 eggs in 365 days by a black Australorp at the Glen Agricultural College laying test, South Africa in 1944–1945.

The largest egg reported is one of eight ounces laid at Windlesham, Surrey, in March 1950.

CHEESE

The largest Cheshire cheeses ever made weighed 300 lb. each. They were produced by Mr. Percy Cooke in 1909.

RATTING

All rat-killing records are held by Mr. J. Shaw's "Jacko" which in killing 1,000 rats in under 1 hour 40 minutes in London on 1st May, 1862, accounted for the first 100 in 5 minutes 28 seconds.

VEGETABLE RECORDS

The most outsize vegetables reported from British Flower Shows and in the Horticultural press since 1930 are as follows :—

Beetroot	12½ lb. at Melton Mowbray, Leicestershire.
Cabbage	21 feet 3 inches in circumference, Lincolnshire; 75 lb., Bolton, Lancashire.
Cauliflower	5 feet 4 inches tall, Devon.
Mangold	43½ lb. grown by M. Crabb, Devon, 1943.
Marrow	96 lb., Suffolk.
Mushroom	39 inches in circumference and 2 lb. 10 oz. in weight.*
Onion	5 lb. 2 oz. in weight.
Parsnip	41½ inches long, Devon.
Pear	2 lb. 1 oz. for a Catillac.
Potato	5 lb. 4 oz. tuber grown by A. Thompson, Grimethorpe, Barnsley, Yorks., October 1953.
Pumpkin	92 lb. Port Talbot, Glamorgan, 1930.
Runner Bean	27½ inches in length.

* On 1st September, 1902, a mushroom of 53 inches in circumference weighing 2 lb. 15½ oz. was gathered at Plumpton, Sussex.

TEN

ACCIDENTS AND DISASTERS

The greatest human disaster of all time was the Black Death which raged from 1347 to 1351 and caused about 25 million deaths in Europe including over 45 per cent. of the population of Britain. Some authorities state that including the Orient the total number of fatalities was of the order of 75 million.

PANDEMIC

In recent times the greatest loss of life was in the Influenza Pandemic of September — November 1918 with a total loss estimated at 21,640,000 deaths. The deaths in the British Isles were England and Wales 200,000, Scotland 19,000 and Ireland 18,400.

FLOODS

The greatest recorded flood disaster was that in the Honan province of China in 1887, when the Hwang Ho river overflowed with 900,000 perishing.

The worst British floods were those on 31st January, 1953, which inundated large areas of East Anglia, resulting in 307 deaths.

EARTHQUAKES

The worst earthquake was the Chinese shock of 23rd January, 1556 (see page 8), when over 830,000 were killed from all causes.

TORNADO

The worst recorded tornado disaster was the 'Tri-State' tornado of 1925 which killed 689 people in Missouri, Illinois and Indiana, U.S.A.

LANDSLIDE

The greatest recorded loss of life in a landslide occurred in Central Java on 17th April, 1955, when 405 people were killed and many cattle were buried. Some bamboo houses were swept more than $\frac{1}{4}$ of a mile.

FIRE

The greatest number of people killed in a single building was the 2,500 who were burned to death in the Church of La Compañía, Santiago, Chile, on 8th December, 1863.

Apart from fires consequent upon earthquakes, the most destructive fire was the Chicago Fire of 8th October, 1871, which destroyed over 17,400 buildings in 2,124 acres and caused $200,000,000 (£71,400,000) of damage and 250 deaths.

The fire which followed the Kwanto earthquake (see page 8) killed about 60,000 people and the total damage, including the results of the tremors, was £1,000 million.

The worst fire within the last century in the British Isles was that which gutted the Victoria Hall, Sunderland, Durham, in 1883, and in which 183 children died on the staircase. The death roll in the Great Fire of London, 2nd-4th September, 1666, was 8, but the damage over 436 acres was then estimated at £10,750,000.

FOREST FIRES

The worst recorded forest fire was the Peshtigo Fire, Wisconsin, U.S.A., in October 1871, which destroyed 1,280,000 acres of forest and resulted in 1,152 deaths. In acreage however this fire was surpassed by some in Russia in 1921 and 1932 in which years over 5,000,000 acres were burnt down and the forest fire in Maine and New Brunswick which razed 3,000,000 acres in 1825.

MINING

The world's worst mining disaster occurred in the Honkeiko Colliery in Manchuria on 26th April, 1942, when 1,549 miners were killed. The worst coal-mining accident in the United Kingdom was the explosion at the Senghenydd Colliery, Glamorganshire, on 14th October, 1913, with 439 fatalities. The worst disaster in England was that at the Oaks Colliery, Yorkshire, on 12th December, 1866, with 361 killed and the worst in Scotland that at Blantyre Colliery, Lanarkshire, on 22nd November, 1877, when 207 miners were killed. The greatest rescue was that at Knockshinnock Colliery, Lanarkshire, when on 7th September, 1950, heavy rains caused an inrush of surface moss which entombed 129 miners of whom 116 were rescued.

MARINE

The worst marine disaster of all time occurred on 18th February, 1945, when the 25,000 ton German merchantman "Wilhelm Gustloff" was torpedoed off Danzig and sank within a few minutes. The ship was carrying 5,000 refugees and 3,700 U-Boat personnel, a total of 8,700 of whom over 7,000 were drowned.

The greatest number of persons lost on a single warship was the 3,033 Japanese lost when the 72,200 ton battleship "Yamato" (See page 52) was sunk off Kyushu Island on 7th April, 1945.

The greatest toll taken in a marine accident in time of peace was when 1,517 were drowned on 14th-15th April, 1912, when the White Star Liner "Titanic" struck an iceberg in the Western Atlantic. On 17th June, 1940, 2,500 were drowned in the torpedoing of the "Lancastria" off St. Nazaire. The largest number lost on a single British warship were on H.M.S. Hood in the Denmark Strait, N. Atlantic, when 1,418 were killed of the 1,421 complement, in May 1941.

SUBMARINE

The worst single submarine disaster in history was the loss of H.M.S. "Thetis" in Liverpool Bay on 1st June, 1939, when 99 passengers and crew were entombed.

LIFEBOAT

The worst British lifeboat disaster was that of 10th December, 1886, when attempting to save the crew of the barque "Mexico" 27 members of the crews of the Southport and St. Anne's, Lancashire, lifeboats were drowned.

The greatest British lifeboat rescue was that of 17th March, 1907, when 456 people from the 12,000 ton White Star Liner S.S. "Suevic" were rescued from the Maenheere Reef off the Lizard, Cornwall. The greatest number of lives saved by R.N.L.I. boats was the 2,056 in 1940. The most called lifeboats are those of Great Yarmouth and Gorleston which have been launched 1,117 times and rescued 1,748 lives. Since the war the busiest lifeboat has been that at Ramsgate, whose record is 993 launchings and 1,652 lives saved. Coxswain William G. Fleming, G.C. (1865-1954), of the Gorleston Crew, Norfolk, has contributed to the saving of the record total of 1,182 lives.

RAILWAYS
World

The worst disaster in world railway history occurred on 12th December, 1917, at Modane, France, when an overloaded leave train left the rails and crashed, killing 543 persons.

British Isles

The highest toll in any railway crash in the British Isles was at Quintinshill in Southern Scotland on 22nd May, 1915, when 227 troops were killed when a military train was involved in a collision.

England

The worst railway accident in England was the triple collision at Harrow on 8th October, 1952, when the final death roll reached 118.

Ireland

Ireland's worst rail crash was the Armagh collision of 12th June, 1889, when 80 were killed.

AIR
World

The world's worst air accident occurred on 18th June, 1953, when a U.S. Air Force C-124 (Globemaster) crashed near Tokyo, Japan, killing 129 persons including the crew of seven.

British Isles

The worst air accident in the British Isles occurred on 12th March, 1950, at Sigingstone, Glamorganshire, when an Avro Tudor V attempting to land at Llandow crashed, killing 81 of the 83 passengers.

AIRSHIP

The worst airship disaster was that of 4th April, 1933, when the U.S. dirigible Akron crashed into the sea off the New Jersey coast killing 73 personnel. The worst airship accident in the United Kingdom was the loss of the R.38 (American designation Z.2-Z) which broke in two on a trial flight near Hull, Yorkshire, on 24th August, 1921, killing 62 people. The better known R.101 disaster on 5th October, 1930, occurred near Beauvais, resulting in 47 deaths.

ROAD

The world's earliest fatal motor accident occurred on 13th September, 1895, when a Mr. W. H. Bliss was knocked down and killed in New York, U.S.A. Since that time in the U.S.A. there have been 1,115,000 killed (up to 1955) with 1937 being the worst year with a toll of 39,643 (over 108 a day) killed.

Britain's first motor-car fatality occurred on 17th August, 1896, when a Mrs. Bridget Driscoll was run down and killed at the Crystal Palace, South London. Since that time up to 1st January, 1955, approximately 229,400 have been killed in Britain. The worst year was 1941 with 9,169 (over 26 a day) killed. The worst single car accident on record occurred near Whitesburg, Kentucky, U.S.A., when on 31st July, 1954, a car ran into a cliff and burnt out, killing 11 and injuring 1. Though there are no collated world statistics it is believed that the worst road accident of any kind occurred outside Guatemala City, Guatemala, on 27th July, 1954, when 47 were killed and 27 injured when a bus crashed over a cliff edge.

The worst road accident in Britain took place at Gillingham, Kent, on 4th December, 1951, when a double-decker bus ran into a marching column of Royal Marine Cadets killing 17 outright with 7 later dying in hospital, and only 10 of the 52 escaping injury.

SPORTS DISASTER

The worst disaster in sporting history occurred at Le Mans, France, in the annual 24-hour motor race on 11th June, 1955, when a Mercedes 300 SLR driven by the Frenchman, Pierre Levegh, collided with another car when travelling at 160 m.p.h. and leapt the barrier and exploded among the crowd killing 82.

The worst sports crowd disaster in the British Isles took place on 9th March, 1946, at a cup-tie football match at the Bolton Wanderers' Ground at Burden Park, Bolton, Lancs., when 33 were killed when sections of the stands collapsed. The game, against Stoke City, was played to a finish.

AIR ATTACK

Raids

The greatest number of civilian casualties caused in any single raid was the estimated 20,000 killed and 60,000 wounded in the R.A.F.'s 1,000 bomber "saturation" attack on Hamburg, Germany, on the night of 25th-26th July, 1943.

The worst raid in Britain was on London (1,224 alerts) on the night of 10th-11th May, 1941, when 1,436 were killed and 1,792 injured.

The worst raid in World War I was that of 3rd September, 1917, in which a single bomb on a Chatham drill hall killed 107 and wounded 86.

The most sustained attack was 57 consecutive nights (7th September to 2nd November, 1940) on London.

Flying Bomb

The worst V.1 incident occurred at Korte van Ruysbroeckstraat, Antwerp, at 8.19 p.m. on 21st January, 1945, when 76 were killed and 57 wounded.

Rockets

The worst V.2 incident occurred at the Cinema Rex, Avenue de Keyser, Antwerp, at 3.23 p.m. on 16th December, 1944, when 567 persons were killed and 291 wounded.

The worst of the 1,050 V.2 incidents during the 199-day assault on Southern England occurred at the premises of F. W. Woolworth & Co. Ltd., 279-281 New Cross Road, South London, on 25th November, 1944, when 164 were killed.

Atom Bombs

Of the two atom bombs dropped during World War II, that causing the greater casualties was the one dropped from the U.S. B-29 bomber "Enola Gay" piloted by Col. Paul W. Tibbets, Jnr., over the Japanese town of Hiroshima (pop. 343,000), at 9.15 a.m. on 6th August, 1945, which caused 91,233 deaths.

ELEVEN

HUMAN ACHIEVEMENTS

1. Honours, Decorations and Awards

OLDEST ORDERS and MEDALS

The Knights of the Order of the Hospital of St. John of Jerusalem were recognized by Papal bull in 1113 for the care of sick pilgrims. The Grand Priory of the Order of the Hospital of St. John of Jerusalem in England received a Royal Charter on 14th May, 1888, with objects of the promotion of ambulance, hospital and other charitable work.

The prototype of the princely Orders of Chivalry is the Most Noble Order of the Garter founded in c.1348 by King Edward III. The earliest campaign medals were those issued by Queen Elizabeth to senior officers engaged in the defeat of the Spanish Armada in 1588 but these were, in fact, in the nature of decorations. The earliest campaign medal issued to officers and men was the Dunbar Medal, struck in gold and silver by Cromwell for his victory over the Scots on 3rd September, 1650. The first general issue war medal was the Waterloo Medal of 1815. A bar for the Battle of the Glorious First of June of 1794 was, however, included among those authorised for the first Naval General Service Medal which was not issued until 1849.

RAREST DECORATIONS and MEDALS

The rarest medal is the Conspicuous Gallantry Medal (Flying) of which only 107 were awarded in the Second World War. Of War Medals, only two Naval General Service Medals were issued with seven bars and only two Military General Service Medals (1793-1815) with fifteen bars.

Unique British decorations are:—D.S.C. and 3 bars, Cdr. N. E. Morley, R.N.V.R. (1939–45); C.G.M. and bar, C.P.O. A. R. Blore (1914–18); D.S.M. and 3 bars, P.O. W. H. Kelly (k. 1944) and M.M. and 3 bars, Stretcher-Bearer E. D. Correy (1914–18).

COMMONEST DECORATIONS

Of gallantry decorations, the most unsparingly awarded was the M.M. which was awarded to 115,589 recipients between 1916 and 1919. The most frequently awarded decoration in the 1939-45 war was the D.F.C. which was awarded (with bars) 21,000 times.

HIGHEST PRICED DECORATION

The highest price ever found for a medal group was the £420 in July 1955 for the medals and sword of Assistant Surgeon T. E. Hale, V.C., won Sebastapol in 1855.

MOST HIGHLY DECORATED OFFICERS

Of the 3 soldiers ever to have achieved a bar to the Victoria Cross, one also won a Military Cross. He was Capt. Noel Godfrey Chavasse, V.C.*, M.C., R.A.M.C. The most highly decorated non-commissioned officer is C.S.M. John H. Williams, V.C., D.C.M., M.M.*. See Plate 11.

The most highly decorated woman is Mrs. Odette Churchill (née Brailly) G.C., M.B.E., Légion d'Honneur.

MOST RIBBONS

The greatest number of medal ribbons ever worn by any officer is the 38, usually in 10 rows, by the Field Marshal the Viscount Montgomery of Alamein, K.G., G.C.B., D.S.O. The greatest number of sets of initials borne by any officer was by Admiral of the Fleet, H.R.H. the Duke of Windsor during the time he was King Edward VIII. In addition to the K.G., K.T., K.P., G.C.B., G.C.S.I., G.C.M.G., G.C.I.E., G.C.V.O., G.B.E., and I.S.O., he was an M.C. and also sovereign of the Order of Merit (O.M.), the Royal Order of Victoria and Albert (V.A.), Imperial Order of the Crown of India (C.I.), Order of the Companion of Honour (C.H.), the Distinguished Service Order (D.S.O.) and the Royal Red Cross (R.R.C.) making 17 of which he carried only the initials for the first-mentioned 11.

Of subjects of the crown, those with seven sets of initials have been Field Marshal the Earl Roberts of Kandahar, Pretoria and Waterford, V.C., K.G., K.P., G.C.B., O.M., G.C.S.I., G.C.I.E. (d. 14th November, 1914), and Lord Hardinge of Penshurst, K.G., G.C.B., G.C.S.I., G.C.M.G., G.C.V.O., G.C.I.E., I.S.O. (d. 1944).

MOST DECORATED FAMILY

Three members of the Gough family were awarded the V.C. — Major C. J. S. Gough (Indian Mutiny 1857-58), his brother Lt. H. H. Gough (Indian Mutiny 1857) and his son Major J. E. Gough (Somaliland 1903). The family with the greatest number of honours is the Howard family of whom twenty-three members have been invested with the K.G., while the closely allied Mowbrays and Fitzalans have eleven, making a total of thirty-four.

YOUNGEST AWARDS

The youngest person ever to be awarded a British decoration was Anthony Farrer, aged 8, who was awarded the Albert Medal of the Second Class in 1916 for saving the life of an 11-year-old girl from an attack by a cougar on Vancouver Island, British Columbia, Canada. The youngest award of a V.C. was posthumously to Boy (1st Class) J. T. Cornwell, R.N., of H.M.S. " Chester " for bravery in the Battle of Jutland when not yet 16½ years. The youngest award of a G.C. was on 16th December, 1952, to John Banford, 15, of Newthorpe, Nottinghamshire, for saving life in a fire.

PEERAGE

MOST ANCIENT CREATION

The year A.D. 1223 has been ascribed to the Premier Irish barony of Kingsale (formerly of Courcy) though on the Order of Precedence the date is listed as 1397. The premier English barony De Ros, at present held by a Baroness in her own right and 26th in her line, dates from 1264.

MOST TITLED PEER

The peer with the greatest number of titles is the Duke of Atholl who is also the Marquess of Atholl, Marquess of Tullibardine, Earl of Atholl, Earl of Tullibardine, Earl of Strathtay and Strathardle, Earl Strange, Glenalmond, and Glenlyon, Viscount of Balquhidder, Lord

Murray, Balvenie, and Gask, Baron Strange, Baron Percy, Baron Murray of Stanley, Lord Murray of Tullibardine and Baron Glenlyon — nineteen titles in all.

OLDEST

Collated records do not exist but the greatest age established for any peer is the 98 years 99 days of the 1st Earl Halsbury (born 3rd September, 1823, died 11th December, 1921). The oldest age at which any person has been raised to the peerage is 84 in the case of William Francis Kyffin Taylor, G.B.E., K.C. (born 9th July, 1854) who was created Baron Maenan of Ellesmere, County Salop in 1948.

The oldest living peer is the Marquess of Winchester, Premier Marquess of England, who was 92 on 30th October, 1954.

HIGHEST NUMBERING

The highest succession number borne by any peer is that of the present 34th Baron of Kingsale.

CREATIONS

The largest number of new peerages created in any year was the fifty-four in 1296. The greatest number of extinctions in a year was the sixteen in 1923 and the greatest number of deaths forty-four in 1935.

2. *Endurance and Endeavour*

CIRCUM-NAVIGATION

Man's earliest circumnavigation of the world was achieved by Sebastian del Cano in the Spanish ship *Vittorio* on 6th September, 1522. Del Cano was a navigator to the Portuguese-born explorer Ferdinand Magalhâes (Magellen) (c. 1470–1521) who, having sailed westward from the estuary of the Guadalquivir, Spain, on 20th September, 1519, with five ships, was killed on 27th April, 1521, on Mactan Island in the Philippines.

ATLANTIC CROSSING

The smallest boat ever to cross the Atlantic from West to East was the *Sapolio*—a canvas covered folding boat, 14 feet 6 inches by 5 feet 5 inches by 3 feet. W. A. Andrews left Atlantic City in the *Sapolio* on 2nd July, 1892, and landed at Fuzetta, South Portugal, 2,845 miles away, on 24th September, 1892—eighty-four days later.

The only two men to have rowed the Atlantic were George Haroo and Frank Samuelson, who left New York on 6th June, 1897, and covered 3,075 miles in fifty-five days, landing at St. Mary's, Scilly Isles. Their boat was 18 feet, 5 feet beam, clinker built double ender, and had no mast or sails in its equipment. They stowed five pairs of oars.

POLAR

The conquest of the North Pole was first achieved on 6th April, 1909, by the U.S. Naval Officer, Cdr. Robert E. Peary (1856–1920) accompanied by Matthew Henson and four Eskimos (see page 109). Peary's party stayed at the Pole for thirty-six hours.

The conquest of the South Pole was first achieved on 14th December, 1911, by the Norwegian Roald Amundsen (1872–1928) in a fifty-three-day southward march from the Bay of Whales which he had reached in the *Fram*.

MOUNTAINEER-ING

The conquest of the highest point on Earth, Mount Everest (29,160 feet), was first achieved at 11.30 a.m. on 29th May, 1953, by Sir Edmund P. Hillary, K.B.E., and the Sherpa, Tensing Norkay, G.M. (see page 19) and frontispiece.

The highest human settlement of which there is evidence is the remains of a South American Indian settlement one hundred feet below the summit of the dormant volcano Llullaillaco (21,719 feet) on the borders of Chile and Argentina.

OCEAN DEPTH

The deepest penetration yet made into the ocean's depths is the 13,287 feet (2·52 miles) 160 miles S.W. of Dakar, French West Africa, in the bathyscaphe *F.N.R.S.* 3, manned by Lt.-Cdr. Georges S. Houet and Lt. Pierre Henri Willm on 14th February, 1954. The vessel dived at 10.08 a.m. and touched the bottom at 1.30 p.m. where the water pressure was 5,900 lb. (2·63 tons) per square inch. After thirty-six minutes on the bottom it ascended to break the surface at 3.21 p.m.

DIVING

The greatest descent made in a flexible diving suit is 550 feet by Diver J. E. Johnstone to recover bullion from a wreck in the Hauriki Gulf, New Zealand in 1949.

The deepest salvage operation ever planned is that by a British salvage team in 1955 on the " Konsigurd " 680 feet below the surface of Oslofjord.

MINING DEPTH

Man's deepest penetration made into the ground is at the Kolar Gold Field, Mysore State, South India, where in the Champion Reef mine a working depth of 9,811 feet (1·86 miles) below the surface has been attained (see also page 108).

ALTITUDE

The highest altitude yet obtained by man in the stratosphere is subject to U.S. Air Force security regulations but is believed to be 90,000 feet (17·04 miles) by Major Arthur Murray in a Bell X-1A over California during 16th June, 1954 (see page 55 and Plate 2).

The record altitude achieved by a manned balloon is 72,394 feet (13·17 miles) by " Explorer II " over South Dakota, U.S.A., at 11.40 a.m. on 11th November, 1935, manned by Capt. Albert Stevens and Capt. Orvil Anderson.

The greatest known altitude attained by a large unmanned balloon is 22 miles (116,160 feet) by the 3·2 million cubic feet Super Skyhook released from the University of Minnesota, U.S.A., in August 1954. Smaller meteorological balloons may have attained 130,000 feet before bursting.

The greatest published altitude for any rocket is 250 miles achieved by a two-stage 5,000 m.p.h. V2/WAC Corporal rocket, separating at twenty miles, over White Sands, New Mexico, U.S.A., on 24th February, 1949. A temperature of 1,898°F. was recorded at the high point. The highest published figure for a one-stage rocket is 158 miles by a 4,300-m.p.h. Viking rocket reported in May 1954.

TOP AIR ACES

The top score of any fighter pilot in the 1914–1918 war was 80 kills by the German Manfred von Richthofen. Major Erich Hartman of the Luftwaffe, released from Russia in 1955, is reputed to have shot down 352 allied aircraft in the 1939–45 war.

The highest score credited to a British fighter pilot is 73 enemy aircraft destroyed, also in the 1914–18 war, by Major E. Mannock, V.C., D.S.O.**, M.C.*. The top score in the 1939–45 war was 38 'planes by Group-Capt. J. E. Johnson, D.S.O.**, D.F.C. The greatest success against flying bombs was achieved by Squad/Ldr. Berry, D.F.C.*, who brought down 60 in 1944–1945.

ANTI-SUBMARINE SUCCESSES

The highest number of U-Boat kills attributed to one ship in the 1939–45 war was 13 to H.M.S. *Starling* (Capt. F. J. Walker, C.B., D.S.O.***, R.N.). Capt. Walker was in overall command at the sinking of a total 25 U-Boats between 1941 and the time of his death in 1944.

SPEED AIR

For details of world air speed record see page 55. The highest speed ever achieved by a woman pilot is the 708·362 m.p.h. by Jacqueline Auriol, 37, in a Mystère jet near Paris, in June 1955.

SPEED LAND

The fastest speed ever achieved on land is the 632 m.p.h. by Lt.-Col. John L. Stapp in an experimental rocket sled at the Air Development Center, Alamogordo, U.S.A. Running on rails and impelled by nine rockets with a total thrust of 40,000 lb., the top speed is reached within five seconds. See Plate 10. An un-manned rocket attained 1292 m.p.h. at Edwards Field, Calif. in September 1955.

The fastest speed ever achieved by a wheeled vehicle is the 403·135 m.p.h. by John Cobb's Railton Special, in one direction, on the Bonneville Salt Beds, U.S.A., on 16th September, 1947. The mean for two runs in opposite directions and the official World Land Speed Record, is 394·196 m.p.h. The timing mile was covered in 9·1325 seconds. The car was powered by two, 12-cylinder Napier-Lion engines of 478,728 c.c. developing 2,860 h.p. See Plate 11.

WATER

The fastest speed ever achieved on water was the 215·08 m.p.h. by Donald Campbell (Great Britain) on 23rd July, 1955, in his first run. His mean speed over two runs, and the world's water speed record is 202·32 m.p.h., in the turbo-jet engined " Bluebird " K7 on Ullswater, England.

Wood-Cutting

The world record for cutting six " shoes " to ascend and sever the top of a 12-inch diameter log is the 1 minute 46 seconds set by the Tasmanian axeman, Ray Youd, at the Sandfly Sports, Tasmania, on 12th March, 1955.

Brick-Laying

The world record for brick-laying was established by Joseph Raglon of East St. Louis, U.S.A., in 1937 who, supported by assistants, laid 3,472 bricks in 60 minutes—at a rate of nearly 58 a minute.

Barrel-Jumping

The greatest number of barrels jumped on ice is fifteen (total length 28 feet 7 inches) in January 1955 at Grossinger, New York, by Leo Lebel, 24. The women's world record was set at the same competition by Lebel's sister, Aldrina, 23, who cleared eight barrels (18 ft. 3 in.).

Juggling

The only juggler in history able to juggle—as opposed to " shower " —ten balls or eight plates was the Italian Enrico Rastelli who was born in Samara, Russia, on 19th December, 1896, and died on 13th December, 1931, in Bergamo, Italy.

Tightrope Walking

The greatest tightrope walker of all-time was the Frenchman, Jean François Gravelet ("Blondin") (1824–1897) who made the earliest crossing of the Niagara on a 1,100-foot long 3-inch rope, 160 feet above the Falls on 30th June, 1859. He also made a crossing with an assistant, Harry Colcord, pick-a-back.

The world tightrope endurance record is 113 hours by Willi Pischler, 23, ending on 12th July, 1955.

The highest high-wire act was that of the Germans Alfred and Henry Traber on a 520-feet rope stretched from the Zugspitze (9,750 feet) to the Western Peak, Bavaria, during July and August, 1953. See Plate 11.

Trapeze Artistry

The greatest aerialist of all time was the Mexican, Alfredo Codona, who, in 1920, became the first man ever to perfect a triple somersault.

Stilt-Walking

The highest stilts ever successfully mastered were 22 feet from the ankle to the ground by Harry Yelding (" Harry Sloan ") of Great Yarmouth, Norfolk, England.

Lion-Taming

The greatest number of lions mastered and fed in a cage by an unaided lion-tamer was forty by " Captain " Alfred Schneider in 1925.

Bull-Fighting

The highest paid bull-fighter in history was Manuel Laureano Rodriguez y Sanchez known as Manolete who, immediately prior to being killed at Linares, Spain, on 27th August, 1947, was receiving up to £9,000 for an appearance.

Morse

The highest speed at which anyone has received morse code is 75·2 words per minute—over seventeen symbols per second. This was achieved by Ted R. McElroy of the United States in a tournament at Asheville, North Carolina, on 2nd July, 1939.

Typewriting

International competitions in typewriting have occurred between only 1906 and 1946.

The highest speeds attained with a ten-word penalty per error on a manual machine are:—

One Minute: 170 words Margaret Owen (U.S.A.) (Underwood Standard) New York, 21st October, 1918.

One Hour: 147 words (net rate per minute) Albert Tangora (U.S.A.) (Underwood Standard) 22nd October, 1923.

The official hour record on an electric machine is 9,316 words (forty errors) giving a net rate of 149 words per minute by Margaret Hamma (U.S.A.) in Brooklyn, New York, on 20th June, 1941, on an I.B.M. machine. Since then, in unofficial tests, Miss Stella Pajunas has attained 200 words per minute on an I.B.M. machine.

Shorthand

The earliest record of shorthand dates from 63 B.C. as used by Marcus Tullius Tiro in recording the speeches of Caesar and Cicero in Rome. The Tironian system was in fact only a highly abbreviated form of longhand. Shorthand proper dates from a treatise by Dr. Timothy Bright in 1588.

The highest speeds ever attained under championship conditions are:—

300 w.p.m. (99·64 per cent. accuracy) for five minutes and 350 w.p.m. (99·72 per cent. accuracy, that is, two insignificant errors) for two minutes by Nathan Behrin (U.S.A.) in New York in December 1922. Behrin (born 1887) used the Pitman system invented in 1837.

In the British Isles the only four shorthand writers to pass official Pitman tests at 250 w.p.m. are:—

Mr. G. W. Bunbury of Dublin on 23rd March, 1894.
Miss Edith Ulrica Pearson of London on 30th June, 1927.
Miss Emily Doris Smith of London on 22nd March, 1934.
Miss Beatrice W. Solomon of London in March 1942.

Most Marriages

Mrs. Beverly Nina O'Malley, 45, a Los Angeles, U.S.A. barmaid set a world record in May 1955 by obtaining her thirteenth divorce to marry Gabriel Avery, her fourteenth husband.

Greatest Money Makers

Transcending all other personal fortunes is that of Dr. J. T. Williamson, the Canadian geologist, who discovered and staked in 1934 the Mwadui diamond mine near Shinyanga, Tanganyika, East Africa.

Turning from largely unexploited but wholly owned capital assets to income, the highest ever attained is that of £1,000,000 every ten days (£36,500,000 per annum) stemming from oil-rights which accrued to His Late Majesty Abdul Aziz Ibn Abdul Raham al Faisal Al Saud, King of Saudi-Arabia, Lord of Arabia and Guardian of the Holy City of Mecca.

Richest Woman

The largest estate ever left by a woman financier was the $95 million (£33,900,000) by Mrs. Hetty Green Wilks, 80, in March 1952. She had a balance of over $31,400,000 in one bank alone. Her will was found in a tin box with four pieces of soap.

Biggest Wills

The wealthiest man in the British Isles is usually allowed to be Sir John Reeves Ellerman, the shipowner, whose father left the largest ever proved will in the United Kingdom of over £36,684,994 in 1933.

The greatest will proved in Ireland was that of the 1st Earl of Iveagh who died in 1927 leaving £13,486,146.

Richest Families

The greatest number of millionaires in one family is probably the eighty-three members, each worth over $5,500,000, of the Lykes family of Florida. This represents over 1 per cent. of all America's 8,000 dollar millionaires.

The largest number of millionaires in one family in the British Isles is that of the Wills family of the Imperial Tobacco Company, of whom thirteen members have left estates in excess of £1,000,000 since 1910.

Greatest Bequests

The greatest bequests in a life-time of a millionaire were those of the late Andrew Carnegie (1835–1919), who left only £4,430,000. His major bequests totalled $309,940,000 (£110,700,000). The greatest benefactions of a living British millionaire are those of Viscount Nuffield which, in an era of very much higher taxation, total some £27 million to date.

Most Travelled Man

The British pilot with the greatest flying mileage in the world is Capt. Oscar Philip Jones, C.V.O., O.B.E., who retired as the Senior Captain of the British Overseas Airways Corporation in May 1955, aged 56. Capt. Jones, who began flying with the Royal Flying Corps in 1917, totalled 21,600 hours and 4,200,000 miles in his 38-year career. The pilot credited with most trans-Atlantic crossings is Capt. S. W. A. Scott of the B.O.A.C. who made his first crossing in 1941 and his five-hundredth on 17th May, 1955.

Gastronomic Records

Records for eating and drinking by trenchermen do not match those suffering from the rare disease of bulimia (morbid desire to eat) and polydipsia (pathological thirst). Some bulimia patients have to spend fifteen hours a day eating, with an extreme consumption of 384 lb. of food in six days in Mortimer's Case of 1743. Some polydipsomaniacs are unsatisfied by less than ninety-six pints of liquid a day.

Specific records have been claimed as follows:—

Raw Eggs

24 in 14 minutes, by Glen Johns (Canada) in Ontario, Canada, on 14th March, 1955.

Hamburgers — 77 at a sitting, by Philip Yazdzik (U.S.A.) in Chicago, Illinois on 25th April, 1955.

Oysters — 480 in 60 minutes, by Joe Garcia (Australia) in Melbourne on 5th February, 1955.

Meat — One whole roast ox in 42 days by Johann Ketzler of Germany in 1880.

Beer — 24 pints in 52 minutes by Auguste Maffrey of France.

Wine — 40 pints in 59 minutes by a Spaniard, Dionsio Sanchez.

ENDURANCE

Running — The greatest non-stop run recorded is the 127 miles 275 yards by J. Saunders round a track in New York in a " Go as You Please " race on 21st–22nd February, 1882. Saunders covered this distance in 22 hours 49 minutes.

The greatest distance covered in twenty-four hours is the 159 miles 562 yards of W. H. Hayward (South Africa) at Motspur Park, Surrey, England, from 11 a.m. 20th November to 11 a.m. 21st November, 1953. He consumed 2 lb. of sugar and 16 eggs during the trial but lost 7 lb. in weight. The distance comprised 2 miles 12 yards more than six marathons and entailed over 637 laps of the track. See Plate 11.

The greatest distance covered in six days is 623 miles 1,320 yards between 25th November and 1st December, 1888 by George Littlewood of England on a track in New York.

Walking — The longest officially recorded walking race was that of 3,415 miles from New York to San Francisco, U.S.A., from 3rd May to 24th July, 1926 by A. L. Monteverde, 60, occupying 79 days 10 hours 10 minutes.

Longest on a Raft — The longest recorded survival alone on a raft is 133 days (4½ months) by Second Steward Poon Lim of the British Merchant Navy whose ship was torpedoed in the Atlantic. He was picked up by a fishing boat and was awarded the B.E.M. in July 1943.

Swimming — The longest duration swim ever recorded is the 292 miles of John V. Sigmund (U.S.A.) who swam down the Mississippi River, U.S.A., from St. Louis to Caruthersville in 89 hours 48 minutes ending on 29th July, 1940.

The longest duration swim by a woman was 87 hours 27 minutes in a pool by Mrs. Myrtle Huddleston of New York in 1931.

Underwater — The world record for staying underwater was set on 2nd November. 1912, at the Piscine de la Gare, Paris, by the bath-master, Georges Pouliquen, with 6 minutes 29·8 seconds, so beating the previous record by 1 minute 43·6 seconds.

The longest submergence in a frogman's suit is the 25 hours 6 seconds at the Salon du Sportsmen, Montreal, Canada, by Guy Cadieux, 27, who entered the water (88–92°F.) at 9.49 a.m. on 28th March, 1955 and emerged at 10.49 a.m. on 29th March.

Cycling — The duration record for cycling on a track is 125 hours by Anandrao Halyalkar, 22, at Shivaji Park, Bombay, from 1 p.m. on 14th April to 6 p.m. 19th April, 1955. The monocycle duration record is 11 hours 21 mins. (83·4 miles) by Raymond Le Grand at Maubeug, France on 12th September, 1955.

Talking — The world record for non-stop talking was set at Oldham, Lancashire, England, by Kevin Sheenhan of Limerick, Ireland, with 127 hours (5 days 7 hours) in October 1954.

The longest running commentary was one of 27 hours 15 minutes by Pierre Chouinard of CKAC Station, Montreal, Canada, when reporting a piano-playing marathon starting at 7.30 p.m. on 25th February, 1955.

Filibuster

The longest filibuster in the history of the United States Senate is that of Senator Morse (Independent, Oregon) on 24th–25th April, 1953, when he spoke on the Tidelands Oil Bill for 22 hours 26 minutes without once being able to resume his seat.

Sermon

The longest sermon on record was delivered by Clinton Locy of West Richland, Washington, U.S.A., in February 1955. It lasted 48 hours 18 minutes and ranged through texts from every book in the Bible.

Dancing

Marathon dancing must be distinguished from dancing mania which is a pathological condition. The worst outbreak of dancing mania was at Aachen, Germany, in July 1374 when hordes of men and women broke into a frenzied dance in the streets which lasted for hours till injury or complete exhaustion ensued.

Of organised marathon dancing that of the greatest duration was one in Detroit, U.S.A., in which relays of dancers stayed in action for 106 days before the police intervened to break it up.

Ballet

Among the world's greatest ballet dancers, the Russian-born Pole Vaslav Nijinsky (1890–1950) was alone in being able to execute the *entrechat dix*—crossing and uncrossing the feet ten times in a single elevation.

The greatest number of spins called for in classical ballet choreography is the thirty-two *fouettés en tournants* in Swan Lake. Miss Rowena Jackson of New Zealand has achieved 121 such turns in class in Melbourne in 1940.

Rocking-Chair

The longest recorded duration of a " Rockathon " is 92 hours by two Canadians ending on 27th March, 1955 in Hawkesbury, Canada.

Piano-playing

On 1st May, 1955, in Berlin, Heinz Arntz set a world record by playing the piano non-stop, except for refreshment intervals, for 423 hours (17 days 15 hours). The British record is 194 hours (8 days 2 hours) set by J. D. Strickland at Bolton, Lancs., on 20th May, 1951.

The women's world record is 132 hours (5 days 12 hours) 5 minutes, starting on 25th April and finishing at 11.5 p.m. on 30th April, 1955, at Shepherd's Hall, Old Market, Bristol, by Marie Ashton.

Pole-Squatting

There being no international rules, the " standards of living " atop poles vary widely. The record squat for men is 196 days by William L. Howard, 34, at Portland, Oregon, U.S.A., ending on 25th December, 1952. The women's record is 152 days by Miss Erma Leach, 25, at San Francisco on a 51-foot pole ending on 1st January, 1951.

The British record is 31 days 7 hours by Victor Reeves, 23, of Walsall, England, in a 28-inch diameter barrel on a 40-foot pole ending 19th August, 1952. This is claimed as a world record for a barrel.

Modern records do not, however, compare with that of the Syrian monk, Simeon the Stylite, in the fifth century A.D., who spent over thirty years on a 50-foot high stone pillar at Qualat-Seman, near Aleppo, Syria.

Pipe-Smoking

The world record for keeping a pipe alight (3·3 grams of tobacco and two matches) is 1 hour 55 minutes 11 seconds by Paul Lauderback of Los Angeles, U.S.A., in an international contest in March 1954.

Fasting

Most humans experience considerable pain after an abstinence from food for even twelve hours. Records set free from unremitting medical surveillance are of little value.

The world " record " is claimed by Mrs. Cornelia Foster, 61, of Kew Township, Johannesburg, South Africa, who claims to have lived 102 days on nothing but water and soda water. An earlier claim of 210 days had been made for a seventeen-year-old Indian girl Dhanalakshim of Mercara in South India in November 1952.

Hunger Strike

The longest recorded hunger-strike is that of the Irish playwright Terence MacSweeney in Brixton Prison, London which lasted seventy-four days before death ensued on 25th October, 1920.

Sleeplessness

The most extreme case of survival without sleep is that of the Italian Ugo Dell'aringa, a bank clerk from Lucca, who has only been observed to have one hour's sleep in the thirty-eight years since 1917, when privations in an Austrian Prisoner of War Camp affected his centres of sleep.

PARACHUTING

Earliest Descent

The earliest demonstration of a parachute was by the Frenchman Sebastien Lenormand from the tower of Montpellier Observatory, France, in 1783. Ten years later in 1793 J. P. Blanchard made a descent from a balloon but broke a leg. The first successful parachute jump from a balloon was by Jacques Garnerin (1769–1823) from 2,230 feet over Monceau Park, Paris, on 22nd October, 1797. The earliest descent from an aeroplane was that of Captain Berry, U.S. Army over St. Louis, Missouri, in 1912.

Highest

Captain Edward Sperry and First-Lt. Henry P. Nielsen of the U.S. Army in ejection tests from a B.47 jet bomber over the Gulf of Mexico in the summer of 1954 parachuted from a height of 45,200 feet.

Lowest

The lowest recorded voluntary jump is the 154-foot jump by John Tranum (G.B.) from Pasadena Bridge, California, U.S.A., in October 1927.

Longest Delayed Drop

In August 1945 Lt.-Col. Vasiliy Romanuk of Russia jumped from 43,005 feet and fell 39,833 feet (7·54 miles) before his 'chute was opened at 3,172 feet. The time taken for such a fall at a terminal velocity of 120 m.p.h. would be $3\frac{3}{4}$ minutes. In the seventeen years from 1934 to 4th September, 1951, when he made his two-thousandth jump, Romanuk logged 150 parachuting hours. The feminine record for a free fall is 26,230 feet from a height of 27,430 feet by Mlle. Odette Rousseau, near Paris on 24th August, 1955.

Frequency

Sgt. Bonvizotto made fifty jumps in 4 hours 41 minutes (one every 5 minutes 37·2 seconds) in a specially staged Argentine army test near Buenos Aires on 6th April, 1954.

Heaviest Load

The greatest load ever dropped by parachute is 5·35 tons of lead and cement from 2,300 feet at El Centro, California, in a U.S. army test in June 1952. The nylon parachute with an area of three-quarters of an acre was the largest ever used.

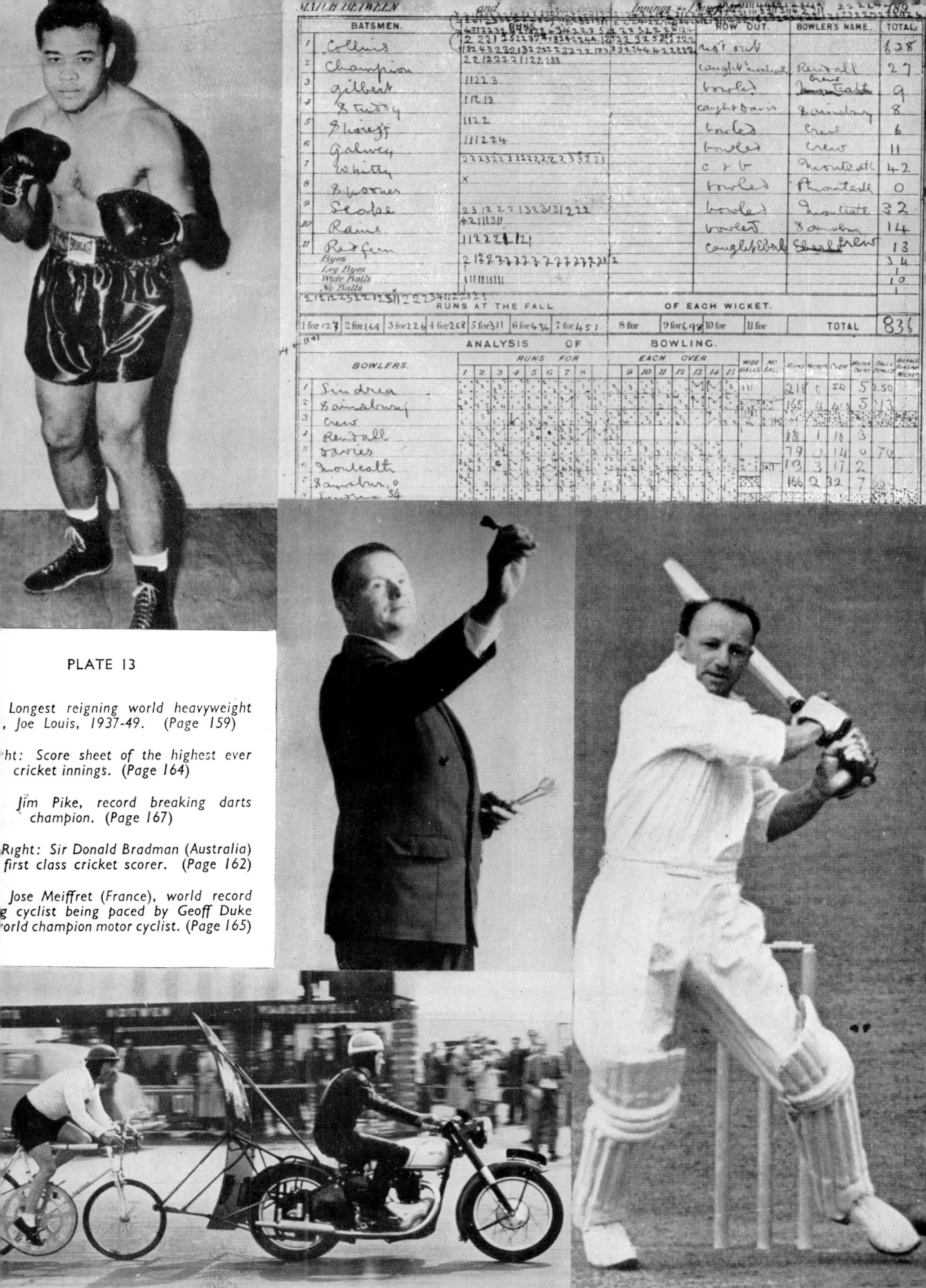

MATCH BETWEEN and Innings

	BATSMEN.	RUNS	HOW OUT.	BOWLER'S NAME.	TOTAL
1	Collins	[illegible]	not out		628
2	Champion	2212222112 2283	caught Monteath	Rendall	27
3	Gilbert	11223	bowled	Crew	9
4	Sturdy	11213	caught Davis	Sainsbury	8
5	Sharp	1122	bowled	Crew	6
6	Galway	111224	bowled	Crew	11
7	Whitty	2223222222222223 3221	c & b	Monteath	42
8	Spooner	x	bowled	Monteath	0
9	Leake	231227132313 1222	bowled	Monteath	32
10	Raine	4211311	bowled	Sainsbury	14
11	Redfern	11222 1 2 1	caught Ebel	Crew	13
	Byes	2 1 7 7 7 7 7 7 7 7 7 7 7 7 7 2 1 2			34
	Leg Byes				1
	Wide Balls	1111111111			10
	No Balls				1

RUNS AT THE FALL OF EACH WICKET.

1 for 127	2 for 164	3 for 226	4 for 268	5 for 311	6 for 436	7 for 451	8 for	9 for 698	10 for	11 for	TOTAL	836

ANALYSIS OF BOWLING.

	BOWLERS.	Runs	Wickets	Overs	Maiden Overs
1	Sindrea	218	0	50	5
2	Sainsbury	165	4	43	5
3	Crew				
4	Rendall	18	1	10	3
5	Davies	79	0	14	0
6	Monteath	113	3	17	2
7	Sainsbury	166	2	32	7

PLATE 13

Longest reigning world heavyweight , Joe Louis, 1937-49. (Page 159)

ht: Score sheet of the highest ever cricket innings. (Page 164)

Jim Pike, record breaking darts champion. (Page 167)

Right: Sir Donald Bradman (Australia) first class cricket scorer. (Page 162)

Jose Meiffret (France), world record g cyclist being paced by Geoff Duke orld champion motor cyclist. (Page 165)

Above: Billy Wright, the most capped footballer. (Page 168)

Above: Hans Jeppson, the world's most expensive footballer. (Page

PLATE 14

Below: Huaso, ridden by Capt. A. L. Morales (Chile) (Page 167)

Below. K. J. Jones (Wales), most capped Rugby footballer. (Pa

TWELVE

SPORT

ANGLING

LARGEST CATCHES

The largest fish ever caught on a rod is the, as yet unratified, 2,536 lb., 16 feet 9 inches long man-eating White Shark (*Carcharodon carcharias*) by A. Dean at Denial Bay, near Ceduna, Australia, on 12 April, 1955. The largest fish ever caught by a woman was the 882 lb. Bluefin (*Tuna*) by Mrs. B. D. Crowninshield off Wedgeport, Nova Scotia, on 6 Sept., 1947. A Bluefin weighing 977 lb. was caught by a man in 1950.

The largest fish ever taken underwater was a 628 lb. Jew fish (*Giant Sea Bass*) by Arnaldo Borges, south of Rio de Janeiro on 14 Jan., 1954.

The world surf casting record is 660 feet made at San Francisco in 1938 with a nine-foot bamboo rod by Prima Livernais.

BRITISH ROD-CAUGHT RECORDS

(as supplied by the Chairman of the National Federation of Sea-Anglers, Mr. L. A. Hastilow)

Species	Weight lb.	ozs.	Angler	Location	Year
Bass	18	2	F. C. Borley	Felixstowe	1943
Black Sea-Bream	6	5	M. J. Browne	Menai Strait	1935
Red Sea-Bream	7	8	A. F. Bell	Fowey	1925
Brill	13	10	J. L. Williams	Brighton	1933
Bull Huss (Greater Spotted Dog-fish)	21	0	F. C. Halse	Poole	1939
Coalfish	23	8	H. Millais	Lands End	1921
Cod	42	0*	I. L. Stewart	Ballycotton	1921
Conger	84	0	H. A. Kelly	Dungeness	1933
Dab	2	9½	M. L. Watts	Morfa Beach	1939
Flounder	4	5	E. F. J. Plumridge	Fowey	1928
Grey Mullet	10	1	P. C. Libby	Portland	1952
Haddock	8	4*	A. Attenborough	Ballycotton	1912
Hake	17	8	Mrs. J. T. Ashby	Penzance	1911
Halibut	152	12*	E. C. Henning	Valencia	1926
John Dory	8	8	J. F. Vallin	Mevagissy	1922
Ling	45	0	H. C. Nicholl	Penzance	1912
Mackerel	4	0½	Fl./Lt. P. Porter	Peel, Isle of Man	1952
Plaice	7	0	T. Farrow	Hastings	1913
Pollock	21	0	H. Millais	Lands End	1931
Pouting	4	10	H. B. Dare	Coverack	1935
	4	10*	W. G. Pales	Ballycotton	1937
Ray (Thornback)	38	0	E. C. Henning	Rustington	1935
Scad	3	3	J. B. Thornton	Deal	1934
Skate (Common)	336	0		Beer	1910
Shark (Blue)	155	0	J. F. Barlow	Looe	1954
Shark (Porbeagle)	365	0*	Dr. O'D. Browne	Achill	1932
Sole	4	0	M. Sinton	Clevedon Pier	1943
Tope	62	11	J. Drew	Herne Bay	1911
Tunny	851	0	L. Mitchell-Henry	Whitby	1933
Turbot	27	14	F. S. Stenning	Salcombe	1907
Whiting	6	0	E. H. Tame	Shieldaig	1940
Wrasse	12	12	F. A. Mitchell-Hedges	Looe	1912

(*Also Irish Record)

IRISH ANGLING RECORDS (Sea)

Species	Weight lb.	ozs.	Angler	Location	Year
Bass	16	0	Major Windham	Waterville	1909
Bream (Red)	5	0	W. R. Harrison	Ballycotton	1908
Coalfish	22	0	Baroness Bouck	Ballycotton	1910
Cod	42	0	I. L. Stewart	Ballycotton	1921
Conger	72	0	J. Green	Valencia	1914
Dab	1	8	Mrs. J. S. Dunn	Ballycotton	1911
Flounder	3	0	T. L. Ashby	Ballyconneely	1908
Gurnard	8	0	W. J. Edwards	Valencia	1919

IRISH ANGLING RECORDS (Sea)—*continued*

Species	Weight lb. ozs	Angler	Location	Year
Haddock	8 4	A. Attenborough	Ballycotton	1912
Hake	14 0	Mr. Taffler	Ballycotton	1946
Halibut	152 12	E. C. Henning	Valencia	1926
Ling	44 0	E. Graham Falcon	Ballycotton	1915
Monkfish	52 0	W. W. Hewetson	Clew Bay	1933
Pollock	19 3	J. N. Hearn	Ballycotton	1904
Pouting	4 10	W. G. Pales	Ballycotton	1937
Shark (Blue)	122 0	J. R. Pickup	Ballycotton	1937
Shark (Porbeagle)	365 0	Dr. O'D. Browne	Keem Bay, Achill	1932
Skate	221 0	T. Tucker	Ballycotton	1913
Tope	56 0	Mr. Tite	Derrynane	1939
Turbot	26 8	J. F. Eldridge	Valencia	1915
Whiting	4 0	W. R. Harrison	Ballycotton	1908

(Fresh Water)

Species	Weight lb. ozs	Angler	Location	Year
Bream	11 8	A. Pike	River Blackwater	1882
Perch	5 8	S. Drum	Lough Erne	1946
Pike	53 0‡	J. Garvin	Lough Conn	1920
Salmon	57 0*	M. Maher	River Suir	1874
Trout (Brown)	30 8†	J. W. Pepper	Lough Derg	1861
Trout (Sea)	7 8	B. H. Fry	Cloonaghlin Lough	1927
	7 8	Hon. M. Biddulph	Easkey Lough	1945

* A 58 lb. salmon was reported from the River Shannon in 1872 while one of 62 lb. was taken in a net on the lower Shannon on 27 March, 1925.

† A 35½ lb. Brown Trout is reputed to have been caught at Tarlaghvam, near Tuam, in Aug. 1738.

‡ A pike in excess of 92 lb. is reputed to have been landed from the Shannon at Portumna c. 1796.

ENGLISH FRESH WATER RECORDS

Species	lb. oz. dr.		Year
Gudgeon	4 4	from the Thames at Datchet, by G. Cedric	1933
Bleak	5 4	from the Trent at Radcliffe, by H. Stubbins	1890
Dace	1 8 5	from a tributary of the Avon (Hampshire), by R. W. Humphrey	1932
Roach	3 14	from a reservoir at Molesey, Middlesex, by W. Renny	1938
Rudd	4 8	from Mere near Thetford, Norfolk, by Rev. E. E. Alston	1933
Perch	6 0 14	from the Stour (Bures), by P. Clarke	1950
Grayling	7 2	from the Melgum by J. Stewart	1939
Chub	8 8	from the Rother, by D. Deekes	1951
Tench	8 8	from the Leicester Canal, by M. Foode	1950
Common Bream	13 8	from Castle Lake, Chiddingstone, by E. G. Costin	1945
Barbel	14 6	from the Thames, by T. Wheeler	1888
	14 6	from the Avon (Hampshire), by H. D. Tryon	1934
	14 6	from the Avon (Hampshire), by F. W. K. Wallis	1937
Pike	37 8	from the Avon (Hampshire), by C. Warwick	1944
Carp	44	from Redmire Pool, Herefordshire, by R. Walker	1952

GAME FISH	Salmon (rod and line)	64 lb., Tay, in 1922, by Miss G. W. Ballantine.
	Brown Trout (lake)	39½ lb., Loch Awe, 1866, by W. C. Muir (on a salmon rod).
	Trout (river)	27¾ lb., River Tay (Murthly), in 1842, by Col. Dobiggin.
	Trout (sea)	22½ lb., River Frome (Dorset), in 1946, by S. R. Dwight.
SEA	Tunny	852 lb., off Scarborough, September 1949, by J. H. Lewis.

ARCHERY

EARLIEST REFERENCES

Palaeolithic drawings of archers indicate that bows and arrows are an invention of at least 20,000 years ago. Archery developed as an organised sport at least as early as the fifth century A.D. The oldest archery body in the British Isles is the Royal Company of Archers, the Sovereign's bodyguard for Scotland, dating from 1676 though the Ancient Scorton Arrow meeting in Yorkshire was first staged in 1673.

FLIGHT SHOOTING

The world's greatest distances were achieved in Turkey, near Istanbul, in 1798, when a distance of 967 yards was attained by Sultan Selim.

The modern world flight shooting freestyle record is 719 yards 2 feet by Paul Berry (U.S.A.) at Middletown, Ohio, in 1949.

The regular style (standing stance) record is 640 yards by J. Stewart at Austin, Texas, in 1949.

The British record is 490 yards set by J. Flinton at Radley, 2 July, 1955.

TARGET SHOOTING

(Highest score, a " gold " value 9 points).

The British records for standard rounds are:—

HIGHEST SCORES

York Round (6 dozen at 100 yards, 4 dozen at 80 yards and 2 dozen at 60 yards)
Single Round 913, J. B. Collyer, Oxford, 22 July, 1954
Double Round 1,677, J. B. Collyer, Oxford, 22 July, 1954

Western Round (4 dozen at 60 yards and 4 dozen at 50 yards)
Championship 698, G. Arthur, Oxford, 1950
Club Shoot 742, H. N. P. Payton, 19 July, 1953

American Round ($2\frac{1}{2}$ dozen at 60 yards, 50 yards and 40 yards)
County Championship 688, T. C. Morgan, Derbyshire, 1952
Club Shoot 730, H. N. P. Payton, Henley, 3 Oct., 1953

Hereford (women) (6 dozen at 80 yards, 4 dozen at 60 yards and 2 dozen at 50 yards).
Single Round 875, Miss J. Warner, Winchester, 27 May, 1955
Double Round 1,725, Miss J. Warner, Winchester, 27 May, 1955

MOST TITLES

The greatest number of world (Fédération Internationale de Tir à l'Arc) titles (instituted 1911), won by a man is 5 by H. Deutgen (Sweden) from 1947-1950 and 1952. The greatest number won by a woman is also 5 by Janina Kurkowska (Poland) winning the last in 1946.

The greatest number of British Championships is 12 by Horace Ford between 1849 and 1867.

ATHLETICS—TRACK AND FIELD

EARLIEST REFERENCES

Track and field athletics date from the ancient Olympic Games. The earliest recorded Olympiad dates from the 21 or 22 July, 776 B.C., at which celebration Coroebas won the foot race.

The earliest meetings in the British Isles were probably those at the Royal Military Academy, Sandhurst, c. 1810. The race with the longest history is the Rugby School Crick Run which has records back to 1837. The oldest athletic club in the world is Exeter College A.C., Oxford, which was founded in the autumn of 1850. Amongst its captains have been Dr. J. E. Lovelock and Dr. R. G. Bannister, both former holders of the world one-mile record.

FASTEST RUNNER

In May 1949 Melvin Patton (U.S.A.), co-holder of the world's 100 yards record, running the last stage of a sprint relay was timed to cover a flying 100 yards in 8·3 seconds, giving an average of 24·64 m.p.h. However, there is evidence that another Californian sprinter, Harold Davis, well surpassed 25 m.p.h. in the latter half of the Amateur Athletics Union 100 metre championship final in New York on 20 June, 1943. See Plate 12.

HIGHEST JUMPER

There are several reported instances of high jumpers exceeding the official world record height of 6 feet $11\frac{5}{8}$ inches. The earliest of these came from unsubstantiated reports of Watussi tribesmen in Central Africa clearing up to 8 feet $2\frac{1}{2}$ inches, probably however, from inclined take-offs. Other jumpers reputed to have cleared 7 feet in practice are W. Stewart (U.S.A.) (7 feet 0 inches in 1941), L. Steers (U.S.A.) (over 7 feet 0 inches in 1941), C. Holding (U.S.A. (7 feet 0 inches on 24 April, 1954, at Commerce, Texas) and W. F. Davis, the Olympic record holder (7 feet 0 inches). The greatest height cleared above an athlete's own head is the 13 inches by E. A. Ifeajuna (Nigeria), at Vancouver on 31 July, 1954, when winning the British Empire Title at 6 feet 8 inches. The highest cleared by a woman above her own head is $2\frac{1}{4}$ inches by Mary Donaghy (New Zealand), at Paeroa, New Zealand, on 29 March, 1955, when jumping 5 feet $4\frac{1}{4}$ inches.

MOST OLYMPIC GOLD MEDALS

Ray C. Ewry (U.S.A.) between 1900 and 1908 won 8 individual Olympic gold medals. His standing long jump record of 11 feet $4\frac{7}{8}$ inches at St. Louis in Aug. 1904 remains unsurpassed. Paavo Johannes Nurmi (Finland) won 7 individual and 2 team race gold medals between 1920 and 1928. The greatest number of medals won in a single celebration is 4 by A. C. Kraenzelin (U.S.A.) in 1900, by P. J. Nurmi (Finland) in 1924, J. C. Owens (U.S.A.) (100 and 200 metres, the long jump and first stage in the 4 × 100 metre relay) at Berlin in 1936, and the 4 of Francina E. Blankers-Koen (Netherlands), (100 and 200 metres, 80 metre hurdles, and last stage in the women's 4 × 100 metre relay) at Wembley, London, in 1948.

MOST A.A.A. TITLES

The greatest number of national A.A.A. titles amassed by an individual athlete is the 14 individual and two relay titles by E. McDonald Bailey from 1946 to 1953.

The greatest consecutive number of title wins stands to the credit of D. Horgan of Ireland (Shot Putt, 1893-1899), A. A. Cooper (2 miles walk, 1932-1938), D. O. Finlay (120 yards hurdles, 1932-1938) and H. Whittle (440 yards hurdles, 1947-1953) each with 7.

EARLIEST LANDMARKS

The first time 10 seconds (" even time ") was bettered under championship conditions was in the 1890 A.A.U. Championships at Analostan Island, Washington, by John Owen who recorded 9 4/5th seconds. The first recorded instance of 6 feet being cleared in the high jump was on 17 March, 1876, at Marston, near Oxford, England, by the Hon. Marshall Jones Brooks with 6 feet 0⅛ inches. The breaking of the " 4 minute barrier " in the one mile was first achieved at 6·10 p.m. on 6 May, 1954, on the Iffley Road track, Oxford, by Dr. Roger Gilbert Bannister, C.B.E. (Great Britain) with 3 minutes 59·4 seconds.

WORLD'S RECORDS (MEN)

The complete list of World's Records for the fifty scheduled men's events passed by the International Amateur Athletic Federation as of 1 November, 1955.

RUNNING

Event	Mins. Secs.		Place	Date
100 yards	9·3	Melvin Emery Patton (U.S.A.)	Fresno, U.S.A.	15 May, 1948
	9·3	Hector Dennie Hogan (Australia)	Sydney, Australia	3 Mar., 1954
	9·3*	James J. Golliday (U.S.A.)	Evanston, U.S.A.	14 May, 1955
220 yards	20·2	Melvin Emery Patton (U.S.A.)	Los Angeles, U.S.A.	7 May, 1949
440 yards	46·0	Herbert Henry McKenley (Jamaica)	Berkeley, U.S.A.	5 June, 1948
880 yards	1:47·5*	Lawrence Spurrier (U.S.A.)	Berkeley, U.S.A.	26 Mar., 1955
1 mile	3:58·0	John Michael Landy (Australia)	Turku, Finland	21 June, 1954
2 miles	8:33·4*	Sándor Iharos (Hungary)	London, England	30 May, 1955
3 miles	13:14·2*	Sándor Iharos (Hungary)	Budapest, Hungary	23 Oct., 1955
6 miles	27:59·2	Emil Zátopek (Czechoslovakia)	Brussels, Belgium	1 June, 1954
10 miles	48:12·0	Emil Zátopek (Czechoslovakia)	Stará Boleslav, CSR.	29 Sept., 1951
15 miles	1H14:01·0*	Emil Zátopek (Czechoslovakia)	Prague, CSR	29 Oct., 1955
100 metres	10·2	James Cleveland Owens (U.S.A.)	Chicago, U.S.A.	20 June, 1936
	10·2	Harold Davis (U.S.A.)	Compton, U.S.A.	6 June, 1941
	10·2	Lloyd Berrington LaBeach (Panama)	Fresno, U.S.A.	15 May, 1948
	10·2	Henry Norwood Ewell (U.S.A.)	Evanston, U.S.A.	9 July, 1948
	10·2	Emmanuel McDonald Bailey (Trinidad and G.B.)	Belgrade, Jugoslavia	25 Aug., 1951
	10·2	Heinz Fütterer (Germany)	Yokohama, Japan	31 Oct., 1954
200 metres	20·2	Melvin Emery Patton (U.S.A.)	Los Angeles, U.S.A.	7 May, 1949
400 metres	45·4*	Louis Jones (U.S.A.)	Mexico City	18 Mar., 1955
800 metres	1:45·7*	Roger Moens (Belgium)	Oslo, Norway	3 Aug., 1955
1,000 metres	2:19·0*	Audun Boysen (Norway)	Göteborg	30 Aug., 1955
	2:19·0*	István Rózsavölgyi (Hungary)	Budapest, Hungary	21 Sept., 1955
1,500 metres	3:40·8*	Sándor Iharos (Hungary)	Helsinki, Finland	28 July, 1955
	3:40·8*	László Tábori Talabercsuk (Hungary)	Oslo, Norway	7 Sept., 1955
	3:40·8*	Gunnar Nielsen (Denmark)	Oslo, Norway	7 Sept., 1955
2,000 metres	5:02·2*	István Rózsavölgyi (Hungary)	Budapest, Hungary	2 Oct., 1955
3,000 metres	7:55·6*	Sándor Iharos (Hungary)	Budapest, Hungary	14 May, 1955
5,000 metres	13:40·6	Sándor Iharos (Hungary)	Budapest, Hungary	23 Oct., 1955
10,000 metres	28:54·2	Emil Zátopek (Czechoslovakia)	Brussels, Belgium	1 June, 1954
20,000 metres	59:51·8	Emil Zátopek (Czechoslovakia)	Stará Boleslav, CSR.	29 Sept., 1951
25,000 metres	1H16:34·6*	Emil Zátopek (Czechoslovakia)	Prague, CSR.	29 Oct., 1955
30,000 metres	1H35:23·8	Emil Zátopek (Czechoslovakia)	Stará Boleslav, CSR.	26 Oct., 1952
1 hour (12m. 809yd.)	20.052m.	Emil Zátopek (Czechoslovakia)	Stará Boleslav, CSR.	29 Sept., 1951

RELAYS

Event	Mins. Secs.		Place	Date
4×110 yards	40·2*	Texas University, U.S.A. (Finis Dean Smith, Alvin Frieden, Jerry Prewitt, Robert Whilden)	Modesto, U.S.A.	21 May, 1955
4×220 yards and 4×200 metres	1:24·0	University of Southern California, U.S.A. (George Pasquali, Ronald Frazier, Norman Stocks, Patton)	Los Angeles, U.S.A.	20 May, 1949
4×440 yards	3:08·8	Amateur Athletic Union Team, U.S.A. (Gerald Eugene Cole, John William Mashburn, Reginald Pearman, Whitfield)	London, England	9 Aug., 1952
4×880 yards	7:27·3	Fordham University, U.S.A. (Terrence Foley, Frank Tarsney, William Persichetty, Thomas Courtney)	Los Angeles, U.S.A.	21 May, 1954
4×1 mile	16:41·0	Great Britain and Northern Ireland Team (C. J. Chataway, G. W. Nankeville, D. C. Seaman, R. G. Bannister)	London, England	1 Aug., 1953
4×100 metres	39·8	United States Olympic Games Team (Owens, Ralph H. Metcalfe, Foy Draper, Frank C. Wykoff)	Berlin, Germany	9 Aug., 1936
4×400 metres	3:03·9	Jamaican Olympic Games Team (Arthur Stanley Wint, Leslie Alphanzo Laing, McKenley, Rhoden)	Helsinki, Finland	27 July, 1952
4×800 metres	7:26·4*	Soviet Army Team (Gennadiy Modoy, Georgiy G. Ivakin, Sergey Sukhanov, Oleg Ivanov Ageyev)	Riga, Latvia	2 Aug., 1955
4×1,500 metres	15:14·8*	Budapest Honved Sport Egyesulet (Ferenc Mikes, László Tábori Talabercsuk, István Rózsavölgyi, Sándor Iharos)	Budapest, Hungary	29 Sept., 1955

HURDLING

Event	Mins. Secs.		Place	Date
120 yards (3′ 6″)	13·5	Richard Harold Attlesey (U.S.A.)	Fresno, U.S.A.	13 May, 1950
	13·5	Richard Harold Attlesey (U.S.A.)	Helsinki, Finland	10 July, 1950
220 yards (2′ 6″)	22·3	William Harrison Dillard (U.S.A.)	Salt Lake City, U.S.A.	21 June, 1947
440 yards (3′ 0″)	51·3	Yuriy Nikolayvich Lituyev (U.S.S.R.)	London, England	13 Oct., 1954
110 metres (3′ 6″)	13·5	Richard Harold Attlesey (U.S.A.)	Helsinki, Finland	10 July, 1950
200 metres (2′ 6″)	22·3	Frederick Wolcott (U.S.A.)	Princeton, U.S.A.	8 June, 1940
	22·3	William Harrison Dillard (U.S.A.)	Salt Lake City, U.S.A.	21 June, 1947
400 metres (3′ 0″)	50·4	Yuriy Nikolayvich Lituyev (U.S.S.R.)	Budapest, Hungary	20 Sept., 1953
3,000 metres S'chase	8:40·4*	Jerzy Chromik (Poland)	Budapest, Hungary	11 Sept., 1955

WORLD'S RECORDS (MEN)—*continued*

FIELD EVENTS

Event	ft. ins.	Metres		Place	Date
High Jump	6′ 11½″	(2·12 m.)	Walter Francis Davis (U.S.A.)	Dayton, Ohio, U.S.A.	27 June, 1953
Pole Vault	15′ 7¾″	(4·77 m.)	Cornelius Anthony Warmerdam (U.S.A.)	Modesto, U.S.A.	23 May, 1942
Long Jump	26′ 8¼″	(8·13 m.)	James Cleveland Owens (U.S.A.) See plate 12	Ann Arbor, U.S.A.	25 May, 1935
Hop, Step and Jump	54′ 3¾″	(16·56 m.)	Adhemar Ferriera da Silva (Brazil)	Mexico City	16 Mar., 1955
Shot Putt	60′ 10″	(18·54 m.)	William Parry O'Brien (U.S.A.)	Los Angeles, U.S.A.	11 June, 1954
Discus Throw	194′ 6″	(59·28 m.)	Fortune Everette Gordien (U.S.A.)	Pasadena, U.S.A.	22 Aug., 1953
Hammer Throw	211′ 8½″	(64·52 m.)	Mikhail Petrovich Krivonosov (U.S.S.R.)	Belgrade, Jugoslavia	19 Sept., 1955
Javelin Throw	268′ 2½″	(81·74 m.)	Franklin W. Held (U.S.A.)	Modesto, U.S.A.	21 May, 1955
Decathlon		7,980* points.	Rafer Johnson (U.S.A.)	Kingsburg, U.S.A.	10/11 June, 1955

(1st day: 100 m. 10·5; Long Jump 24′ 6⅜″; Shot Putt 45′ 3¼″; High Jump 6′ 0¾″; 400 m. 49·7.
2nd day: 110 m. Hurdles 14·5; Discus 154′ 10¾″; Pole Vault 12′ 8½″; Javelin 193′ 10⅝″; 1,500 m. 5:01·5). See Plate 12.

WORLD'S RECORDS (WOMEN)

The complete list of Women's World's Records passed by the International Amateur Athletic Federation as at 1 Nov., 1955

RUNNING

Event	Mins. Secs.		Place	Date
100 yards	10·4	Marjorie Jackson (Australia) See Plate 12	Sydney, Australia	8 Mar., 1952
220 yards	23·8*	Christa Stubnick-Seliger (Germany)	Erfurt, Germany	29 May, 1955
880 yards	2:08·4	Nina Grigorievna Otkalenko (1) (U.S.S.R.)	Moscow, U.S.S.R.	18 July, 1954
60 metres	7·3	Stanislava Walasiewiczowna (Poland)	Lemberg, Poland	24 Sept., 1933
100 metres	11·4	Marjorie Jackson (Australia)	Gifu, Japan	4 Oct., 1952
200 metres	23·4	Marjorie Jackson (Australia)	Helsinki, Finland	25 July, 1952
800 metres	2:05·0	Nina Grigorievna Otkalenko (1) (U.S.S.R.)	Zagreb, Jugoslavia	25 Sept., 1955

RELAYS

Event	Mins. Secs.		Place	Date
4×110 yards	46·3	Australian National Team (Shirley Barbara Delahunty (2), Verna Johnson, Winsome Cripps (3), Jackson)	London, England	4 Aug., 1952
4×220 yards	1:39·9	Great Britain and Northern Ireland Team (Anne Pashley, Jean Newboult, Shirley Hampton, Ann Elaine Johnson)	London, England	30 Sept., 1953
3×880 yards	6:36·2	Hungarian National Team (Anna Bácskai, Agnes Oros, Aranka Kazi)	Tata, Hungary	21 July, 1954
4×100 metres	45·6	U.S.S.R. National Team (Vyera Kalashnikova, Zinaida Safronova, Nadezhda Dvalishvili (4), Irina Robertnova Turova)	Budapest, Hungary	20 Sept., 1953
	45·6*	U.S.S.R. National Team (Porlinithenko, Galina Vinogradova, Zinaida Safronova, Mariya Itkina)	Moscow, U.S.S.R.	11 Sept., 1955
4×200 metres	1:36·4	U.S.S.R. National Team (Vyera Kalashnikova, Zinaida Safronova, Flora Kazantseva, Nadezhda Dvalishvili)	Bucharest, Rumania	9 Aug., 1953
3×800 metres	6:27·6*	U.S.S.R. National Team (A. Lapshina, Ludmila Lysenko, Nina Grigorievna Otkalenko (1))	Moscow, U.S.S.R.	11 Sept., 1955

HURDLES

Event			Place	Date
80 metres	10·8*	Galina Yermolenko (U.S.S.R.)	Leningrad, U.S.S.R.	6 July, 1955

FIELD EVENTS

Event	ft. ins.	Metres		Place	Date
High Jump	5′ 8″	(1·73 m.)	Aleksandra Georgievna Chudina (U.S.S.R.)	Kiev, U.S.S.R.	22 May, 1954
Long Jump	20′ 7½″	(6·28 m.)	Yvette Winifred Williams (5) (N.Z.)	Gisborne, N.Z.	20 Feb., 1954
	20′ 7½″	(6·28 m.)	Galina Vinogradova (U.S.S.R.)	Moscow, U.S.S.R.	11 Sept., 1955
Shot Putt	53′ 6½″	(16·32 m.)	Galina Ivanovna Zybina (U.S.S.R.)	Stalinabad, U.S.S.R.	24 Oct., 1955
Discus Throw	187′ 1″	(57·04 m.)	Nina Dumbadze (U.S.S.R.)	Tbilisi, U.S.S.R.	18 Oct., 1952
Javelin Throw	182′ 0″	(55·48 m.)	Nadezhda Efimova Konyayeva (U.S.S.R.)	Kiev, U.S.S.R.	6 Aug., 1954

PENTATHLON

		Place	Date
4,977* points	Nina Martyenko (U.S.S.R.)	Leningrad, U.S.S.R.	8 July, 1955

(200 metres 25·8; 80 metre H. 11·3; High Jump 1·62 m. (5′ 3¾″); Long Jump 5·92 m. (19′ 5⅛″); Shot Putt 13·54 m. (44′ 5¼″).)

(1) née Pletnyeva; (2) née Strickland; (3) now Mrs. Dennis; (4) née Khnykina; (5) now Mrs. Corlett

* Performance not yet ratified as of 1st November, 1955

UNITED KINGDOM BEST PERFORMANCES

Event	Time hr. min. sec.	Holder	Place	Date
100 yards	9·7	Eric Liddell	London	7 July, 1923
	9·7	Cyril Holmes	Sydney	5 Feb., 1938
220 yards	21·2	William Applegarth	London	4 July, 1914
	21·2	Cyril Holmes	Sydney	10 Feb., 1938
440 yards	47·6	Godfrey Brown	London	1 Aug., 1938
880 yards	1 48·6	Brian Hewson	London	13 Aug., 1955
1 mile	3 58·8	Roger Bannister	Vancouver	7 Aug., 1954
2 miles	8 34·8	Kenneth Wood	London	30 May, 1955
3 miles	13 23·2	Christopher Chataway	London	30 July, 1955
6 miles	28 19·4	Gordon Pirie	London	10 July, 1953
10 miles	50 11·0	Ian Binnie	Dunoon	28 Aug., 1953
15 miles	1 19 19·4	John Stone	Walton	23 Oct., 1954
100 metres	10·4	Arthur Sweeney	Wupperthal	2 July, 1937
200 metres	21·2	George Ellis	Berne	29 Aug., 1954
400 metres	46·7	Godfrey Brown	Berlin	7 Aug., 1936

UNITED KINGDOM BEST PERFORMANCES—*continued*

Event	Time hr. min. sec.	Holder	Place	Date
800 metres	1 47·4	Derek Johnson	Berne	28 Aug., 1954
1,000 metres	{ 2 20·2	Brian Hewson	Manchester	21 June, 1955
	2 20·2	Brian Hewson	Aldershot	2 July, 1955
1,500 metres	3 42·2	Roger Bannister	Vancouver	7 Aug., 1954
2,000 metres	5 09·4	Christopher Chataway	London	11 June, 1955
3,000 metres	8 06·2	Christopher Chataway	London	7 June, 1954
5,000 metres	13 51·6	Christopher Chataway	London	13 Oct., 1954
10,000 metres	29 17·2	Gordon Pirie	Stockholm	3 Sept., 1953
25,000 metres	1 23 45·8	Ernest Harper	Berlin	25 Aug., 1929
Marathon	2 17 39·4*	James Peters	Chiswick	26 June, 1954
1 hour	11 miles 1,575 yds.	Ian Binnie	Dunoon	28 Aug., 1953
120 yards Hurdles	14·3 *m*	Donald Finlay	Paris	4 Sept., 1938
	14·3	Jack Parker	London	30 July, 1955
220 yards Hurdles (straight)	23·3	Peter Hildreth	London	29 Aug., 1955
220 yards Hurdles (turn)	23·7	Paul Vine	London	15 July, 1955
440 yards Hurdles	51·8	Harry Kane	London	13 Oct., 1954
2 miles Steeplechase	9 44·0	John Disley	London	21 June, 1952
3,000 metres Steeplechase	8 44·2	John Disley	Moscow	11 Sept., 1955
4×100 metres Relay	40·6	G.B. Olympic Team (E. McDonald Bailey, W. Jack, J. A. Gregory, B. Shenton)	Helsinki	27 July, 1952
4×400 metres Relay	3 09·0	G.B. Olympic Team (F. F. Wolff G. L. Rampling, W. Roberts, A. G. K. Brown)	Berlin	9 Aug., 1936
High Jump	6′ 7½″	{ A. S. Paterson	Glasgow	2 Aug., 1947
		Peter Wells	Papakura, N.Z.	11 Dec., 1954
Pole Vault	14′ 1¼″	Geoffrey Elliott	Berne	28 Aug., 1954
Long Jump	24′ 8¾″	Kenneth Wilmshurst	Vancouver	5 Aug., 1954
Hop, Step and Jump	50′ 8″	Kenneth Wilmshurst	London	30 May, 1955
Shot Putt	55′ 2″	John Savidge	Cardiff	8 May, 1954
Discus Throw	169′ 11″	Mark Pharaoh	Prague	15 Sept., 1955
Hammer Throw	192′ 6″	Ewan Douglas	Edinburgh	28 April, 1955
Javelin Throw	223′ 1″	Peter Cullen	Coventry	29 Aug., 1955
Decathlon	6,044 pts.	Geoffrey Elliott	Helsinki	25/26 July, 1952

*World's Fastest ever recorded (26 miles 385 yards) *m*—made over 110 metres.

LONGEST TUG O'WAR

The longest recorded pull was that of 2 hours 41 minutes between "H" Company and "E" Company of the 2nd Derbyshire Regiment at Jubbulpore, India, on 12 Aug. 1889.

The longest pull recorded under A.A.A. rules (in which lying on the ground is not permitted) is the 8 minutes 18·2 seconds in the first pull between R.A.S.C. (Feltham) and the Royal Marines (Portsmouth Division) at the Royal Tournament of June 1938.

THREE-LEGGED RACE

The fastest recorded time for a 100 yards three-legged race is 11·0 seconds made at Brooklyn, New York, by Harry L. Hillman and Lawson Robertson on 24 April, 1909.

GREATEST CABER TOSS

The 21-foot long, 230 pound, Braemar Caber defied all comers until it was successfully tossed at the Braemar Gathering of 6 Sept., 1951, by George Clark.

WOMEN'S ATHLETICS

BEST UNITED KINGDOM PERFORMANCES

Event	mins. secs.	Holder	Place	Date
100 yards	10·9	A. Pashley	White City	14 Aug., 1954
	10·9	M. Francis	White City	1 Aug., 1955
200 metres	24·2	J. Scrivens	Budapest	3 Oct., 1954
220 yards	24·3	J. Scrivens	White City	13 Aug., 1955
440 yards	56·6	D. S. Leather	White City	21 Aug., 1954
880 yards	2 09·0	D. S. Leather	White City	19 June, 1954
Mile*	4 45·0	D. S. Leather	White City	21 Sept., 1955
80 metres hurdles	11·0	P. G. Seaborne	Budapest	3 Oct., 1954
High Jump	5 ft. 7½ ins.	S. Lerwill	White City	7 July, 1951
Long Jump	20 ft. 0⅛ ins.	J. Desforges	Nienburg	30 Aug., 1953
Shot Putt	41 ft. 8 ins.	S. Farmer	Nienburg	30 Aug., 1953
Discus	143 ft. 1½ ins.	S. Farmer	Nienburg	30 Aug., 1953
Javelin	148 ft. 7½ ins.	D. Coates	White City	14 June, 1952

*World's best performance

BADMINTON

The game was devised at the end of the 1860's at Badminton Hall in Gloucestershire, the seat of the Dukes of Beaufort.

MOST TITLES

Most wins in the All-England Championships (instituted 1899).

Event	Times	Holder	Dates
Men's Singles	6	J. F. Devlin	1925, 26, 27, 28, 29, 31.
Women's Singles	6	Miss M. Lucas	1902, 05, 07, 08, 09, 10.

Most titles (i.e. including doubles):—

Men	21	G. A. Thomas (later Sir George Thomas, Bart.)	from 1903 to 1928.
Women	17	Miss M. Lucas	from 1899 to 1910.

Most international appearances:—

	Times	Men	Times	Women
England	36	R. C. F. Nicholls, 1930 to 1951.	37	Mrs. H. S. Uber, 1926 to 1951.
Ireland	32	J. L. Rankin, 1929 to 1949.	20	Mrs. J. A. Macnaughton (née Hamilton) 1930 to 1939.
Scotland	25	E. W. Wilson, 1931 to 1950.	26	Mrs. J. A. S. Armstrong (née Anderson) 1933 to 1952.
Wales	16	R. J. Evans, 1928 to 1936. C. G. Gooding, 1930 to 1939.	22	Mrs. L.W. Myers, 1928 to 1939.

MOST INTERNATIONALS

BASEBALL

EARLIEST GAME

The earliest recorded baseball game under the pioneer Cartwright rules was at Hoboken, New Jersey, on 19 June, 1846, with the New York Nine beating the Knickerbockers 23–1.

HIGHEST BATTING AVERAGE

The highest average in a career is ·367 by Tyrus Cobb of Detroit and Philadelphia who was in the game from 1905 to 1928. During his career Cobb made 2,244 runs from 4,191 hits on 11,429 times at bat.

MOST HOME RUNS HIT

The highest number of home runs hit in a career is the 714 by George H. "Babe" Ruth of New York between 1915 and 1935. His American League record for home runs in one year is 60 in 151 games between 15 April and 30 Sept., 1927.

The National League record is 56 in a year by Lewis R. Wilson of Chicago in 1930.

HIGHEST EARNINGS

The greatest earnings of a baseball player is the $1,091,477 amassed between 1914 and 1938 by Ruth with a peak of $80,000 in both 1930 and 1931.

The longest measured home run is 565 feet by Mickey Mantle (Yankees) in Washington Stadium on 17 April, 1953. The longest throw is 411 feet 6 inches by Raymond Tran of California 1939. The fastest time for circling bases is 13·6 seconds by Donald Weir of University of California in 1943.

BASKETBALL

Perhaps the only game completely the product of the United States is Basketball devised by Dr. James A. Naismith at the International Y.M.C.A. Training School at Springfield, Mass., in 1891 and first played on 20 Jan., 1892. The game is now a global activity. The Amateur Basketball Association of England and Wales was founded in 1936.

Largest Ever Gate

Harlem Globetrotters played to 75,000 at the Olympic Stadium, Berlin, in 1951.

Greatest Playing Record

Harlem Globetrotters in their silver jubilee season of 1951–52 set unapproached attendance and scoring records. They won 333 games and lost 8 before over 3,000,000 spectators and travelled over 75,000 miles to achieve such figures.

American Professional Records

Most points scored in a season: George Mikan, a member of Minneapolis scored 1,932 points 1950–51.

Most points scored in a single game: Joe Fulks, a member of Philadelphia scored 62 points against Indianapolis on 10 Feb., 1949.

Most points scored by a team: Sheboygan scored 141 against Denver (104) on 10 March, 1950 (in regulation time).

Largest field goal on record is 84 feet 11 inches by George Linn, 20, of Alabama against North Carolina at Tuscaloosa in January 1955.

BILLIARDS

EARLIEST MENTION

The earliest mention of Billiards was in a poem of the Frenchman Marot (d. 1544) while the earliest mention in England was in 1591 by Spenser. The first recorded public billiards room in England was the Piazza, Covent Garden, in the early part of the last century. Slate-beds came in in 1827 and rubber cushions in 1835.

HIGHEST BREAKS

In 1907, Tom Reece (England), using the anchor cannon, made an unfinished break of 499,135. The highest certified break is the 42,746 of W. Cook (England) in 1907. The official world record under present rules is 1,784 by Joe Davis in the 1936 United Kingdom Championship. The amateur record is 702 by Robert Marshall in the 1953 Australia Amateur Championship. Davis has an unofficial personal best of 2,501.

FASTEST CENTURY

On 10 October, 1952, Walter Lindrum (Australia) made a 100 break in 27·5 seconds.

MOST WORLD TITLES

The greatest number of world titles (instituted 1870) won by a player is the 8 of John Roberts, jun. (England), 1870 (twice), 1871, 1875 (twice), 1877 and 1885 (twice). The greatest number of United Kingdom titles (instituted 1934) won by a player is the 7 (1934-39 and 1947) by Joe Davis (England), who also won 4 world titles (1928-30 and 1932) before the series was discontinued in 1934.

MOST AMATEUR TITLES

The greatest number of Amateur Championships (instituted 1888) won is the 6 by H. C. Virr (1907-08, 1911-14). A. P. Gaskell, between 1888 and 1891, also gained 6 titles but that of 1889 was by declaration.

SNOOKER

EARLIEST MENTION

Research has established that snooker was originated as a variation of " black pool " in Jubbulpore, India, in 1875 by Col. Sir Neville Chamberlain. It did not reach England till 1885.

HIGHEST BREAKS

The official world break record is the 146 by Joe Davis (b. Whitwell, Derbyshire, 15 April, 1901) made at Manchester on 7 March, 1950, when one pink intervened for a black and so thwarted a maximum possible score of 147. An unratified 147 was achieved by the Australian O'Donoghue in Australia in 1928, by the amateur Leo Levitt at Montreal, Canada, on 24 Nov., 1948, by Clark McConachy in a practice match at the Beaufort Club, London, on 19 Feb., 1952, and by Rex Williams on 6 May, 1955.

The only time 147 has been made under standard conditions, as laid down by the Billiards Association and Control, was at Thurston's, Leicester Square, by Joe Davis on 23 January, 1955. This was the 575th of his 599 centuries to 1 Aug., 1955.

The official world break record for an amateur is 104, by Frank Edwards.

MOST CENTURIES

Joe Davis secured his 500th century on 18 Feb., 1953, at which time the game's next most prolific scorer was his brother Fred with 144 centuries.

MOST TITLES

Joe Davis won every one of the world's professional championships from its institution in 1927 to 1940 and his fifteenth title in 1946 after which he retired from the event. The greatest number of title wins in the Amateur Championship is the 4 of P. H. Matthews (1928, 1931, 1936 and 1938).

BOWLS (LAWN)

ORIGINS

Bowls can be traced back to at least the thirteenth century in England. The Southampton Town Bowling was formed in 1299. After falling into disrepute the game was rescued by the bowlers of Scotland who headed by W. W. Mitchell framed the modern rules in 1848–49.

MOST TITLE WINS

The greatest number of wins in the annual international Championships (instituted 1903) is by Scotland with 19. The longest string of successes are also by Scotland with 4 from 1907–10 and 4 from 1912–14 resuming in 1919.

ENGLISH TITLES

The only man to have won four Singles Titles (instituted 1905) is E. P. Baker (Poole Park, Dorset) in 1932, 1946, 1952 and 1955. The most Pairs Titles (instituted 1912) have been won by Poole Park with three in 1926, 1927 and 1950. The Triples Title (instituted 1945) has never been twice won. Three clubs have won the Rinks (instituted 1905) twice—Wellingborough 1909 and 1912, Belgrave (Leicestershire) 1922 and 1954 and Oxford City and Country 1948 and 1951.

MOST INTERNATIONALS

The greatest number of international seasons by an English bowler is 19 by J. G. Carruthers (Muswell Hill) between 1905 and 1939.

BOXING

EARLIEST REFERENCES

The origins of fist-fighting belong to Greek mythology. The earliest prize-ring code of rules were formulated in England in 1743 by the champion pugilist Broughton. Boxing, which had in 1865 come under the Queensberry Rules, was not established as a legal sport in Britain until after the ruling by Mr. Justice Grantham after the death of Billy Smith at Covent Garden, London, on 24 April, 1901.

Earliest World Title Fight

The first world heavyweight title fight, with gloves, and 3-minute rounds, was on 7 Sept., 1892, between John L. Sullivan and James J. Corbett in New Orleans, U.S.A.

Longest Fight

The longest recorded fight with gloves was between Andy Bowen and Jack Burke on 6 April, 1893, at New Orleans, U.S.A. The fight lasted 110 rounds and 7 hours 19 minutes but was declared a no contest. The record duration for a bare knuckle fight was 6 hours 15 minutes between James Kelly and Jack Smith at Melbourne, Australia, on 19 Oct., 1856.

Shortest Fight

The extreme case is recorded of a knockout in 10½ seconds (including a 10 second count) on 24 Sept., 1946, when Al Couture struck Ralph Walton while the latter was adjusting a gum shield in his corner. If the time was accurately taken it is clear that Couture must have been more than half-way across the ring from his own corner at the opening bell.

The shortest world heavyweight title occurred in Dublin, Ireland, on 17 March, 1908, when Tommy Burns knocked out Jem Rocke in 1 minute 28 seconds. The shortest world title fight was on 6 April, 1914, when Al McCoy knocked out George Chip for the middleweight crown in New York in 45 seconds. The same time was required by Tommy McGovern to knock out the lightweight Billy Thompson in Wandsworth, London, on 28 Aug., 1951, for the shortest ever British title fight.

Tallest and Heaviest

The tallest boxer of all time was the Canadian negro Harry Gunson who boxed from 1898 to 1900. He was 7 feet 2 inches tall.

The heaviest ever boxer is the 7 feet 1 inch Ewart Potgieter (South Africa) who has weighed in at 326 lb. (23 stone 4 lb.).

WORLD HEAVYWEIGHT CHAMPIONS

Longest & Shortest Reigns

The longest reign of any world heavyweight champion is the 11 years 8 months 9 days of Joe Louis from 22 June, 1937, when he knocked out Jim Braddock in the eighth round at Chicago. During his reign Louis made a record number of 25 defences of his title. The shortest reign was by Primo Carnera (Italy) at 350 days from 29 June, 1933, to 14 June, 1934. However, if the disputed title claim of Marvin Hart is allowed, his reign from 3 July, 1905, to 23 Feb., 1906, is only 235 days. See Plate 13.

Heaviest & Lightest

The heaviest world champion was Primo Carnera of Italy who won the title on 29 June, 1933, at Long Island, U.S.A. He was scaled 270 lb. (19 stone 4 lb.). The lightest champion was Bob Fitzsimmons (b. Cornwall, England, 4 June, 1862), who won the title on 17 March, 1897, at Carson City, Nevada, U.S.A., at 167 lb. (11 stone 13 lb.).

The greatest differential in a fight was the 94 lb. (6 stone 10 lb.) between Carnera (270 lb. or 19 stone 4 lb.) and Tommy Loughran (U.S.A.) (186 lb. or 13 stone 4 lb.) when the former won on points at Miami, U.S.A., on 1 March, 1934. The greatest "tonnage" in a world title fight was 488¾ lb. (34 stone 12½ lb.) when Carnera (259½ lb.) fought Uzcudun (229½ lb.) on 22 Oct., 1933, in Rome.

Tallest & Shortest

The tallest world champion was the 6 feet 6¾ inches tall Jess Willard (U.S.A.) who won the title by knocking out Jack Johnson in the 26th round at Havana, Cuba, on 5 April, 1915. The shortest was Tommy Burns (1881-1955), world champion from 1906-08, at 5 feet 7 inches.

Youngest

The youngest age at which the world title has been won is 23 years 1 month by Joe Louis (b. 13 May, 1914) on 22 June, 1937.

WORLD CHAMPIONS (any weight)

Longest and Shortest Reign

Joe Louis's heavyweight record stands for all divisions. The shortest reign was 47 days by the flyweight Emile Pladner.

Youngest and Oldest

The youngest at which any world title has been claimed is 18 years 8 months 6 days by the featherweight Abe Atell in 1901. The oldest world champion was Bob Fitzsimmons who held his light-heavyweight title till 20 Dec., 1905, when he was 43 years 6 months old. Fitzsimmons also had the longest career of any official world title-holder with 33 years from 1882-1914.

Longest Fight

The longest world title fight (under Queensberry Rules) was that between the lightweight Joe Gans and Battling Nelson at Goldfield, Nevada, on 3 Sept., 1906, which was terminated in the 42nd round when the former was declared the winner after a foul.

Biggest weight span

The only man to hold world titles at 3 weights simultaneously was Henry Armstrong (U.S.A.) at featherweight, lightweight and welterweight in 1938.

Most Knockdowns

Max Baer knocked down Primo Carnera 12 times in 11 rounds in their heavyweight title fight in New York on 14 June, 1934, before the referee stopped the fight.

Biggest Purse

The greatest purse was the $990,445 (£373,480) received by Gene Tunney for his fight against Jack Dempsey in Chicago on 22 Sept., 1927.

BIGGEST GATE

This was accumulated at the above fight at Soldiers' Field, Chicago, when receipts totalled $2,658,660 (£949,500). The promoter, Ted Rickard, took a profit of $475,690 (£169,880).

HIGHEST ATTENDANCES

The greatest paid attendance at any boxing fight was the 120,757 at the Sesquicentennial Stadium, Philadelphia, on 23 Sept., 1926, for the Tunney *v.* Dempsey world heavyweight title fight.

The highest non-paying attendance is 135,132 at the Tony Zale *v.* Billy Prior fight at Milwaukee, Wisconsin, U.S.A., on 18 Aug., 1941.

HIGHEST EARNINGS IN CAREER

The largest fortune made in a fighting career is the $3,800,000 (£1,357,700) amassed by Joe Louis from 1934 to 1951. Including exhibitions, radio and television income his total has been estimated at $4,625,000 (£1,651,000). Including $3,000,000 earnings for refereeing Jack Dempsey has grossed over $6,100,000 (£2,178,000).

MOST KNOCK DOWNS

The greatest recorded number of knock-downs in a fight is 38. This occurred in the fight between Joe Jeanette (27) and Sam McVey (11) in Paris on 17 April, 1907.

Greatest Number of Knock-outs

The greatest number of knock-outs in a career is 127 by "Young" Stribling (William Lawrence) (1921–1933).

Greatest Number of Fights The greatest number of fights in a career is the 1,309 fought by Abe the Newsboy (U.S.A.) (Abraham Hollandersky) in the fourteen years from 1905 to 1918.

Biggest Weight Difference The greatest weight difference recorded in a major bout is 10 stone (140 lb.) at Brooklyn, U.S.A., on 30 April, 1900, between Bob Fitzsimmons (12 stone 4 lb.) and Ed Dunkhorst (22 stone 4 lb.). Fitzsimmons won in two rounds.

MOST A.B.A. TITLES

Class	Instituted	Champion	Year
Flyweight 5 (8 stone or under)	1920	T. Pardoe	1929-33
Bantam 4 (8 stone 7 lb. or under)	1884	W. W. Allen	1911-12, 1914, 1919
Feather 5 (9 stone or under)	1888	G. R. Baker	1912-14, 1919, 1921
Lightweight 4 (9 stone 7 lb. or under)	1881	M. Wells	1904-07
		F. Grace	1909, 1913, 1919-20
Light-Welterweight (10 stone or under)	1951	No champion has yet retained or regained the title.	
Welterweight 2 (10 stone 8 lb. or under)	1920	P. O'Hanrahan	1924-25
		D. McCleave	1932, 1934
		D. Lynch	1935, 1937
		CSMI J. Ryan	1946-47
		J. P. Maloney	1951-52.
Light-Middleweight 2 (11 stone 2 lb. or under)	1951	B. Wells	1953-54
Middleweight 5 (11 stone 11 lb. or under)	1881	R. C. Warner	1899, 1901, 1903, 1907, 1910
		H. W. Mallin	1919-23
		F. Mallin	1928-32
Light-Heavyweight 4 (12 stone 10 lb. or under)	1920	H. J. Mitchell	1922-25
Heavyweight 5 (any weight)	1881	F. Parks	1899, 1901-02, 1905-06

LONGEST SPAN The greatest span of A.B.A. title-winning performances is that of H. P. Floyd in the heavyweight division who won in 1929 and gained his fourth title 17 years later in 1946.

CONTRACT BRIDGE

EARLIEST REFERENCES Bridge (a corruption of Biritch) is of Levantine origin, being played in Greece in the early 1880's. The game was known in London in 1886 under the title of "Biritch or Russian Whist".

HIGHEST POSSIBLE SCORES

Opponents bid 7 of any suit or No Trumps doubled and redoubled and vulnerable. Opponents make no trick.

Above Line	1st undertrick	400
	12 subsequent undertricks at 600 each	7,200
	All Honours	150
		7,750

Bid 7 no trumps, double and redouble, vulnerable.

Below Line	1st trick (40 × 4)	160
	6 tricks (30 × 6 × 4)	720
Above Line	2nd game of 2-Game Rubber (worth)	350
	Grand Slam	1,500
	All Honours (4 aces)	150
	(Highest Possible Positive Score)	2,880

CANOEING

The acknowledged pioneer of canoeing as a sport is John Macgregor, a British barrister, in 1865. The Royal Canoe Club was formed on 26 July of that year.

MOST OLYMPIC GOLD MEDALS Gert Fredriksson of Sweden won the Kayak singles 1,000 m. in 1948 and retained the title in 1952. In 1948 he also won the 10,000 m. Kayak singles.

MOST BRITISH TITLES G. Colyer (Richmond Canoe Club) most individual titles with 7 (1951-54) while R. Prout (Canvey Island C. C.) holds 9 kayak pairs titles (1951-54) and the 1951 10,000 m. singles title.

CHESS

ORIGINS Chess, derived from the Persian word *shah*, spread from India in the seventh century A.D. reaching England c.1255. The *Fédération Internationale des Echecs* was established in 1924.

LONGEST GAMES The most protracted chess match on record was one drawn on the 191st move between H. Pilnik (Argentina) and M. Czerniak (Israel) at Mar del Plata, Argentina, in April 1953. The total playing time was 20 hours. A game of 21½ hours but drawn on the 171st move (average over 7½ minutes per move) was played between the Russians Makagonov and Chekover at Baku in 1945.

MOST OPPONENTS Records by chess masters for numbers of opponents tackled simultaneously depend very much whether or not all the opponents are replaced as defeated, are in relays, or whether they are taken on in a simultaneous start.

The greatest number tackled on a replacement basis is 400 (379 defeated) by the Swedish master G. Stahlberg in 36 hours play in Buenos Aires, Argentina, in 1946.

The blindfold record is 45 opponents (43 defeated) in Buenos Aires in 1947 by the Argentinian Miguel Najdorf. The exact conditions of this record are not clear, but in 1937 in Glasgow G. Koltanowski (Belgium, now of U.S.A.) tackled 34 opponents blindfold in a simultaneous start.

COURSING

The sport of dogs chasing hares is centuries old. The classic event is the annual "Waterloo Cup" instituted in 1836 at Altcar near Liverpool.

The most successful Waterloo Cup dog recorded was Colonel North's "Fullerton" sired by Greentich which tied first in 1889 and then won outright in 1890, 1891 and 1892.

The longest authenticated course is 4 minutes 10 seconds on 2 Mar., 1934, when Major C. Blundell's "Blackmore" beat "Boldon" in a Barbican Cup decider.

CRICKET

EARLIEST MATCH

The earliest evidence of the game of cricket is from a drawing depicting two men playing with a bat and ball dated c.1250. The earliest major match of which the score survives is the Kent *v.* England match of 1744 at the Artillery Ground in London.

BATTING INNINGS

Highest

The highest recorded innings in cricket is the 1,107 runs made by Victoria against New South Wales in the Inter-State match at Melbourne of 1926–27.

The highest innings ever made in England is the 903 for 7 wickets declared in the 1938 Test against Australia at the Oval, London.

The highest innings recorded by English County sides are as follows:—

Yorkshire	887	*v.* Warwickshire	at Birmingham	1896
Surrey	811	*v.* Somerset	in London, Oval	1899
Kent	803 for 4	*v.* Essex	at Brentwood	1934
Lancashire	801	*v.* Somerset	at Taunton	1895
Nottinghamshire	739 for 7	*v.* Leicestershire	at Nottingham	1903
Sussex	705 for 8	*v.* Surrey	at Hastings	1902
Leicestershire	701 for 4	*v.* Worcestershire	at Worcester	1906
Somerset	675 for 9	*v.* Hampshire	at Bath	1924
Hampshire	672 for 7	*v.* Somerset	at Taunton	1899
Warwickshire	657 for 6	*v.* Hampshire	at Birmingham	1899
Gloucestershire	653 for 6	*v.* Glamorganshire	at Bristol	1928
Derbyshire	645	*v.* Hampshire	at Derby	1898
Middlesex	642 for 3	*v.* Hampshire	at Southampton	1923
Worcestershire	633	*v.* Warwickshire	at Worcester	1906
Glamorgan	587 for 8	*v.* Derbyshire	at Cardiff	1951
Northamptonshire	557 for 6	*v.* Sussex	at Hove	1914

Lowest

The lowest recorded innings is the 12 made by Oxford University *v.* the Marylebone Cricket Club (M.C.C.) at Oxford in 1877 and the 12 by Northamptonshire *v.* Gloucestershire at Gloucester in 1907. On the occasion of the Oxford match however the University batted a man short.

Biggest Victory

The greatest margin of victory occurred in the 1922–23 Australian season when Victoria defeated Tasmania at Melbourne by an innings and 666 runs. The largest margin in England is the innings and 579 runs by England over Australia in the 1938 Test at the Oval. The most one-sided county match was at the Oval in 1888 when Surrey defeated Sussex by an innings and 485 runs.

FASTEST SCORING

In a Day

The greatest number of runs scored in a day is the 721 runs all out (10 wickets) by the Australians against Essex at Southend in 1948.

The fastest recorded exhibition of hitting occurred in the Kent *v.* Gloucestershire match of 1937 at Dover when Kent scored 219 runs for 3 wickets in 71 minutes or at the rate of 156 runs for each 100 balls bowled.

The fastest 50 ever hit was completed in 11 minutes by C. I. J. Smith (66) in the Middlesex *v.* Gloucestershire match at Bristol in 1938 in 12 scoring strokes.

The fastest century ever hit was completed in 35 minutes by P. G. H. Fender (113 not out) for Surrey *v.* Northampton at Northampton in 1920. The most prolific scorer of centuries under the hour was G. L. Jessop with nine between 1897 and 1913.

The fastest double century was completed in 120 minutes by G. L. Jessop (286) for Gloucester *v.* Sussex at Hove in 1903.

The fastest treble century was completed in 181 minutes by D. C. S. Compton (300) for the M.C.C. *v.* N.E. Transvaal at Benoni in 1948–49.

The fastest time recorded for running 4 runs with full equipment is 12·3 seconds by R. Todd in Melbourne in 1940.

SLOWEST SCORING

The longest time a batsman has ever taken to open his innings is 1 hour 37 minutes by T. G. Evans (10 not out) for England *v.* Australia at Adelaide in 1946–47 Tests. At Nottingham in 1882 the Lancashire batsman R. G. Barlow utilized 2½ hours to score 5 not out, during which innings his score remained unchanged for 80 minutes.

The slowest century on record is by the Pakistan batsman Hanif Mohammed (142) in the Bahawalpa Test *v.* India in 1954–55. He required 7 hours 48 minutes to reach 100. The slowest double century recorded is S. G. Barnes' 10 hours 42 minutes for 234 for Australia *v.* England at Sydney in the 1946–47 Test.

HIGHEST INDIVIDUAL INNINGS

The highest individual innings recorded is the 452 not out by Sir Donald Bradman batting for New South Wales against Queensland at Sydney in the 1929–30 Australian season. See Plate 13.

LONGEST INNINGS

The longest innings on record was L. Hutton's 364 runs in 13 hours 20 minutes for England *v.* Australia at the Oval in 1938.

BIGGEST SCORERS

The greatest number of runs scored in a season is the 3,816 by D. C. S. Compton in 1947. His batting average was 90·85.

The record for the greatest number of centuries in a season is also held by Compton with eighteen in 1947. With their restricted fixture list the Australian record is eight by Sir Donald Bradman in the 1947–48 season.

The most centuries in a career is the 197 of Sir John (J. B.) Hobbs (1905–1934). The Australian record is Sir Donald Bradman's 117 centuries.

The highest recorded seasonal batting average in England is Bradman's 115·66 for 26 innings in the 1938 season in England and for a complete career (1927–1949) 95·14 for 338 innings, also by Bradman.

Most runs in a career

The greatest aggregate of runs in a career is the 61,237 by Sir John Hobbs for 1905 to 1934.

Least Runs in a career

S. Clark, the Somerset wicket-keeper, played five matches for his county in 1930 scoring nine successive 0's.

Most runs off an Over

No batsman has yet scored the possible of 36 runs off a six-ball over. The nearest approach is the 32 by C. Smart (6, 6, 4, 6, 6, 4) off G. Hill at Cardiff in the 1935 Glamorgan-Hampshire match. E. Alletson in the 1911 Nottinghamshire *v.* Sussex match at Hove scored 34 off E. H. Killick in an over (4, 6, 6, 4, 4, 4, 6) but the over included two no-balls.

LONGEST HIT

The longest measured drive is the 175 yards by the Rev. W. Fellows of Oxford University in 1856.

MOST SIXES IN AN INNINGS

The highest number of sixes hit in an innings is eleven by C. K. Nayudu for the Hindus *v.* the M.C.C. in Bombay in 1926–27, by C. J. Barnett for Gloucestershire against Somerset at Bath in 1934 and R. Benaud for the Australians *v.* T. N. Pearce's XI at Scarborough in 1953.

MOST BOUNDARIES IN AN INNINGS

The highest number of boundaries in an innings is the 68 by P. A. Perrin for Essex *v.* Derbyshire at Chesterfield in a 343 not out innings in 1904.

LARGEST NUMBER OF RUNS OFF A BALL

The most runs scored off a single hit is the 10 by S. H. Hill-Wood off C. J. Burnup in the Derbyshire *v.* M.C.C. match of 1900 at Lord's.

GREATEST PARTNERSHIP

The record stand for any partnership is the 577 by the Indians Gul Mahomed and V. S. Hazare in the Baroda *v.* Holkar match at Baroda in 1946–47.

The records for each wicket are as follows:—

1st wicket	555	P. Holmes and H. Sutcliffe for Yorkshire *v.* Essex at Leyton in 1932.
2nd wicket	455	B. B. Nimbalkar and K. V. Bhandakar for Maharashtra *v.* W. Indian States at Poona in 1948-49.
3rd wicket	445	P. E. Whitelaw and W. N. Carson for Auckland *v.* Otago at Dunedin, N.Z. in 1936-37.
4th wicket	577	As above.
5th wicket	405	S. G. Barnes and D. G. Bradman for Australia *v.* England at Sydney in 1946-47.
6th wicket	487*	G. Headley & C. C. Passailaigue for Jamaica *v.* Lord Tennyson's XI at Kingston in 1931-32.
7th wicket	348	D. Atkinson and C. Depeiza for West Indies *v.* Australia at Bridgetown, Barbados in 1954-55.
8th wicket	433	V. T. Trumper and A. Sim for an Australian XI *v.* Canterbury at Christchurch, N.Z., in 1913-14.
9th wicket	283	J. Chapman and A. R. Warren for Derbyshire *v.* Warwickshire at Blackwell in 1910.
10th wicket	307	A. F. Kippax and J. E. H. Hooker for New South Wales *v.* Victoria at Melbourne in 1928-29.

The English records where differing are as follows :—

2nd wicket	429*	J. G. Dewes and G. H. G. Doggart for Cambridge University v. Essex at Cambridge in 1949.
3rd wicket	424*	W. J. Edrich and D. C. S. Compton for Middlesex v. Somerset at Lord's in 1948.
4th wicket	448	R. Abel and T. Hayward for Surrey v. Yorkshire at the Oval in 1899.
5th wicket	393	E. G. Arnold and W. B. Burns for Worcestershire v. Warwickshire at Birmingham in 1909.
6th wicket	411	R. M. Poore and E. G. Wynyard for Hampshire v. Somerset at Taunton in 1899.
7th wicket	344	K. S. Ranjitsinhji and W. Newham for Sussex v. Essex at Leyton in 1902.
8th wicket	292	R. Peel and Lord Hawke for Yorkshire v. Warwickshire at Birmingham in 1896.
10th wicket	235	F. E. Woolley and A. Fielder for Kent v. Worcestershire at Stourbridge in 1909.

* unbroken partnership

BOWLING

GREATEST NUMBER OF WICKETS

In a Season The largest number of wickets gained in a season is the 304 by the Kent bowler A. P. Freeman in the 1928 season. Freeman bowled 1,976·1 overs of which 423 were maidens with an average of 18·05.

In a Career The greatest wicket taker in history is W. Rhodes who from 1898 to 1930 took 4,188 wickets.

Greatest Number of Consecutive Wickets No bowler in first class cricket has yet achieved five wickets with five consecutive balls. The nearest approach is that by C. W. L. Parker for Gloucestershire v. Yorkshire at Bristol in 1922, who struck the stumps with five successive balls but the second was called as a no-ball. The only man to have taken four wickets with four consecutive balls more than once is R. J. Crisp for West Province v. Griqualand West at Johannesburg in 1931–32 and again v. Natal at Durban in 1933–34.

Greatest Number of Hat Tricks The greatest number of " hat tricks " is the seven by D. V. P. Wright (Kent) between 1937 and 1949. In his own benefit match at Lord's in 1907 A. E. Trott bowling for Middlesex took four Somerset batsmen with four consecutive balls and then later in the same innings achieved a " hat-trick."

Most Wickets in an Innings The taking of all ten wickets by a single bowler has been many times recorded but has only been achieved on three occasions by one bowler—A. P. Freeman of Kent against Lancashire at Maidstone in 1929 against Essex at Southend in 1930 and against Lancashire at Manchester in 1931. The feat has been performed at the least expense of runs by H. Verity (Yorkshire) when he had Nottinghamshire out at Leeds in 1932 at a personal cost of 10 runs in 52 balls in 1932. The only bowler to have clean bowled a whole side out was J. Wisden of the North who bowled out all ten South batsmen at Lord's in 1850.

Most Wickets in a Match No bowler in first-class cricket has yet achieved 18 wickets in a match though this feat was actually performed in a minor County match at Swindon in 1937 for the Kent 2nd XI v. Wiltshire by N. W. Harding. A. P. Freeman took ten wickets or more in a match on 137 occasions.

Most Wickets in a Day The record number of wickets taken in a day's play is 17 by C. Blythe for 48 runs for Kent against Northamptonshire at Northampton in 1907, by H. Verity for 91 runs for Yorkshire v. Essex at Leyton in 1933 and by T. W. Goddard for 106 runs for Gloucestershire v. Kent at Bristol in 1939.

Most Expensive Bowling The greatest number of runs ever knocked off a bowler in one innings is the 362 off A. A. Mailey in the New South Wales v. Victoria inter-State match at Melbourne in 1926–27. The greatest number of runs conceded in a match is the 428 runs off C. S. Nayudu in the Holkar v. Bombay match at Bombay in 1944–45, when he also made the record number of 917 deliveries. The most balls bowled in an innings is the 555 of Ghulam Ahmed for Hyderabad v. Holkar at Indore in 1950–51.

Most Maidens The greatest number of consecutive maiden overs ever bowled is 17 (105 balls) by H. L. Hazell for Somerset v. Gloucestershire at Taunton in 1949.

Most Balls The greatest number of balls sent down by any bowler in a season is the 12,234 by A. P. Freeman (Kent) in 1933.

Best Average The lowest bowling average recorded is that of 8·61 runs per wicket by A. Shaw (177 wickets for 1,525 runs in 1880).

Longest Spell The longest recorded spell of uninterrupted bowling is the 66 overs by J. Iremonger for Nottinghamshire v. Hampshire at Southampton in 1914.

FIELDING

Most Catches No fielder has yet held 7 catches in an innings but several players have held six including W. R. Hammond for Gloucestershire on three occasions, against Surrey at Cheltenham in 1928, against Worcestershire also at Cheltenham in 1932 and against Nottinghamshire at Bristol in 1933.

In a Match In the 1928 match (above) Hammond held a record total of 10 catches in the whole match.

In a Season The record number of catches in a season is 78 by W. R. Hammond in 1928. The most catches in a career is the 913 of F. E. Woolley (1906–1938).

THROWING

Longest The longest recorded throw of a cricket ball is 140 yards 2 feet (422 feet) by R. Percival on Durham Sands Racecourse on Easter Monday, 1884.

MOST DISMISSALS BY A WICKETKEEPER

In an Innings The record of dismissals in an innings by a wicket-keeper is seven. The English record is held by E. J. Smith for Warwickshire against Derbyshire at Birmingham in 1926, W. F. Farrimond for Lancashire *v.* Kent at Manchester in 1930 and W. F. Price (all caught) for Middlesex *v.* Yorkshire at Lords in 1937. The Australian record of seven is shared by D. Tallon for Queensland *v.* Victoria at Brisbane in 1938–39 and R. A. Saggers (all caught) for New South Wales *v.* Combined XI, also at Brisbane, in 1940–41.

In a Match The greatest number of dismissals by a wicket-keeper in a match is twelve by E. Pooley for Surrey *v.* Sussex at the Oval in 1868 and by D. Tallon for Queensland *v.* New South Wales at Sydney in 1938–39.

In a Season The record number of dismissals for any wicket-keeper in a season is 127 in 1929 by L. E. G. Ames of Kent. The record for the number stumped is also by Ames with 64 in 1932. The highest total of dismissals in a wicket-keeping career is the 1,468 of H. Strudwick of Surrey (1902–1927) with 1,215 catches and 253 stumpings. Most stumpings in a career is the 413 of Ames (1926–1950).

Least Byes The best wicket-keeping record for preventing byes is that of A. P Wickham when, keeping for Somerset *v.* Hampshire at Taunton in 1899, he did not concede a single bye in a total of 672 runs. The Test record is no byes in 659 runs by T. G. Evans for England *v.* Australia at Sydney in 1946–47.

Most Byes The record at the other extreme is that of P. H. Stewart-Brown of Harlequins who in 1927 let through 46 byes in an Oxford University innings of only 188.

ENGLISH COUNTY CHAMPIONSHIP The County Championship of England was inaugurated in 1873. The greatest number of victories have been secured by Yorkshire with twenty-two wins. They have never been lower than twelfth (in 1953) on the table. The most "wooden spoons" have been won by Northamptonshire with ten since 1923. They did not have a single win between May 1935 and May 1939. The greatest number of consecutive appearances in the series is 421 by J. Vine of Sussex.

Oldest and Youngest County Cricketer The youngest player to represent his county was W. W. F. Pullen for Gloucestershire against Yorkshire at Sheffield in 1882 at 15 years 11 months. The oldest regular County player has been W. G. Quaife of Warwickshire (b. 16 April, 1871) who played during the 1927 season when 56.

RECORD ATTENDANCES The world record attendance for a cricket match is 350,534 for the Third Test of 1936–37 between Australia and England at Melbourne. On 4 Jan., 1937 for the third day 87,798 people attended. For the whole series the figure was a record 933,513. The English record for a match is 158,000 in the 1948 Test between England and Australia at Leeds and the record for one day probably a capacity 46,000 at Old Trafford, Manchester in August 1926.

HIGHEST BENEFIT The highest "benefit" ever accorded a player is £14,000 for C. Washbrook in the Lancashire *v.* Australians match at Manchester in 1948.

LONGEST MATCH The lengthiest recorded cricket match was the "timeless" Test England *v.* South Africa of 1938–39 which went on for ten days after which it was abandoned.

MINOR CRICKET RECORDS (where excelling those in First Class Cricket)

Highest Individual Innings In the Junior House match Clark's House, Clifton College *v.* North Town in 1899 A. E. J. Collins over five afternoons and 5 hours 50 minutes batting scored an unprecedented 628 not out, carrying his bat through the innings of 836. See Plate 13.

Fastest Scoring S. K. Coen (South Africa) scored 50 runs (11 fours and 1 six) for Gezira *v.* R.A.F. in 1942 in 7 minutes compared with the First Class record of 11 minutes. C. Pepper in a Services match in Palestine in 1943 hit a century in 24 minutes.

C. I. J. Smith hit 9 successive sixes for a Middlesex XI *v.* Harrow and District at Rayner's Lane, Harrow, in 1935. This feat was repeated by A. D. Nourse, Jun., at Cairo in 1942–43 in a South African XI *v.* Military Police match.

Biggest Stand T. Patten and N. Rippon playing for Buffalo *v.* Whorouly at Gupstend, Victoria in 1913–14 made a Third wicket stand of 641.

Greatest Number Successive Wickets

P. Hugo in a school match Smithfield *v.* Alwal North in South Africa in 1930–31 took 9 wickets with 9 successive deliveries, taking all ten wickets for 3 runs.

Wicket-keeping Most Dismissals

In a Repton College house match for Priory *v.* Mitre, H. W. P. Middleton in 1930 caught one and stumped eight batsmen in one innings.

CROQUET

EARLIEST REFERENCES

Croquet, in its present day form, originated as an English country house lawn game c.1856.

MOST CHAMPIONSHIPS

The greatest number of Croquet Championship victories (instituted 1867) is the 7 of H. O. Hicks (1932, 1939, 1947–50, 1952). Hicks also has 5 Doubles and 2 Mixed Doubles Titles.

Miss D. D. Steel, fifteen times winner of the Women's Championship (1919–39), is the only woman to have won the Croquet Championship (1925, 1933, 1935–36). She has also 3 Doubles and 7 Mixed Doubles Titles making a total of 29 titles.

HIGHEST HANDICAP

The highest current playing handicap is that of H. O. Hicks (Devon) with —5½.

LARGEST CLUB

The largest number of courts of any club is the eleven of the Sussex County (Brighton) Croquet and Lawn Tennis Club.

CROSS COUNTRY AND ROAD RACING

INTERNATIONAL CROSS-COUNTRY CHAMPIONSHIP

The earliest recorded international cross-country race took place over 9 miles at Ville d'Avray, outside Paris on 20 March, 1898, between England and France (England won 21 points to 69). The inaugural International Cross-Country Championships took place at the Hamilton Park Racecourse, Scotland, on 28 March, 1903. The greatest margin of victory is the 56 seconds (representing 390 yards) by Holden at Ayr Racecourse, Scotland, on 24 March, 1934. The narrowest wins are those of A. E. Wood (England) in 1909, T. Evenson (England) in 1930 and A. Mimoun-o-Kacha (France) in 1949, each of whom won by the official margin of 1 second.

The greatest team win was England's in 1924 at Newcastle and in 1932 in Brussels with her first six men home in the first six.

LARGEST NUMBER OF INTERNATIONAL APPEARANCES

The runners of participating countries with the largest number of international championship appearances are:—

Wales	14	D. Phillips, 1922, 1924, 1926–37.	Ireland	8	J. Marshall, 1946, 1949–55.
England	12	J. T. Holden, 1929–39, 1946.	N. Ireland	7	M. Gorman, 1933–39.
Scotland	11	J. C. Flockhart, 1933–39, 1946–49.	Spain	5	V. J. Guixa, 1950–53, 1955.
,,	11	D. McL. Wright, 1920–1930.	Eire	4	T. F. Smythe, 1929–32.
Belgium	11	O. Van Rumst, 1929–39.	Netherlands	3	S. Bobeldyk, 1950–51, 1953.
France	10	R. Rerolle, 1929–38.			

ENGLISH CHAMPIONSHIP

The English Cross-Country Championship was inaugurated at Roehampton, South London, in 1877. The greatest number of individual titles achieved is the 4 of P. H. Stenning (Thames Hare and Hounds) (1877–80) and A. Shrubb (South London Harriers) (1901–04). The most successful club in the team race has been Birchfield Harriers from Birmingham with 27 wins and one tie between 1880 and 1953.

CYCLING

Earliest Race

The earliest recorded bicycle race was a velocipede race at the Parc de St. Cloud, Paris, on 31 May, 1868, over two kilometres.

Fastest Speed

The highest speed ever achieved on a bicycle is 109·12 m.p.h. by Jose Meiffret of France using a 275-inch gear behind a windshield on a racing car near Bordeaux in October 1951. See Plate 13.

The greatest distance ever covered in one hour is 76 miles 504 yards by Leon Vanderstuyft (Belgium) on the Montlhéry Motor Circuit, France, in September 1928. This was achieved from a standing start paced by a motor cycle.

WORLD RECORDS Open Air Tracks

Professional Unpaced Standing Start

1 km.	1 8·6	R. H. Harris	Milan	20 Oct., 1952
10 kms.	12 53·0	M. Archambaud	Milan	28 Oct., 1937
20 kms.	25 59·6	M. Archambaud	Milan	28 Oct., 1937
1 hour	28 m. 805 yds.	F. Coppi	Milan	7 Nov., 1942

CYCLING (Open Air Tracks)—*continued*

Amateur Unpaced Standing Start

1 km.	1 10·2	R. Vargachkin	Toula	21 June, 1954
5 kms.	6 25·6	A. Kazianka	Milan	26 Oct., 1954
10 kms.	13 03·4	F. Aureggi	Milan	30 Oct., 1952
20 kms.	26 29·6	E. Baldini	Milan	30 Oct., 1954
100 kms.	2 29 08·2	G. B. Milesi	Milan	2 Nov., 1954
1 hour	27 m. 1,549 yds.	E. Baldini	Milan	30 Oct., 1954

Professional Motor-paced

1 hour	44 m. 53 yds.	R. Oubron	Toulouse	12 Oct., 1949

Covered Tracks

Professional Unpaced Standing Start

1 km.	1 09·0	R. H. Harris	Paris	9 Nov., 1952
5 kms.	6 24·4	G. Messina	Paris	28 Nov., 1954
10 kms.	12 51·8	G. Messina	Paris	28 Nov., 1954

Amateur Unpaced Standing Start

1 km.	1 10·2	R. Gaignard	Paris	28 Nov., 1954
1 hour	26 m. 1,633 yds.	Wimmer	Paris	19 Dec., 1954

Professional Motor-paced

100 kms.	1 29 37·2	J. Lohmuller	St. Etienne	22 Aug., 1952
1 hour	44 m. 499 yds.	A. Le Strat	Paris	9 Jan., 1955

MOST WORLD TITLES

The greatest number of world titles won since the institution of the amateur championships in 1893 and the professional championships in 1895 are:—

Amateur Sprint	4	W. J. Bailey (G.B.)	1909–11 1913
Amateur 100 kms.	7	L. Meredith (G.B.)	1904–05, 1907–09, 1911, 1913.
Amateur Road Race	2	G. Martano (Italy)	1930 1932.
Professional Sprint	6	T. Ellegaard (Denmark)	1901–03, 1906, 1908, 1911.
	7	J. Scherens (Belgium)	1932–47.
Professional 100 kms. Paced	4	V. Linart (Belgium)	1921. 1924, 1926–27.

MOST OLYMPIC TITLES

Cycling has been on the Olympic programme since the revival of the Games in 1896. The greatest number of gold medals won is three by P. Masson (France) 333·3 m. 2 kms. and 10 kms. in Athens in 1896 and three by F. Verri (Italy) 333·3 m., 1,000 m. and 5 kms. in the 1906 Games also at Athens.

MOST BRITISH TITLES

The greatest number of National Cycling Championship titles secured by an individual rider is twelve by A. White (1920–1925) ranging from the ¼ mile to 25 miles.

ROAD CYCLING RECORDS (BRITISH) as recognised by the Road Time Trials Council

MEN

	hrs. mins. secs.	
25 miles	55 49·0	W. Holmes.
30 miles	1 07 30·0	R. Jowers.
50 miles	1 56 44·0	G. K. Bentley.
100 miles	4 04 30·0	R. Booty.
12 hours	264·87 miles	K. H. Joy.
24 hours	478·75 miles	K. Brice.

WOMEN

	hrs. mins. secs.	
25 miles	1 04 01·0	G. Tilly.
30 miles	1 19 28·0	E. Sheridan.
50 miles	2 11 44·0	J. Harris.
100 miles	4 34 03·0	M. Dawson.
12 hours	237·98 miles	C. M. Watts.

PLACE TO PLACE RECORDS (as recognised by the Road Records Association)

	days	hrs.	mins.	secs.	
London to Bath and back (210 miles)		9	36	23	K. H. Joy, 1953.
London to Brighton and back (104½ miles)		4	25	33	K. H. Joy, 1953.
Land's End to John O'Groats (872 miles)	2	6	33		S. H. Ferris, 1937.

DARTS

The origins of darts date from the use by archers of heavily weighted ten-inch throwing arrows for self-defence in close quarter fighting. These "dartes" were used in Ireland in the sixteenth century and darts was played on the "Mayflower" by the Plymouth pilgrims in 1620. Today there are an estimated 6,000,000 dart players in the British Isles—a higher participation than in any other sporting pastime.

No national or international controlling organisation for the game has existed which has collated records and conditions of play. The throwing distances and boards, vary considerably from one locality to another.

LOWEST POSSIBLE SCORES

The lowest number of darts to achieve standard scores are: 201 4 darts, 301 6 darts, 501 9 darts, 1,001 17 darts.

The 4 and 6 darts "possibles" have been many times achieved, the 9 darts 501 occasionally but never the 17 darts 1,001 which would require 15 treble 20's, a treble 17 and a 50.

The lowest even number which cannot be scored with three darts (ending on a double) is 162. The lowest odd number which cannot be scored with three darts (ending on a double) is 159.

PLATE 15

Left· Ben Hogan (U.S.A.) co-holder of lowest 72 holes golf aggregate. (Page 172)

Above: Jean Borotra (France) who made 26 appearances, at Wimbledon. (Page 180)

Right. Sonja Henie (Norway), 10 times world figure skating champion. (Page 178)

Below: The Irish bred Tulyar which sold for £250,000. (Page 175)

PLATE 16

Above: Stirling Moss (G.B.) record holder of
Miglia. (Page 182)

Top Left: Jack Wardrop (Scotland) world 2
record holder. (Page 187)

Left: World's greatest weight lifter, Paul Anderso
pressing 403½ lb. (Page 191)

Below: World's record ski jumper Tauno Luiro. (

The fastest time taken for a match of three games of 301 is 2½ minutes by Jim Pike at Broadcasting House, Broad Street, Birmingham, in 1952. See Plate 13. FASTEST MATCH

The record time for going round the board in "doubles" at arm's length is 14·5 seconds by Jim Pike at the Craven Club, Newmarket, in 1944. His match record for this feat at the nine-feet throwing distance, retrieving his own darts, is 3 minutes 30 seconds at King John's Head, Blackfriars, London, in 1937. FASTEST "ROUND THE BOARD"

The largest attendance at any darts match was the 17,000 at the Agricultural Hall, Islington, London, at the finals of the 1939 "News of the World" Contest. GREATEST CROWD

Re-instituted in 1947, the annual "News of the World" England and Wales Individual Championships consists of the best of 3 legs 501 up, "straight" start and finish on a double with an 8-foot throwing distance. To date no player has won more than once and the only county to provide more than one winner is Middlesex with:— MOST TITLES

1948–49	J. Boyce	Social Club, New Southgate, Middlesex.
1950–51	H. Perryman	Home Office Social Club, Greenford, Middlesex.

EQUESTRIAN SPORTS

Evidence of horse-riding dates from an Egyptian statuette dated c.2000 B.C. Pignatelli's academy of horsemanship at Naples dates from the sixteenth century. ORIGIN

Equestrian events have been included in the Olympic Games since 1912.

The greatest number of Olympic Gold Medals by a horseman is four by Lt. C. F. Pahud de Mortanges (Netherlands) who won the individual three-day event in 1928 and 1932 and was in the winning team in 1924 and 1928. MOST OLYMPIC MEDALS

The most team wins in the Prix de Nations is three by Sweden in 1912, 1920 and 1924. MOST TEAM WINS

No rider has yet succeeded in retaining an individual Olympic Prix de Nations. The lowest score obtained by a winner was by F. Ventura (Czechoslovakia) at Amsterdam in 1928 with no faults.

The official Fédération Equestre Internationale high jump record is 8 feet 1¼ inches by Huaso ridden by Capt. A. L. Morales (Chile) at Santiago, Chile, on 5 Feb., 1949. See Plate 14. JUMPING

At the Diamond Jubilee Show, Tenterfield, New South Wales, in March 1937 Lookout cleared a measured 8 feet 3 inches. The British record stands at 7 feet 6½ inches by Swank at Olympia, London, on 25th June, 1937. On the same day Lady Wright of Durley set the best ever recorded height for an equestrienne on Jimmy Brown at 7 feet 4 inches.

FENCING

The sport of fencing grew up with the prohibition of duelling. In England this occurred c.1842.

The greatest number of individual Olympic gold medals won is three by Nedo Nadi (Italy) 1912 and 1920 (2) and Ramon Fonst (Cuba) 1900, 1904 (2). MOST OLYMPIC TITLES

The greatest number of Amateur Fencing Association Titles have been won as follows:— MOST A.F.A. TITLES

Foil	(Instituted 1898)	7	J. Emrys Lloyd	1928, 1930–33, 1937–38.
Epée	(Instituted 1904)	5	R. Montgomerie	1905, 1907, 1909, 1912, 1914.
Sabre	(Instituted 1898)	5	Dr. R. F. Tredgold	1937, 1939, 1947, 1948, 1949.
Foil (Ladies)	(Instituted 1907)	5	Miss G. Sheen	1949, 1951, 1952, 1953, 1954.

FOOTBALL (ASSOCIATION)

Football derived from local mob games and became standardized with the formation of the Football Association in England on 23 Oct., 1863. The oldest club is Sheffield F.C. formed in 1855. ORIGINS

The highest score recorded in a first-class match is 36. This occurred in the Scottish Cup match between Arbroath and Bon Accord on 5 Sept., 1885, when Arbroath won 36–0 on their home ground. HIGHEST SCORES Teams

The highest score recorded in an international match is 17. This occurred in the England *v.* Australia match at Sydney in 1951 when England won 17–0. The highest in British Isles occurred at Sunderland in 1899 when England beat Ireland 13–2. The highest score in an F.A. Cup match is 26 when Preston North End beat Hyde by 26–0 in 1887. The highest score in a final tie is 6 when Bury beat Derby County 6–0 in 1903 in which year Bury did not concede a single goal in Cup matches.

The highest score in a Football League (Division I) match is 12 goals in 1892 when West Bromwich Albion beat Darwen 12–0, and in 1909 when Nottingham Forest beat Leicester Fosse by the same score.

Individuals

The most goals scored by one player in a first-class match is 13 by J. Petrie of Arbroath v. Bon Accord in the Scottish Cup match above. The record in League Football is 10 by J. Payne for Luton Town v. Bristol Rovers on 13 April, 1936, at Luton in a 3rd Division South match. The English 1st Division record is 7 goals by E. Drake for Arsenal v. Aston Villa at Birmingham on 14 Dec., 1935, and J. Ross for Preston North End v. Stoke at Preston on 6 Oct., 1888. The Scottish 1st Division record is 8 goals by J. McGrory for Celtic v. Dunfermline Athletic on 14 Jan., 1928.

The record for individual goal-scoring in an International is 6 by J. Bambrick for Ireland v. Wales at Belfast on 1 Feb., 1930.

The best season records are 60 goals in 39 games by W. R. Dean for Everton (Division I) in 1927–28, and 66 goals in 38 games by J. Smith for Ayr United (Scottish Division II) in the same season.

The best career record in first-class football (1922–38) is 550 goals by James McGrory of Glasgow Celtic. The English record is 379 goals by W. R. Dean.

Most Caps Total

The greatest total of full international caps won is the 68 of W. A. (Billy) Wright of Wolverhampton Wanderers with 26 International Championship appearances (1945–55) and 42 foreign internationals and World Cup matches (1946–55). See Plate 14.

Including war-time internationals, Stanley Matthews has a total of 71 international appearances but of these only 20 are in full international championship matches and 25 in full foreign internationals.

England

The greatest number of England caps secured in the International Championship is 34 by Robert Crompton (Blackburn Rovers) from 1902 to 1914. Crompton also had 8 internationals against foreign teams.

Wales

The record number of Welsh caps in the International Championships is 48 by W. (Billy) Meredith (Manchester City and United) from 1895 to 1920. This is a record for any of the four home countries.

Scotland

The Scottish record for International Championship matches is 30 by Alan Morton (Queen's Park and Glasgow Rangers) from 1920 to 1932. Morton also had a single foreign international making a total of 31 caps.

Ireland

The greatest number of Irish caps recorded in the International Championship is 31 by Elisha Scott (Liverpool and Belfast Celtic) from 1920 to 1936. Ireland also have the youngest ever cap in W. K. Gibson (Cliftonville) who played against England in 1894 at 17. England's youngest international was probably E. C. Bambridge (Swifts) who was 17 when playing against Scotland in 1876.

TRANSFER FEES

The most expensive footballer in history is Juan Alberto Schiaffino who was bought by Milan F.C. from Penerol F.C. of Uruguay in June 1954 for £72,000. Of this figure his personal signing fee of £24,000 did not however match that of the Swede Hans Jeppson (See Plate 14), who received £39,000 of the £60,375 involved in his transfer from Napol to Genoese Atlanta in May 1952.

The British and English record is the £34,000 paid by Sheffield Wednesday to Notts. County for the English International inside forward J. Sewell in March 1951. The Scottish record is £17,500 paid by Dundee to Derby County for W. (Billy) Steel in September 1950.

CROWDS

The world record association football crowd is 200,000 on the occasion of the Brazil v. Uruguay World Cup match in Rio de Janeiro on 1 July, 1950.

The British record paid attendance is 149,547 at the Scotland v. England International of 17 April, 1937, at Hampden Park. It is, however, probable that this total was slightly exceeded on the occasion of the F.A. Cup Final between Bolton Wanderers and West Ham United at Wembley Stadium on 28 April, 1923, when the crowd broke in on to the pitch and the start was delayed 40 minutes until the pitch was cleared. The counted admissions were 126,047.

The Scottish Cup record attendance is 146,433 at Hampden Park in 1937 when Celtic played Aberdeen. The British Club match record is 143,570 at the Rangers v. Hibernian match of 1948 at Hampden Park, Glasgow.

F.A. CUP TITLES

The greatest number of F.A. Cup wins is 6 by: Blackburn Rovers 1884–86, 1890–91, 1928 (seven final appearances); Aston Villa 1887, 1895, 1897, 1905, 1913, 1920 (eight final appearances); Newcastle United 1910, 1924, 1932, 1951–52, 1955 (ten final appearances). The greatest number of Scottish F.A. Cup wins is 17 by Celtic: 1892, 1899–1900, 1904, 1907–08, 1911–12, 1914, 1923, 1925, 1927, 1931, 1933, 1937, 1951, 1954.

MOST LEAGUE CHAMPIONSHIPS

The greatest number of League Championships (Division I) is 7 by: Arsenal 1931 (record points 66), 1933, 1934, 1935, 1938, 1948, 1953.

WORLD CUP

The Fédération Internationale de Football (F.I.F.A.) was founded in April 1904 in Paris and instituted the World Cup Competition in 1930, two years after the four British Isles' associations had resigned.

The only countries to win twice are Uruguay in 1930 and 1950, and Italy in 1934 and 1938.

MOST OLYMPIC WINS

The only countries to have won the Olympic Football title twice are the United Kingdom (1908 and 1912) and Uruguay (1924 and 1928). These contests have now virtually ceased to be amateur. The highest Olympic score is Denmark 17 *v.* France "A" 1 in 1908.

HIGHEST SCORES

The highest score in a home Amateur International is 11 goals in the England *v.* Scotland match of 1939 (8–3) at Dulwich. The foreign record is 15 goals in 1906 when England beat France 15–0 in Paris.

The highest score in an F.A. Amateur Cup Final is 8 in 1926 when Northern Nomads beat Stockton 7–1 and in 1932 when Dulwich Hamlet beat Marine (Liverpool) by the same score.

The highest individual scores in amateur internationals are 6 by W. C. Jordan for England *v.* Holland (12–0) at Park Royal, London, on 23 March, 1908, and by V. J. Woodward for England *v.* Holland (9–1) at Stamford Bridge, London, on 11 Dec., 1909.

MOST CAPS

The record number of England amateur caps is held by V. J. Woodward (Chelmsford, Tottenham Hotspurs, and Chelsea) who, between 1903 and 1912, made 60 appearances in amateur and full internationals and in the Olympic Games.

F.A. AMATEUR CUP TITLES

The greatest number of F.A. Amateur Cup (instituted 1893) wins is 8 by Bishop Auckland who won in 1896, 1900, 1914, 1921–22, 1935, 1939 and 1955.

RECORD ATTENDANCE

The highest attendance at an amateur match is 100,000 at the 1953 Cup Final between Pegasus and Harwich at Wembley when there was also a receipts record of £29,247.

FOOTBALL POOLS

The largest single win ever recorded on the football pools was £104,417 won by a Hornsey, London man, father of six children, in November 1950. In December 1950, a £108,309 treble chance win was shared by two undisclosed persons.

FOOTBALL (GAELIC)

EARLIEST REFERENCES

The game developed from inter-parish "free for alls" with the formation on 1 Nov., 1884, of the Gaelic Athletic Association in Thurles, Ireland.

MOST TITLES

The greatest number of All-Ireland Championships won by one team is the seventeen by Kerry (1903–53). The greatest number of successive wins is four by Wexford (1915–18) and four by Kerry (1929–32).

HIGHEST SCORE

The highest score in an All-Ireland final was in 1911 when Cork (6 goals, 6 points) beat Antrim (1 goal, 2 points).

MOST APPEARANCES

The most appearances in All-Ireland finals are by Dan O'Keefe (Kerry) with ten, of which seven were on the winning side.

FOOTBALL (RUGBY LEAGUE)

ORIGIN

Rugby League arose from the secession of twenty North of England clubs from the Rugby Union due to the Union's refusal to recognize compensation for loss of working time. The Northern Union, formed 1896, changed its title to the Rugby League in 1922 and adopted full professionalism and reduced the number of players on each side from 15 to 13.

MOST WINS

The greatest number of wins in the Challenge Cup competition (instituted 1897) is five by Huddersfield in 1913, 1915, 1920, 1933 and 1953. The only Club to have appeared in four consecutive Finals was Oldham in 1924–5–6–7.

HIGHEST SCORES

The highest score in a test match, Great Britain *v.* Australia (instituted 1908) is 59 points at Brisbane on 3 July, 1954, when Great Britain won 38–21 with the winners scoring a record of 10 goals.

The greatest winning Test margin is 25 points when Australia beat Great Britain by 33–8 at Birmingham on 1 Jan., 1912, and when Great Britain beat Australia 37–12 at Sydney on 12 June, 1954.

MOST CAPS

The most appearances by a British player against Australia is fifteen by J. Sullivan (Wigan) between 1924 and 1933.

RECORD ATTENDANCES

The record attendance is 102,575 at Odsal Stadium, Bradford, at the Warrington v. Halifax Challenge Cup replay on 5 May, 1954. The record gate is £29,691 at the same drawn final at Wembley Stadium on 24 April, 1954.

LONGEST KICK

The record in a kicking-for-distance contest is 77 yards 2 feet 3 inches by M. Hodgson at Swinton, England, on 13 April, 1940.

FOOTBALL (RUGBY UNION)

The game is traditionally said to have originated from a breach of the rules of the football played in Nov. 1823 at Rugby School. This handling code of football evolved gradually during the last century but the Rugby Football Union was not founded until 1871.

MOST CAPPED PLAYERS

By any Country	42	G. V. Stephenson (Ireland)	1920–30
By England	31	W. W. Wakefield	1920–27
By Scotland	37	J. M. Bannerman	1921–29
By Wales	39	K. J. Jones (See Plate 14)	1947–55

Players from the three Dominion Unions — South Africa, Australia and New Zealand—obviously have less opportunity to win international caps. The most capped player from South Africa—which is generally conceded to be the premier Rugby country in the world—is M. M. Louw with 18 caps from 1928–38.

Highest Scores

In club matches scores of over 100 points by one side have been recorded but the highest aggregate for any match played under the auspices of the " International Rugby Union Football Board " since 1905 when modern scoring values came in is:—

England beat Ireland by 36 points to 14 at Dublin in 1938.

The greatest winning margin was 29 points when Wales beat Ireland by 29 points to 0 at Cardiff in 1907.

It has to be noted, however, that in 1881 England beat Wales by 7 goals, 1 drop goal and 6 tries to nil which would amount in modern terms to a score of 56 points.

The highest score by any Dominion side in an International in the British Isles was when South Africa beat Scotland by 44 points to 0 at Murrayfield on 24 Nov., 1951.

The highest score in any international was in the 1924 Olympic Games when France beat Rumania in Paris by 61 points to 3.

The highest in the " International Championship " in which France (which is not a member of the International Board) takes part was when Wales beat France by 49 points to 14 in 1910 at Swansea.

The greatest winning margin in the " International Championship " was 42 points when Wales beat France by 47 points to 5 in 1909 in Paris.

SCORING RECORDS — AGGREGATE and MARGIN of VICTORY in the ten annual internationals in the " International Championship " (since modern scoring values came in in 1905.)

	Match	Pts.	Record Aggregate	Pts.	Record Margin
1.	England v. Scotland	47.	Scotland won 28–19 in 1931	19.	England won by 19–0 in 1924 and 24–5 in 1947.
2.	England v. Wales	45.	Wales won 27–18 in 1908	22.	Wales won by 22–0 in 1907 and by 28–6 in 1922.
3.	England v. Ireland	50.	England won 36–14 in 1938	22.	England won by 36–14 in 1938 and Ireland by 22–0 in 1947.
4.	England v. France	54.	England won 41–13 in 1907	37.	England won by 37–0 in 1911.
5.	Scotland v. Wales	45.	Scotland won 35–10 in 1924	25.	Scotland won by 35–10 in 1924.
6.	Scotland v. Ireland	46.	Scotland won 29–17 in 1913	21.	Ireland won by 21–0 in 1950.
7.	Scotland v. France	34.	Scotland won 31–3 in 1912	28.	Scotland won by 31–3 in 1912.
8.	Wales v. Ireland	32.	Wales won 28–4 in 1920	29.	Wales won by 29–0 in 1907.
9.	Wales v. France	63.	Wales won 49–14 in 1910	42.	Wales won by 47–5 in 1909.
10.	Ireland v. France	30.	Ireland won 25–5 in 1911	24.	Ireland won by 24–0 in 1913.

LONGEST KICKS

The longest recorded successful drop-goal is 90 yards by G. Brand for South Africa v. England at Twickenham, London, in 1932.

The place kick record is reputed to be 100 yards at Richmond Athletic Ground, Surrey, by D. F. T. Morkell in an unsuccessful penalty for South Africa v. Middlesex in 1906. This was not measured until 1932.

GLIDING

	WORLD RECORDS		BRITISH RECORDS	
DURATION				
Multi-Seater	57 hrs. 10 mins.	B. Dauvin and H. Couston (France) in a Kranich III from Romanin-les-Alpills on 6/8 April, 1954.	22 hrs. 14 mins.	Fl./Lt. W. B. Murray and Lt./Cdr. (A) J. S. Sproule, R.N., in a Falcon III from Dunstable, Beds., on 9/10 July, 1938.
Solo	56 hrs. 15 mins.	C. Atger (France) in an Arsenal Air 100 from Romanin-les-Alpills on 2/4 April, 1952.	15 hrs. 47 mins.	Sub/Lt. A. N. Young in a Falcon II from Long Mynd, Shropshire, on 18 Aug., 1938.
DISTANCE				
Solo	535·17 miles	R. H. Johnson (U.S.A.) in a Ross-Johnson N 3722 from Odessa, Texas, to Sabina, Kansas, on 5 Aug., 1951.	257 miles	Fl./Lt. A. W. Bedford, A.F.C., in an Eon Olympia from nr. Farnborough, Hants., to Usworth, Northumberland, on 2 May, 1951.
GOAL FLIGHT				
Solo	395·73 miles	U. I. Efimenko (U.S.S.R.) in an A-9 from Grabtsevo to Mélovoé on 6 June, 1952.	257 miles	As above.
GOAL AND RETURN				
Multi-Seater	270·92 miles	E. Dommisse and S. J. Barker (S. Africa) in a Kranich II Z S-G from Keetmanshoop to Mariental, S. Africa, and return on 9 Feb., 1952.	77·2 miles	J. W. S. Pringle, M.B.E., and J. Grantham in a Kranich from Cambridge to Dunstable and return on 12 Aug., 1949.
Solo	*260·35 miles	W. H. Coverdale, Jnr. (U.S.A.) in a Schweizer I-23 from Grand Prairie, Texas, to Brownwood, Texas, on 22 Aug., 1952.	163 miles	P. A. Wills in a Weihe from Redhill to Little Rissington and return on 3rd June, 1951.
ABSOLUTE ALTITUDE				
Multi-Seater	44,255 feet	L. E. Edgar and H. E. Klieforth (U.S.A.) in a Pratt-Read from Bishop, California (released at 9,830 feet) on 19 Mar., 1952 (also record altitude gain—34,425 feet).	———	No absolute record but record altitude gain 15,240 feet Flt./Lt. A. D. Piggott and Cadet Flt./Sgt. B. Whatley from Sedborgh, Yorks., on 27 July, 1953.
Solo	42,100 feet	W. S. Ivans, Jnr. (U.S.A.) in a Schweizer S.G.S. I-23 from Bishop, California (released at 12,000 feet) on 30 Dec., 1950 (also record altitude gain—30,100 feet).	30,400 feet	P. A. Wills in a Weihe from Simons Hill, Fairlie, New Zealand (released 2,200 feet) on 29 Dec., 1954 (also record altitude gain—28,200 feet).
SPEED				
Triangular 100 km. Course—Solo	58·85 m.p.h.	J. Wojnar (Poland) in a 'Jaskolka S.P. 1325' from Leszno, Poland, on 15 May, 1954.	37·0 m.p.h.	D. Smith in a 'Jaskolka' from Leszno, Poland, on 25 June, 1954.

* An, as yet, unratified record of 305 miles was set by Lyle Maxey (U.S.A.) from El Mirage Field, Calif., on 5 Sept., 1955.

GOLF

The earliest international match was on Leith Links in 1657 between James, Duke of York and John Paterson representing Scotland v. two English peers and resulted in a win for Scotland.

CLUBS

The oldest club of which there is written evidence is the Gentlemen Golfers (now the Honourable Company of Edinburgh Golfers) formed in March 1744—10 years prior to the Institution of the Royal and Ancient. The oldest club in America is St. Andrew's, New York, founded in 1888.

Largest

The largest club in the world is the Johannesburg Country Club in South Africa with a membership of 4,500. The club with the highest membership in the British Isles and England is North Shore, Skegness, Yorkshire (membership 1,100). The largest in Scotland is the Royal and Ancient Golf Club of St. Andrews, Fife (1,050) and the largest in Ireland is Elm Park, Dublin (850).

COURSES

Highest

The highest golf course in the world is that of the La Paz Golf Club, La Paz, Bolivia, 12,000 feet above sea level. Golf, however, has been played in Tibet at an altitude of over 16,000 feet.

The highest golf course in Great Britain is at Leadhills, 1,500 feet above sea level.

Lowest

The lowest golf club in the world is at Kallia, on the north eastern shores of the Dead Sea, 1,250 feet below sea level.

Longest Hole

The two longest holes in the world are at Cohanzick Country Club, New Jersey, and the Hot Springs Golf Club, Arkansas, U.S.A., which both have 700 yard holes. The longest hole on a championship course in Great Britain is the sixth at Troon, Ayrshire, which stretches 580 yards.

LOWEST SCORES

9 holes and 18 holes

The lowest recorded score on an 18 hole course is the 55 (15 under bogey) of A. E. Smith, the Woolacombe professional on his home course on 1 Jan., 1936. The course measured 4,248 yards and had a bogey 70. The detail was 4, 2, 3, 4, 2, 4, 3, 4, 3 = 29 out and 2, 3, 3, 3, 3, 2, 5, 4, 1 = 26 in. The last 9 were also a record low. The lowest recorded score on a long course (6,000 yards) is 58 by J. L. Black of Claremont, California, on 18 June, 1914.

The record low score for a first class professional tournament in Great Britain is 62 by the Australian Peter Thomson at the Oakdale course, Harrogate, Yorks., in July 1951. In a 63 round at Mere in 1949 Fred Daly did the first nine in a British Tournament record of 29.

72 holes

The lowest recorded score on a first class course is 259 (21 under par) by Byron Nelson (U.S.A.) in the Seattle Open Championship at the par-70 6,200 yard long Broadmoor Course, Washington, on 11–14 Oct., 1945, with rounds of 62, 68, 63, 66, and 259 by Ben Hogan (U.S.A.) in the Greenbriars Tournament at the Old White par-70 6,368 yard course at White Sulphur Springs on 2–7 May, 1950, with 64, 64, 65, 66. See Plate 15.

The lowest 72 holes in a national championship is 262 by Percy Alliss (G.B.) in the Italian Open Championship at San Remo in 1935 with 67, 66, 66, 63. The lowest for four rounds in a British first class tournament is 266 by Richard Burton in the "News Chronicle" Tournament at Hollingbury Park, Brighton, on 16–18 August, 1949, with 68, 66, 64, 68.

YOUNGEST AND OLDEST CHAMPIONS

The youngest winner of the British Open was Tom Morris, Jnr., in 1868 aged 18. The youngest winner of the British Amateur title was A. G. Barry at Prestwich in 1905 at 19. Barry had a distinction shared by only one other man in that he won Blues at Oxford (1914) and Cambridge (1906–07). The oldest winner of the British Amateur was the Hon. Michael Scott at Hoylake in 1933 at 54. The oldest British Open Champion was H. Vardon in 1914 at 44. The oldest American Amateur Champion was J. Westland in 1952 at 47.

HIGHEST SCORES

The highest score for a single hole in the British Open is 21 by a player in the inaugural meeting at Prestwich in 1860. Double figures have only once been recorded on the card of the winner when in 1883 at Musselburgh, W. Fernie scored a 10.

The most shots recorded for a hole in a professional tournament is variously 21 or 23 for the 17th by the 1927 American Open Champion T. Armour in the Shawnee Open Championship of that year.

FASTEST AND SLOWEST ROUNDS

With such variations in the lengths of courses, speed records even for rounds under par are of little comparative value. It is recorded that on 20 Sept., 1938, K. Bousfield completed the 18 holes of the Burnham Beeches course in 91 minutes, scoring 69, one over the course record, to complete 6 rounds in 3 minutes outside a 12 hour target. In 1939 a large team of players propelled a ball round the famous Tam O'Shanter Course at Niles, Illinois, in 17 minutes 20 seconds, hence maintaining an average of 57·8 seconds per hole.

The slowest round recorded in the finals of the British Amateur Championships is the 3 hours 40 minutes at St. Andrews in 1950 between F. R. Stranahan and R. D. Chapman. The slowest recorded round in a professional match was one of 4 hours 15 minutes at Walton Heath in 1938 between T. H. Cotton and R. A. Whitcombe *v.* A. D. Locke and S. Brews in a 4-ball match for a stake of £500 a side.

LONGEST DRIVE

In long-driving contests 280 yards is rarely surpassed. However, under freak conditions of wind, slope, parched or frozen surfaces or ricochet from a stone or flint much greater distances are achieved. The greatest recorded, and the only drive in excess of a ¼ mile, is that by E. C. Bliss (1863–1917), a 12 handicap player, at the 9th hole of the Old Course, Herne Bay, Kent, in August 1913 at 445 yards. Bliss, 6 feet tall and over 13 stone, drove to the back of the green on the left-handed dog-leg. The drive was measured by a government surveyor, Capt. Lloyd, who also measured the drop from tee to resting place as 57 feet.

RECORDS

In British "Open"

The British Open was inaugurated in 1860 at Prestwick, Ayrshire. The lowest 9 holes was recorded by C. H. Ward in 1950 who did the inward half of the Old Troon Course, Ayrshire, in 30.

The lowest scoring round is 63 in a qualifying round by Frank Jowle, 43, at the New Course, St. Andrews (6,526 yards) on 4 July, 1955. The best by an amateur in the "Open" is 66 by F. R. Stranahan (U.S.A.) at the same championship. The lowest 72 hole aggregate is the 279 (69, 72, 70, 68) by the South African A. D. Locke again at Troon in 1950.

The lowest score for the British Amateur Championship (inaugurated in 1885) 9 holes is 29 by R. D. Chapman (U.S.A.) at Sandwich in 1948. British Amateur

The American Open Championship was inaugurated in 1894. The lowest 72 hole aggregate is 276 by Ben Hogan at the Riviera County Club, Los Angeles, in 1948. American Open

The American Amateur Championship was inaugurated in 1893. The lowest score for 9 holes is 30 by F. Ouimet in 1932. American Amateur

MOST INTERNATIONALS

Amateur

The greatest number of amateur internationals won are as follows:—

England	L. G. Crawley (Brancepeth Castle)	38 times	1931–1954
Ireland	R. C. Ewing (County Sligo)	42 times	1934–1954
Scotland	E. A. McRuvie (Leven Thistle)	21 times	1929–1936
Wales	A. D. Evans (Brecon)	41 times	1931–1954
	S. B. Roberts (Prestatyn)	41 times	1932–1954

The England *v.* Scotland Professional Internationals were instituted in 1903 but discontinued in 1938. The greatest number of internationals is 15 by T. Dobson (East Renfrewshire) 1932–1938. Professional

The greatest prize money from a single meeting is the $22,500 (£8,035) won by Lloyd Mangrum during the 1948 Tam O'Shanter tournaments. Highest Prize Money

MOST TITLES

The most titles won in the world's major championships are as follows:—

British Open	H. Vardon	6	1896–98–99, 1903, 1911–14.
British Amateur	John Ball	7	1888–90–92–94–99, 1907–10.
American Open	W. Anderson	4	1901–03–04–05.
	R. T. Jones	4	1923–26–29–30.
American Amateur	R. T. Jones	5	1924–25–27–28–30.
British Ladies'	Miss C. Leitch	4	1914–20–21–26.
	Miss J. Wethered now (Lady Heathcoat-Amory)	4	1922–24–25–29.

LONGEST HOLE IN ONE

The longest hole ever driven in one is the par four (425 yards) ninth hole at Hillcrest Golf Club, Winston-Salem, North Carolina, U.S.A., by Cardwell, in 1939. This green has many times been driven in one in dry weather particularly with, as on this occasion, a strong following wind.

The longest hole in one performed in the British Isles is the 365 yards by Kenneth Saunders at the tenth hole on the Harewood Downs G. C., Amersham, Bucks., course on 8 July, 1955.

The greatest number of holes in one in a career is 23 by C. T. Chevalier between June 1918 and 1954. Holes in One Most

There is no recorded instance of a golfer performing three consecutive holes in one but there are three cases of aces being achieved in two consecutive holes:—

A. Duthie	Vancouver Golf and Country Club, Canada	1911
Cpl. R. Halverty	Recreation Park, Long Beach, California, U.S.A.	Aug. 1945
W/Cdr. T. R. Vickers	Changi Golf Course, Singapore	June 1950

The youngest golfer recorded to have shot a hole in one was Peter Toogood aged 8, at the 7th (110 yards) at Kingston Beach Golf Club. The oldest golfer to have performed the feat is T. S. South aged 91 at the seventh (110 yards) at Highcliffe Castle Golf Club, Hampshire, in 1952. Youngest and Oldest

The oft-repeated claim for a 435 yard hole in one in 1953 at the first hole of the Hermitage Country Club, Richmond, Virginia, U.S.A., was in fact achieved by a ball-testing driving machine built by the Achushnet Co.

GREYHOUND RACING

EARLIEST MEETING

Modern greyhound racing originated with the perfecting of the mechanical hare by O. P. Smith at Emeryville, California, U.S.A., in 1919. The earliest greyhound track race in the British Isles was at Manchester on 24 July, 1926.

DERBY

The only dog to have twice won the British Greyhound Derby, held each year (except 1940) over 525 yards at the White City Stadium, London, since 1927, was "Mick the Miller" in 1929 and 1930.

The fastest time for a winner of this race or any classic is 28·50 seconds (hand-timed) by "Endless Gossip" in 1952, so striking an average of 37·68 m.p.h.

GRAND NATIONAL

The only dog to have twice won the British Greyhound Grand National (instituted 1927), over 525 yards and 4 flights at the White City Stadium, London, is "Juvenile Classic" in 1938 and 1940.

The fastest time was 29·43 seconds (photo-timed) by " Barrowside " in May 1955. " Barrowside " failed to secure the " double " by placing second in the Derby—27 inches behind the winner, but displaced the previous record of " Dangerous Prince " which was second in both races 1949.

GYMNASTICS

EARLIEST REFERENCES Gymnastics were widely practised in Greece during the period of the ancient Olympic Games (776 B.C. to A.D. 392). They were not, however, revived until c.1780.

MOST OLYMPIC WINS Italy has won most Olympic team titles with four victories in 1912, 1920, 1924 and 1932.

The most individual gold medals have been won by Anton Heida (U.S.A.) with four (All-round title, long horse, side horse and horizontal bar) all in 1904. At Helsinki in 1952 Viktor Tchoukarine (U.S.S.R.) won three gold medals for Combined Exercises, Pommelled Horse and Long Horse and two silver medals for Parallel Bars and Rings.

ROPE CLIMBING The American Amateur Athletic Union records are tantamount to world records:
20 feet (hands alone) 3·1 seconds, Don Perry (U.S.A.) at State College, Pennsylvania, 1 May, 1948, and Sandford Werner (U.S.A.) at Detroit, 4 May, 1951.
25 feet (hands alone), 4·7 seconds, Garvin S. Smith at Los Angeles, 19 April, 1947.

CHINNING THE BAR It is recorded that the professionals A. Cutler (England) achieved twelve successive chins with one arm in 1878 and A. Lewis (England) 78 chins with both arms in 1913.

GREATEST TUMBLER The greatest tumbler of all-time is Dick Browning (U.S.A.) who in April 1954 at Santa Barbara, California, made a backward somersault over a 7 feet 6 inch bar. In his unique repertoire is a " Round-off," backward handspring, backward somersault with half-twist, walk-out, tinsica tigna round-off, backward handspring, double backward somersault.

LARGEST GYMNASIUM The world's largest gymnasium is Yale University's Payne Whitney Gymnasium at New Haven, Connecticut, U.S.A., completed in 1932 and valued at $18 million (£6,430,000). The building, known as the " Cathedral of Muscle ", has nine stories with wings of five stories each. It is equipped with four basket ball courts, three rowing tanks, twenty-eight squash courts, twelve hand-ball courts, a roof jogging track and twenty-five yard by forty-two foot swimming pool on the first floor and a fifty-five yards long pool on the third floor.

HOCKEY

A representation of two hockey players in an orthodox " bully " position exists in Copenhagen Museum on an altar pot dated A.D. c.1330 and there are British references to the game from the same century.

MEN'S

Earliest International The first international matches date from the Wales *v.* Ireland match at Rhyl in Jan. 1895.

Highest International Score The greatest number of goals scored in an international match was the 16 when England defeated France 16–0 at Beckenham in 1922.

Greatest Number of Caps
England 37, S. H. Saville (1913–1930).
Wales 36, G. B. Dadds (1932–1955).
Scotland 33, A. B. Burt (1905–1922).
Ireland 34, S. de Lacy (1937–1954).
Great Britain 11, J. A. Cockett (England).

WOMEN'S

The All England Women's Hockey Association was founded in 1895.

Earliest International The first international match dates from the England *v.* Ireland game in Dublin in 1896.

Highest International Score The highest score in a women's international match occurred in 1923 when England defeated France by 23 goals to nil.

Most Caps The greatest number of international representations are those of Miss Mabel Bryant who represented England for 14 years between 1907 and 1929.

HORSE RACING

RACECOURSE The earliest course was the Smithfield, London, opened c. A.D. 1175. The earliest trophy is the Chester Cup contested since 1512.

The world's largest racecourse is the 320 year old Newmarket, Cambridgeshire, England, on which the Beacon Course is 4 miles 397 yards long and the Rowley Mile is 167 feet wide.

ALL TIME WORLD RECORDS

¼ mile, 20·8 seconds, Big Racket, 4, Mexico, 5 Feb., 1945.
½ mile, 45·4 seconds, Tie Score, 4, Mexico City, 1 April, 1945.
1 mile (straight) 1 minute 32 seconds, Mopsus, 3, Brighton, England, 22 June, 1939.
1 mile, 1 minute 33·6 seconds, Citation, 5, Albany, California, 3 June, 1950.
2 miles, 3 minutes 15 seconds, Polazel, 3, Salisbury, England, 8 July, 1924.

JOCKEYS (Flat Racing) MOST WINNERS

Sir Gordon Richards (G.B.), retired in 1954, having won 4,870 races from 21,834 mounts. He has won more races than any other jockey since his career started in 1921. He won the Derby in 1953 for the first time in 28 attempts.

MOST PURSE MONEY

Eddie Arcaro (U.S.A.) retired in 1952 having earned £4,922,000 in 21 years—more than any other jockey. Arcaro, oddly enough, lost 250 races before registering his first win.

OLDEST

Levi Burlingame (U.S.A.) rode his last race at the age of 80 years at Stafford, Kansas, in 1932.

YOUNGEST

Jimmy Taylor (G.B.) was licensed by the Jockey Club and rode his first race at the Catterick Bridge Course in 1939 at the age of 10.

LIGHTEST

The lightest winner ever recorded was Kitchener who won the Chester Cup on "Red Deer" in 1844 at 3 stone 7 lb. He died in 1872.

MOST WINS IN SUCCESSION

Sir Gordon Richards (G.B.) won the last race on 3 Oct., 1933, all the six next day and the first five on 5 Oct.—total twelve.

(Steeplechase) MOST WINNERS

Dolly Byers (U.S.A.) starting in 1916 rode in 446 steeplechases and won 152 races.

MOST JOCKEYS IN ONE RACE

There were 66 jockeys in the Grand National in 1929 at Liverpool which is also a world record field for any horse race.

HORSES FASTEST

"Devineress", a three-year-old travelled the 5 furlongs of the Belmont Handicap at Epsom on 2 June, 1933, in 54·6 seconds = 41·2 m.p.h.

MOST ENGAGED IN A DAY

In eight races at the National Hunt meeting at Worcester on 16 March, 1955, 361 horses were engaged.

The most in a flat race meeting was the seven races at Nottingham on 11 Oct., 1941, when 346 horses were engaged.

MOST RUNNERS AT ONE MEETING

(Flat) 214 in seven races at Newmarket, 15 June, 1915.
(National Hunt) 158 in six races at Wetherby, 20 Jan., 1951.

MOST RUNNERS IN ONE RACE

66 (a world record) in the Grand National on 22 March, 1929.
58 in the Lincolnshire Handicap on 13 March, 1948, is the flat racing record.

MOST ENTRIES

483 horses were entered for the 1952 Derby.

WINNER OF MOST RACES

23 races in a season were won by "Fisherman" in 1857. 79 out of 174 races were won by "Catherina" in a career lasting from 1833 to 1841.

MOST SUCCESSFUL SIRE

"Stockwell's" progeny won 1,153 races between 1858 and 1876 and in 1866 set a season record with 132 races won.

MOST EXPENSIVE (in training)

£60,000 was paid for "Call Boy" at a private sale in July 1927 by Sir H. Mallaby-Deeley to the executors of the late Mr. F. Curzon. This record was equalled at a private sale in June 1938 when £60,000 was paid for "Nearco".

MOST EXPENSIVE STALLION

£250,000 was paid in February 1953 for "Tulyar" by the Irish National Stud to H. H. Aga Khan. "Tulyar" has the highest covering fee of any serving stallion at 600 sov. See Plate 15.

HIGHEST STAKE WINNER

Although only raced for two seasons, H.H. Aga Khan's "Tulyar" (1951–52) aggregated a record of £76,417 10s. 0d. In the 1952 season alone, in seven races, it achieved the figure of £75,173 10s. 0d.

GREATEST RACE VALUE

"Supreme Court's" race value at the King George VI and Queen Elizabeth Stakes at Ascot on 21 July, 1951, was £25,172 10s. 0d.

MOST SUCCESSFUL IN THE CLASSICS

A horse has yet to win all five classics. Nearest approach was in 1902 when "Sceptre" won the 1,000 Guineas and 2,000 Guineas, Oaks and St. Leger. In 1868, "Formosa" won the same four events, but deadheated the 2,000 Guineas.

MOST WINS IN A SEASON

Most races won in a single season was in 1947 when Sir Gordon Richards won 269 races.

OWNERS

Lord William Beresford won 69 races with his horses in the 1899 season.

MOST SUCCESSFUL

The highest amount of stake money won in a season was £92,518 13s. 0d. by H.H. Aga Khan in 1952.

H.H. Aga Khan from 1922 to 1954 had won 773 races, value £978,927.

THE DERBY

Greatest of England's five classic races, the Derby was inaugurated in 1780. It has been run over 1 mile 885 or 880 yards since 1784 at Epsom Downs except for the two war periods when it was run at Newmarket. The race is for three year old colts carrying 9 stone and fillies carrying 8 stone 9 lb.

MOST WINS

G. Robinson won six times: 1817, 1824, 1825, 1827, 1828 and 1836.

RECORD TIME

The record time for the Derby is 2 minutes 33·8 seconds (35·06 m.p.h.) by "Mahmoud" ridden by C. Smirke owned by H.H. Aga Khan, trained by F. S. Butters, which won by 3 lengths in 1936 from a field of 22 at 100 to 8.

SMALLEST FIELD
SMALLEST HORSE

The smallest field was 6 in 1783 and the largest 34 in 1862. "Little Wonder", the 1840 winner, stood only 14 hands 3½ inches.

MOST SUCCESSFUL TRAINER

John Porter of Kingsclere trained seven winners — "Blue Gown" (1868), "Shotover" (1882), "St. Blaise" (1883), "Ormonde" (1886), "Sainfoin" (1890), "Common" (1891) and "Flying Fox" (1899).

GRAND NATIONAL

Instituted in 1837 (under present conditions in 1839), the Grand National is a steeplechase for six year olds and over. The course at Aintree, near Liverpool, is 4 miles 856 yards and over 30 jumps.

MOST WINS

No horse has won three times but six share the record of two wins:

Peter Simple	1849 and 1853	The Colonel	1869 and 1870
Abd-el-Kader	1850 and 1851	Manifesto	1897 and 1899
The Lamb	1868 and 1871	Reynoldstown	1935 and 1936

Poethlyn won in 1919 having won the war-time Gatwick race in 1918.

Manifesto was entered eight times between 1895 and 1904—winning twice, coming third three times and fourth once.

FASTEST TIME

Golden Miller, a seven-year old ridden by G. Wilson carrying 12 stone 2 lb. owned by Miss D. Paget, won by 5 lengths from a field of 30 with odds of 8 to 1 in 9 minutes 20·4 seconds (28·82 m.p.h.) in 1934.

HIGHEST JUMP

The "Open Ditch", the 15th Jump, is 5 feet 2 inches high, 3 feet 9 inches wide. The ditch on take-off side is 6 feet wide, guard rail in front of ditch 1 foot 6 inches in height.

FIELD

The largest field was the 66 starters in 1929 and the smallest 6 in the inaugural race of 1837.

DEAD HEATS

There is no recorded case in turf history of a quintuple dead heat. The nearest approach was at the Astley Stakes, at Lewes, England, in August 1880 when Mazurka, Wandering Nun and Scobell triple dead-heated for first place, just ahead of Cumberland, and Thors who dead heated for fourth place. Each of the five jockeys thought he had won. The only two examples of a quadruple dead heat known are that of 1851 in an open hunters' stakes at Chester, England, between The Squire, Pulcherrima, The Defaulter and Reindeer, and at the Houghton Meeting at Newmarket in 1855 between Overreach, Lady Go-Lightly, Gamester and The Unexpected. The earliest recorded photo-finish dead heat in Britain occurred in the 5 furlong Beechfield Handicap at Doncaster on 22 Oct., 1947, between Phantom Bridge and Resistance.

LONGEST RACE

The longest recorded horse race was one of 1,200 miles in Portugal, won by a horse Emir bred from Egyptian-bred Blunt Arab stock. The holder of the world's record for long distance racing and speed is Champion Crabbet who covered 300 miles in 52 hours 33 minutes carrying 17½ stone in 1920.

GAMBLING
Highest Odds

The highest recorded odds secured by a backer was the 60,640 : 1 secured on 15 June, 1951, by Mr. Pratley, of Coventry, England, on a 1s. each-way accumulator which built up to £3,032. His wins were on "Guerrier," "Val d'Assa," "Pun" and "Donore."

The world record odds on a "double" are 24,741 : 1 secured by Mr. Montague Harry Parker of Windsor, England, for £1 each-way "double" on "Ivernia" and "Golden Sparkle".

Tote Record

The British record for a Tote dividend is 3,410 : 1 received by Mrs. Answorth on "Coole" at Haydock Park, England, on 30 Nov., 1929, when, from a 2s. bet, she received £341 2s. 6d.

The American Pari-Mutuel record pay-off is the $941·75 : 1 on "Wishing Ring" at Laytonia, Kentucky, in 1912.

Shortest Price

The shortest ever odds, quoted on any race horse is the 100 : 1 on, on the American horse "Man O'War" on three separate occasions in 1920.

FOX HUNTING

EARLIEST REFERENCES

Hunting the fox in Britain dates only from the middle of the 17th century. Prior to that time hunting was confined principally to the deer or the hare. The fox was only hunted by mistake.

OLDEST PACK

The oldest pack of foxhounds in existence in England is the Sinnington (1680) but the old Charlton Hunt in Sussex, now extinct, and the Duke of Buckingham in the Bilsdale country, Yorkshire, hunted foxes prior to that time.

LARGEST PACK

The pack with the greatest number of hounds has been the Duke of Beaufort's hounds maintained at Badminton, Gloucestershire, since c.1780. At times hunting eight times a week, this pack had 120 couple.

LONGEST HUNTS

The longest hunts on record are the Coplow to Endersby Gorse run by the Quorn on 24 Feb., 1800, of 28 miles and the Greatwood run of 22 Feb., 1871, when the Duke of Beaufort's hounds found close to Greatwood and marked their fox to ground close to Highworth having covered also 28 miles in 3½ hours. The longest hunt in Ireland is probably that by the Scarteen Hunt, County Limerick, in 1914 in a 24-mile run from Pallas to Knockkoura. The longest duration hunt is that of 26 Jan., 1736, when the Charlton Hunt of Sussex ran from East Dean Wood from 7·45 a.m. to kill over 24½ miles away at 5.50 p.m. after 10 hours 5 minutes.

HURLING

EARLIEST REFERENCE

A game of very ancient origin, hurling only became standardized with the formation of the Gaelic Athletic Association in Thurles, Ireland, on 1 Nov., 1884.

MOST TITLES

The greatest number of All-Ireland Championships won by one team is twenty by Cork (1890–1954). The greatest number of successive wins is four by Cork (1941–44).

HIGHEST SCORE

The highest score in an All-Ireland final was in 1896 when Tipperary (8 goals, 14 points) beat Dublin (0 goals, 4 points).

MOST APPEARANCES

The most appearances in All-Ireland finals is nine by Christie Ring (Cork) of which eight were on the winning side.

ICE HOCKEY

The game probably originated in 1855 at Kingston, Ontario, Canada, but Montreal and Halifax also lay claims as the originators. Twenty-two countries were members of the international body—Ligue Internationale de Hockey sur Glace—at the time of the last Winter Olympic Games at Oslo 1952.

MOST OLYMPIC CHAMPIONSHIPS

Canada has won the Olympic title six times—that is at every Winter Olympic celebration except in 1936 when Great Britain won at Garmisch-Partenkirchen, Germany.

STANLEY CUP RECORDS

(This cup became emblematic of world professional team supremacy several years after the first contest in 1893.)

MOST WINS

Seven times by the Montreal Canadians: 1916, 1924, 1930, 1931, 1944, 1946, 1953.

LONGEST MATCH

2 hours 56 minutes 30 seconds at Montreal when Detroit Red Wings eventually beat Montreal Maroons 1–0 in the sixth period of overtime.

MOST GOALS

(a) By one side: 11, when Montreal Canadians beat Toronto.

(b) Aggregate: 13, when Montreal Canadians beat Toronto 10–3, on 29 March, 1945. Most cup goals in a season: Maurice Richard of Montreal Canadians—54 goals.

REGULAR SEASON RECORDS

MOST GOALS

The most goals scored by one side is 15 when Detroit Red Wings beat New York Rangers 15–0 at Detroit on 23 Jan., 1945. The most goals (aggregate) was 21 when Montreal Canadians beat Toronto 14–7 on 10 Jan., 1920.

HIGHEST SCORE

The greatest number of goals recorded in a British League game is the 24 when Wembley Lions beat Wembley Monarchs 16–8 on 25 Jan., 1940. The highest individual score in a game in English League is 7 goals of Bud McEachern for Streatham *v.* Harringay Greyhounds on 5 May, 1948. The Scottish League record is 8 by Hal Schooley for Paisley Pirates *v.* Fife Flyers on 11 Dec., 1953. The fastest scoring recorded in a British League game is 4 goals in 31 seconds by Wembley Lions *v.* Harringay Racers on 29 Dec., 1938.

ICE SKATING

ORIGINS

The earliest reference to ice skating is that of a Danish writer dated 1134. The earliest English account of 1180 refers to skates made of bone. Metal blades date from probably c.1600. The oldest skating club is the Edinburgh Skating Club formed in 1642. The earliest artificial ice rink in the world was built in Chelsea, London, in 1876.

LARGEST RINK

The world's largest artificial ice rink is the Pan-Pacific Auditorium, Los Angeles, California, U.S.A. It has an ice area of 300 × 100 feet. The largest in the U.K. is the Crossmyloof Ice Rink, Glasgow, with an ice area of 225 × 97 feet.

SPEED RECORDS

Men	500 m.	40·8	Jurij Sergyer (U.S.S.R.)	Alma Ata	19 Jan., 1955
	10,000 m.	16 32·6	Hjalmar Andersen (Norway)	Hamar	10 Feb., 1952

MOST TITLES

The greatest number of world speed skating titles (instituted 1893) won by any skater is five by O. Mathisen (Norway) 1908–09, 1912–14, and Clas. Thunberg (Finland) 1923, 1925, 1928–29, 1931. The most Ladies' titles is three by Mlle. M. Isakova (U.S.S.R.).

The most British titles ($1\frac{1}{2}$ miles) won is four by A. E. Tebbitt (1895, 1900, 1902, 1905) and by C. W. Horn (1927, 1929, 1933(2)).

FIGURE SKATING

The greatest number of world figure skating titles (instituted 1896) is ten by U. Salchov between 1901 and 1911. The women's record is ten titles by Frk. Sonja Henie (Norway), (1927–36). See Plate 15.

JUDO

ORIGIN

Jiu Jitsu (Jujutsu) is of Chinese origin in the pre-Christian era but has been greatly developed by the Japanese, particularly since 1880. There are no world championships, largely due to the fact that Japanese domination would be a foregone conclusion.

HIGHEST GRADE

The highest grade is the Black Belt (*dan*) in which there are degrees ranging from 1 to 7 (fighting degrees) and 8 to 10 (rare honorary degrees). The highest degree, Tenth *Dan*, is currently held by Mifune of Japan. The highest grade of any judoka in Britain is Seventh *Dan* held by the coach G. Koizumi.

LAWN TENNIS

(The modern game is generally agreed to have started with Major W. Wingfield's patent for "sphairistike" taken out in February 1874. This game soon became known as lawn tennis.)

ALL TIME RECORDS

MOST GAMES Singles Match

The greatest number of games ever played in a singles match is 100. J. Drobny (Egypt) and J. E. Patty (U.S.A.) divided their match on an indoor court at Lyons, France, on 20 Feb., 1955, with the score at 21–19, 8–10, 21–21 (Drobny's score first) after four hours' play.

Doubles Match

The greatest number of games ever played in a doubles match is 135. F. R. Schroeder and R. Falkenburg beat R. A. Gonzalez and H. W. Stewart (all U.S A.) 36–34, 3–6, 4–6, 6–4, 19–17 at Los Angeles, U.S.A., on 15 May, 1949, after $4\frac{3}{4}$ hours of play.

Mixed Doubles Match

The most games played in a mixed doubles match was 71 when, in the semi-finals of the American Championship of 1948, W. F. Talbert and Mrs. W. du Pont (U.S.A.) beat R. Falkenburg and Miss G. Moran (U.S.A.) 27–25, 5–7, 6–1.

Set

The most games ever recorded in a set is the 70 in the first set of the 1949 Los Angeles doubles match quoted above. For singles, the most games in a set was 54 when J. Coughlin beat E. Miles 28–26 in the 1933 American Inter-Collegiate Championships.

LONGEST SET

At Beaulieu on the French Riviera in 1937, Mme. R. Mathieu (France) took two hours to win a first set 7–5 against Mrs H. Sperling (Germany).

LONGEST MATCH

It took six hours playing time for F. G. Lowe (G.B.) to beat A. J. Zerlendi (Greece) in the second round of the Olympic Games singles championship at Antwerp in 1920. The match was subjected to interruptions owing to the weather. The score was 14–12, 8–10, 5–7, 6–4, 6–4.

MOST DECISIVE DEFEAT

Miss Huiskamp, having won her previous round 6–0, 6–0 in the Washington State Championships in 1910, was beaten by Miss Hazel V. Hotchkiss (now Mrs. George Wightman), then the American champion, 6–0, 6–0, without winning a single point.

GREATEST DOMINATION

The earliest occasion upon which any player secured all four of the world's major titles was in 1935 when F. J. Perry (G.B.) won the French title, having won Wimbledon (1934), the American title (1933–34) and the Australian title (1934).

The earliest example of a man holding all four titles at the same time was J. D. Budge (U.S.A.) who won Wimbledon (1937), America (1937), Australia (1938), France (1938), Wimbledon (1938) and America (1938)—a unique run of successes.

The earliest example of a woman player winning all four major titles and, furthermore, holding them all at the same time, was Miss Maureen Catherine Connolly (U.S.A.). She won the American title in 1951, Wimbledon in 1952, retained the American title in 1952, won the Australian in 1953, the French in 1953 and Wimbledon again in 1953. She won her third American title in 1954, her second French in 1954, and her third Wimbledon in 1954. Miss Connolly (now Mrs. Norman Brinker) was seriously injured in a riding accident shortly before the 1954 American championships.

FASTEST SERVICE

The fastest service of any player was that of the U.S. Davis Cup player Lester Stoefen who, in 1935, was measured to drive a ball at 131 m.p.h.

GREATEST CROWD

The greatest crowd at a tennis match was 25,578 at the first day of the Davis Cup Challenge Round between Australia and the United States at the White City, Sydney, on 27 Dec., 1954.

DAVIS CUP RECORDS

(This international knock-out team championship was instituted in 1900 and has been contested to date by no less than 49 nations).

MOST GAMES

Singles

The greatest number of games in a Davis Cup singles rubber was 78, when J. Drobny (Czechoslovakia) beat A. K. Quist (Australia) in the 1948 Inter-Zone final at Boston, Mass., U.S.A., 6–8, 3–6, 18–16, 6–3, 7–5.

Doubles

The greatest number of games in a Davis Cup doubles rubber was 81 when W. T. Tilden and R. N. Williams (U.S.A.) beat J. O. Anderson and J. B. Hawkes (Australia) 17–15, 11–13, 2–6, 6–3, 6–2, in the Challenge Round at Forest Hills, U.S.A., on 1 Sept., 1923, and again when J. D. Hackett and M. Murphy (Ireland) beat V. Skonecki and J. Chytrowski (Poland) 10–8, 8–10, 12–14, 7–5, 6–1, in the third round of the European Zone at Warsaw in 1950.

Set

The most games in any set in a Davis Cup match was 34 in the 1948 Inter-Zone final (see above).

LONGEST SPAN

Dr. J. C. Gregory (G.B.) who first played for England in 1926 and finally for Great Britain in 1952—26 years later, holds this record. Gregory came into the game in 1952 because of an injury to G. L. Paish, and partnered by A. J. Mottram, won the doubles in the fifth set against Yugoslavia in Zagreb.

MOST DECISIVE RUBBERS

On 6 occasions, a rubber has been won 6–0, 6–0, 6–0. In March 1955 at Rangoon, Burma, the Philippines secured the necessary three rubbers to win the tie with the loss of only 4 games against the Burmese Ko Ko and Maung-Maung in the two singles. A Burmese pair failed to register a single game in the doubles.

TIES

Longest

In 1946, at Paris, Yugoslavia, having lost the two opening singles in the fifth set, then went on to win the tie 3–2 by winning the doubles and reverse singles each in the fifth set. The total number of games was 261.

Shortest

Argentina, in 1931, on March 26-28 beat Paraguay at Asuncion, 5–0, losing only 15 games. Paraguay has not entered the competition since. On April 2-4, 1931, at Buenos Aires, Argentina beat Uruguay 5–0 again also losing only 15 games.

Most Representations

G. von Cramm (Germany) played 102 rubbers (between 1932 and 1953) winning 82 and losing only 20 matches.

BRITISH DAVIS CUP RECORDS

("British Isles" 1900-1921, "England" 1922-1928, "Great Britain" since 1929.)

Most Representations A. J. Mottram (1947-55) appeared for Great Britain in 56 rubbers. F. J. Perry appeared in 52 rubbers between 1931-36.

BEST PLAYING RECORD H. L. Doherty played in 12 rubbers all in the Challenge Round between 1902 and 1906 and won them all. This is the only immaculate Davis Cup record by any player in the Challenge Round.

LONGEST PARTNERSHIP A. J. Mottram and G. L. Paish played in 16 double rubbers as a pair from 1947 to 1955. F. J. Perry and G. P. Hughes made 14 appearances.

YOUNGEST PLAYER R. K. Wilson was selected for the tie against Norway in 1953 at the age of 17 years but was not called upon to play. Roger Becker was selected for the tie against Yugoslavia in 1952 at the age of 18 and played a singles match, losing in the fifth set.

OLDEST PLAYER Dr. Colin Gregory won a doubles rubber partnered by A. J. Mottram against Yugoslavia at Zagreb in 1952 when 48 years of age.

WIMBLEDON RECORDS (The first Championship was in 1877).

MOST GAMES Singles The most games in a singles match at Wimbledon was 93 when J. Drobny (Egypt) beat J. E. Patty (U.S.A.) 8–6, 16–18, 3–6, 8–6, 12–10 in the 3rd round on 25 June, 1953.

Doubles The most games in a doubles match at Wimbledon was 94 when J. E. Patty and M. A. Trabert (U.S.A.) beat K. McGregor and F. A. Sedgman (Australia) 6–4, 31–29, 7–9, 6–2 in the quarter finals of 1950.

Set The most games in a set at Wimbledon was 60—also the longest time taken by a set which was 2½ hours—in the record doubles match mentioned above.

MOST GAMES IN FINALS The most games in a Wimbledon men's singles final was 58 when J. Drobny (Egypt) beat K. R. Rosewall (Australia) 13–11, 4–6, 6–2, 9–7 in 1954.

The most games in a Wimbledon women's singles final was 44, when Mlle. Suzanne Lenglen (France) beat Mrs. Lambert-Chambers (G.B.) 10–8, 4–6, 9–7 in 1919.

The most games in a Wimbledon men's doubles final was 64, on two occasions. First when J. O. Anderson and R. Lycett beat G. L. Patterson and P. O'Hara Wood 3–6, 7–9, 6–4, 6–3, 11–9 in 1922 and secondly when G. M. Lott and J. van Ryn (U.S.A.) beat H. Cochet and J. Brugnon (France) 6–2, 10–8, 9–11, 3–6, 6–3 in 1931.

The most games in a Wimbledon ladies' doubles final was 38 when Mme. R. Mathieu and Miss E. Ryan beat Miss F. James and Miss A. M. Yorke 6–2, 9–11, 6–4 in 1933.

The most games in a Wimbledon mixed doubles final was 38 when F. J. Perry and Miss D. Round (G.B.) beat J. D. Budge and Miss S. Fabyan (U.S.A.) 7–9, 7–5, 6–4 in 1936.

LONGEST MATCH The longest Wimbledon match was the 4¼ hours required by the 1953 Drobny *v.* Patty match (see above).

YOUNGEST CHAMPIONS The youngest ever champion at Wimbledon was Miss Charlotte Dodd (b. Sept. 29, 1871) who was 15 when she won in 1887.

The youngest male champion was Wilfred Baddeley (b. 11 Jan., 1872) who won the Wimbledon title in 1891 at the age of 19.

The youngest doubles champions were the 18 year old Australian Lewis A. Hoad (b. 23 Nov., 1934) and his partner Kenneth R. Rosewall, who was born only 3 weeks before, who won the title in 1953.

MOST APPEARANCES Jean Borotra (France) first entered Wimbledon in 1922 (the wettest-ever Wimbledon) and appeared without a break to 1955, except for the years 1946-1947—26 appearances in all. See Plate 15.

MOST WINS Miss Elizabeth Ryan (U.S.A.) won her first title in 1914 and her nineteenth in 1934. (12 women's doubles with 5 different partners and 7 mixed doubles with 5 different partners).

The greatest number of wins by a man at Wimbledon was by William C. Renshaw (G.B.) who won 7 singles titles (1881-2-3-4-5-6-9) and 7 doubles (1880-1-4-5-6-8-9) partnered by his twin brother Ernest.

The greatest number of singles wins were those of Mrs. Helen Wills-Moody (U.S.A.) (now Mrs. Roark) who won her 8th singles title in 1938.

The greatest number of singles wins by a man were those of William C. Renshaw as quoted above.

The greatest number of doubles wins by men was 8 by R. F. and H. L. Doherty, brothers. They won each year from 1897 to 1905 except for 1902.

The most doubles titles won by a woman were the 12 by Miss Elizabeth Ryan mentioned above.

The greatest number of mixed doubles wins were the 7 times by Miss Elizabeth Ryan as noted above. Randolf Lycett (G.B.) 1919-21-23 and E. Victor Seixas (U.S.A.) 1953-54-55 are the only men who have had three wins.

MODERN PENTATHLON

Modern Pentathlon (Riding, Fencing, Shooting, Swimming and Running) was inaugurated into the Olympic Games at Stockholm in 1912. The Modern Pentathlon Club in Britain was founded in 1923 and changed its title to the Modern Pentathlon Association of Great Britain in 1929.

MOST WORLD TITLES

The only man to have retained a world title is the Swede Lars Hall, the 1952 Olympic champion, who having won in Bern in 1950 won again in Halsingborg, Sweden, in 1951.

MOST BRITISH TITLES

No pentathlete has won three titles. Those who have won two are:—

Cdt. (later 2nd/Lt.) V. W. Barlow	1929, 1930.
Lt. (later Capt.) C. P. D. Legard	1932, 1935.
Cdt. (later 2nd/Lt.) R. A. Hosman	1937, 1938.
L/Cpl. A. C. Martin	1947, 1948.
Capt. D. A. Duckworth	1949, 1951.
C.S.M.I. G. R. Norman	1953, 1954.

MOTOR CYCLING

OLDEST RACE

The oldest motorcycle races in the world are the A.-C.U. Tourist Trophy series, first held on a 15¾-mile course in the Isle of Man in 1907 and still run in the Island, on the 37¾-mile "Mountain" circuit and the 10¾-mile Clypse circuit.

LONGEST CIRCUIT

The "Mountain" circuit, over which the two main T.T. races are run, is the longest used for a "classic" motorcycle race.

FASTEST CIRCUIT

The fastest circuit is the 4¾-mile Hockenheim track near Heidelberg in Germany, lapped by G. E. Duke on a 500 c.c. Italian Gilera at 123·8 m.p.h. in May, 1955. The fastest English circuit is Silverstone, which Duke lapped on a Gilera at 94·82 m.p.h. in April, 1955.

Of the Grand Prix races, the French, run over the 5·2-mile Rheims circuit, is the fastest, Duke having lapped there in 1955 at 116·7 m.p.h. The Senior T.T. in the Isle of Man is the longest, covering seven laps of the "Mountain" course (264¼ miles) and is generally regarded as the most difficult.

The 2⅜-mile Barcelona circuit over which the Spanish Grand Prix is run is the most fatiguing, however, for it consists almost entirely of corners and the 500 c.c. race covers no fewer than 53 laps. The lap record, held in 1955 by C. Bandirola, on an Italian M.V.-Agusta, stands at 69·5 m.p.h.

MOST SUCCESSFUL RIDERS

With 10 T.T. victories between 1923 and 1939, the Irishman S. Woods has a record which has still to be beaten in the Isle of Man.

Since 1949, the Fédération Internationale Motocycliste has conducted World Championships. Duke, five times a T.T. winner, has won the 500 c.c. championship four times and the 350 c.c. title twice, giving him the highest total of successes. He and the sidecar driver, E. S. Oliver are the only men to have held one title for three consecutive seasons.

MOST SUCCESSFUL MACHINES

Since the first T.T. was run, the British Norton factory has won 32 races in the series, more than any other make. In the past few years, however, the Italian Gilera has been outstanding, with five 500 c.c. Championship wins out of seven.

RELIABILITY TRIALS

The most important and longest trial, covering approximately 1,250 miles, is the F.I.M.'s International Six Days, first held in 1913. It has been won by a British team sixteen times out of thirty.

The toughest trial is the Scottish Six Days, in which B. H. M. Viney, captain of the British I.S.D.T. team, has the unique distinction of being the winner in three consecutive years—1947–48–49 and also 1953.

The solo Trials Drivers' Star, awarded by the British Auto-Cycle Union for the most consistent performance of the year in national one-day trials was won in 1953 by J. V. Smith, at the age of 19 and again in 1954.

WORLD RECORDS

The fastest speed ever attained on a motor cycle is the 193·72 m.p.h. achieved by J. Allen (U.S.A.) at Bourneville Salt Flats, Utah, U.S.A., on 25 Sept., 1955 riding a 649 c.c. unsupercharged Triumph.

The official world record (ratified by the F.I.M.) is 185 m.p.h. set by New Zealander R. Wright on 2 July, 1955 at Invercargill, New Zealand on a 998 c.c. unsupercharged Vincent. On the same machine, the same day, R. Burns, a Scot, raised his own flying kilometre sidecar record to 163 m.p.h. The fastest speed achieved with the smallest recognized engine is $93\frac{1}{2}$ m.p.h. for the flying kilometre achieved by H. Baumm on a 49 c.c. N.S.U. near Munich on 10 May, 1955.

The longest listed motorcycle record is the 30,998 miles in 19 days at an average speed of 68 m.p.h. set by a group of French Army officers on a Gnôme et Rhône " Yacco " machine at Montlhéry from the 19 June to 8 July, 1939.

MOTOR RACING

OLDEST RACE

The oldest motor race in the world still being regularly run is the R.A.C. Tourist Trophy—first held in the Isle of Man in 1905. It is currently run on the Dundrod course outside Belfast, Northern Ireland.

The oldest Continental races are the French Grand Prix and the Targa Florio, which both began in 1906.

LONGEST CIRCUIT

The longest motor racing circuit in the world is the Mille Miglia which has been run in Italy since 1927. The 1955 course measured 992·37 miles, starting and finishing at Brescia. The record average speed attained on the course, which is held on public roads is 97·96 m.p.h. by Stirling Moss (G.B.) driving a Mercedes Benz in 1955. On the last 85 miles of the race from Cremona to Brescia Moss averaged 123 m.p.h. See Plate 16.

FASTEST CIRCUITS

The fastest motor racing circuit in the world is the Avus track near Berlin. In 1937, Rosemeyer (Germany) in a 6 litre Auto Union lapped at a record speed of 171 m.p.h.

The fastest English circuit is Silverstone which has been lapped at 100·16 m.p.h. by G. Farina (Italy) in the Thinwall Special.

TOUGHEST CIRCUITS

The Targa Florio is acknowledged to be the most difficult and arduous circuit. Held in Sicily on the Madonie Circuit it is 45 miles in length and over the eight laps of the race it involves the negotiation of approximately 6,800 corners, over severe mountain gradients and narrow rough roads. The lap record is 57·82 m.p.h. by E. Castellotti (Italy) in a sports Lancia in 1955.

The most difficult Grand Prix circuit is generally regarded to be the Monaco, run through the streets of Monte Carlo. It is 1·9 miles in length and has ten pronounced corners and several sharp changes of gradient. The race is run over 100 laps and involves on average some 1,500 gear changes. The record lap stands at 68·70 m.p.h. by J. M. Fangio (Argentina) in a Mercedes Benz in 1955.

LONGEST AND FASTEST

The most important sports car race is the Le Mans 24 hours Grand Prix d'Endurance held on the 8·35 mile Sarthe circuit in France. The longest distance ever covered is 2,594·58 miles by M. Hawthorn and I. Bueb in a Jaguar in 1955. Their average speed for the whole distance was 107·072 m.p.h. The fastest speed ever recorded in the race was 181·57 m.p.h. over the measured kilometre by J. M. Fangio in a Mercedes Benz in 1955.

Since its inception in 1923 it has been won five times by Bentley cars in 1924–27–28–29 and 1930, (more than any other single make) once by Lagonda in 1935 and three times by Jaguar 1951–53–55.

MOST SUCCESSFUL DRIVERS

Based on the World Drivers' Championships inaugurated in 1950, the most successful drivers have been J. M. Fangio (Argentine) who won twice in 1951 and 1954 and A. Ascari (Italy) who also won twice in 1952 and 1953.

Before the inception of the Drivers' Championship there was no official basis for comparison, but of major races Nuvolari (Italy) won 42 between 1927–46, A. Ascari 45 between 1947–55, R. Caracciola (Germany) 27 between 1926–39, J. M. Fangio 35 between 1949–55.

The most successful British 500 c.c. driver based on the National 500 c.c. Championships is Don Parker who won in 1952–53.

The British Racing Drivers' Club "Gold Star" award has been made four times to J. R. Cobb (track racing and record breaking) and four times to S. Moss (road racing).

MOST SUCCESSFUL RALLY DRIVERS

Based on overall performances in ten rallies the European Grand Touring Championships has been won twice since its inception in 1953 by W. Schlüter of Germany in 1953–54 driving a Fiat (Italian), Porsche and D. K. W. (German) Cars.

MOST SUCCESSFUL HILL CLIMB DRIVER

The British National Hill Climb Championship inaugurated in 1947 has been won four times by K. Wharton in 1951–52–53–54. Raymond Mays has won the Shelsley Walsh hill climb seventeen times between 1923 and 1948.

LAND SPEED RECORDS

The most successful land speed record breaker was Sir Malcolm Campbell. He broke the record nine times between 1924, with 146·16 m.p.h. in a Sunbeam and 1935 with 301·13 m.p.h. in the Rolls Royce engined "Bluebird."

The land speed record now stands at 394·196 m.p.h. achieved by John Cobb. (See page 145.)

The longest duration world record is the 300,000 kilometre (186,410 miles) covered in 133 days 17 hours 37 minutes 38·64 seconds, an average of 58·08 m.p.h. achieved at Montlhéry, France, in March–July 1933 by a Citröen car with a team of eight drivers.

The world speed record for compression ignition engined cars is 169·3 m.p.h. by Dana Fuller, Jnr., in the Fuller Diesel 6/71 on 11 Sept., 1953, at Bonneville Salt Beds, U.S.A.

The slowest international class record is the "J" class (up to 350 c.c.) 2,000 kilometres (1,242·7 miles) held by a Citröen-Barbot at 52·8 m.p.h. and achieved at Montlhéry in 1953.

OLYMPIC GAMES

The earliest celebration of the ancient Olympic Games of which there is a record is that of July 776 B.C. The ancient Games were terminated by decree of the Roman Emperor Theodosius in A.D. 392.

The Olympic Games of the modern era were inaugurated in Athens in April 1896.

Celebrations have been allocated as follows:—

I	Athens	1896	IX	Amsterdam	1928
II	Paris	1900	X	Los Angeles	1932
III	St. Louis	1904	XI	Berlin	1936
	†Athens	1906	XII	*Tokyo, then Helsinki	1940
IV	London	1908	XIII	*London	1944
V	Stockholm	1912	XIV	London	1948
VI	*Berlin	1916	XV	Helsinki	1952
VII	Antwerp	1920	XVI	Melbourne	1956
VIII	Paris	1924	XVII	Rome	1960

*Cancelled due to World Wars. †Intercalated Celebration.

The Winter Olympics were inaugurated in 1924 and have been allocated as follows:—

I	Chamonix	1924	V	St. Moritz	1948
II	St. Moritz	1928	VI	Oslo	1952
III	Lake Placid	1932	VII	Cortina, Italy	1956
IV	Garmisch-Partenkirchen	1936			

OXFORD *v.* CAMBRIDGE

Sporting Contests between representatives of Oxford and Cambridge Universities began with the cricket match of 4–5 June, 1827, at Lord's. The use of distinctive shades of Blue grew up from 17 June, 1836, on the occasion of the second Boat Race.

The record number of representations by an individual is 16 by K. C. Gander-Dower (Trinity, Cambridge) at the six sports of Billiards, Eton Fives, Rugby Fives, Lawn Tennis, Squash Rackets and Tennis between 1928 and 1931. At "full" blue sports the only quintuple blues have been:—

Oxford: C. J. Ottaway (Brasenose) athletics, cricket, Association football, rackets and tennis. 1870–1874.

Cambridge: Hon. A. Lyttelton (Trinity) athletics, cricket, Association football, rackets and tennis 1875–1879.

PIGEON RACING

EARLIEST REFERENCES

Pigeon Racing was the natural development of the use of homing pigeons for the carrying of messages—a quality utilized in the ancient Olympic Games (776 B.C.–A.D. 392). The earliest major long-distance race was from Crystal Palace, South London in 1871. The earliest recorded occasion on which 500 miles was flown in a day was by "Motor" (owned by G. P. Pointer of Alexander Park Racing Club) which released from Thurso, Scotland on 30 June, 1896, covered the 501 miles at a speed of 1,454 yards per minute (49½ m.p.h.).

LONGEST DURATION

The greatest recorded homing flight was that by a pigeon, owned by the Duke of Wellington which was released from a sailing ship off the Ichabo Islands, West Africa, on 1 June, 1845. It dropped dead a mile from its loft at Nine Elms, London, 55 days later, having flown an airline route of 5,400 miles but an actual flight of probably 7,000 miles to avoid the Sahara Desert. The official British duration record (into England) is 1,093 miles, Rome to Spennymoor by "Prince of Rome" (Vester and Scurr) liberated 4.30 a.m. 29 June, homed 8.44 a.m., 17 August, 1913.

BEST SPEEDS

The fastest speed recorded in any race is 2,744 yards per minute (93·55 m.p.h.) by H. Mussen's winner of the 1914 Malahide (Ulster Federation) Race over 80 miles.

The 500 mile record is 2,095 yards per minute (71·42 m.p.h.) by W. Reed's winner of the Thurso Race in 1948. The world's 24 hour record is 751 miles by Edfeldt and Wahiström's winner of the 1951 Lulea Race to Ystrad, Sweden—liberated 1 a.m., flying time 15 hours 52 minutes, velocity 47·25 m.p.h.

The best 24 hour performance into Britain is 682 miles from A. R. Hill's winner of the 1952 race from Hanover, Germany—velocity, 44·6 m.p.h.

POLO

EARLIEST GAMES

There is record of polo being played in Persia in 525 B.C. though the name is derived from the Tibetan word *pula*. The game was introduced into England from India in 1869 and the earliest match was that on Hounslow Heath, West of London, in July 1871 between 9th Lancers and the 10th Hussars. The first All-Ireland Cup match was at Phoenix Park, Dublin in 1878. The earliest international match England *v.* America was in 1886.

The game is played on the largest pitch of any ball game in the world. A ground measures 300 yards long by 160 yards wide with side boards or, as in India, 200 yards wide without boards.

HIGHEST HANDICAP

The highest handicap based on eight 7½ minute " chukkers " is 10 goals. The top handicap players currently are R. Cavanagh and E. Alberdi in Argentina; S. Igleheart, C. Smith and R. Skene (Australia) in U.S.A. all at 10.

HIGHEST SCORE

The highest score in an international match is 23 goals in the second match of the 1930 Westchester Cup at Meadow Brook, U.S.A., in which U.S.A. won 14 goals to England's 9.

HIGHEST PRICED PONY

The highest price ever paid for a polo pony is $22,000 (£7,600) for Mr. L. Lacey's Argentine pony " Jupiter " by Mr. Sandford in America in 1928.

MOST INTERNATIONALS

The greatest number of times any player has represented England is three in the case of F. M. Freake, Capt. L. Cheape, Col. V. Lockett and G. Balding.

RACKETS

EARLIEST WORLD CHAMPION

The first world rackets champion was Robert Mackay who claimed the title in London in 1820. The first closed court champion was Francis Erwood at Woolwich in 1860.

LONGEST REIGN

Of the 18 world champions since 1820 the longest reign has been that of Peter Latham who won the title in Manchester in 1887 and resigned after a record of 4 successful defences 15 years later in 1902.

MOST AMATEUR TITLES

Singles

Since the Amateur singles championships were instituted in 1888 the most titles won by an individual were the 9 by E. M. Baerlein between 1903 and 1923.

Doubles

Since the institution of the Amateur doubles championships in 1890 the most shares in titles have been by Lord Aberdare (formerly Hon. C. N. Bruce) with 10 between 1910 and 1934.

ROLLER SKATING

ORIGIN

Roller Skating is of Dutch origin c.1770. The earliest reference in Britain is dated August 1823. The sport boomed from 1903 to 1909.

LARGEST RINK

The largest roller rink ever laid down was that at Olympia, West London, in 1890 which had a track 4½ laps to the mile (391 yards).

MOST TITLES

The greatest number of Great Britain One Mile titles won is five by J. Reed (1929–30, 1932–33, 1937).

FASTEST MILE

The British Amateur Mile record (paced) is 2 minutes 48·4 seconds set at Olympia in 1911 by A. R. Eglington. The unpaced record is 2 minutes 58·4 seconds by J. Struggles at Birmingham in 1952.

The professional hour record is 19 miles 651 yards by A. R. Eglinton at Holland Park, London, in 1911.

ROWING

OLDEST RACE

The earliest established sculling race is the Doggett's Coat and Badge which was first rowed on 1 Aug., 1715, on a course from London Bridge to Chelsea and is still being rowed every year over the same course, under the administration of the Fishmongers' Company.

The first English Regatta probably took place in 1775 on the Thames by the Ranelagh Gardens, near Putney.

BOAT RACE

The earliest University Boat Race, which Oxford won, took place on 10 June, 1829 at Henley. In the 100 races since then, Cambridge have won 54 times, Oxford 45 times and there has been 1 dead heat.

The record time for the 4¼ mile course (Putney to Mortlake) is 17 minutes 50 seconds by Cambridge in 1948.

The record for the distance was made in 1954 by Thames Rowing Club in the Boustead Cup Race with 17 minutes 27 seconds rowing Mortlake to Putney.

The heaviest man ever to row in a University boat was J. J. Toogood of Balliol, 1829's No. 5 who is reputed to have weighed 14 stone 10 lb.

The lightest oarsman was the 1882 Oxford Stroke A. H. Higgins at 9 stone 6½ lb. The lightest cox was F. H. Archer (Oxford) in 1862 at 5 stone 2 lb.

The smallest winning margin of a University Boat Race is Oxford's win by a canvas in 1952. The greatest margin (apart from sinking) is Cambridge's win by 20 lengths in 1900.

HENLEY ROYAL REGATTA

The annual regatta at Henley-on-Thames was inaugurated on 26 March, 1839

The course, except in 1923, has been 1 mile 550 yards since 1839. Prior to 1922 there were two slight angles. Classic Records:—(Year in brackets, date instituted).

Grand Challenge (1839)	8 oars	Leander Club 1952	6m 38 secs.
Ladies' Plate (1846)	8 oars	Lady Margaret 1949	6 : 43
Thames Challenge (1868)	8 oars	Princeton U.S.A. 1953	6 : 45
Stewards' Challenge (1841)	4 oars	Trinity, Oxford 1949	7 : 13
Visitors' Challenge (1847)	4 oars	Pembroke, Cambridge 1952	7 : 15
Silver Goblets (1895)	Pair oar	R. Baetens and M. Knuysen (Belgium) 1953	7 : 51
Diamond Challenge (1844)	Sculls	R. George (Belgium) 1953	8 : 0

SHOOTING

WORLD RECORDS

Free Pistol	50 m. 6 × 10 shot series Poss. 600—	559 T. E. Ullman (Sweden)	Berlin	Aug., 1936
Free Rifle	300 m. 3 × 40 shot series Poss. 1,200—	1,133 A. Bogdanov (U.S.S.R.)	Caracas	Nov., 1954
Small Bore Rifle	50 m. 3 × 40 shot series Poss. 1,200—	1,174 A. Bogdanov (U.S.S.R.)	Caracas	Nov., 1954

Bench Rest ·22 Rifle: ten shots put through a hole ·2402 in dia. at 100 yards by O. A. Rinehart (U.S.A.).

The world's record stag, shot near Moritzburg, Germany, in 1699 by Frederick I, was a 66-pointer.

RECORD BAGS

The record bag for one gun in a day is 1,070 grouse by Lord Walsingham at Blubberhouse, Yorkshire, in Sept. 1888.

Rabbits	6,943	5 guns	Blenheim, Oxfordshire	7 Oct., 1898
Partridge	2,119	6 guns	Rothwell, Lincs.	12 Oct., 1952
Pheasants	3,937	7 guns	Hall Barn, Bucks.	18 Dec., 1913

SKI-ING

ORIGINS

The earliest mention of ski-ing exists in a work by Procopius A.D. c.550. The earliest recorded competition was in Norway in 1767. The Winter Olympics were inaugurated in 1924.

MOST OLYMPIC MEDALS

The most Olympic gold medals won by an individual for ski-ing is three by Torleif Haug (Norway) who, in 1924, won the Ski-ing Combined Event, the 18 kilometre and the 50 kilometre event. The only woman to have won two gold medals is Mrs. Andrea Mead Lawrence (U.S.A.) who at Oslo in 1952 won both the Slalom and the Giant Slalom.

MOST BRITISH TITLES

The greatest number of British Ski-running Titles won is three by Leonard Dobbs (1921, 1923–24) and W. R. Bracken (1929–31). The most Ladies Titles is four by Miss I. M. Roe (1938–39, 1948–49). The most wins in the British Ski-jumping Championships (discontinued 1936) is Colin Wyatt (1931, 1934, 1936). Wyatt set the official British record of 57 metres (187 feet) in 1931.

FASTEST SPEED

The fastest recorded speed attained on ski is 109·11 m.p.h. by Ralph Miller (U.S.A.) at Portillos, Chile, in July 1955.

LONGEST JUMP

The world's greatest ski-jump was achieved on the Oberstdorf Jump in Bavaria on 3 March, 1951, by the nineteen-year-old Finn, Tauno Luiro, who covered 456 feet (139 metres). The vertical height of the run is 161 metres (528·2 feet). See Plate 16.

SPEEDWAY

MOST WORLD TITLES

The world speedway championship was instituted in 1936 since when only two riders have won twice—the Australian, Jack Young (West Ham) in 1950 and 1953 and Fred Williams (Wembley) in 1951 and 1952.

MOST LEAGUE WINS The League was instituted in 1932 and was won first by the Wembley Lions who have since won in 1946–47 and 1949–53 making the record total of eight victories. The highest winning League total is 62 points by Belle Vue in 1933.

TRACK RECORDS Track records of First and Second Division Speedway tracks (all over 4 laps) are as follows:

FIRST DIVISION

Track	Time (secs.)	Holder
Belle Vue	70·2	Peter Craven (Belle Vue).
Birmingham	69·6	Alan Hunt (Birmingham).
		Split Waterman (West Ham).
		Dan Forsberg (Sweden).
Norwich	71·0	Fred Williams (Wembley).
Odsal (Bradford)	65·8	Eddie Rigg (Odsal).
Wembley	68·4	Split Waterman (West Ham).
West Ham	70·6	Jack Young (West Ham).
Wimbledon	62·2	Ronnie Moore (Wimbledon).

SECOND DIVISION

Track	Time (secs.)	Holder
Bristol	60·8	Dick Bradley (Bristol).
Coventry	66·4	Ken McKinlay (Leicester).
Exeter	72·0	Goog Hosking (Exeter).
Ipswich	71·6	Junior Bainbridge (Ipswich).
		Ken McKinlay (Leicester).
Leicester	66·8	Len Williams (Leicester).
Oxford	66·0	Keith Gurtner (Australia).
Poole	70·0	Olle Nygren (Sweden).
Rayleigh	69·0	Ken McKinlay (Leicester).
Southampton	63·2	Dudley Smith (Southampton).
Swindon	71·0	Dick Bradley (Bristol).

SQUASH RACKETS

EARLIEST CHAMPION Although the game was evolved in the middle of the last century at Harrow School (England) there was no recognized champion of any country until J. A. Miskey of Philadelphia won the American Amateur Singles Championship in 1906.*

MOST WINS

Open Championship The most wins in the open championship (amateur or professional), held annually in Britain, are the five by Abdel Fattah Amr Bey (later Pasha) of Egypt who won in 1932-4-5-6-7 ; also Hashim Khan of Pakistan, who won in 1950-1-2-3-4.

Amateur Championship The most wins in the amateur championship are the six by Abdel Fattah Amr Bey of Egypt, later appointed Ambassador in London, who won in 1931-2-3-5-6-7.

Professional Championship The most wins in the professional championship are the five by J. P. Dear (Great Britain) (1935-6-7-8-9) and Hashim Khan (Pakistan) (1950-1-2-3-4).

United States (Amateur) The most wins in the United States Amateur championship are the six by Stanley W. Pearson who won in 1914-15-16-20-21-22. (Note. Stanley W. Pearson Junior won in 1947).

Most International Selections The record for international selections is held by J. P. MacHale (Ireland) with 21 between 1948 and 1954.

England The record for England is held by A. A. T. Seymour-Haydon with 15 from 1947-1954.

Scotland The record for Scotland is held by P. Harding-Edgar with 18 from 1938-1952.

Wales The record for Wales is held by L. J. Verney with 18 from 1949-1954.

Longest Span of INTERNATIONAL APPEARANCES P. Harding-Edgar first played for Scotland in 1938 and last played 15 years later in 1952.

YOUNGEST AND OLDEST CHAMPIONS The youngest ever amateur champion was Abdel Fattah Amr Bey who was 21 when he first won the title in 1931. The youngest ever competitor was N. H. R. A. Broomfield who reached the third round at the age of 16 years 10 months.

The oldest ever amateur champion was J. E. Palmer-Tomkinson who was 47 years old when he won in 1926.

LONGEST CHAMPIONSHIP MATCH The longest recorded championships match was the two hours required for D. G. Butcher to beat J. P. Dear in the second leg of the professional championship at Prince's Club in 1933. Butcher won 10–8 in the 5th game. One rally went to 183 strokes.

MOST WINS IN A WOMEN'S CHAMPIONSHIP The most wins in the Women's Squash Rackets Championship are the six by Miss Janet R. M. Morgan (England) in 1949-50-51-52-53-54. Miss Morgan won all three of the world's major titles, the Australian, British and U.S. championships in 1954.

* 1906 indicates 1906-7 season and similarly throughout.

SWIMMING

EARLIEST REFERENCES Competitive swimming originated in London c.1837 at which time there were 5 or more pools.

MOST WORLD RECORDS Men, 31, Arne Borg (Sweden) 1921–1929.
Women, 41, R. Hveger (Denmark) 1936–1941.

MOST OLYMPIC TITLES The record number of individual Olympic gold medals by a swimmer is the four won by C. M. Daniels (U.S.A.) in 1904, 1906 and 1908. The greatest individual number on the current programme on the four year cycle is three in 1924 and 1928 by J. Weissmuller (U.S.A.) who also won two further gold medals in relays.

The greatest number by a British swimmer is 3 by J. Jarvis who took the 100 metres, 400 metres and 1,000 metres titles in Paris in 1900, and 3 individual and 1 relay gold medal by H. Taylor at the 1906 and 1908 celebrations.

Four women swimmers have won 2 gold medals of whom H. Mastenbroek (Netherlands) at Berlin in 1936, won a silver medal in addition to two gold.

MOST A.S.A. TITLES

The greatest number of A.S.A. titles won by an individual is the 38 amassed between 1912 and 1927 by J. G. Hatfield (Middlesborough). The greatest number by a woman swimmer is the 19 by Miss Joyce Cooper (Mermaid) between 1927 and 1933.

The greatest number of diving titles won is ten by L. W. G. Marchant (1933-1950). The women's record is 7 by both Miss Esna Child (1946-1949) and Miss Ann Long (1950-1954).

DIVES EASIEST MOST DIFFICULT

The dive with the lowest tariff (degree of difficulty 1·0) is the "jump forward standing straight" from the 1 metre (1 yard 3¼ inches) board while that with the highest tariff (degree of difficulty 2·7) is the "three and a half somersaults forward with pike" from the 10 metre (32 feet 9 inches) board. The Mexican diver Joaquin Capilla has performed a 4½ somersaults from a 10 metre board but this dive is not on the International tariff.

PLUNGING RECORDS

No world records are recognized in plunging but the following are British records (limit of 60 seconds from the start of the dive) which are both superior to the American records:—

Men: 86 feet 8 inches. F. Parrington (Liverpool) Bootle 20 Sept., 1933.

Women: 71 feet 3½ inches. Miss E. Todd (Everton) Seacombe, 17 Nov., 1937.

WORLD RECORDS

(as recognized by the Fédération Internationale de Natation Amateur)

Distance	Name	Time	Date	Venue	Length of course
MEN:		FREESTYLE			
100 yards	R. Cleveland (U.S.A.)	49·2	23.2.52	Columbus	25 yards
100 metres	R. Cleveland (U.S.A.)	54·8	1.4.54	New Haven	25 metres
200 metres	J. C. Wardrop (G.B.) See Plate 16	2 03·4	4.3.55	Columbus	25 yards
220 yards	J. C. Wardrop (G.B.)	2 03·4	4.3.55	Columbus	25 yards
400 metres	F. H. Konno (U.S.A.)	4 26·7	3.4.54	New Haven	25 yards
440 yards	J. B. Marshall (Australia)	4 28·1	17.2.51	New Haven	25 yards
800 metres	F. H. Konno (U.S.A.)	9 30·7	7.7.51	Honolulu	100 metres
880 yards	J. B. Marshall (Australia)	9 37·5	23.7.50	Seattle	55 yards
1,500 metres	H. Furuhashi (Japan)	18 19·0	16.8.49	Los Angeles	50 metres
1,760 yards	J. B. Marshall (Australia)	19 49·4	7.7.50	New Haven	55 yards
		BREAST STROKE			
100 yards	M. Furnkawa (Japan)	1 01·4	1.10.55	Tokyo	25 metres
100 metres	M. Furnkawa (Japan)	1 08·3	1.10.55	Tokyo	25 metres
200 metres	M. Furnkawa (Japan)	2 31·0	1.10.55	Tokyo	25 metres
220 yards	M. Furnkawa (Japan)	2 31·9	1.10.55	Tokyo	25 metres
		BUTTERFLY STROKE			
100 yards	A. Wiggins (U.S.A.)	54·7	22.1.55	Chapel Hill	25 yards
100 metres	A. Wiggins (U.S.A.)	1 01·5	2.4.55	New Haven	25 metres
200 metres	T. Ishimoto (Japan)	2 20·8	1.10.55	Tokyo	25 metres
220 yards	T. Ishimoto (Japan)	2 21·6	1.10.55	Tokyo	25 metres
		BACK STROKE			
100 yards	Y. Oyakawa (U.S.A.)	55·7	27.2.54	Columbus	25 yards
100 metres	G. Bozon (France)	1 02·1	27.2.55	Troyes	25 metres
200 metres	G. Bozon (France)	2 18·3	26.6.53	Algiers	25 metres
220 yards	VACANT. Basic time 2 mins. 20·0 secs.				
		INDIVIDUAL MEDLEY			
400 yards	J. C. Wardrop (G.B.)	4 36·9	1.4.55	New Haven	25 yards
400 metres	V. Stroujanov (U.S.S.R.)	5 15·4	2.10.54	Minsk	25 metres
		FREESTYLE RELAY			
4×100 yards	Yale University (U.S.A.) (K. Donovan, H. Gideonse, D. Armstrong, J. Niles).	3 21·3	1.2.55	New Haven	25 yards
4×100 metres	National Team (Japan) (H. Suzuki, A. Tani, N. Goto, M. Kogo)	3 46·8	16.8.55	Tokyo	50 metres
4×200 yards	Yale University (U.S.A.) (W. Moore, J. McLane, M. Smith, D. Sheff).	7 39·9	14.2.53	New Haven	25 yards
4×200 metres	Yale University (U.S.A.) (W. Moore, J. McLane, D. Sheff, R. Thomas).	8 29·4	16.2.52	New Haven	25 metres
		MEDLEY RELAY			
4×100 yards	Ohio State University (U.S.A.) (Y. Oyakawa, B. Ledger, A. Wiggins, R. Cleveland).	3 48·0	22.1.55	Columbus	25 yards
4×100 metres	National Team (Japan) (K. Hasi, M. Furakawa, T. Ishimoto, M. Kogo)	4 15·7	13.8.55	Tokyo	50 metres

WORLD RECORDS—*continued*

WOMEN:

FREESTYLE

Distance	Name	Time	Date	Venue	Length of course
100 yards	J. Alderson (U.S.A.)	58·1	30.7.54		
100 metres	W. den Ouden (Netherlands)	1 04·6	27.2.36	Amsterdam	25 metres
200 metres	R. Hveger (Denmark)	2 21·7	11.9.38	Aarhus	25 metres
220 yards	R. Hveger (Denmark)	2 22·6	23.4.39	Copenhagen	25 yards
400 metres	R. Hveger (Denmark)	5 00·1	15.9.40	Copenhagen	25 metres
440 yards	A. Curtis (U.S.A.)	5 07·9	3.5.47	Seattle	25 yards
800 metres	V. Gyenge (Hungary)	10 42·4	28.6.53	Budapest	50 metres
880 yards	L. de Nijs (Netherlands)	10 58·1	18.8.55	Utrecht	50 metres
1,500 metres	L. de Nijs (Netherlands	20 46·5	22.7.55	Utrecht	50 metres
1,760 yards	L. de Nijs (Netherlands)	22 05·5	12.8.55	Utrecht	50 metres
	BREAST STROKE				
100 yards	VACANT. Basic time 1 min. 09·2 secs.				
100 metres	VACANT. Basic time 1 min. 18·2 secs.				
200 metres	VACANT. Basic time 2 min. 48·5 secs.				
220 yards	VACANT. Basic time 2 min. 50·0 secs.				
	BUTTERFLY STROKE				
100 yards	B. Mullen (U.S.A.)	1 05·4	8.4.55	Daytona Beach	25 yards
100 metres	A. Voorbij (Netherlands)	1 13·2	28.8.55	Algiers	25 metres
200 metres	VACANT. Basic time 2 min. 48·0 secs.				
220 yards	VACANT. Basic time 2 min. 49·5 secs.				
	BACK STROKE				
100 yards	G. Wielema (Netherlands)	1 04·6	13.3.50	Hilversum	25 metres
100 metres	C. Kint (Netherlands)	1 10·9	22.9.39	Rotterdam	25 metres
200 metres	G. Wielema (Netherlands)	2 35·3	2.4.50	Hilversum	25 metres
220 yards	VACANT. Basic time 2 min. 37·0 secs.				
	INDIVIDUAL MEDLEY				
400 yards	S. Mann (U.S.A.)	5 18·6			25 yards
400 metres	E. Szekely (Hungary)	5 40·8	13.7.55	Budapest	33⅓ metres
	FREESTYLE RELAY				
4×100 yards	Walter Reed S.C. (U.S.A.) (K. Knapp, S. Mann, W. Werner, M. Gilett).	3 59·2	16.4.54	Daytona Beach	25 yards
4×100 metres	National Team (Hungary) (I. Novak, J. Temes, E. Novak, K. Szoke).	4 24·4	1.8.54	Helsinki	50 metres
	MEDLEY RELAY				
4×100 yards	Walter Reed S.C. (U.S.A.) (S. Mann, M. Gillett, D. Gray, W. Werner)	4 30·5	19.8.55	Montreal	25 yards
4×100 metres	National Team (Hungary) (E. Pajor, E. Szekely, R. Szekely, K. Zoke)	4 57·8	3.9.55	Budapest	50 metres

BRITISH NATIVE RECORDS

MEN:

Distance	Time	Name	Date	Venue	Length of Course
100 yards	52·2	J. C. Wardrop (Scotland)	6. 9.52	Dundee	25 yards
110 yards	58·0	R. Roberts (England)	2. 9.55	*Blackpool	55 yards
220 yards	2 08·0	J. C. Wardrop (Scotland)	20. 8.54	Rothesay	25 yards
440 yards	4 39·5	N. McKechnie (England)	19. 7.55	*Wallasey	25 yards
880 yards	10 03·6	J. C. Wardrop (Scotland)	10. 7.52	*Skegness	110 yards
One mile	20 53·2	J. C. Wardrop (Scotland)	19. 7.52	Henleaze	55 yards
100 yards Ba.	58·3	W. J. Brockway (Wales)	25. 9.54	Newport	33⅓ yards
110 yards Ba.	1 04·2	J. C. Wardrop (Scotland)	24. 8.54	Dundee	25 yards
100 yards Br.	1 06·1	P. C. Jervis (England)	1.10.54	*Wallasey	25 yards
110 yards Br.	1 12·6	P. C. Jervis (England)	1.10.54	*Wallasey	25 yards
200 yards Br.	2 28·0	J. B. Service (Scotland)	2.10.53	Glasgow	25 yards
220 yards Br.	2 44·7	P. C. Jervis (England)	9.10.54	*Wallasey	25 yards
100 yards Bu.	59·3	G. Symonds (England)	28. 9.55	Coventry	30 yards
110 yards Bu.	1 06·7	J. I. Hale (England)	19. 5.55	*Wallasey	25 yards
200 yards Bu.	2 14·5	J. I. Hale (England)	1.10.54	*Wallasey	25 yards
220 yards Bu.	2 30·0	J. I. Hale (England)	30. 9.54	*Wallasey	25 yards

WOMEN:

Distance	Time	Name	Date	Venue	Length of Course
100 yards	1 00·3	F. Ewart (England)	17. 9.55	Aberdeen	33⅓ yards
110 yards	1 07·1	F. Ewart (England)	3. 9.55	*Blackpool	55 yards
220 yards	2 29·2	C. Gibson (Scotland)	25. 7.47	*Hastings	110 yards
440 yards	5 16·8	D. Wilkinson (England)	24. 5.52	Croydon	25 yards
880 yards	11 43·5	D. Wilkinson (England)	25. 8.53	Uxbridge	73⅓ yards
One Mile	23 56·4	D. Wilkinson (England)	25. 8.53	Uxbridge	73⅓ yards
100 yards Ba.	1 06·3	J. Grinham (England)	23. 5.55	Hounslow	25 yards
110 yards Ba.	1 14·0	M. Edwards (England)	9.12.54	Heston	33⅓ yards
100 yards Br.	1 14·9	M. Grundy (England)	29. 5.55	Lowermoor	25 yards
110 yards Br.	1 24·5	H. O. Gordon (Scotland)	11. 9.54	Dundee	25 yards
200 yards Br.	2 37·4	M. Grundy (England)	17. 9.55	Aberdeen	33⅓ yards
220 yards Br.	2 58·8	H. O. Gordon (Scotland)	22.10.54	Hamilton	25 yards
100 yards Bu.	1 08·7	A. Morton (England)	8.10.55	Aberdeen	33⅓ yards
110 yards Bu.	1 17·7	C. Macadam (England)	3. 9.55	*Blackpool	55 yards

Abbreviations: (used throughout lists)

Ba. = Back-stroke
Br. = Breast-stroke
Bu. = Butterfly-stroke
IM = Individual Medley
* = Salt water course

CHANNEL SWIMMING

The first cross English Channel swim (without a life jacket) was achieved on 24-25 Aug., 1875, by Capt. Matthew Webb (G.B.) from Dover, England, to Cape Gris Nez, France, in 21 hours 45 minutes. Webb swam an estimated 38 miles to make the 21 mile crossing. The first reverse crossing from France to England was achieved by Enrique Tiriboschi (Argentina) in 16 hours 33 minutes on 11 Aug., 1923.

The first woman to succeed was Gertrude Ederle (U.S.A.) from France to England on 6 Aug., 1926, in the then record time of 14 hours 31 minutes. The first woman to swim from England to France was Florence Chadwick (U.S.A.) in 16 hours 22 minutes on 11 Sept., 1951, having on 8 Aug., 1950, already achieved France to England in 13 hours 23 minutes.

The first man to complete a crossing both ways was Edward H. Temme (G.B.) who swam from France to England (14 hours 29 minutes) on 5 Aug., 1927, and England to France (15 hours 54 minutes) on 19 Aug., 1934.

Fastest

The cross-channel record is the 10 hours 50 minutes set by the Egyptian Hassan Abd-el-Rheim on 22 Aug., 1950, on which day 8 other swimmers succeeded.

An unrecognized claim of 10 hours 45 minutes was made by Vencesles Spacek (Austria) in 1927.

The official record for the England to France crossing is 13 hours 55 minutes by Miss Florence Chadwick (U.S.A.) on 11 Oct., 1955.

Slowest

The slowest crossing was the 3rd ever made when Henry Sullivan (U.S.A.) on 5-6 Aug., 1923, was in the water for 27 hours 25 minutes.

Most in a Day

The record number of successful crossings in a day is 18 on 16 Aug., 1951 (12 men, 6 women) all from France to England with the fastest time by Mareeh H. Hamad (Egypt) at 12 hours 12 minutes.

TABLE TENNIS

EARLIEST REFERENCE

The earliest evidence relating to a game resembling table tennis has been found in the catalogues of London sports goods manufacturers in the 1880's. The old Ping Pong Association was formed in 1902 but the game proved only a temporary craze until resuscitated in 1921.

MOST WINS IN WORLD CHAMPIONSHIPS (Instituted 1926-7)

Event	Holder	Times	Date
Men's singles (St. Bride's Vase)	G. Viktor Barna (Hungary)	5	1930, 32, 33, 34, 35
Women's Singles (G. Geist Prize)	Angelica Roseanu (Rumania)	6	1950, 51, 52, 53, 54, 55
Men's Doubles	G. Viktor Barna (Hungary) with 3 different partners	8	1929, 30, 31, 32, 33, 34, 35, 39
Women's Doubles	M. Mednyanszky (Hungary) with 3 different partners	8	1927, 29, 30, 31, 32, 33, 34, 35
Mixed Doubles (Men)	Ferenc Sido (Hungary)	4	1949, 50, 52, 53
(Women)	M. Mednyanszky (Hungary)	6	1927, 28, 30, 31, 33, 34

G. Viktor Barna gained a personal total of 15 world titles, while 19 have been won by Mlle. M. Mednyanszky.

MOST TEAM TITLES

Event	Holder	Times	Date
Men's Team (Swaythling Cup)	Hungary	11	1927, 28, 29, 30, 31, 33, 34, 35, 38, 49, 52
Women's Team (Marcel Corbillon Cup)	Rumania	4	1951, 52, 54, 55

MOST WINS IN ENGLISH OPEN CHAMPIONSHIPS (Instituted 1921)

Event	Holder	Times	Date
Men's Singles	Richard Bergmann (Poland then G.B.)	6	1939, 40, 48, 50, 52, 54
Women's Singles	Miss K. M. Berry (G.B.)	3	1923, 24, 25
Men's Doubles	G. Viktor Barna (Hungary then G.B.)	6	1933, 34, 35, 38, 39, 49
Women's Doubles	Diane and Rosalind Rowe (G.B.)	6	1950–55
Mixed Doubles (Men)	G. Viktor Barna (Hungary then G.B.) with 4 different partners	8	1933, 34, 35, 36, 38, 40, 51, 53
(Women)	Miss M. Osborne (Birmingham)	4	1935, 36, 38, 40

The highest total of English titles for men is 20 by G. V. Barna and 9 for women by Miss M. Osborne and Miss R. Rowe.

Longest Match

The longest recorded match occurred in the 1935 Swaythling Cup final between M. Haguenauer (France) *v.* Marina (Rumania) which was unfinished after 7 hours play. In the same meeting A. Ehrlich (Poland) played Paneth (Rumania) for over 125 minutes for a single point.

Shortest Match

The shortest title match on record was in the 1955 world men's single final when T. Tanaka (Japan) beat Z. Dolinar (Jugoslavia) in 3 straight games in a total time of 13 minutes including the time spent retrieving balls and changing ends.

TENNIS

(Sometimes known as " Real " or " Royal " Tennis).

OLDEST COURT

The oldest of the 45 recorded Tennis Courts in the British Isles is the Royal Tennis Court at Hampton Court Palace, Middlesex, built by Henry VIII in 1530 and rebuilt by Charles II in 1660. The only closed court in Ireland built at St. Stephen's Green, Dublin, by Sir Edward Guinness in 1885 is now owned by the Eire Office of Public Works, but has not been in use since 1940.

The first recorded World Tennis champion was the Frenchman, Clerge, c.1720.

LONGEST REIGN

The longest reign of any of the 15 world champions since Clerge is that of Pierre Etchebaster who won the title in Paris in 1928, last defended it in New York (winning 7–0) in 1950 and retired undefeated in 1954 after 26 years. Etchebaster also holds the record for the greatest number of successful defences of his title with seven.

MOST AMATEUR CHAMPIONSHIPS

The greatest number of Amateur Tennis titles won is the 11 of E. M. Baerlein between 1912 and 1930.

MOST INTER-NATIONALS

Lord Aberdare (formerly Hon. C. N. Bruce) represented Great Britain against U.S.A. and France on 14 occasions between 1922 and 1939.

WALKING

WORLD RECORDS

	hrs. mins. secs.	Holder	Country	Date	Place
2 miles	12 45·0	W. Hardmo	Sweden	1 Sept., 1945	Sweden
5 miles	34 32·8	J. Dolezal	Czechoslovakia	15 Oct., 1955	England
7 miles	48 15·2	W. Hardmo	Sweden	9 Sept., 1945	Sweden
10 miles	1 10 45·8	J. Dolezal	Czechoslovakia	30 Apr., 1954	Czechoslovakia
20 miles	2 33 09·4	J. Dolezal	Czechoslovakia	14 May, 1954	Czechoslovakia
30 miles	4 21 11·0	J. A. Ljunggren	Sweden	8 Aug., 1953	Sweden
3,000 metres	11 51·8	W. Hardmo	Sweden	1 Sept., 1945	Sweden
5,000 metres	20 26·8	W. Hardmo	Sweden	31 July, 1945	Sweden
10,000 metres	42 39·6	W. Hardmo	Sweden	9 Sept., 1945	Sweden
15,000 metres	1 05 59·6	J. Dolezal	Czechoslovakia	30 Apr., 1954	Czechoslovakia
20,000 metres	1 30 2·8	V. Golubnitshi	U.S.S.R.	4 Oct., 1955	U.S.S.R.
25,000 metres	1 56 43·0	J. Dolezal	Czechoslovakia	14 May, 1955	Czechoslovakia
30,000 metres	2 21 38·6	J. Dolezal	Czechoslovakia	12 Oct., 1952	Czechoslovakia
50,000 metres	4 26 18·2	A. Roka	Hungary	9 Aug., 1953	Rumania
1 hour	8 m. 1,025 yds.	J. F. Mikaelsson	Sweden	1 Sept., 1945	Sweden
2 hours	15 m. 1,708 yds.	J. Dolezal	Czechoslovakia	14 May., 1955	Czechoslovakia

The unofficial 24 hour record is 125 miles 1,591 yards by Claud Hubert (France) at Motspur Park on 4/5 July, 1953.

BRITISH AMATEUR RECORDS

	hrs. mins. secs.	Holder	Place	Date
2 miles	13 11·4	G. E. Larner (G.B.)	Manchester	13 July, 1904
5 miles	35 15·0	R. Hardy (G.B.)	White City	31 May, 1952
7 miles	49 28·6	R. Hardy (G.B.)	White City	31 May, 1952
10 miles	1 14 30·6	F. J. Redman (G.B.)	White City	26 May, 1934
15 miles	1 56 41·4	R. Bridge (G B.)	Stamford Bridge	2 May, 1914
20 miles	2 46 10·0	G. T. Galloway (G.B.)	White City	26 May, 1934
30 miles	4 29 31·8	H. H. Whitlock (G.B.)	White City	5 Oct., 1935
1 hour	8 miles 474 yds.	A. H. G. Pope (G.B.)	White City	31 Aug., 1932
2 hours	15 miles 701 yds.	R. Bridge (G.B.)	Stamford Bridge	2 May, 1914

WATER POLO

Water Polo was developed in England in c.1870 and was first included in the Olympic Games at St. Louis, U.S.A., in 1904.

MOST OLYMPIC WINS

Hungary tied Great Britain's record of three Olympic team titles (1908, 1912 and 1920) when, at Helsinki in 1952, they added to their wins of 1932 and 1936.

MOST A.S.A. WINS

The club with the greatest number of Amateur Swimming Association titles is Plaistow United Swimming Club of Essex with eleven from 1928 to 1954.

In the Inter-County contest most wins have been secured by Lancashire with eighteen between 1896 and 1951.

HIGHEST INTER-NATIONAL SCORE

The greatest number of goals scored by an individual in a home international is eleven by T. C. Miller (Plaistow United) when England defeated Wales 13–3 at Newport in 1951.

MOST CAPS

International matches since 1946 have been subject to ill defined rulings as to whether or not they are " official " internationals. In some cases, no ruling has been made. It is, however, estimated that T. C. Miller (Plaistow United) holds the " cap " record with a total of 40 to 45.

WEIGHTLIFTING

ORIGINS

Amateur weightlifting is of comparatively modern origin, having been introduced in the Olympic Games at Athens in 1896. Prior to that time weightlifting consisted of professional exhibitions in which some of the advertised poundages were open to doubt.

GREATEST EVER LIFT

The greatest weight ever raised by a human being is 4,133 lb. (1·84 tons) by the 25 stone French-Canadian, Louis Cyr (1863–1912) in Chicago in 1896 in a back-lift (weight raised off trestles). Cyr had a 60½ inch chest and 22 inch biceps.

The greatest overhead lift ever made by a woman, also professional, is 282 lb. by Katie Sandwena (Germany) c.1926 in a continental clean and jerk. This is equivalent to seven 40 pound office typewriters.

MOST OLYMPIC WINS

The only lifters to win two Olympic gold medals are L. Hostin (France) who won the light-heavyweight title in 1932 and 1936 and J. Davis (U.S.A.) who won the heavyweight title in 1948 and 1952. Davis was the youngest lifter to win a world title when he took the 1938 light-heavyweight title in Vienna aged 17 years.

WEIGHTLIFTING RECORDS

		WORLD	lb.	BRITISH	lb.
Bantam weight	Press	V. Stogov, U.S.S.R.	235¾	A. Greenhaigh	193¼
	Snatch	C. Vinci, U.S.A.	225¾	J. Creus	201
	Jerk	V. Stogov, U.S.S.R.	286½	J. Creus	260½
	Total	V. Stogov, U.S.S.R.	738	J. Creus	655½
Feather weight	Press	I. Udodov, U.S.S.R.	245¾	S. Whiting	203
	Snatch	R. Chimishkyan, U.S.S.R.	242½	J. Creus	221½
	Jerk	R. Chimishkyan, U.S.S.R.	315	J. Creus	276¾
	Total	R. Chimishkyan, U.S.S.R.	771	J. Creus	680
Light weight	Press	F. Nikitin, U.S.S.R.	265½	A. Carroll	237½
	Snatch	N. Kostilev, U.S.S.R.	271	J. Halliday	246¼
	Jerk	I. Shams, Egypt	338¼	J. Halliday	310¼
	Total	N. Kostilev, U.S.S.R.	843	J. Halliday	760
Middle weight	Press	T. Kono, U.S.A.	292	J. Lockwood	238
	Snatch	Y. Duganov, U.S.S.R.	293	J. Halliday	260¾
	Jerk	T. Kono, U.S.A.	371¼	J. Halliday	325¼
	Total	T. Kono, U.S.A.	903½	J. Halliday	800
Light heavy weight	Press	G. Novak, U.S.S.R.	315¼	P. Caira	265¼
	Snatch	A. Vorobyev, U.S.S.R.	299¾	J. Halliday	260¾
	Jerk	T. Lomakin, U.S.S.R.	381¼	S. Harrington	341
	Total	T. Kono, U.S.A.	958¾	P. Caira	830
Middle heavy weight	Press	A. Vorobyev, U.S.S.R.	319½	J. M. Barnett	275¼
	Snatch	A. Vorobyev, U.S.S.R.	309½	J. Halliday	260¾
	Jerk	N. Schemansky, U.S.A.	399	S. Harrington	341
	Total	A. Vorobyev, U.S.S.R.	1013¾	J. M. Barnett	855
Heavy weight	Press	P. Anderson, U.S.A.	408¾	J. M. Barnett	290½
	Snatch	N. Schemansky, U.S.A.	330½	R. Walker	297½
	Jerk	P. Anderson, U.S.A.	433	R. Walker	363¾
	Total	P. Anderson, U.S.A.	1129½	R. Walker	887

WORLD RECORDS AWAITING RATIFICATION

			lb.				lb.
Light heavy weight	Press	T. Kono, U.S.A.	316¼	Total	T. Kono, U.S.A.		964¼
	Snatch	D. Sheppard, U.S.A.	303				
Middle heavy weight	Snatch	D. Sheppard, U.S.A.	316¼				
Heavy weight	Snatch	N. Schemansky, U.S.A.	333¾	Jerk	P. Anderson, U.S.A.	See Plate 16	434½
				Jerk	P. Anderson, U.S.A.		436½

WRESTLING

EARLIEST REFERENCES

Wrestling holds and falls, depicted on the walls of the Egyptian tombs of Beni Hasan, prove that wrestling dates from 3,000 B.C. or earlier. It was introduced into the ancient Olympic Games in the 18th Olympiad c.704 B.C. The Graeco-Roman style is of French origin and arose about 1860.

GREATEST NUMBER OF OLYMPIC TITLES

No wrestler has yet won more than two Olympic titles. Those with two Gold Medals are :—

K. Ware (Finland), Graeco-Roman, Lightweight, 1912 and 1920.
J. Richtohoff (Sweden), Freestyle, Heavyweight, 1928 and 1932.
K. Pihlajamaki (Finland), Freestyle, Featherweight, 1932 and 1936.
K. Palusalu (Estonia), Freestyle and Graeco-Roman, Heavyweight, both in 1936.
A. Gronberg (Sweden), Graeco-Roman, Middleweight, 1948 and 1952.

LONGEST BOUT

The longest recorded bout was in the light-heavyweight division in the Olympic Games at Stockholm in 1912, when A. Ahlgren (Sweden) and F. Boling (Finland) wrestled for over 9 hours in the final with no decision.

MOST BRITISH TITLES

Heavyweight	9	F. Oberlander	1939-47.
Middleweight	4	S. J. Bissell	between 1930 and 1938.
Lightweight	7	A. Thompson	1934-40.
Bantamweight	6	J. Reid	1930-35.

GREATEST RANGE

V. Bensen, the British Amateur Wrestling Association lightweight champion 1919-21 and 1925 and 1926, won also in 1926 the welterweight, middleweight and light-heavyweight titles. In 1924, he won also the heavyweight title thus amassing 10 titles ranging between lightweight and heavyweight.

LONGEST SPAN

The longest span for B.A.W.A. titles is the 25 years of G. Mackenzie, who won his first title in 1909 and his last in 1933. Mackenzie also holds the record of having represented Great Britain in five successive Olympiads from 1908 to 1928.

HEAVIEST HEAVYWEIGHT

The heaviest heavyweight champion in British wrestling history was A. Dudgeon (Scotland) who won the 1936 and 1937 B.A.W.A. heavyweight titles scaling 22 stone.

YACHTING

ORIGINS

Yachting in England dates from the Restoration of Charles II in 1660. The earliest club is the Royal Cork Yacht Club (formerly the Cork Harbour Water Club) established in Ireland in 1720. The elements of tide and wind make record times in yachting of no comparative value.

HIGHEST SPEED

The highest authenticated speed attained by any yacht is 16·5 knots by the schooner " Rainbow " in 1898.

A 17-foot sliding-seat canoe, sailed and designed by Uffa Fox (G.B.), has attained 16·3 knots over a measured half mile.

MOST SUCCESSFUL

The most successful racing yacht in history was the Royal Yacht " Britannia " (1893–1935) owned by King George V which in 625 starts won 231 races.

The America's Cup races, open to challenge by any nation's yachts, began in 1870 with the unsuccessful attempt by J. Ashbury's " Cambria " (G.B.) to capture the trophy from the " Magic " owned by F. Osgood (U.S.A.). Since then the cup has been challenged by Great Britain in sixteen contests but the American or Canadian (in 1876 and 1881) holders have never been defeated.

In Olympic yachting events, which were inaugurated in 1904, the only two yachts to win gold medals twice were the " Llanoria " (U.S.A.) 6 metre class, in 1948 and 1952 and the " Pan " (Norway) Dragon class, also in 1948 and 1952.

LARGEST and SMALLEST CLASSES

The largest class under the new rules for International Cruiser/Racers are the 12-metre boats, which have waterline length of 39 feet 4 inches to 41 feet 9 inches and overall length of about 62 feet.

The most numerous international class is the Star class, which originated in the U.S.A. in 1911. They have a waterline length of 15 feet 6 inches, 22 feet 9 inches overall and a sail area of 281 square feet. There are more than 3,000 registered Stars.

One of the smallest " one-designs " is the British Moth Boat, with a waterline length of 8 feet 6 inches, 11 feet overall and a sail area of 63 square feet.

INDEX